Adam Feinste

AUTISM AND THE LAW

Navigating a legal minefield

Illustrations by Daisy Whittle

Autism and the Law

Published by:

Pavilion Publishing and Media Ltd
Blue Sky Offices, 25 Cecil Pashley Way
Shoreham by Sea, West Sussex
BN43 5FF

Tel: 01273 434 943
Email: info@pavpub.com
Web: www.pavpub.com

Published 2024

A catalogue record for this book is available from the British Library.

ISBN: 978-1-803883-20-5

Pavilion Publishing and Media is a leading publisher of books, training materials and digital content in mental health, social care and allied fields. Pavilion and its imprints offer must-have knowledge and innovative learning solutions underpinned by sound research and professional values.

Author: Adam Feinstein
Editor: Mike Benge
Cover design: Daisy Whittle
Page layout and typesetting: Phil Morash, Pavilion Publishing and Media Ltd
Printing: CPI Antony Rowe

About the author

Adam Feinstein is an acclaimed British author, autism researcher, poet, translator, Hispanist, journalist and film critic. He has an autistic son, Johnny, and has written widely on autism including *A History of Autism: Conversations with the Pioneers* (Wiley-Blackwell, 2010) and *Autism Works: A Guide to Employment Across the Entire Spectrum* (Routledge, 2019), both of which received much international praise.

In 1998 Feinstein launched an international autism magazine, *Looking Up*, and as editor of the Autism Connect web portal, he organised regular online autism conferences attended by more than 10,000 delegates and involving the participation of many of the world's leading autism authorities.

Feinstein is also the English-language biographer and translator of the Nobel Prize-winning Chilean poet, Pablo Neruda. His own poems and his translations (of Neruda, Federico García Lorca, Mario Benedetti and others) have appeared in many magazines, including *Agenda, Acumen, PN Review, Poem* and *Modern Poetry in Translation*.

Feinstein has given numerous lectures on autism, Neruda and cinema around the world, including Mexico, Argentina, Chile, Nicaragua, Guatemala, the United States, Russia, China, India, Spain, Italy, Germany, Switzerland and the Netherlands. He broadcasts regularly for the BBC and writes for the *Guardian*, the *Observer*, the *Financial Times*, the *Times Literary Supplement* and the *New Statesman*. He has been a Royal Literary Fund Fellow.

Acknowledgments

As always, my first, and largest, debt of gratitude must go to the remarkable Dame Stephanie Shirley – known to her many friends around the world as Steve. Once again, she has not only shown herself to be immensely generous in personally financing this book, but offered her unfailing, and hugely appreciated, support throughout the writing process. I would also like to express my thanks and appreciation to the other members of the book's steering committee – John Carrington and Eileen Hopkins – for their experience and their constant backing at every stage. As ever, John, the project manager, ensured a calm and smooth running of the financial elements of the entire operation.

I am enormously grateful to Ekaterina Harrison for her invaluable input throughout the writing of this book. Katya is an autistic lawyer, senior associate of the international law firm, Katten Muchin Rosenman LLP, and has three autistic children, so she not only has vast professional knowledge of legal matters but, like me, has intensely personal experiences as a parent. She read every chapter of this book and her comments proved crucial.

Space does not allow me to thank each and every one of the numerous people I interviewed while writing this book. You all offered me vital insights which I profoundly appreciate. Allow me, though, to express my heartfelt appreciation to Patricia Alban-Stanley, whose autistic son, Sammy, died at the age of 13 in 2020 after years of neglect, for her courageous campaign for justice; to Steve Broach KC, for his comments on the Autism Act (2009) and the Equality Acr (2010) and to Luke Clements and Anna Moore for their observations on assessment of needs and other issues.

I am extremely grateful to Yo Dunn and Dr Lucy Series for explaining the intricacies of the Mental Capacity Act (2005) and crucial aspects of deprivation of liberty and to Alexis Quinn for sharing her extraordinary account of her own years in detention in hospital before she managed to escape. I again thank Yo Duun, as well as Belinda Schwehr and the lawyer Alex Rook, for their important analysis, variously, of the Care Act (2014) the Health and Care Act (2022) and judicial reviews.

I greatly appreciate the information offered by George Andruszkiewicz on mediation in the workplace. Many people provided invaluable assistance in navigating the complexities of the criminal justice system. I must thank Professor Glynis Murphy, Dr Richard Mills, Dr Dermot Bowler, Dr Katie Maras, Dr Chloe Holloway-George and Cos Michael for their authoritative observations on various critical aspects, including the conditions in police custody, the police interview and the plight of autistic individuals both in prison and after their release. My gratitude goes to the appropriate adult, Sarah Doyle, for her enlightening personal insights and to Charotte Henry for her brave battle for justice for her brother, Alex, a victim of the so-called Joint Enterprise common law. I am also extremely grateful to Barry Sheerman MP, chairman of the Westminster Commission on Autism, who has likewise campaigned forcefully against Joint Enterprise.

On the civil and family justice systems, Nadine Finch, a former family barrister, offered helpful insights and I am also grateful to Jon Adams, a talented artist with Asperger's syndrome, dyslexia and synaesthesia for his personal views in this area.

Dr Michael Fitzpatrick provided invaluable assistance in the chapter on mis-medication, malpractice, quack 'cures' and the MMR controversy, for which I am profoundly grateful. I again congratulate Barry Sheerman MP for his Westminster Commission's energetic campaign against the use of untested 'treatments; for autism.

Of those I do not quote directly, I would like to thank Jonathan Andrews, the first lawyer to whom I spoke when I began writing this book (he works for Reed Smith and is, himself, autistic, and he raised the important issue of autism in the civil courts); Jolanta Lasota, chief executive of the UK national charity, Ambitious about Autism, for her helpful advice; Estelle Christmas and Philippa Stannard at Autism at Kingwood, the charity and social care provider, for their useful guidance on the issue of autistic individuals' right to vote; Philip Waite, the autistic policeman with whom I spent some time at Bishopsgate Police Station in east London; Virginia Bovell, who among other things, drew my attention to the significant matter of cuckooing, and Professor Francesca Happé and Professor Patricia Howlin, of the Institute of Psychiatry in London, for their observations.

My deep gratitude naturally goes to the publisher, Pavilion, for taking on this project – and specifically to Louisa Robertson and the copy editor, Mike Benge, for their expertise, attention to detail, patience and understanding. And of course, my thanks and admiration must also go to the illustrator, Daisy Whittle, whose wonderful drawings adorn this book - including its striking cover.

I must also thank Adam Micklethwaite, director of the excellent Autism Alliance – a national UK partnership of charities sporting autistic people and their families. Adam read through every chapter of this book and made important comments. The Autism Alliance offers access to relevant legal information resources, together with commentary on the key legislation relevant for autistic people and their families in England, and will provide details of any major changes made to this legislation.

Last, but very much not least, let me express my immeasurable love and gratitude to my own beautiful family for their unfailing support: my wife, Kate, and my three children: Lara, Katriona and Johnny, as well as my first grandchild, Jasmine, who was born during the writing of this book.

Adam Feinstein

Special thanks for input to the book's development from:

AUTISM
ALLIANCE UK

Contents

Online resources are available at
www.pavpub.com/autism-and-the-law-resources
from where they can be downloaded and printed.

Foreword

Dame Stephanie Shirley CH
Sponsor

Autism is a developmental condition which affects communication, forming relationships and the way people make sense of the world. More than one in 100 people is autistic.

My focus is on pioneering, strategic projects in the field of autism. Initiated in 2022, *Autism and the Law: Navigating a Legal Minefield* is a comprehensive reference book designed to help parents, professionals and anyone in caring positions understand the relevant law in England.

I knew and admired the author Adam Feinstein from the portal site, Autism Connect, and had earlier commissioned two of his books: *A History of Autism: Conversations with the Pioneers* (2010) and *Autism Works: A Guide to Successful Employment Across the Entire Spectrum* (2018). We share the searing experience of our autistic sons being also profoundly learning-disabled; and hence, also, a pertinent interest in how autistic people interact with the legal framework. He proves to be a lucid advocate of the complex legalities of English law.

The project was driven by a volunteer steering group consisting of myself and Eileen Hopkins of Ai-Media, who is an autism consultant, and chaired by businessman and academic John Carrington. We were well supported by the autistic lawyer, Ekaterina Harrison, Senior Associate of Katten Muchin Rosenman LLP and author of *The EHCP Handbook: How to Make an Effective Education Health and Care Plan, A Guide for Parents and Carers* (also published by Pavilion).

The contents of the book will be kept up-to-date online by the Autism Alliance, the UK partnership of not-for-profit organisations that support autistic people and their families.

A note on terminology

Identity-first language

Wherever possible in this book, I have preferred to use the identity-first expression, 'autistic individual', rather than the person-first 'individual with autism', on the basis that many autistic people consider that person-first language isolates individuals from their diagnosis. In direct quotations, I have endeavoured to respect the descriptor used by the commentator or by the subject of a particular case study. I also continue to use the term 'Asperger's syndrome' as appropriate, despite its official removal as a separate classification from DSM-5 in 2013, because so many individuals prefer to keep this label.

English law

This book is about English law. Whenever this book alludes to the UK Parliament or Government, this is a reference to the Westminster Parliament in London and therefore the legislation discussed pertains to the situation in England. There may, however, sometimes be overlaps with the legal position in the devolved nations (Scotland, Wales and Northern Ireland).

For readers wishing to find out more, the Autism Alliance, a UK partnership of not-for-profit organisations that support autistic people and their families, provides access to relevant legal information resources, together with commentary on the key legislation relevant for autistic people and their families in England, and any major changes made to this legislation.

To find out more see:
www.autism-alliance.org.uk/autism-and-the-law

Introduction

One of the main aims of this book is to tackle the considerable gap between the way the law exists in England in terms of protection for autistic individuals and their families, and the way it could (and should) be. This applies throughout the process, from the initial diagnosis through to subsequent education and employment, potential involvement in the criminal and civil justice systems, through to the much-neglected stage of life as an older autistic person. The book will highlight how autistic individuals in England are not being granted the human rights laid down in national and international legislation. By exploring the disparity between the laws as they exist and the way they are applied in practice, and by offering guidance on how to obtain these unmet human rights, this book aims to expose the legislative shortcomings, as well as explain the significance of instances of malpractice on both a local and national level, with the objective of helping those in similar situations to avoid a similar fate.

This book is designed, then, as an accessible 'self-help' guide to help families of people with autism, autistic individuals and carers negotiate the legal minefield and avoid the appalling traps that lie in wait for them. But it could also be seen, as Ekaterina Harrison – the autistic lawyer whose insights have proven invaluable throughout the writing of this book – notes, as a comprehensive primer:

> 'It introduces readers to complex subjects and provides some foundation for understanding, before diving into more advanced material It also points out areas needing attention and brings in insights from professionals in the field. It offers a broad panorama of what is going on. This approach opens up new horizons and hints at where more research could be carried out. offering a compassionate survey of the issues. You offer a compassionate survey of the issues. Your book functions as a guiding light, directing individuals towards areas ripe for improvement. And that, to me, is its real strength.'[1]

I have, indeed, tried to write compassionately and un-stuffily, rather than dispassionately. After all, Dr Martha Nussbaum, professor of law and ethics at the University of Chicago, told me: 'I reject the contrast between the emotional and the "rational". I argue that emotions embody thoughts about our deepest commitments.'[2]

I naturally hope that professionals working in the legal professions, as well as the police and the health services, will find this book a valuable resource. There has been progress among professional bodies in understanding autism and neurodivergent individuals. Britain now has a National Police Autism Association, a privately run group of UK police officers and staff supporting colleagues affected by autism and other neurodivergent conditions such as dyslexia, dyspraxia and ADHD. Nevertheless, the neurodiversity training introduced by some police forces remains generally patchy across the UK as

1 Ekaterina Harrison, personal communication, February 28, 2024.

2 Professor Martha Nussbaum, personal communication, December 7, 2023. See also her 2004 book, *Hiding from Humanity: Disgust, Shame and the Law.*

a whole. There is also a Legal Neurodiversity Network, a network of neurodivergent employees, partners and allies working in the UK legal services sector. However, a 2022 survey of 93 defence lawyers found that only half of autistic people (52%) were considered by the police to be vulnerable adults, even though the law recognises all autistic people as vulnerable. Over a third (35%) of autistic defendants were not given an 'appropriate adult' during police investigations, even though their diagnosis was known to police, and despite all autistic people being entitled under the law to have an appropriate adult present when being interviewed by the police. And only a quarter (25%) of autistic people were given 'reasonable adjustments' (see Chapter 6).

A new review published in July 2023 indicated that 'dehumanising policies' leave autistic people in the United Kingdom struggling to access health, education and housing. In the review, Aimee Grant, a senior lecturer in public health and Wellcome Trust Career Development Fellow at Swansea University, who is herself autistic, wrote that, under the Equality Act (2010), autistic people should receive reasonable adjustments – meaning that organisations must make changes to how they provide their services to remove environmental and social barriers:

> 'Despite this, autistic people often experience society as highly disabling. We die between 16 and 30 years younger than non-autistic people and have a suicide rate nine times higher. Autistic people are often misunderstood by non-autistic people who fail to recognise how autistic people show empathy. This misunderstanding is embedded in many government bodies, which can result in dehumanising policies and services that do not meet autistic people's needs.'[3]

Grant and her colleagues reviewed the evidence from a range of government and non-government research and reviews to understand how well autistic people fare in relation to government services. They analysed the areas described by William Beveridge, founder of the UK welfare state, as the 'five giants': health, education, employment, poverty and housing. Their findings were decidedly bleak. Many government services designed to support autistic people are not available without diagnosis. However, most autistic people are not yet diagnosed in the UK. Waiting lists are astonishingly long. Even with a diagnosis, autistic people often do not receive the healthcare that meets their needs. The review found that some individuals did not even tell doctors they were autistic because they expected to be treated badly. Of those who did inform their GP, more than 75% said that the GP had not made any reasonable adjustments, such as allowing extra processing time during appointments:

> 'Being expected to phone to book appointments is also difficult for nearly two-thirds of autistic people, yet many GP surgeries insist on phone calls to book appointments. Autistic people also report that clinical spaces are painfully bright, busy and loud, which can make it harder for us to explain what is wrong to the doctor'[4] [see Chapter 1]

3 Grant A & Williams K (2023) 'Dehumanising policies' leave autistic people struggling to access health, education and housing – new review [online]. Available at: https://nation.cymru/news/dehumanising-policies-leave-autistic-people-struggling-to-access-health-education-and-housing-new-review/ (accessed March 2024).

4 Ibid.

Under the Children and Families Act (2014), local authorities have a duty to identify needs in their area and commission services to support children and young people with special educational needs and disabilities (SEND). In January 2015, the government published a SEND code of practice. Even after an appropriate school has been found, the threat of unlawful exclusion remains a very real one. Autistic people often struggle in educational institutions because these institutions rarely meet their needs:

> 'This can mean, for example, that autistic children are labelled as "trouble-makers" by teachers, rather than disabled. Despite the fact that autistic people account for only 3 per cent of the population, around 80 per cent of those sent to pupil referral units are autistic. This has life-long effects, as only 8 per cent of students with an education, health and care plan (EHCP) progress to university, compared with 50 per cent of non-disabled people.'[5] [see Chapter 2]

British teachers are required to have a clear understanding of the needs of pupils with SEND, including autism, as part of the Teachers' Standards. The 2021-26 autism strategy committed £600,000 for staff autism training and professional development in schools and colleges in 2021/22. The SEND system does not extend to higher education, which is education generally undertaken in universities. Providers are, instead, bound by different statutory duties under the Equality Act (2010) when it comes to supporting autistic students in higher education.[6]

Under the Care Act (2014), local authorities have duties relating to the provision of adult social care services which apply to everyone, including autistic adults. Guidance for social workers is provided in a government-commissioned Capabilities Statement. The government is also rolling out a qualification for commissioners who work with autistic people. Guidance on identifying local demand and developing services for autistic people was published alongside the 2021-26 autism strategy. Many specialists consider the Care Act a positive initiative, but a serious lack of resources means that the theoretical protection the Act offers is not implemented in practice (see Chapter 4).

The 2023 review found that autistic people are more likely to live in poverty than non-autistic individuals. A 2009 report had already shown that one-third of autistic people in the UK were not in paid work or getting benefits. One reason for this is that the benefits designed to stop disabled people living in poverty, such as the personal independence payment (PIP), can be hard to apply for, especially for autistic people. 'And for people

5 Grant A & Williams K (2023) 'Dehumanising policies' leave autistic people struggling to access health, education and housing – new review [online]. Available at: https://nation.cymru/news/dehumanising-policies-leave-autistic-people-struggling-to-access-health-education-and-housing-new-review/ (accessed March 2024).

6 An appalling example was that of Natasha Abrahart, a 20-year-old physics student with chronic social anxiety disorder who took her own life in April 2018 on the day of a 'truly terrifying' oral exam. Bristol University argued that they did not owe Natasha a duty of social care because she was protected by the Equality Act. In May 2022, however, a senior county court judge found there had been breaches of the Equality Act by the university amounting to disability discrimination. The university was ordered to pay more than £50,000 in damages, which included the costs of Natasha's funeral. Bristol University appealed against the decision but the High Court rejected the university's appeal in February 2024.

who manage to apply for PIP, autism falls within the "psychiatric disorders" category, which means they are least likely to receive the award and most likely to lose their PIP upon renewal.'[7] (For more, see Chapter 10.)

Furthermore, around 12% of British autistic people are homeless. As rent typically costs far more than the amount of money awarded in housing benefit, and autistic people are less likely to be in work or have access to benefits, they are more likely to struggle to pay for housing. As the 2023 review noted, 'this can be made worse by the "bedroom tax", which is when tenants in social housing have their benefit reduced if they have spare bedrooms. This affects single people under 35 especially, as they are only eligible for the shared accommodation rate. Autistic people can find it hard to live with other people due to their sensory needs, and there are few one-bedroom properties.' Autistic people who do not have somewhere to live are more likely to be placed in secure residential care, where they are subjected to similar confines to people in prison, by staff who may have limited understanding of autism. They can also be subjected to questionable clinical 'treatment'. 'Worse, some autistic people in residential care have experienced abuse by staff. In the most severe cases, autistic people have died due to abusive and/or negligent treatment while in residential care.'[8] (For more, see Chapter 3.)

The 2023 Aimee Grant review concluded:

> 'In every area of government services, we found policies that failed to account for known autistic needs. These failures have a cumulative impact throughout life. A lack of accommodations in education leads to less likelihood of securing accessible employment and greater reliance on benefits and social housing. To improve this, the policy-making process needs to be made accessible to disabled people, so that services meet our needs. This could include ensuring that consultation processes reach out to a broader range of autistic people and then meet their needs to submit evidence. It is also important that policymakers put evidence from the autistic community ahead of evidence provided by non-autistic "experts" who fundamentally misunderstand autism, can have conflicts of interest and thus cannot speak on our behalf.'[9]

Baroness Sheila Hollins published a damning report in 2023 condemning the UK government's 'inhumane' treatment of people with learning disabilities and autism who had been locked in solitary confinement for up to 20 years. The report said that patients were being 'warehoused' in hospital wards unsuitable for their needs, despite repeated government pledges to stop the practice. These patients are held in rooms in isolation, some for decades, because there is nowhere to house them in the community. Many are being treated unnecessarily with anti-psychotic medication. The government first promised in 2013 that it would end the practice of admitting people with learning disabilities and autism to hospitals without there being a medical need to do so. However,

7 Grant A & Williams K (2023) 'Dehumanising policies' leave autistic people struggling to access health, education and housing – new review [online]. Available at: https://nation.cymru/news/dehumanising-policies-leave-autistic-people-struggling-to-access-health-education-and-housing-new-review/ (accessed March 2024).

8 Ibid.

9 Ibid.

according to the British daily, *The Independent*, a decade later, in 2023 there were 2,005 people in the UK with learning disabilities or autism – 205 of them children – who were being forced to stay in inappropriate care because there were no community care spaces available. Half of them had been detained for more than two years.[10] In her report, Baroness Hollins wrote: 'My heart breaks that after such a long period of work, the care and outcomes for people with a learning disability and autistic people are still so poor, and the very initiatives which are improving their situations are yet to secure the essential funding required to continue this important work.'[11]

Only around 16% of autistic adults in the UK are in full-time employment, despite many having good intelligence and considerable talents. The UK's Autism Act (2009) stipulates that autistic people should be supported in order to be able to work. However, according to the 2023 review (see Chapter 3):

> '...autistic people are less likely to be in work than non-autistic people. Access to work is a UK government scheme to pay disabled people for the extra costs of working, but the application and claiming processes are complicated. Of the 42 per cent of autistic adults who say they need help to access work, only 12 per cent are getting it.'[12]

Indeed, as I explained in my book, *Autism Works*, autism can frequently prove an *advantage* in the workplace.[13] In February 2024, as this book was going to press, Sir Robert Buckland – the former British Justice Secretary who has an autistic son – published his Autism Employment Review, which assesses the barriers preventing autistic people from entering the workforce and recommends a series of measures to tackle them, including improving access to supported internships, apprenticeships and better practical support in employment.

In response, Dr James Cusack, chief executive of the research charity Autistica, who is himself autistic, declared: 'To be their best and to ensure they can get the best out of their whole workforce, including autistic people, employers need to change the way that they recruit and support staff. This is not about reasonable adjustments for a small number of people – it's about changes that benefit everyone, because we all think and work differently.'[14] Jolanta Lasota, chief executive of Ambitious About Autism, also welcomed the Buckland Review. She added: 'We would like to see a step change in support for autistic pupils at school – including mandatory training for teachers and careers advice tailored to autistic pupils. As one of our young campaigners explained, "If there's a gap, we fall down it"... We are therefore calling for the piloting of Employment Health and Care plans, a continuation of the Education Health and Care plans that already exist, which

---

10 Thomas R (2023) 'Scandal of patients with learning disabilities locked in 'inhumane' solitary confinement for 20 years'. 08 November. The Independent. Available at: www.independent.co.uk/news/health/autism-learning-disabilities-hollins-inquiry-b2443821.html (accessed March 2024).

11 Ibid.

12 Ibid.

13 Feinstein A (2019) *Autism Works: A Guide to Successful Employment Across the Entire Spectrum*. London: Routledge.

14 Rafiq M & Fox N (2024) *Autistic people held back by job interview questions – report* [online]. Available at: www.bbc.co.uk/news/uk-68381352?xtor=AL-72-%5Bpartner%5D-%5Byahoo.north.america%5D-%5Bheadline%5D-%5Bnews%5D-%5Bbizdev%5D-%5Bisapi%5D (accessed March 2024).

provide a legal obligation for autistic young people to be supported in school, where necessary. We believe the same is needed for the world of work, as the requirement for support does not end when a young person leaves school or college.'[15]

The Autism Act (2009) was the first-ever condition-specific law to be introduced in England. The Act, which applies to adults only, laid down an obligation on the government in Westminster to meet the needs of autistic adults by producing an autism strategy and statutory guidance for England's local authorities and organisations forming part of the National Health Service. A ten-year follow-up in 2019 on the impact of the Autism Act highlighted profoundly concerning unmet needs and insufficient services for autistic adults. Barry Sheerman, the Labour MP who founded and chairs the Westminster Commission on Autism and who has an autistic grandson, told me that the Autism Act is 'pretty toothless. It does not really work. Local authorities hide behind the scaling back of the Department of Education centrally. The marginalisation of local authorities in delivering education has actually resulted in the one area for which local authorities now have responsibilities for, alongside social care, being the most expensive to provide. And with the dramatically reduced budget, the local authorities are forced to limit the number of calls on resources for children on the autism spectrum.'[16]

A leading disability lawyer, Steve Broach KC, told me that he considers the Equality Act (2010) infinitely more useful than the Autism Act (2009). He explained his reasoning:

> 'The Autism Act merely requires (1) publication of an autism strategy, and (2) publication of guidance on the implementation of that strategy, which relevant public bodies must act under (follow, unless there is good reason not to do so). As such, the "teeth" of the Autism Act are entirely dependent on the content of the strategy and guidance, and these documents, in any event, apply only to a limited number of bodies. By contrast, the Equality Act applies to almost all areas of life and requires bodies subject to it to refrain from discriminating against autistic people, including through failing to make reasonable adjustments.'[17]

In 2019, the UK government undertook a comprehensive review of the autism strategy and planned to extend it to include children and young people for the first time. A call for evidence was launched in March 2019, with a summary of the findings published in July 2021. The findings from this and other reports were used to inform a new autism strategy, 'The national strategy for autistic children, young people and adults: 2021 to 2026.'

There have also been successive health policies aimed at improving outcomes for people with autism. The NHS Long Term Plan (2019) featured several objectives for people with autism, including: the introduction of a 'digital flag' in the patient record by 2023/24 to ensure staff know a patient has autism; ensuring reasonable adjustments are made so wider NHS services can support people with learning disabilities or autism; and piloting the introduction of a specific health check for people with autism. In November 2022, it

15 See: https://www.fenews.co.uk/skills/ambitious-about-autism-response-to-the-buckland-review-on-autism-employment/ (accessed January 2024).

16 Barry Sheerman, personal communication, September 7, 2022.

17 Steve Broach, personal communication, September 12, 2022.

was announced that the so-called Oliver McGowan mandatory training was to be launched for health and care staff in England to support people with a learning disability and autism following the four-year campaign of Oliver's grieving mother, Paula. Nevertheless, there have been alarming examples of malpractice and/or failure to introduce reasonable adjustments (see Chapter 9).[18]

The 2021-26 autism strategy says autistic people may be over-represented among people who come into contact with the criminal and youth justice systems, as victims, witnesses or defendants. It references evidence that autistic people often have poor experiences with these systems, can find prison environments overwhelming and that staff do not always understand their needs. The strategy commits to developing a better view of existing provision for neurodivergent adults, including autistic adults, through a call for evidence on neurodiversity in the criminal justice system.

The social model of disability recognises that many people with disabilities do not consider themselves to be 'vulnerable'. Nevertheless, it is important to acknowledge that many autistic individuals may have vulnerabilities which can lead to encounters with the law – specifically, drugs, cuckooing, disability hate crime, autistic victims of the asylum battle, alleged links with terrorism and the dangers of the internet. The dreadful murder of the transgender autistic teenager Brianna Ghey in 2023 promoted her mother, Esther, to call for the introduction of measures to prevent cyber-bullying (see Chapter 8).

Each chapter of this book includes the latest research findings and illuminating case studies. The Autism Alliance – a UK partnership of not-for-profit organisations that support autistic people and their families - is a useful resource for anyone who wants to be kept up-to-date with any major changes made to the legislation discussed in the book. It signposts relevant legal resources and provides commentary on the key legislation relevant for autistic people and their families in England. For more information see: www.autism-alliance.org.uk/autism-and-the-law.

The structure of the book allows readers to consult a relevant section quickly and easily. The hope is that they do not feel alone and that, armed with the appropriate information, they are in a position in law which will support them in persuading the authorities to realise that they (parents, individuals and carers) are acting within the law in fighting to ensure that their legal rights – which are fundamental human rights – are met.

18 One of the most recent, and tragic, instances was that of Mattheus Vieira, a 11-year-old autistic boy, who died of sepsis at the Queen Elizabeth Hospital in King's Lynn, Norfolk, in April 2022. An inquest in Norwich heard in February 2024 that hospital staff had described Mattheus as 'uncooperative' and 'very difficult to examine'. Mattheus, who had communication difficulties, did not like to be touched and would sit in his pram looking at his tablet computer. Yvonne Blake, area coroner for Norfolk, said: 'He wasn't writhing about – he was sitting quietly playing and people might have been reassured by that'. She said that Mattheus could communicate in single words – saying the word for 'shoe' in Portuguese when he wanted to go out. He died on the afternoon of April 12 as his condition worsened and as staff were preparing to transfer him to a paediatric intensive care unit in Cambridge. Recording a narrative conclusion, the coroner said: 'Mattheus died from sepsis which was not recognised in a timely fashion, and appropriate treatment was not instigated. His death was contributed to by neglect.'

Chapter 1: Pre-assessment, diagnosis and obtaining the appropriate initial services

This chapter will focus on:

- Pre-assessment and ways of obtaining a diagnosis.
- Safeguarding and the pervasive culture of parent-blaming.
- Coming to terms with an autism diagnosis.

Pre-assessment and pathways to obtaining a diagnosis

If you are an autistic individual, the parent or carer of an autistic person and you have an apparent need, you have a right to an assessment of your support requirements. This could be because you have recently received an autism diagnosis and have been told you might need extra support in your daily life. You will need to have this assessment before your local council can recommend a service, such as help from a paid carer or access to day and respite services.

Free needs assessment

You are entitled to a free needs assessment if you have an autism diagnosis and you think you might need more support. The Autism Act (2009) guidance states that, regardless of whether you have other disabilities or not, you are entitled to a needs assessment if you are autistic. Your local authority's website should tell you how to apply for a needs assessment. There is no time limit for your local authority to do the needs assessment. If you have not received a reply within six weeks, contact them to find out what is happening.[19]

19 See www.autism.org.uk/advice-and-guidance/topics/social-care/social-care-england/assessments-and-care-plans (accessed March 2024).

According to the Care Act (2014), the assessor must have a good understanding of your condition or they must consult someone who has. You can have a family member, friend or advocate to be with you during the assessment. If you have substantial difficulty in being involved in the planning process, social services must provide an advocate. If you have a carer, social services must involve them in the assessment, as long as you are happy with this involvement.

A social worker or a community care officer will usually visit you at home to conduct the assessment. They might ask you to complete some forms yourself (a self-assessment). You do not have to agree to this if you would rather not do such a self-assessment. Your local authority must take into account your preferences and needs when deciding when, where and how to do the assessment. If you do not have mental capacity, then a face-to-face assessment should be arranged.[20]

Before the assessment, the local authority must provide you with a list of the questions they will ask. The assessment should include needs you may have in the future. It should consider whether your well-being is likely to deteriorate in the near future if support is not put in place, and you should provide as much detail as you can. The assessor should listen to

20 Ibid.

what outcomes you would like to achieve. This is known as a 'person-centred' approach, and social services must adopt such an approach.

Not everyone who has a needs assessment will be entitled to acquire support. Your local authority will help you to obtain support if your needs meet the national eligibility criteria. If you are eligible for support, social services should develop a care and support plan with you, usually after a needs assessment has taken place. This is sometimes called a care plan. The plan will say the type of support you need and how your care and support needs will be met. It will help you to receive the care you need and also help your friends and family understand how they can better support you.[21]

Your local authority must review your support at least once a year to ensure that it still meets your needs. If you decide you are unhappy with a part of your care plan, you can contact your local authority to ask for a review. If your local authority decides that you no longer qualify for local authority support, they should give you information about other help available.

Getting a diagnosis

Autism is a diagnosis that is being given more and more frequently. A 2022 study conducted by Professor Ginny Russell and colleagues[22] tested whether the proportion of people receiving a new diagnosis of autism had been increasing over a 20-year period, both overall and by sub-groups. The study found an exponential 787% increase in recorded incidence of autism diagnoses in the UK between 1998 and 2018. The researchers concluded: 'Increases could be due to growth in prevalence or, more likely, increased reporting and application of diagnosis. Rising diagnoses among adults, females and higher-functioning individuals suggest augmented recognition underpins these changes.'

Diagnosing autism can be difficult because there is no medical test, such as a blood test, that can diagnose the condition. Doctors look at the child's developmental history and behaviour to make a diagnosis. Autism can sometimes be detected at 18 months of age or younger. By the age of two, a diagnosis by an experienced professional can be considered reliable. However, many children do not receive a final diagnosis until much older. Some people are not diagnosed until they are adolescents or adults. This delay means that people with autism might not receive the early assistance they require. Diagnosing children with autism as early as possible is important to make sure children receive the services and support they need to reach their full potential.

Screening tests for autism are available in the UK, but these should not be seen as an alternative to proper assessment and diagnosis. If your child is pre-school age (between 18 and 24 months), your health visitor or GP may carry out a 'screening interview' called M-CHAT (Modified Checklist for Autism in Toddlers). This aims to identify children at high risk of social-communication differences such as autism. This will not give you a diagnosis, but it is a way of indicating whether your child may be autistic. Other tools, sometimes available online or as smartphone apps, also claim to be able to screen for

21 Ibid.

22 Russell G *et al* (2022) Time trends in autism diagnosis over 20 years: a UK population-based cohort study. *Journal of Child Psychology and Psychiatry* **63** (6) 674–682.

autism. The use of screening or testing tools is potentially problematic because many factors can affect a child's development, and many other sensory, physical and mental health conditions will require specialist investigation. Once again, the use of such screening tools should not be considered as alternatives to proper assessment and diagnosis. The UK government does not recommend screening because, it says, 'there is not currently a test that is good enough for screening the general population [and] it is not known if screening would improve long-term outcomes for children with autism'.[23] Nevertheless, it has been pointed out that screening and assessment are closely linked stages in the diagnostic process, and they each play a distinct role that cannot be replaced by the other. [24]

Because autism is so frequently associated with epilepsy, neurologists will sometimes conduct EEG scans. There is no evidence that seizures or epilepsy (that is, recurrent seizures) cause autism. Various studies have shown that intellectual disability (ID) is the major risk factor for autistic people developing epilepsy. The risk for epilepsy in autistic children without an ID is 8%, increasing to 20% in those with an ID. The risk can be as high as 40% in those with severe intellectual disability. Epilepsy is more likely to occur if someone in the family is autistic. Autism is also more likely in families who have a history of epilepsy. Research also indicates a higher prevalence of epilepsy in women and girls. My son, Johnny, underwent a number of brain scans, all of which were negative. But this told me very little: the way a neurologist (or paediatrician) diagnoses seizures or epilepsy is the same whether or not the person is autistic. However, there are some characteristics associated with autism that can be confused with signs of seizures, such as staring or repetitive movements.

If you are the parent of a child being assessed for autism, you should be wary of those who diagnose your child in absentia, based only on your description of your child's behaviour. Having said that, sometimes these informal diagnoses can prove accurate. Before Johnny was diagnosed, I was on a flight and began describing my concerns to the passenger in the seat next to me: three-year-old Johnny had stopped speaking and was no longer playing with his peers in the playgroup at the end of the road. The passenger remarked: 'I would suggest that Johnny has autism'. I was rightly sceptical of anyone proposing a diagnosis without even observing my son in person. Nevertheless, I took the man's business card without looking at it. Several months later, Johnny was indeed diagnosed with autism by Professor Jeremy Turk at St George's Hospital in south London. It was only then that I decided to look at that business card: it belonged to Professor Éric Fombonne, one of the world's leading autism authorities. Now, whenever I meet Fombonne around the world, he always asks me: 'How's the young man I diagnosed at 30,000 feet?'

Common signs

The characteristics of autism vary from one person to another, but for a diagnosis to be made, a person will usually be assessed as having had persistent difficulties with social communication and social interaction and restricted and repetitive patterns of behaviours,

23 See https://view-health-screening-recommendations.service.gov.uk/autism/ (accessed March 2024)

24 Ekaterina Harrison, personal communication, October 15, 2023.

activities or interests. Unfortunately, the criteria for autism remain largely defined by a medical, deficit-based model.

Some of the main signs that a child may be autistic include:

- Not drawing their parents' or others' attention to objects or events, for example not pointing at a toy or a book, or at something that is happening nearby (a lack of shared attention).
- Carrying out activities in a repetitive way, for example always playing the same game in the same way, or repeatedly lining toys up in a particular order.
- Being resistant to change.
- Emerging difficulties with social interaction and social communication.
- Behaviour such as biting, pinching, kicking, pica (putting inedible items in the mouth), or self-injury.[25]

Health services involved

In the UK, autism diagnoses are made in specialised health services, known as 'secondary care', and not by general practitioners (GPs). GPs will refer a suspected case to secondary care, where autism is normally assessed by a multi-disciplinary team. Referrals may also come directly from young people, families, schools and social workers. The secondary care service for adults is in specialist autism or neurodevelopmental services, or, for those younger than 19 years old, at Child and Adolescent Mental Health Services (CAMHs), or a specialist neurodevelopmental or autism service. Younger, pre-school children are most often diagnosed by community paediatric teams.

In other words, there are several routes to diagnosis, but all flow through secondary care. This means that there is a risk that information about diagnoses may not be passed from secondary to primary care (paediatricians or CAMHs to GP sources), may not be communicated (as parents may not approve of sharing the diagnosis with their GP) or may be incorrectly recorded. The pathways above relate to the NHS, which is free at the point of delivery but which suffers from long waiting lists, leading some families to seek assessment from private practitioners.

Diagnoses made by private services are not routinely fed back to GPs. Instead, clients (parents or adults) are provided the diagnosis by private companies to use as they will. Indeed, there has been a huge surge in the number of Google searches for private autism assessments in the UK, according to a new analysis by the digital innovation healthcare company, Brain in Hand, published in August 2023. The report stated that, between May and August of that year, there had been a staggering 900% increase in searches related to private autism and ADHD assessment. Furthermore, there had been an average of 5,000 searches per month for 'private autism assessment', and a 5,000% increase in searches for terms such as 'high-functioning autism' and 'stimming' in the last quarter.[26]

25 See www.autism.org.uk/advice-and-guidance/topics/diagnosis/pre-diagnosis/parents-and-carers (accessed January 2024)

26 See https://bdaily.co.uk/articles/2023/08/08/uk-sees-900-rise-in-searches-for-private-autism-diagnoses-as-many-call-for-transformative-change-to-address-assessment-backlog (accessed March 2024)

Dr Sarah Lister Brook, the clinical director at Britain's National Autistic Society (NAS), said the decisions of independent diagnostic assessments could not necessarily be relied on: 'There are many providers out there now, some for profit and others not-for-profit. Some are regulated – many are commissioned by the NHS to deal with NHS waiting lists – but some operate with minimal regulation or oversight, so the quality is variable.'[27]

It is important to realise that some UK local authorities may not accept the results of private diagnoses. They might insist upon an NHS diagnosis before they will provide services to you and your child. With this in mind, it is recommended that you stay on the waiting list for an NHS assessment, even if you also decide to go privately.

It is also worth noting here that a diagnosis of autism is not a prerequisite for receiving accommodations in education for children and young people. Typically, needs are evaluated on a functional level by professionals such as educational psychologists, speech and language therapists, and occupational therapists. It is also worth mentioning that self-identification as autistic is gaining acceptance. It is recognised that obtaining an official diagnosis can be challenging, and not everyone has access to the necessary services or resources to pursue it.[28]

Ways to seek a diagnosis

You have a choice of ways of seeking a diagnosis. If you want to approach a GP, keep a file with information on why you think your child may be autistic. Bear in mind that one study indicated that 40% of British GPs said they had received no training on autism at degree level, in training or in practice, so take some information on what autism and Asperger's syndrome are. In the file, include information on anything different you noticed during the pregnancy and childhood (if known) to the present day, including information from school, friends, college, family and work colleagues. Also include any incidents that have happened which make you think autism may be the diagnosis. Ask the GP for a referral for assessment. If the GP disagrees or cannot refer you, contact your local Patient Advisory Liaison Service (PALS) for details of how to obtain a second opinion.

You have the right to complain if you are unhappy about any aspect of referral, diagnosis or care that your child has received from an NHS service. (The complaints procedure is different in each UK nation, but this book specifically focuses on the situation in England.) If your GP cannot refer, or if you disagree with your GP or the second opinion, you could consider a private assessment. If you manage to obtain a private diagnosis, take all paperwork back to your GP to request further help from the NHS.

As of June 2023, 143,119 people were waiting for an autism assessment in England, new NHS data have revealed. This is a 47% increase in just one year.[29] National Institute for Health and Care Excellence (NICE) guidelines state that no one should wait longer than three months between being referred and first being seen, but these data show that the vast majority of people (83%) have been waiting longer than 13 weeks.

27 See https://amp-theguardian-com.cdn.ampproject.org/c/s/amp.theguardian.com/society/2024/mar/04/some-nhs-centres-twice-as-likely-to-diagnose-adults-as-autistic-study-finds (accessed March 2024).

28 Ekaterina Harrison, personal communication.

29 See www.autism.org.uk/what-we-do/news/autism-assessment-waiting-times-3 (accessed January 2024)

A damning report published by the Disability Law Service (DLS) in 2020 revealed a large number of unlawful restrictions on the rights of disabled children with autism to social care needs assessments. The report showed that at least 41 local authorities across England are breaking the law by discriminating against autistic children. The law requires all disabled children to be given proper care, but many councils have adopted a policy that excludes autistic children from an appropriate assessment unless they (for example) also have another disability. The case studies in the report are particularly heartbreaking.[30]

The research underpinning the DLS report considered the legality of restrictions put in place by some local authorities which impede the rights of disabled children with autism to an assessment of their needs and to support required to meet those needs. The policies of 149 English local authorities were considered, although only 93 were identified as having 'functional' eligibility policies for such support. Of the policies that were considered as functional, 41 (44.08%) made specific mention of autism when determining whether a child would be assessed by or supported by their Children with Disabilities Team. These authorities generally linked autism to an additional requirement (or requirements), for example, that the child had another impairment or a formal diagnosis. These criteria are referred to as 'Autism Plus' policies. Such 'Autism Plus' policies constitute unlawful discrimination under the Equality Act (2010). They indirectly discriminate against disabled children with autism, compared to other disabled children. 'Autism Plus' policies of this kind, which predicate support on the existence of a formal diagnosis of autism, would appear also to represent unlawful discrimination under the Equality Act (2010) on grounds of sex – as materially more young men have an autism diagnosis than young women. It is arguable that 'Autism Plus' policies of this kind also constitute *direct* discrimination under the Equality Act. Eligibility policies which require disabled children with autism to have received a formal diagnosis of autism before accessing disabled children's assessment and support services constitute a non-statutory barrier to disabled children's support services under the Children Act (1989) and the Chronically Sick and Disabled Persons Act (1970) and are, in consequence, unlawful.

Luke Clements, professor of law at the University of Leeds, pointed out:

> 'We identified 41 English authorities which had Autism Plus policies. We followed these up and found that 30 had changed their policies. On the other hand, other authorities now have them which did not use to. In any case, even if an authority changes the policy, their practices may continue to be exactly the same. On their website, they no longer refer to autism distinctly. It is good that 30 of them have officially changed their policies, but we do not know whether they have altered their training or staff. So they might have "changed their name and done the same".'[31]

30 See https://cerebra.org.uk/research/41-local-authorities-are-unlawfully-discriminating-against-autistic-children/ (accessed March 2024)

31 Luke Clements, personal communication, February 20, 2023.

Eligibility criteria

Navigating the eligibility criteria in social care can be quite complex. Local authorities can establish a threshold at which they deem it necessary to address the child's needs. As Baroness Hale pointed out in R (KM) v Cambridgeshire CC: 'The uncomfortable reality is that the same level of presenting need may qualify for services in one authority area but not in another.'[32]

Nevertheless, it has been pointed out that the local authority needs to apply its eligibility criteria in accordance with the law, such as fulfilling their public sector equality duty, among other considerations. 'A thorough legal analysis is necessary to determine the lawfulness of certain exclusions, such as the absence of a diagnosis or the requirement for additional factors alongside an autism diagnosis,' the autistic lawyer, Ekaterina Harrison, observed.[33]

The issue of access was also a major concern of the DLS research team. Local authorities are under a duty to publish their eligibility criteria for disabled children's assessment and support services as part of their 'local offer'. In many cases, the relevant criteria were not accessible and in many cases they were identified only after a prolonged period of searching or through the use of information gained from Freedom of Information requests.

The DLS called for immediate action by the local authorities to rectify the 'systemic' failings in their eligibility criteria for the assessment and support of disabled children – and to ensure that these were published in a readily accessible form. The UK government should also bring forward legislation to put eligibility criteria on a statutory footing – as has been done for (among others) disabled adults in England and disabled children in Wales. All authorities with 'Autism Plus' policies should withdraw these as a matter of great urgency.[34]

Jane Harris, the former Director of External Affairs at the National Autistic Society, declared:

> 'This is a damning report, revealing how autistic children are routinely being failed by a social care system starved of investment. Parents tell us they're asking for help in desperate situations, but too often they're being turned away. It is completely unacceptable for a council to deny a child an assessment simply because an autistic child does not have another condition. It is equally wrong for a council to withhold support from someone just because they do not have a formal diagnosis. Families are left struggling to support their children without training or funding. And without extra help (like short breaks), they can end up isolated and alone, unable to function on a daily basis. Councils should make decisions about support based on a child's needs. Without this, autistic children will struggle at home and at school and could end up isolated. No one would accept this situation for their child. And we won't accept it for autistic children. The government must make sure councils follow the law and have funding to support autistic children properly.'[35]

32 See www.supremecourt.uk/cases/docs/uksc-2011-0005-judgment.pdf (accessed March 2024).

33 Ekaterina Harrison, personal communication.

34 See https://cerebra.org.uk/research/41-local-authorities-are-unlawfully-discriminating-against-autistic-children/ (accessed January 2024).

35 Ibid.

The Westminster Commission on Autism review on the pre-assessment phase while seeking a diagnosis found that this was a stage of extremely high levels of stress. Only a quarter of those questioned by the Commission declared themselves satisfied with the provisions or support available to them or their child while waiting for the autism assessment. One parent of an autistic child observed: 'It was one of the most stressful periods of my life, mainly because of watching my son struggle and having no clue how to help him, despite being very proactive in trying to get help'. Another parent suggested that everyone – the school nurse, teachers, the GP, health visitors – appeared to be 'passing the buck' when assuming responsibility for referring the child. Being female was another challenge when seeking an autism diagnosis. Many professionals continue to assume that autism is a male condition.[36] In fact, the frequency of 'masking' or 'camouflaging' among females has led to an under-diagnosis of girls and women, which can be problematic in many areas of life, including in the workplace.[37]

Very recent research from University College London (UCL) suggests that people have an 85% chance of being diagnosed as autistic in some NHS centres, compared with a 35% chance in others. Dr William Mandy, a professor of neurodevelopmental conditions at UCL who led the 2024 research across several NHS foundations in southern England, said the wide variation suggested a lack of consistency between centres. He said it raised fears that lives could be badly affected by inaccurate diagnoses and called for 'radical changes' to the system: 'Our results worryingly suggest that people are being over-diagnosed in some areas and underdiagnosed in others,' said Professor Mandy, adding: 'The fact is that the diagnostic manuals are open to a lot of interpretation and so there is fundamentally a lack of consensus as to where the right boundaries of autism are... Our findings worry me because this is a high-stakes assessment that is really important in affecting somebody's identity, their access to services and funds, and their life decisions.'[38]

Although the UK government's 2010 autism strategy recommended the establishment of specialist, community-based, multi-disciplinary teams to provide, co-ordinate and oversee services. there is no guidance as to the staffing or operation of these teams. As a consequence, a number of different models have emerged. Dr Bryony Beresford, a professor at the University of York, conducted the first national evaluation of specialist autism team service models in 2020.[39] 'Each team differed in their diagnostic assessment protocols and each was unique,' she said. 'In addition, unlike some diagnoses, clinical judgement is central to the autism diagnostic process and this will contribute to variation. Does this mean we can't trust diagnoses? We just don't yet have the evidence to say yes or no to that question.'[40]

36 See www.bath.ac.uk/announcements/report-highlights-need-for-greater-support-for-individuals-awaiting-autism-diagnostic-assessment/ (accessedMarch 2024)

37 See: Afam Feinstein: *Autism Works: A Guide to Successful Employment Across the Entire Spectrum*. London: Routledge, 2019.

38 See https://amp-theguardian com.cdn.ampproject.org/c/s/amp.theguardian.com/society/2024/mar/04/some-nhs-centres-twice-as-likely-to-diagnose-adults-as-autistic-study-finds (accessed March 2024).

39 Beresford BA, Mukherjee SKM, Mayhew ET, et al. (2020): The SHAPE project: Supporting adults with High-functioning Autism and asPerger syndromE. Mapping and evaluating Specialist Autism Team service models. *Health Services and Delivery Research*. p. 1. ISSN 2050-4357.

40 See https://amp-theguardian com.cdn.ampproject.org/c/s/amp.theguardian.com/society/2024/mar/04/some-nhs-centres-twice-as-likely-to-diagnose-adults-as-autistic-study-finds (accessed March 2024).

Useful resources and further guidance

- Your child does not have to be diagnosed to be considered in need. You should contact your local social services (in England and Wales) – or the social work department (in Scotland) or Health and Social Care Trust (in Northern Ireland) – to ask for an assessment of your child's particular needs. You can also ask for an assessment of your needs as a carer. You might be able to access a variety of support such as short breaks. Your family may also be eligible for benefits such as Disability Living Allowance and Carers Allowance.
- The social care assessment is not the sole option for aiding individuals with special needs. Another option, for instance, is the education, health and care assessment, which is accessible to children and young people up to the age of 25.
- Luke Clements' *Accessing Public Services Toolkit: A problem-solving approach:* www.lukeclements.co.uk/wp-content/uploads/2018/11/Toolkit-final-2017.pdf

Safeguarding and the pervasive culture of parent-blaming: how to play the 'game'

The appalling cases of the deaths of Sammy Alban-Stanley (see **Case study 2** on p.24) and Oskar Nash (see **Case study 6** on p.42) highlighted the horrendous defects inherent in a system in which the emphasis on safeguarding led to the parents being blamed, without any justification whatsoever. As Anna Moore, a solicitor working for Leigh Day specialising in Court of Protection and Human Rights Act cases involving children and vulnerable adults, explained to me:

> 'In the cases of Oskar and Sammy, the focus on the social services' interventions was not on supporting the disabled child but rather on safeguarding. So they concentrated on short-term interventions which sought to resolve safeguarding issues but were inappropriate in these cases. In other words, the structure of support was not fit for purpose. With child protection, workers are trained to scrutinise what is happening in the home. In both of these cases, there were loving families trying to do their best.'[41]

Moore continued:

> 'Autism often falls into the gap: it is not a physical disability – so it is not always picked up by the Children with Disabilities Team, even though that would be the most appropriate team provided they were properly trained. What was clear in the cases of both Oskar and Sammy was that the NHS Trust was saying that it was a social care issue, while the social services were saying that it was not a safeguarding issue. So no one was willing to pick the cases up. And the parents came to be blamed. This was unfounded, as both coroners agreed, but incredibly distressing.

41 Anna Moore, personal communication, February 23, 2023.

The whole system is not fit for purpose. Of course, safeguarding is important, but not the right intervention for the disabled children.'[42]

Case study 1: Child Z versus Sefton Council

The family of an autistic child, known as Child Z, is due to be paid £1,000 and receive an apology from Sefton Council, near Liverpool, after 'unacceptable delays' in assessing the child's needs. The payout is in addition to £3,000 already offered to the family by the local authority after it failed to provide appropriate levels of special educational needs provision to the family.[43]

The ruling follows a complaint submitted on behalf of the family to the Local Government Ombudsman about the way the child was treated by Sefton Council, alleging it had failed to deliver specialist therapies listed in an education, health and care plan (EHC Plan). The complaint also alleged that there had been repeated delays in having the child's EHC Plan reviewed over several years, including most recently in 2021, when this was completed only after the family had threatened legal action – according to a report recently released by the Local Government Ombudsman (LGO).

After investigating, the complaint was upheld by the LGO in a ruling which also stated that Sefton Council needed to 'make improvements to its service to ensure it complies with SEN statutory timescales and requirements'.

Child Z had been assessed and provided with an EHC Plan in 2018. As part of that plan, the child was entitled to occupational therapy and speech and language support, which was commissioned by the council. According to the LGO decision notice, the child's speech and language therapy provider claimed that, in early 2019, the family had agreed to reduce the amount of support the child received. The family 'strongly refutes' this claim. A couple of months later, the council, school and family met to complete an annual review, a copy of which 'does not appear' to have been sent to the family, nor was a finalised EHC Plan issued for that year, according to the LGO. The service provider maintained that, by July 2019, the family had once again agreed to a reduction in provision. The child's mother again 'strongly refutes' this claim. A further review of the child's EHC Plan was conducted during the Covid pandemic in June 2020, when the child was not attending school due to lockdown. By April 2021, the council 'appears to have started another annual review', according to the LGO. When this was not received by the family, they wrote to the council in October 2021 threatening legal action. Shortly afterwards, the EHC Plan was received and the family initiated an appeal. After the appeal process had been completed in 2022, the child's EHC Plan was amended: a decision made for an alternative school placement where, according to the LGO report, Child Z is now 'thriving'. The LGO said the council was at fault in not providing the family with a copy of the amended EHC Plan in 2019, which meant that they were 'not given access to their appeal rights' or were unable to challenge the level of provision offered. The LGO said that, after a complaint by the family, the council had provided a 'suitable' remedy over the lack of SEN provision by offering £2,000 to compensate for their costs in sourcing private provision and in 'recognition of the time and trouble they had experienced in raising their concerns'. →

42 Ibid.

43 See www.liverpoolecho.co.uk/news/liverpool-news/council-pay-family-autistic-child-27596868 (accessed March 2024).

A further element to the complaint involved an allegation that the council had failed to obtain professional assessments. While the council said they were in the process of organising these when notified by the family that they were sourcing their own, the LGO found this not to be the case. The report notes, however: 'I am equally not persuaded Child Z and their parents suffered injustice as a direct result of the Council's actions' because the reports were not shared with the council until it was too late for them to be included in the review for that year – although they were later factored into an amended plan that was produced following appeal. Recommending that the council pay an additional £1,000 to the family 'in recognition of the uncertainty and distress caused by not completing EHC Plan annual reviews within statutory timescales' or issuing an apology, the report also said the council had agreed to take action to improve its overall service within three months of the decision.[44]

Ekaterina Harrison offered a different perspective:

> 'Parent-blaming typically pertains to situations where concerns about parenting neglect lead to attributions of the issues to inadequate parenting, rather than recognising special needs. As a result, it is not uncommon for parents to be directed towards parenting courses as an initial response to tackle the challenges. In this case, it appears that parents are being held responsible for their struggle in seeking assistance, particularly in terms of articulating the problems to meet eligibility criteria. I hesitate to label this particular example as a culture of parent-blaming. Rather, it seems to be a reflection of a convoluted and user-unfriendly system.' [45]

Anna Moore confirmed that change had occurred as a result of the Alban-Stanley and Nash inquests: 'Even more powerful is the work that people like Sammy's mother, Patricia, go on to do. However, the resource-led approach is getting even stronger. There are very real issues of access to justice: for example, the availability of lawyers and legal aid. It is a very uneven playing-field.'[46]

Case study 2: Sammy Alban-Stanley

Patricia Alban-Stanley went through a living nightmare after two local authorities refused to offer support for her son, Sammy, who died four days after being found at the bottom of a cliff in 2020. He was 13 years old. Alban-Stanley told me that Sammy had been diagnosed with the neurological condition, Prader-Willi syndrome, five weeks after birth. 'We knew he was also autistic. He was under the Children with Disabilities Team in East Hampshire. The problem was that people with neurological conditions do not behave in the way that the local authority expects them to. They don't fit into the disability "box". Sammy was brilliant at making things out of Lego and wood, and he had a good vocabulary. But he had no sense of physical danger. You just cannot win: I worked hard on his diet so that his weight was good – which is unusual in children with Prader-Willi, as the hypothalamus which regulates emotion, mood and appetite is faulty, and muscle tone is low. Shopping in Aldi, I made sure he chose exactly five food items for each meal, a system that I had worked very hard at, basically tapping into his autism to regulate his PWS. But we were penalised for all the work Sammy and I put in, because they could not understand how someone so polite and sweet could sometimes act out of control.'[47] ➔

44 Ibid.

45 Ekaterina Harrison, personal communication.

46 Anna Moore, personal communication.

47 Patricia Alban-Stanley, personal communication, May 17, 2023.

Alban-Stanley continued to explain that East Hampshire 'were itching' to remove the care hours. 'Sammy was functioning,' she said, 'but when I noticed some signs of neurodiversity in my three daughters and asked for one of them to be assessed, they began a full-blown parent-blaming attack. They refused point-bank to assess any of my girls and used the opportunity to remove Sammy completely from the disability services within a month, removing his 15 hours of care. They argued that there had to be something wrong with me. They claimed that Sammy did not have autism with challenging behaviour.

> 'A large proportion of children with Prader-Willi are under the Children with Disabilities Team. All people with the condition battle obesity or and have learning disabilities. But precisely because I had worked with Sammy and he obviously had both strengths and weaknesses, this was used against him. Without the support at home, his terrible, life-threatening episodes began. They often started when he could not find an object, like his charger. Or he couldn't understand something.
>
> For instance, he could not understand why the receptionist at the doctor's surgery was difficult, while the doctor was really nice. Or he could not understand why a shop would not take back something that was faulty. Or there were unexpected changes of routine. His brain snapped. His behaviour would change, his vocabulary would change, and he would be unsafe for the next 45 minutes. I begged East Hampshire to bring him back under their Children with Disabilities Team. In the end, they did another assessment. They refused to help, arguing that Sammy's episodes were "unpredictable" – but that was precisely why we needed help! So we had no support.'[48]

By 2017, Alban-Stanley was at crisis point. Sammy was asked to leave his junior school and the local named special school had turned him down. 'My work as an upholsterer is based in Kent, where I had a house rented out and where we used to spend part of the holidays. Sammy loved the sea. So, I thought, the sensible thing would be to try to get him into a school in Kent. One of them was a perfect fit for Sammy, so I felt a sense of relief It was an autism-specific school called Laleham Gap. I double-checked and phoned Kent County Council to make sure he could have a place there. They told me we had to move to Kent first. So we did just that. The girls then got assessed, were diagnosed with dyslexia and had their needs met, which was good news. But suddenly, I was chastised. I was asked: "Why did you move?" But they were the ones who had told me to move in the first place! Kent County Council spoke to East Hampshire and then refused to assess Sammy. They decided that he did not meet their criteria for falling under the Children with Disabilities Team.

> 'By then, Sammy had nearly died. He had tried to open a car door when I was driving down the A3. He survived only because I did an emergency stop and grabbed hold of him. The A3 had to be closed. It was horrendous. I thought I would definitely receive support after that, but the Children with Disabilities Team insisted that he still did not meet the criteria. We were allocated a social worker, who pushed for the Children with Disabilities Team to become involved, but they refused. In fact, several senior social workers asked for Sammy to be assessed. One of these social workers was very impressive and argued that no one could be expected to handle this situation at home without support. The police had been called out more than 30 times. They were acting as substitute carers. In fact, social services were actually using the police as my care plan. The manager of the Kent Children with Disabilities ➔

48 Ibid.

– Team declared she had looked up Prader-Willi syndrome on Wikipedia where it stated that most children with Prader-Willi did not have a severe learning disability. We discovered all this at Sammy's inquest. It was shocking. If they had come even once to assess Sammy, they would have seen straight away that he had life-long learning disabilities, affecting daily family functioning, so he should have met the criteria. But they never came, even though he was hospitalised several times. Eventually, they agreed to offer ten hours a week of temporary social care, but that support did not begin until January 2020 and it was not what we had asked for. He needed wraparound care. Then Covid arrived, and the lockdown, and a few weeks later, Sammy died. He had never been accepted back under the care of the Children with Disabilities Team. He suffered six years of neglect.'[49]

Another British mother took seven years to get her son diagnosed with autism. She explained that the local authorities were reluctant even to conduct an assessment and made her feel she was to blame, by being too anxious as a mother. It is distressing to learn how widespread this parent-blaming practice is (the mother said it occurred throughout the UK). Having travelled to more than a hundred countries to write my book on the history of autism and finding that, in general, the toxic 'refrigerator mother' approach had largely been eliminated, I was all the more shocked to find how pervasive this new culture of blaming the parents had become in Britain.

There is even a private service in the Midlands advising parents on how to play the 'game' both to prevent the authorities from thrusting the responsibility onto them, as parents, for their child's problems, and to encourage the same authorities to initiate the assessment process.

The mother mentioned above told me:

> 'When I expressed misgivings about my son's not being allowed to do advanced maths at his generic school, the teacher asked me to leave the building. I was told I was being over-anxious about his future. As a parent, apparently, you are not allowed to show any anxiety! That will be used against you. You are causing the problems. You must not express their anxiety, or you have to express it in a very specific way. You do not say: "I am worried about my child". You say: "My child is not accessing this. Do you think this might be to his detriment?"'[50]

Another mother agrees:

> 'Yes, these are the tricks of the trade. You have to learn to play the "game". My daughter has Asperger's syndrome. I have been playing the "game" with the local authorities since she was around seven. She is now 23. I went to a meeting where another mother said to the school: "Can my daughter have a reduced timetable?" I sat there thinking: "Don't say that – that will get thrown back at you." Instead, you should say: "My daughter is struggling to come into school. What do you think we can do to help?" You have to put all the onus back onto the school. Because if

49 Ibid.

50 Personal communication.

> you say that you can't get your child to school, you are considered responsible. You cannot show that you are weak or worried. Do not cry at a meeting, because they will claim you are emotionally unstable.'[51]

Ekaterina Harrison has observed that schools have:

> '... to offer full-time education, making it challenging for them to propose solutions involving reduced hours, which might potentially be considered as unlawful exclusion. In cases where the reasons for a reduced timetable are medical or if the child has an EHC Plan, parents should engage in discussions with the local authority about these matters. It is possible to argue that the school should have the capacity to provide parents with appropriate guidance, regardless of how the question is posed (as a request or as an invitation to give advice). However, it is important to recognise that there is typically a low level of awareness about special needs entitlements, and this knowledge can greatly differ from school to school. When a discussion devolves into emotional blame, it often suggests that the party resorting to this tactic lacks alternative arguments.'[52]

Luke Clements, professor of law at the University of Leeds, explains:

> 'The key thing is to get emotional support from an independent parent-carer group. Parent-carers who do not have networks need emotional support in order to realise that they are not alone. Independent parent-carer groups are very important. They can provide very helpful support, including, for example, flagging up specialists such as lawyers. There is, as always, a problem. Each local authority area has a designated "Parent-Carer Forum" – and these forums are eligible for a Department for Education grant of £17,500. However, in order to obtain this, they must demonstrate that they have the support of their local authority.[53] Objectively, this can compromise their independence: forums that highlight severe local authority failings risk losing their grant – and in practice, this appears to be a real problem. For example, in 2022 it was reported that Bristol City Council attempted to withdraw its support for a forum because it was saying the wrong things.[54] There are, however, many good parent-carer forums and many other parent-carer groups which do not get funding of this kind.
>
> My research indicates that the key point of departure is to get in touch with a support group which can then give you independent advice. If you have a child with challenging behaviour, there is not much cognitive space. Parents are effectively overwhelmed. They need emotional backing. This gives you the resilience to persevere, rather than give up. Lawyers are pretty difficult to get hold of, and they are expensive. Obviously, you need self-help books, like your one.'[55]

51 Personal communication.

52 Ekaterina Harrison, personal communication.

53 See: https://contact.org.uk/wp-content/uploads/2022/08/FINAL-Grant-application-guidance.pdf

54 See: www.lukeclements.co.uk/what-exactly-is-going-on-bristol/

55 Luke Clements, personal communication, February 20, 2023.

Useful resources and further guidance

- Parents should contact others in the same situation through social media, such as on Facebook.
- Every local authority in the UK is legally obliged to make a parents' online forum available. But parents should bear in mind that these forums are run by the local authority and participants tend to be parents who have not encountered difficulties. Hence the importance of 'independent' social media like Facebook.

The immediate post-diagnosis phase

It may be very difficult for a parent to come to terms with an autism diagnosis. You may experience feelings similar to grieving for a lost 'normal' child or you may feel utterly alone – you're not! I personally chose to seek as much information as possible on the condition, so much so that I launched my own international autism magazine, called *Looking Up*, (www.lookingupautism.org), featuring the latest research findings, as well as human-interest stories. Because its first issues came out before the internet even existed and information was therefore scarce, the magazine proved very popular with parents and special schools.

Remember that your child is the same person he or she has always been. But you need to ascertain the child's specific needs as early as possible. A diagnosis can help your child to receive autism-specific support, but this does not happen automatically.

Local authorities in the UK have a duty to provide services for children in need.
The statutory guidance, published in 2015, for local authorities and NHS organisations to support the implementation of the Adult Autism Strategy stated: 'We remain committed to our future vision that all adults with autism are able to live fulfilling and rewarding lives within a society that accepts and understands them, they can get a diagnosis and access support if they need it, and they can depend on mainstream public services to treat them fairly as individuals, helping them make the most of their talents'.

Note the glaringly obvious omission: children. This is because the strategy refers back to the 2009 Autism Act, which relates only to autistic adults – although the UK government has now published a new strategy, 'National strategy for autistic children, young people and adults: 2021 to 2026'.

In reality, the situation can be desperate for newly diagnosed autistic children in some parts of the UK.

The UK's leading autism research and campaigning charity, Autistica, has pointed out: 'Too many autistic people are abandoned after diagnosis with zero effective support... Consistently, the biggest complaint about diagnostic pathways from autistic people, families and clinicians is the lack of support provided post-diagnosis. Individuals and families are given limited hope for the future. Clinicians and commissioners are given limited resources or guidance to improve pathways.'[56]

56 See: www.autistica.org.uk/news/autistica-release-post-diagnosis-support-plan

Autistica has brought together autistic people, parents, service leads and researchers to devise a support plan outlining the tailored support required to ensure that people understand autism, prepare for the future post-diagnosis and have access to life-long support as their needs and individual circumstances evolve.[57]

Useful resources and further guidance

- The Autistica Post-Diagnosis Support Plan can be accessed at: www.autistica.org.uk/downloads/files/Autistica-Support-Plan.pdf#asset:143226:url (accessed January 2024).
- Some useful information from the NHS can be found at: www.nhs.uk/conditions/autism/newly-diagnosed/ (accessed January 2024).
- Your family may be eligible for benefits such as Disability Living Allowance and Carers Allowance.

Summary

The Autism Act (2009) guidance states that, regardless of whether you have other disabilities or not, you are entitled to a needs assessment if you are autistic. By the age of two, a diagnosis of autism by an experienced professional can be considered reliable. However, many children do not receive a final diagnosis until much older, and some people are not diagnosed until they are adolescents or adults. This increasing delay in NHS diagnoses, which means that people with autism might not receive the early assistance they require, has led to a huge surge in the number of quests for private autism assessments in the UK. However, the decisions of independent diagnostic assessments cannot necessarily be relied on and, in any case, some UK local authorities may not accept the results of private diagnoses. If you want to approach a GP, keep a file with information on why you think your child may be autistic, because many British GPs said they had received no training on autism at degree level, in training or in practice. You have the right to complain if you are unhappy about any aspect of referral, diagnosis or care that your child has received from an NHS service. In some cases, the focus on the social services' interventions has been on safeguarding, rather than supporting the disabled child, and this has led to parents being unjustifiably blamed. There needs to be far more support for newly diagnosed autistic children in some parts of the UK. Clinicians and commissioners are given all-too-limited resources or guidance.

57 Ibid.

Chapter 2: Education and the law

This chapter will focus on:

- Your right to an appropriate education – and choosing the right school.
- The lack of legal protection in the transition into education.
- Fighting school exclusions.
- The use of restraints in schools.
- Masking at school: the legal implications.

How to find the right school – and your legal rights

Many parents of autistic children – and their carers – have difficulties finding an appropriate school. The local authorities (LAs) have a duty only to provide an 'adequate' education for your child. They are, however, obliged to provide you with information about available schools and to explain their decision about where they have decided to place your child.

What does an 'adequate' education mean? Under UK law, it is compulsory for children to participate in education starting from the age of five. The responsibility is placed on parents to ensure that their child receives an efficient full-time education which is suitable for their age, ability and aptitude, and any special educational needs they may have (Education Act (1996), Section 7). This education can be provided either at school or through other means (including home-schooling). Local authorities have a corresponding duty to ensure that the local population has access to efficient primary and secondary education which meets their needs.

The terms 'full-time', 'suitable' or 'efficient' lack specific definitions within English statute law. Nevertheless, the courts have offered some legal guidance on these matters. These discussions frequently arise in the context of home-schooling, where the extent of the obligation to provide suitable education is debated most fervently. Home-schooling is an option often chosen by families with autistic children (see the section on Home-schooling and the law below).

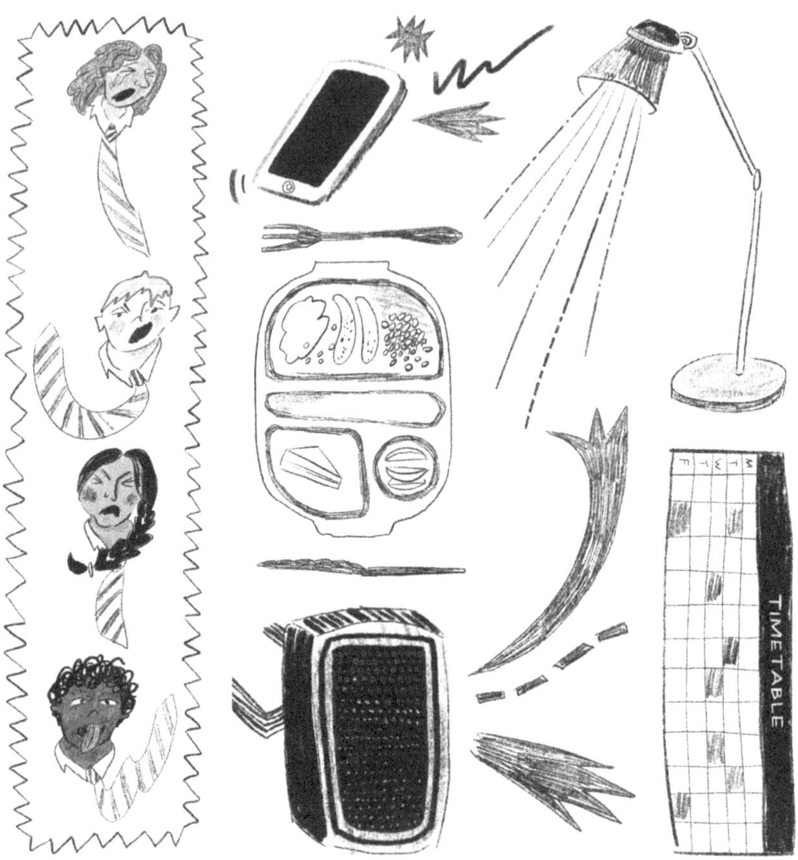

In the UK, the legislative presumption promotes inclusive education for children with special educational needs in mainstream settings. However, parents of autistic children may express a clear preference for special education for their child over a mainstream environment. While the goal of educational inclusion is morally justified in government policies, it remains uncertain whether inclusion has been meeting the needs of children with special educational needs effectively.

It is possible that the emphasis on mainstream education, backed by the presumption in favour of inclusion, has contributed to a decline in the availability of special schools in the UK. Paradoxically, however, according to the Special Needs Jungle website, there has been a large-scale drift of pupils with Education, Health and Care (EHC) Plans away from mainstream schools to special schools for many years, although this has slowed down in recent years due to capacity constraints in special schools.[58] This shift may be influenced by evolving perspectives from experts regarding the desirability of school inclusion.

58 See www.specialneedsjungle.com/send-schools-2021-waiting-other-shoe-drop/ (accessed January 2024).

Notably, Baroness Mary Warnock, who played a crucial role in shaping 'the UK's modern SEN system, revisited the issue and expressed concerns about the effectiveness of inclusion, particularly in secondary schools.[59] She highlighted evidence of bullying faced by children with SEN in mainstream schools and argued that students with statements of SEN (now known as EHC Plans) should be educated in special schools where the necessary provisions could be better offered.

The use of language in this area can prove bewildering, as well as delicate. When talking about state-funded schools that cater to children with special educational needs, it is common to refer to these as 'special' schools. On the other hand, privately owned schools in the same category are often referred to as 'specialist'. It has been suggested that, when discussing the inclusion of autistic children in regular classroom settings, instead of using terms like 'mainstreamed', which can be perceived as insensitive, a more compassionate approach would be to focus on the concept of creating inclusive educational environments that cater to the unique needs of autistic children.[60]

Many autistic children and young people face obstacles that make traditional schooling inaccessible for various reasons. The sensory bombardment (loud noises, fluorescent lighting) may not prove conducive to learning. In such cases, it becomes the responsibility of the local authority to provide a suitable education for children who are unable to attend school due to illness, exclusion or other circumstances, as outlined in Section 19 of the Education Act (2011). Securing appropriate alternative provision is notoriously challenging and may often leave some autistic children without access to education for extended periods, ranging from months to even years.

EHC Plans and assessment

The UK's Equality Act (2010) states that schools must provide all eligible children with free and appropriate public education that meets their unique needs. So, if your child does need extra support, then parents, teachers and the school special educational needs coordinator (SENCO) can work together to request an EHC assessment. If successful, the child can then be given an EHC Plan, which documents exactly what resources and strategies need to be put in place to help the child with his or her learning. The contents of EHC Plans are written based on expert reports from professionals such as occupational therapists, speech and language therapists, and educational psychologists.

The decision on whether to conduct an EHC assessment is based on certain criteria outlined in the Children and Families Act (2014), specifically in Section 36(8). These rules are designed to make it relatively easy for a child to qualify for the assessment. Nevertheless, many local authorities do not appear to have a complete grasp of these requirements, given the significant number of successful appeals against their decisions to deny assessments.

Achieving an actionable plan that is legally enforceable can prove notoriously challenging. EHC Plans have come in for considerable criticism. One common concern is the lack of clear and specific details of the child's needs. This may make it difficult to implement the

59 Warnock M & Norwich B (2005) *Special Educational Needs: A New Look*. Bloomsbury.

60 Ekaterina Harrison, personal communication, May 28, 2023.

necessary and appropriate support. The complex bureaucratic processes involved can be overwhelming for families navigating the system. Insufficient involvement of parents and the students themselves in the planning process is also viewed as a drawback because their input can be extremely valuable. Moreover, inconsistencies and variations across different local authorities may result in unequal access to support services. Limited resources and funding further hinder the effective implementation of these plans, leading to delays and unmet needs.[61]

There are children with special educational needs who do not have EHC Plans, even though they are entitled to this support. If you have a pre-school child who has an EHC Plan or is undergoing an education, health and care needs assessment in preparation for school, your LA must provide you with a list of suitable local schools. They may provide you with a complete list of schools and guidance on which they feel are appropriate or they may just offer a list of selected schools.

It is also a sensible investment of time and money to seek advice from private educational consultants, who possess a deep understanding of schools. Their expertise and insights can provide valuable guidance in selecting the most suitable educational settings for autistic children.

Choosing a school

Every autistic child is unique, with his or her own specific needs. So, although some schools have 'Autism Accreditation' from the UK's National Autistic Society, others may also be more appropriate, for one reason or another. It may be useful to ask professionals who have previously been involved in your child's education or care for their views. This could be an educational psychologist, a speech and language therapist, an occupational therapist, an inclusion support worker, a school special educational needs coordinator (SENCO) or support for learning principal or department head.

Parents are faced with several options when choosing a school for their child. In addition to mainstream and special schools, some schools have bases or units specifically for autistic children and young people. Depending on their needs, it may also be appropriate to consider residential schools or home education for your child. The school environment is crucial: how will your child react to the layout of the school? Is there bright lighting, excessive noise or another specific sensory trigger? Will your child have support in class and during unstructured times such as during breaks and at lunchtime? Can your child manage the journey to and from school, either with or without support? During your visit to the school, attempt to assess the depth of the staff's knowledge of autism, together with what resources and strategies they will use to help your child. Ask whether your child will have access to either a full, reduced or modified curriculum. Will they have the opportunity to learn life skills, achieve qualifications or study subjects of interest? What opportunities will your child have for extracurricular activities, trips and events? Inspection reports and any accreditation awards can also help you.[62]

---

61 See www.ipsea.org.uk/enforcing-your-ehc-plan (accessed March 2024).

62 See www.autism.org.uk/advice-and-guidance/topics/education/education-choices/england/choosing-between-a-mainstream-and-a-specialist-sch (accessed March 2024).

It is important to bear in mind that primary schools are generally more able to accommodate autistic children, especially if they do not have significant learning disabilities. In secondary schools, the larger size and inflexible behaviour-management policies often make it more challenging to cater to their needs.

Special schools for autistic children can be categorised into two types. Some special schools provide a pathway to GCSEs and are suitable for academically capable children. Within this category, there are special schools that offer triple science as part of their GCSE curriculum; this usually indicates a strong emphasis on academic achievement and high aspirations for the students. Other special schools are better suited to autistic children with significant learning disabilities. These can offer vocational pathways.

To ensure an appropriate learning environment for autistic learners, it is crucial for a school to demonstrate its understanding of autism. A general knowledge of special needs may not be sufficient. Examining the school's policies is a good starting point to gain an insight into its specific approach. Certain practices, such as detentions, may not be suitable for autistic children.

In terms of support, small classes can be a viable alternative to one-to-one assistance. This set-up can also benefit children with auditory processing difficulties. Schools with ample natural light and spacious grounds can also contribute positively to the overall sensory experience of autistic learners.

The choice of activities in physical education (PE) is another important factor to consider. Many autistic children find it difficult to participate in team sports. Providing alternative activities which are more inclusive can ensure their active involvement and engagement in PE classes.

Some mainstream schools have autism units, also known as 'resourced provision'. These are considered part of the mainstream school due to their porous nature (the young people can move into and out of the unit from the mainstream school). However, concern has been raised in some circles over the use of these autism units as an intermediary solution between mainstream and special schools. Such units might not facilitate meaningful inclusion at all. On the contrary, they could contribute to the stigmatisation of autistic students by their neurotypical peers.

In recent years, there appears to have been a conspicuous shift away from the model of autism units within mainstream schools across the UK. According to the *Times Educational Supplement*, there was a 14% reduction in such units in secondary schools between 2017 and 2018 alone.[63]

63 Ward H (2018) 'Big drop in mainstream school SEND provision' (TES, July 30). Available at: www.tes.com/magazine/archive/big-drop-mainstream-school-send-provision (accessed March 2024).

Case study 3: 'Peter'

Some autistic children may thrive in a mainstream school. Take the example of Peter (not his real name). He is an autistic boy but, when it came to choosing a school, his mother, Miriam, chose a local mainstream Church of England nursery and school. Peter's autism was not apparent when he started at nursery but came to a head in reception. She was told that he would need a statement (now known as an EHC Plan) if he was to receive the additional support that he needed to stay in school.[64]

Miriam recalled: 'I learned that professional experts would come to assess him – they would make the statement and we would have to sign it to say we agreed. When the statement arrived, we looked at it and I wasn't in agreement with it. What they said didn't match my child. I spoke to the SENCO [Special Educational Needs Coordinator] and told her that I didn't agree with what was written about Peter in the statement. She told us that, if she didn't put these things down, he would never get full-time one-to-one support...'[65]

Miriam was told to go and look at special schools. 'It was only when I went to visit other mainstream schools that I realised there were children with the same disabilities as my child and they were being supported within a mainstream school.' Then Miriam's independent supporter suggested she speak to Laxmi Patel, a solicitor at Boyes Turner's specialist education team. Patel helped Miriam to appeal against the local authority's decision. 'As long as we could find a school which could accommodate my child and meet his needs, then we had a right to challenge the decision. I realised I had power. For the first time, I knew my rights. I knew my child could learn and that his education was worth fighting for.'[66]

Patel and her team took over the appeal and within a short time negotiated an amendment to the statement naming Miriam's preferred school – a mainstream school with a special unit attached in a neighbouring local authority. In addition, Patel secured a financial contribution from the local authority towards the cost of Peter's transport to his new school.

The Equality Act (2010)

The Equality Act (2010) applies to all maintained and independent schools and maintained and non-maintained special schools. According to the 'Equality Act 2010 and Schools' advice, issued by the Department of Education in May 2014, '…in England and Wales, the Act applies to all maintained and independent schools, including Academies, and maintained and non-maintained special schools. In Scotland, it applies to schools managed by education authorities, independent schools and schools receiving grants under Section 73(c) or (d) of the Education (Scotland) Act 1980'. The Act makes it unlawful for schools to discriminate against, harass or victimise a disabled pupil or potential pupil in relation to admissions, exclusions, the way it provides education for pupils, the way it provides pupils access to any benefit, facility or service. A school cannot refuse or omit an application for admission from a prospective pupil due to his or her disability unless it would be detrimental to the education of the pupil or the other pupils in the school. Unfortunately, however, as we shall see, this theoretical legal protection often fails in practice.

64 See www.senexpertsolicitors.co.uk/site/cases/successful-challenge-to-a-local-authoritys-decision

65 Ibid.

66 Ibid.

The Equality Act provides legal protection against discrimination for individuals with protected characteristics. 'Neurodivergence' is not specifically protected under the Equality Act, but disability is. This means that neurodivergence itself is not recognised as a protected characteristic, but individuals who are autistic can be considered disabled under the Equality Act if they have a long-term mental or physical impairment that substantially affects their ability to carry out everyday activities. Not all children with the same neurodivergent condition will necessarily be classified as disabled or not disabled, based on the statutory test. The determination of legal disability status is made on an individual basis, taking into account the extent to which autism affects the person's everyday functioning. Nevertheless, most pupils with an EHC Plan will probably meet the statutory definition of disability. It is essential to assess each individual case on its own merits and develop a legal strategy that aligns with specific objectives.

Case study 4: Lucky Peters

Emma Peters claims that Hull City Council is trying to 'bully' her into sending her six-year-old autistic son, Lucky, to a mainstream school, even though he has an Education and Health Care (EHC) Plan stating that he has severe learning difficulties. She told HullLive: 'We've got that legal document and it says that he can't go to mainstream school but they're still trying to bully me into it. I've said to them on multiple occasions that this is unlawful. I will not send him, it will not happen. They've just ignored everything. They've ignored the law. They've ignored my wishes. They've ignored my son's best interests. It's just what's easy for Hull City Council.'[67]

Emma and Lucky previously lived in Warwickshire, where Warwickshire County Council awarded Lucky a full EHC Plan When she moved to Hull, she says she made it clear that going to a mainstream school was 'off the cards' and that the EHC Plan protected him from the council attempting to force him. She and her son went for a viewing at Tweendykes School, a special school in Hull, but when allocations came back, there were no spaces at any special schools in Hull for Lucky. Emma then told the council that she would home-school him because mainstream school was not an option for Lucky.

She claims that on August 19, 2022, the council rang her and said Lucky sounded like a really good candidate for education outside of the school package. Three days later, however, the council called her again and said that he had been allocated to Wansbeck Primary School, a mainstream school. 'This has all been done behind my back and they've all sat there and agreed to some cosy little agreement and they've just thought that they can bully me into it and, of course, it's not going to happen.'

Emma has been home-schooling her son and says it has been very difficult. His verbal skills are also very limited. Emma said that he can string a sentence together only with the words that come into his head and he can just about convey his very basic needs. She added: 'I'm just trying to teach him skills like life skills and whatever I can get him to learn. I've tried but I'm not qualified to teach a special needs child. I just do my best. I just want what's best for my baby.'[68]

A Hull City Council spokesperson responded: 'We are working with the family to support them with their child's school place. The pupil will have support from the specialist SEND provision at the school that he has been allocated until a permanent place within a special school is available.'

---

67 See www.mirror.co.uk/news/uk-news/mum-accuses-council-bullying-sending-27870369 (accessed March 2024).

68 Ibid.

Alternatives to mainstream schools

Some autistic children are educated in mainstream primary and secondary schools. In some cases, this is the best place for them. In others, they are the worst. My son, Johnny, started to speak at the age of one, lost his language about two years later, and has never regained any speech. He could not possibly survive in a mainstream environment – not just because of his severe needs but because of his hypersensitivity to noise and other incoming sensory bombardments. Bear in mind that governments around the world (and I have visited more than a hundred countries) tend to have an almost dogmatic belief that mainstreaming is the correct approach for all children with special needs, if possible. But in many cases, it is not possible.

For those autistic children who cannot be mainstreamed, the next option is a specialist school: these are schools specifically for children with special educational needs. Some will be just for autistic pupils, while others are for pupils with moderate or severe learning difficulties, physical problems or a combination of both.

Some are day schools, but there are autistic children – like my son, Johnny – who need a 24-hour curriculum in a residential centre to ensure a regular, familiar structure to the day and night. Some have a 52-week placement; others go home at weekends or holidays. A multi-agency plan that establishes joint or three-way funding should be put in place, but the LA is legally responsible for ensuring education. Parents and the LA should agree any special help, such as transport between home and school.

The concept of a 'waking day curriculum' has gained prominence in SEN appeals, although it lacks a specific statutory definition. As a shorthand term, it attempts to capture a type of provision which extends beyond the typical school day. However, its interpretation can vary among different stakeholders. The ruling by the Upper Tribunal in the case of *London Borough of Southwark v WE [2021] UKUT 241 (AAC)* expressed concern over the ongoing use of this expression and argued persuasively for abandoning it altogether.[69]

Non-maintained day or residential schools can be mainstream or special schools, but none of them will be maintained by the local authority. They can charge fees on a non-profit-making basis. Most non-maintained special schools are run by major charities or charitable trusts.

Since special schools are far more expensive to run, there have been instances of local authorities attempting to force parents to choose an inappropriate mainstream school for their autistic child (see **Case study 4** on p.37). Under Section 39 of the Children and Families Act (2014), which applies where the child's parent or the young person has received a draft EHC Plan and has requested that a particular institution be named in the EHC Plan, the local authority is required to consult any institution that it is considering naming in the EHC Plan and, where that institution is maintained by another local authority, the other authority. The local authority must comply with the parent or young person's request, unless the child or young person's attendance at the school would not meet his or her special educational needs or would be incompatible with the efficient education of others or the efficient use of resources. If it believes that these circumstances

69 See www.gov.uk/administrative-appeals-tribunal-decisions/london-borough-of-southwark-v-we-alternative-person-for-oa-2021-ukut-241-aac (accessed March 2024).

apply, the local authority must name the school or other institution, or type of institution, that the local authority considers to be most appropriate for the child or young person (having consulted that institution before naming it in the EHC Plan). A copy of the final EHC Plan must then be sent to the child's parent or the young person and to the school, college or other institution that has been named in the EHC Plan.[70]

Some have argued that cases like Toby Edwards' (see **Case study 5** below) paint a picture of a SEND system in crisis. It is important to note that Toby's story specifically pertains to a child of a particular age and his unique circumstances. It is widely recognised that there is a well-known challenge in the provision of support for individuals with special educational needs once they reach the age of 16 (and Toby was approaching that age). The support system for students beyond this age is an area of significant weakness.

It is essential to recognise that Toby's situation is distinct and should not be conflated with a broader narrative, as the challenges he faces are specific and individual. For their part, schools say they do not receive enough funding to support pupils, while parents complain of having to jump through hoops and endure long delays to obtain the diagnoses and EHC Plans which are necessary to get their children's needs met. Indeed, many believe that the primary challenge lies not in the law itself, but rather in the inadequate funding available to address the issue.

A 2021 survey by the National Autistic Society found that 74% of parents said their child's school place did not fully meet their needs – a figure which has almost doubled since 2017.[71] Of course, these statistics do not tell the full story: the figures may vary across different educational settings, such as primary and secondary schools, as well as between mainstream and special provisions.

Case study 5: Toby Edwards

Toby Edwards, a 15-year-old autistic boy, has gone without schooling for nearly 18 months after being rejected from 12 different special schools because of a lack of places. Toby's parents, who live in south London, have been forced to look as far afield as Cambridge to try to get their son into a school where he can receive the support he needs. Until December 2020, he was being educated in a mainstream state school. His mother, Sally, says he was 'coping in mainstream really well' but things changed because of the Covid-19 pandemic and the onset of puberty.[72]

His parents felt the time had come to put him in a special school. The school and the council, Lewisham, supported the decision, and the family applied to a local special school. However, they received a 'very brutal no'. Since then, Toby has been refused by 11 more schools. 'Every single school has either said they were full or they came up with another reason they couldn't do it', said Sally. For nine months, the family received no support and had to get by with their best efforts at home-schooling. The Covid pandemic made contacting the council almost impossible.[73]

70 See www.ipsea.org.uk/choosing-a-schoolcollege-with-an-ehc-plan (accessed March 2024).

71 See www.autism.org.uk/what-we-do/news/school-report-2021 (accessed March 2024)

72 See https://inews.co.uk/news/education/autistic-schools-special-educational-needs-system-1613079 (accessed March 2024)

73 Ibid.

Transitioning between primary and secondary education

The transition from primary to secondary school provision poses a number of challenges, as the Toby Edwards case study graphically illustrates. As Ekaterina Harrison has pointed out, it is likely that everyone involved in Toby's case may have overlooked the underlying issues until they became more apparent, possibly due to factors such as the Covid-19 pandemic and puberty:

> 'This particular stage, when students are preparing for their GCSEs, is already a challenging period, and being in the right educational setting is absolutely crucial. Transitioning from one school to another, especially from mainstream to special education, can be incredibly difficult for the student, given the combined pressures they face during this time. Furthermore, it is important to consider the possibility that Toby may have been subjected to off-rolling by his mainstream school, particularly if there were concerns about his projected performance in GCSEs.' [74]

(For more on 'off-rolling', see **Fighting school exclusions**.)

Families should be aware that any transitions occurring outside the traditional phase transfer (from primary to secondary school, for example) can be challenging, and should plan their children's future accordingly. 'If a transfer is needed at a different time, it is essential to engage in open communication with the new educational setting to explain the reasons behind the transition,' says Harrison. 'It is worth mentioning that private schools have the right to refuse admission, but state-funded schools can be compelled by the local authority to accept students (although certain processes may need to be followed).'[75]

The Covid pandemic had mixed consequences for children with special educational needs. Many found themselves either struggling to adapt to a radically different classroom environment or to return to school after the lockdowns. In other cases, schools were accused of using 'spurious' risk assessments to stop children from attending class. However, it is worth noting that children with EHC Plans continued to attend school while their classmates were engaged in home-schooling. As a result, some children found themselves in the company of peers who shared similar special educational needs, as they were educated in smaller groups alongside other children with EHC Plans. In some instances, this environment actually helped the formation of friendships and contributed to boosting their confidence.

Lack of protection

Tim Nicholls, head of influencing and research at the National Autistic Society, declared that the education system 'simply isn't working for many autistic children and young people in England. Families can often get the support their children need only after long fights and through expensive and stressful legal action. This is unacceptable.'[76]

---

74 Ekaterina Harrison, personal communication.

75 Ibid.

76 Smith M (2021) *Education system "simply isn't working" for autistic children* [online]. Available at: https://chiswickcalendar.co.uk/education-system-simply-isnt-working-for-autistic-children/ (accessed January 2024)

Some autistic children have an EHC Plan before they start school, while others will go through the EHC needs assessment process once in school. For those with an EHC Plan, parents have the right to request a particular school or college of the following type to be named in the EHC Plan: maintained nursery school, maintained school, academy or free school (mainstream or special), non-maintained special school, further education or sixth-form college, independent school or independent specialist colleges (where they have been approved for this purpose by the Secretary of State) and published on a list (known as the 'Section 41' list, which is available to parents). If you request a placement of the type described above, your LA must comply with your preference and name the school or college in your child's EHC Plan unless it would be unsuitable for your child's age, ability, aptitude or SEN, or incompatible with the efficient education of others, or the efficient use of resources.

If you make representation for a place at an independent school or Independent Specialist Provider (ISP) which is not on the Secretary of State's approved list, your LA must still consider your request. The LA is not under the same conditional duty to name it as described above, but it must have regard to the general principle, as set out in Section 9 of the Education Act (1996) that children should be educated in accordance with their parents' wishes, so long as this is compatible with the provision of efficient instruction and training and does not mean unreasonable public expenditure. You will need to prove that there is a strong case for your child attending that particular school or type of school.

Pupils with an EHC Plan who are moving from primary to secondary school do not follow the usual admissions route. Their LA must amend their statement to name their new school by February 15 in the year of transfer. This is detailed in the Special Educational Needs and Disability (SEND) Code of Practice Section 9.179. The code of practice also suggests that an EHC Plan must be reviewed and amended in sufficient time before the child moves between key phases of education. This is to allow for planning and commissioning of support.

The law should protect children with special needs and smooth the transition into education. All too often, it does not. Patricia Alban-Stanley, whose autistic son, Sammy, died at the age of 13 in 2020 after years of neglect from East Hampshire County Council followed by Kent County Council (see Chapter 1), had been told that she had to move down to Kent into to get Sammy into what she saw as an excellent special school, Laleham Gap. But once Patricia, Sammy and her three daughters were settled in Kent, they were informed that there was no place for Sammy at the school, after all. 'But all the reasons contradicted one another', Patricia explained. 'One was that it was full, one that it was inappropriate for Sammy. But this was ridiculous. I knew it was the right place: I had visited it. And I knew it wasn't full because I had spoken to the school. He was rejected by school after school. Each time, they made excuses. Poor Sammy was beside himself: he did not understand why he could not go to school. It was criminal.'[77]

The situation deteriorated. 'After Sammy had been rejected by three or four schools and the social workers were tearing their hair out, Kent County Council decided to remove his EHC Plan completely. That decision was unlawful. They then said he had to go into

77 Patricia Alban-Stanley, personal communication, May 17, 2023.

mainstream education without support. I considered this extremely dangerous, so I turned to IPSEA [an organisation offering free legal advice to help obtain the appropriate education for children and young people with special needs obtain the education to which they are legally entitled]. IPSEA agreed to take on the case, which was a relief as I was way out of my depth with the way the local authority were trying to mislead me, and how they were even lying at one point to the mainstream school. After weeks of litigation, they finally conceded that Laleham Gap was the right school, but they still fought for two more months to stop him going, backing down at the last minute before the tribunal. So Sammy was strung along for over a year without any school place, during which time he had been in hospital on a number of occasions.'[78]

Case study 6: Oskar Nash

The suicide of Oskar Nash, a 14-year-old boy with Asperger's syndrome from Staines, on January 9, 2020, was contributed to by neglect from Surrey and Borders Partnership NHS Foundation Trust, an inquest concluded. Senior Coroner Richard Travers stated, in his conclusion, that there was neglect in relation to a referral made to children and adolescent mental health services (CAMHS) by Oskar's GP in September 2019. The coroner said there were gross failures in CAMHS' management of the referral, as they had failed to undertake a clinical assessment of Oskar's needs. The coroner found that there was also a series of failures by Surrey County Council (SCC), including a failure to place Oskar in an appropriate school and a failure to ensure that his education health and care plan (EHC Plan) contained sufficient information regarding his health needs and previous suicidal thoughts, as well as a failure to provide effective interventions or support.[79]

Oskar died close to a level crossing in Egham, Surrey. The inquest heard that his mother, Natalia Nash, had experienced a long and difficult struggle to obtain support for Oskar from social services and the community mental health team. She told the inquest how she had desperately tried to get help for Oskar, including contacting social services for help in 2018, telling them she could no longer cope with caring for him. They finally visited Oskar following a serious incident at his school for children with special educational needs, but after only one hour concluded that Natalia 'kept a nice home' and decided to close the case.

Oskar moved from St Dominic's School to Cobham Free School, a mainstream school, in February 2019 and initially everything went well, but his behaviour began to deteriorate in November 2019 and he stopped attending school and began staying out late at night. It emerged during the inquest that Oskar's transfer to Cobham Free School was based on an EHC Plan which was almost three years old. Following repeated calls from Natalia, social services finally appointed Oskar a youth worker, who made one home visit but did little more because Oskar did not want to speak to her.[80]

➔

78 Ibid.

79 See www.inquest.org.uk/oskar-nash-inquest (accessed March 2024).

80 Ibid.

The inquest heard that six weeks before he died, Oskar was at 'red level' on his school's risk register because of incidents of self-harm and absences from school. He had gone missing a number of times, so social services had a duty under Section 47 of the Children Act (1989) to make enquiries in order to decide whether to take any action to safeguard Oskar to protect him from serious harm. A meeting was set up for this purpose in November 2019 but no one was present from the Education Department at Surrey County Council and Natalia knew nothing about it. A further Section 47 meeting was organised but this was abandoned, because the social services representative could not be found. It was then rescheduled at short notice so the school's representative, the deputy head of inclusion, sent a member of the pastoral team in her place. The person chairing the meeting from social services had no knowledge of Oskar's case and important information about Oskar available to social services was not considered in advance. The mental health team was not invited. At this meeting, it was decided Oskar did not meet the threshold for further assessment and support.

Following the conclusion of the inquest, Natalia Nash said: 'Oskar was a boy with a huge smile which could light up thousands of candles. He was a very caring boy who loved exploring nature and making things. Life was not always easy for Oskar, but he showed great courage in overcoming difficulties and managed to achieve even when things were a struggle. I always felt that Oskar wasn't understood by the professionals around him, and as a result, he didn't get the support he needed... Professionals must be properly trained in dealing with autistic children and those with Asperger's syndrome. I would hate for anything like this to happen to another family and I hope that those involved with Oskar will make significant and urgent changes to their procedures going forward.'[81]

Home-schooling and the law

Parents are legally responsible for educating their children. This can be done by sending them to school, but home education is an equally valid and lawful option. There are various possible reasons for choosing to educate an autistic child at home. For sensory reasons, the school environment may be too distracting, the child may be unable to cope with the social aspects of school life, or the parent may feel that their child's needs are not being recognised or supported at school.

If you choose to educate your child at home, the education must be suitable to his or her age, ability and aptitude. Any special educational or additional support needs that they have must also be considered. If your child is not enrolled at school, you do not have to inform your local authority that you are educating your child at home, but they may be able to offer you some appropriate guidance and educational materials. They are unlikely to provide financial help.

You do not need to have any teaching qualifications, follow a fixed timetable, school hours or have any set curriculum. The law does not define how you should home-educate. Most schools follow the National Curriculum in England (Academies do not have to teach the National Curriculum but must teach a broad and balanced curriculum including English, mathematics, science and religious education).

If your child is already enrolled at a state school, you must tell the school in writing that you wish your child's name to be removed from the school register. This will prevent

81 Ibid.

any misunderstanding about your child's non-attendance. If your child goes to a special school, you need permission from your local authority to withdraw your child's name from the school register.

If your child has an EHC Plan, you still have the legal right to home-educate your child. Your local authority will be responsible for maintaining and reviewing the plan for as long as it remains in force.

Useful resources and further guidance

- If your local authority refuses to name the school of your choice, you are entitled to know why and to ask for a review of the decision. If you are having problems in any of these areas then you can contact your Local Information, Advice and Support Service.
- IPSEA (Independent Provider of Special Education Advice) offers free and independent legally based information, advice and support to help acquire the right education for children and young people with all kinds of Special Educational Needs and Disabilities (SEND). www.ipsea.org.uk/

Fighting school exclusions

Every child has a right to a full education and schools should use exclusion only as an absolute last resort. The UK government's guidance has been updated and published in May 2023. It came into force from September 2023, reflecting amendments to underpinning legislation.[82] Unfortunately, however, research by Ambitious About Autism has found that exclusions of autistic pupils have increased significantly in the UK over the past few years. Their research also showed that 56% of autistic children had been sent home from school via unlawful exclusions.[83]

Of considerable concern is the issue of 'unofficial' exclusions and part-time education. Far too often, parents are informed that their child cannot manage full-time attendance and are advised that limited hours or specific staffing arrangements would be a better option. Sometimes, parents are even told to bring their child to school only when certain conditions are met, or that they should go home for lunch. Furthermore, there are instances of parents receiving phone calls asking them to pick up their child due to incidents, meltdowns or signs of struggling. Regrettably, these practices disproportionately impact children with SEN. It is important to emphasise that, unless there are well-documented medical reasons or an EHC Plan in place with a dual schooling arrangement, all of the above-mentioned practices are unlawful.

In the UK, only a headteacher has the authority to exclude a pupil, and this must be on disciplinary grounds. The head can authorise one of two types of exclusions: a fixed-term exclusion, under which a pupil may be excluded for one or more fixed periods up to a

82 Department for Education (2023) *School Suspensions and Permanent Exclusions* [online]. Available at: www.gov.uk/government/publications/school-exclusion (accessed March 2024)

83 See www.ambitiousaboutautism.org.uk/information-about-autism/in-education/exclusions-know-your-rights (accessed March 2024).

maximum of 45 school days in a single academic year, or a permanent exclusion, under which the pupil is permanently excluded and will have to be educated elsewhere.

The new guidance on exclusions, introduced in 2023[84], acknowledges that specific groups of students, such as those with special educational needs, experience higher rates of exclusion. It emphasises the importance of headteachers considering additional support to identify and address the needs of these students, with the aim of reducing the likelihood of exclusion. It is strongly recommended that parents of children with SEN who face exclusion or are at risk of it stay particularly aware of these provisions. They should be prepared to inquire about how schools are precisely implementing these requirements, whenever necessary.

For an exclusion to be legal, the parents of the child must be notified in writing and the exclusion must be formally recorded. A school cannot send a child home to 'cool off' or ask a parent to collect a child from school before the normal end of the school day or bring them in late without formally recording this as an exclusion.

'Off-rolling' has received a lot of interest from the press and among school leaders and teachers recently. This is the practice of removing a pupil from the school roll without using a permanent exclusion, when the removal is primarily in the best interests of the school, rather than the best interests of the pupil. This includes pressuring a parent to remove their child from the school roll. While it may not always be unlawful, Ofsted believes off-rolling is never acceptable.

If a child is excluded because of his or her autism or behaviour linked to it, then it may be unlawful. This can be illustrated by the landmark case featuring an autistic boy in Derbyshire, known only as 'L' (see **Case study 7** on p.49), which dates back originally to February 2016. The case, which was funded by the Equality and Human Rights Commission, was based on the fact that children with disabilities which cause them to have 'a tendency to physically abuse' are not protected by the Equality Act (2010). This means that children like L are not treated as 'disabled' for their physically aggressive behaviour and so cannot challenge decisions to exclude them from school.

The Upper Tribunal made a significant ruling regarding the L case in 2018. They determined that L, falling under the provisions of Regulation 4(1)(c) of the 2010 Regulations, had been wrongly excluded from the definition of 'disability,' as outlined in Section 6(1) of the Equality Act. This decision was deemed a material error based on legal grounds. Importantly, it was acknowledged that Regulation 4(1) conflicted with human rights legislation, and it was recognised that schools should not be excluding children solely based on a 'tendency to physical abuse' connected to their autism. Judge Rowley emphasised that aggressive behaviour is not a deliberate choice for children with autism.[85]

The way Equality Act regulations are currently interpreted means children like L, who are defined as having 'a tendency to physical abuse,' are often not treated as 'disabled' and are

84 See https://assets.publishing.service.gov.uk/media/64ef773513ae1500116e30db/Suspension_and_permanent_exclusion_guidance_september_23.pdf (accessed March 2024).

85 The case name is *C&C v The Governing Body of a School, The Secretary of State for Education (First Interested Party) and The National Autistic Society (Second Interested Party) (SEN) [2018] UKUT 269 (AAC).*

therefore not protected by the Equality Act. The lack of protection under the Equality Act means schools do not have to justify how a decision to exclude a disabled child in these circumstances is proportionate or explain how they have made reasonable adjustments to support the pupil so the behaviour can be prevented or reduced.

In 2016, a report by a House of Lords committee on the impact of the Equality Act on disabled people said the regulations had 'unintentionally discouraged schools from paying sufficient attention to their duties' under the Act. It called for the regulations to be amended 'so that a tendency to physical abuse of other persons ceases to be treated as not amounting to an impairment for the purposes of the definition of "disability"'[86].

Simone Aspis, the campaigns and policy coordinator for the Alliance for Inclusive Education (ALLFIE), pointed to the committee's recommendation and observed: 'If the law was amended to remove this regulation, then we will find that education providers will be required to follow the law and make reasonable adjustments for disabled pupils and students. Too often, schools hide behind this regulation so that they can exclude disabled pupils without good reason, which is totally unacceptable.'[87]

Navin Kikabhai, the chairman of ALLFIE, said the case demonstrated that the Equality Act was 'fundamentally flawed' and 'highlights the increasing erosion of disabled children's rights, and an increasing indifference to children who require multi-disciplinary support'. He added that this support was 'disappearing in increasing numbers from local schooling due to the depletion of local authority support and engagement'.[88]

Polly Sweeney, a human rights partner at solicitors Irwin Mitchell, which represented the family in its appeal against the ruling that found in favour of L's school, declared:

> 'This appeal is about the fundamental right of access to education for disabled children whose conditions, like autism, result in behaviours which can be physically aggressive. The legal definition of "physically abusive" has been stretched to the point that it means disabled children even as young as six or seven who may have displayed only low-level physical aggression on a handful of occasions, or even just once if the physical aggression was significant, are denied protection from discrimination under the law.'[89]

Appealing an exclusion

If your child has been permanently excluded from school, you will be invited to a review meeting with the school's governors. This will happen within 15 school days. You should make sure you are prepared for this meeting, with clear arguments about why the exclusion should be overturned and any evidence you need to support your case. If the governors do not overturn the exclusion, you can ask for an independent review by your local council (or academy trust, if the school is an academy). The school governors

---

86 See https://lordslibrary.parliament.uk/the-equality-act-2010-impact-on-disabled-people/ (accessed March 2024).

87 Pring J (2018) *Autistic teen's legal fight over 'physical abuse' school exclusion* [online]. Available at: www.disabilitynewsservice.com/autistic-teens-legal-fight-over-physical-abuse-school-exclusion/ (accessed January 2024)

88 Ibid.

89 Ibid.

are required to tell you how to ask for an independent review. You can request an independent review by your local council or academy trust. A review panel will conduct a hearing to determine whether the decision to exclude your child was illegal, irrational or did not follow the correct procedure.[90]

The independent review panel cannot overturn the exclusion, but it can take the following actions:

- Uphold the decision to exclude your child.
- Recommend the school's governing body reconsider the decision to exclude.
- Quash the school governors' decision and direct them to reconsider the exclusion.[91]

The Governing Board review and the Independent Review Panel are distinct procedures. Both procedures have certain elements that are particularly relevant to the rights of children with special educational needs. For instance, in the case of an Independent Review, parents have the right to request the appointment of an SEN expert. This expert is designated by the local authority and should have no affiliation or connection with the school. The Independent Review Panel is obligated to consider and take into account the SEN expert's perspective on how the student's SEN may be relevant to his or her exclusion. The updated statutory guidance provides a detailed outline of the available protections in place.[92]

The ombudsman

If your child is still excluded, you can ask the Local Government Ombudsman (or the Education Funding Agency, if the school is an academy or free school) to look at whether your case was handled properly. They cannot overturn the exclusion. The ombudsman's role is limited to reviewing how the case review was handled.

Judicial review

The statutory guidance specifically pertains to the jurisdiction of the school exclusion review process, which encompasses the decision made by the headteacher, the outcomes of the Independent Review Panel and any subsequent reconsideration if applicable. Judicial review operates separately from this process. Judicial review applies to a wide range of public actions and decision-making and has established a vast body of precedent and evolving practices. However, it is a highly specialised area, and individuals considering a claim for judicial review are strongly advised to seek professional legal assistance.[93]

It is also worth noting that the statutory guidance does not extend to independent schools, as the relevant legal provisions are typically outlined in the contract terms of those schools. The school's discipline policy and rules are generally implied terms of the contract, granting the headmaster significant discretion in deciding whether and when to impose exclusions.

90 See https://schoolexclusionproject.com/governing-body-hearing/ (Accessed March 2024).

91 Ibid.

92 Ibid.

93 Ibid.

Discrimination and protected characteristics

If you believe your child was excluded due to discrimination in relation to a protected characteristic, then you can make a claim to an appropriate court or tribunal. This must be done within six months of the exclusion taking place. Making a discrimination claim in relation to a school exclusion can be very challenging. A high standard of evidence is required, so it is essential to seek specialist legal advice. Navigating the legal aspects in this area can be quite intricate. Families who are contemplating such actions are strongly encouraged to seek legal advice or reach out to the Equality and Human Rights Commission for help.[94]

However, bringing a disability discrimination claim also offers significant benefits. Unlike the Independent Review Panel, the tribunal has the power to order reinstatement, which can be a valuable outcome for the individual involved. Moreover, the process is typically expedited, with a shorter timetable of around six weeks, ensuring a relatively swift resolution.

If your child is permanently excluded, your local authority has a legal duty to make arrangements for their full-time education. They should talk through your child's options with you and what you need to do – for example, applying to a different school part way through the academic year, which is known as an 'in year' or 'mid-year' admission.

If this is the first time your child has been permanently excluded, then your local authority still has the normal obligation to comply with your preferences for which school your child should attend wherever possible. However, if your child has been permanently excluded before, then this obligation to comply with your preferences is suspended for two years from the date of the child's most recent exclusion.

If you have any issues with getting your child admitted into a new school, then you should review your right to appeal a school admissions decision.

You can make a claim to a court or a tribunal if you think your child has been discriminated against. You need to do this within six months of the exclusion.

For more general complaints (for example, if you do not want to challenge the exclusion but you are unhappy with the way the school handled it), follow the normal school complaints process.

94 See www.citizensadvice.org.uk/family/education/taking-action-about-discrimination-in-education/#:~:text=Taking%20court%20action,the%20date%20the%20discrimination%20happened. (accessed March 2024),

Case study 7: 'L'

A 13-year-old autistic boy in Derbyshire, known only as 'L', was given a one-and-a-half-day exclusion after he hit a teaching assistant with a ruler, punched her and pulled her hair. In 2018, a judge in the Upper Tribunal ruled that the exclusion had been unlawful because 'aggressive behaviour is not a choice for children with autism'. Campaigners welcomed the ruling, saying it would have a major impact on future generations of autistic children. L's parents said: 'We believe passionately that our son and other children in his position should have equal rights to be able to go to school and receive the support they need to achieve the best possible outcomes. L's autism means that he will grow up in a world where he will face challenges and adversity throughout his life. School should be somewhere he can go without fear of discrimination or exclusion for actions which he has no control over. These rules currently prevent that'. A spokeswoman for the UK Department for Education (DfE) said: 'All schools have a legal duty not to discriminate against disabled pupils, which includes not excluding them from school because of their disability'.[95]

Judge Rowley, who examined whether the school had breached L's and other children's human rights, found that this rule came 'nowhere near striking a fair balance between the rights of children such as L, on the one side, and the interests of the community on the other'. The judge added:

> 'In my judgement, the Secretary of State [for Education] has failed to justify maintaining in force a provision which excludes from the ambit of the protection of the Equality Act, children whose behaviour in school is a manifestation of the very condition which calls for special educational provision to be made for them. In that context, to my mind it is repugnant to define as "criminal or anti-social" the effect of the behaviour of children whose condition (through no fault of their own) manifests itself in particular ways so as to justify treating them differently from children whose condition has other manifestations.'[96]

Useful resources and further guidance

- The National Children's Bureau, the Association of School and College Leaders and IPSEA have published a guide to the legal and unlawful use of exclusions and other practices such as off-rolling. Schools, parents and pupils alike will benefit from clear information about their legal powers and rights. This fact sheet can be accessed at: www.ncb.org.uk/sites/default/files/uploads/files/20190502_ExclusionsFactsheet1.pdf (accessed January 2024).
- If you want to complain about your child's exclusion to the Local Government Ombudsman, go to www.lgo.org.uk/make-a-complaint (accessed January 2024). Remember, however, that the ombudsman cannot overturn the exclusion.
- The Alliance for Inclusive Education (ALLFIE), formed in 1990, is an organisation led by disabled people focused on campaigning and information-sharing on education, training and apprenticeship issues. ALLFIE believes that inclusive education is the basis of life-long equality. For more, visit their website at: www.allfie.org.uk/
- Some other useful websites are:
  - The School Exclusion Project: https://schoolexclusionproject.com/
  - The Communities Empowerment Network: http://cenlive.org/
  - Equality and Human Rights Commission: www.equalityhumanrights.com/en

95 See www.specialneedsjungle.com/against-human-rights-landmark-ruling-against-school-exclusion-for-behaviour-related-to-autism/ (accessed March 2024).

96 Ibid.

The use of restraints in schools

In 2019, the Department of Health and Department for Education issued their revised non-statutory guidance on avoiding the use of restraint and restrictive intervention and also how restraint should be used in health and social care services and special education settings. The guidance was directed at professionals working with children and young people who have learning difficulties, autism and mental health difficulties with challenging behaviour. It aimed to reduce the use of restraints and restrictive intervention, but also to set government guidelines on when such practices are and are not acceptable. Restraint could include physical restraint or restraining someone with the use of mechanical aids such as belts, cuffs and straps. Restrictive intervention could include withdrawal (removing a child or young person involuntarily from a situation) or seclusion (supervised confinement and isolation of a child or young person).

Four years later, in 2023, the UK government was due to update its guidance for schools on the use of physical restraint of pupils and other 'reasonable force' for the first time in a decade. It came after an inquiry by the human rights watchdog found 'inconsistency and uncertainty' over what schools should include in their restraint policies and indicated that a 'significant proportion' of schools wanted 'better and more specific guidance'.[97]

Under the law, school staff have the power to use reasonable force, but only to prevent pupils hurting themselves and others, from damaging property or causing disorder. However, non-statutory guidance has not been updated in almost ten years, and schools' use of the power to restrain children has been questioned in several recent high-profile cases.

In a call for evidence launched in July 2023, the Department for Education said it supported school staff's use of reasonable force 'when it is safe, lawful and absolutely necessary'. But the government also 'recognises that the misuse of reasonable force or restrictive practices can have a significant and long-lasting effect on the pupils, staff members and parents involved, as well as the wider classroom'. Ministers are 'therefore committed to minimising the use of reasonable force, including restraint and other restrictive practices in all schools in England, including special schools and alternative provision'.[98]

IPSEA responded to the consultation about this guidance by expressing two principal concerns. Firstly, the guidance was non-statutory and thus lacked the force of some of the statutory guidance it replaced; and, secondly, it expressly did not apply to maintained mainstream education settings, further education colleges, pupil referral units and providers of alternative provision.

IPSEA declared:

> 'There are children and young people with SEND whose behaviour challenges attending mainstream settings, and we know that physical restraint is sometimes used in these settings. There has also been widespread attention in recent months

97 See https://schoolsweek.co.uk/dfe-plans-update-to-school-restraint-guidance/ (accessed March 2024).

98 See https://consult.education.gov.uk/school-absence-and-exclusions-team/use-of-force-and-restrictive-practices-call-for-ev/supporting_documents/Call%20for%20evidence%20%20use%20of%20reasonable%20force%20and%20restrictive%20practices%20in%20schools%202023%20PUBLISHED.pdf (accessed March 2024).

> regarding the use of isolation in mainstream schools. There is some guidance for these settings on the use of isolation as a disciplinary measure, but IPSEA is concerned that the use of isolation in some mainstream settings goes far beyond a proportionate disciplinary measure. (It is never lawful to use physical restraint as a disciplinary measure.) Challenging behaviour is a common cause of exclusion (lawful and unlawful) from mainstream settings. However, mainstream settings do not have the benefit of clear guidance on how to address challenging behaviour in a positive way. In IPSEA's experience, such settings are more likely to need support, guidance and advice in order to be able to lawfully and appropriately make use of positive behaviour strategies and, in extremis, restraint and restrictive interaction.'[99]

There have been many disturbing examples of deprivation of liberty of children with special educational needs, in both the state and independent school networks across the UK. Some involve the use of restraints (see **Case study 8** on p.52). The use of force is permitted against a pupil for behavioural reasons under Section 93 of the Education & Inspections Act (2006). However, its use on children with special educational needs is controversial and can be considered a breach of their human rights.

An episode of the BBC TV series 'Don't Exclude Me', made in 2021 in collaboration with the Open University, highlighted the use of a 'safe' hold during a special needs school student's restraint. The first restraint was performed by Marie Gentle, OBE, a government behavioural expert, and the second was performed by deputy head teacher, Tom Spence, while Gentle observed and cheered the teacher on for his technique. The schoolboy, Oscar, shrieked in terror and begged to be released. In reaction to the programme, the International Coalition Against Restraint and Seclusion (ICARS), among many others, protested in the strongest terms. ICARS declared:

> 'This restraint has been withdrawn from the Team Teach syllabus – the medical advisers have advised it is not to be used because of the risk of death associated with positional asphyxiation. Yet still, BBC, you are presenting this hold as a safe hold. You have done nothing to put right this wrong and, as a consequence, children's lives are, put bluntly at risk... We suggest that the whole sequence is a masterclass in human rights abuses and how not to use restraint, unless your aim is to engage in practices that could lead to death and go against medical expert and government guidance.'[100]

Jeremy Hayes, the BBC's Complaints Director, responded by saying: 'I consider that what is shown in the programme is consistent with the law and good practice concerning the restraint of children at school'. But for some viewers, this documentary shed light on the misunderstandings surrounding the needs of students with SEN in schools and underscored the urgent need for improved SEN training.[101]

---

99 IPSEA (undated) *New Guidance on Restraint and Restrictive Intervention* [online]. Available at: www.ipsea.org.uk/news/new-guidance-on-restraint-and-restrictive-intervention (accessed March 2024)

100 See https://againstrestraint.com/2022/01/29/the-normalization-of-restraint-in-mainstream-media/ (accessed March 2024).

101 Ibid.

Leigh Day solicitor Catriona Rubens, who represented the Montague family, explained:

> 'Samuel and Jacob were active, sensory seeking children who, because of their autism, interpret the world through movement and touch. It is our view that, by strapping them into mechanical restraint chairs at school, the local authority breached their human rights and failed to deliver any therapeutic benefit to the twins... Restraints against children with special educational needs should only be used in exceptional circumstances, as the least restrictive option to prevent harm to the child. In my view, it is inappropriate to use restraint at school to control the behaviour of autistic children or children with learning difficulties, who may need to move or run around to self-regulate. The law needs to be clearer to prevent this happening. The Department for Education also needs to act quickly to impose a legal duty upon schools to record and monitor every time restraint is used against a child. Without clear records, and good communication between schools and parents, families can be left in the dark about the use of force against their children at school.'[102]

In 2022, Ofsted inspectors expressed concerns over the use of physical restraint on pupils with complex special educational needs (including autism) at a school in Suffolk. Inspectors said safeguarding arrangements at Warren School in Lowestoft were ineffective. Staff told inspectors who visited the school that they did not feel adequately trained to keep all pupils safe. Some said they had raised 'numerous' concerns about pupils' safety, which were not addressed.[103]

Ofsted said inspectors looked at the use of restraint when inspecting any school, but it was used more frequently in some special schools, although there was nothing to suggest it was happening more regularly.[104]

Case study 8: Samuel and Jacob Montague

In 2022, the parents of severely autistic twin brothers, Samuel and Jacob Montague, achieved a landmark successful claim under the Human Rights Act (1998) for the use of mechanical restraint chairs against their sons. Kent County Council agreed to pay £80,000 in compensation after it admitted a school it ran – Five Acre Wood special school in Maidstone – had breached its policy and the Department for Education's guidance by using mechanical restraint chairs against the two boys when they were aged between five and eight years old.

The twins' parents, Annie and Mark, brought a civil case under the Human Rights Act (1998) against the local authority, arguing that the restraints had been used unlawfully because the school had failed to consider less restrictive options and had failed to put in place a plan to reduce the use of restraint. Annie and Mark first saw their sons in the so-called 'Hardrock' chairs at a school concert in 2010, when they were wheeled out on to the stage. The parents took their children out of the school and home-schooled them, and the boys have now flourished. ➔

102 Leigh Day (2022) *Special school apologises for use of mechanical restraint against severely autistic twin boys* [online]. Available at: www.leighday.co.uk/news/news/2022-news/special-school-apologises-for-use-of-mechanical-restraint-against-severely-autistic-twin-boys/ (accessed March 2024)

103 See www.theguardian.com/education/2022/sep/26/ofsted-concerns-physical-restraints-on-pupils-in-special-needs-school-warren-school-lowestoft-suffolk#: ~ :text = The%20report%20said%20pupils%20are,than%20not%2C%20the%20staff.%E2%80%9D (accessed March 2024).

104 Ibid.

A spokesperson for Kent County Council expressed sincere apologies for the experiences Samuel and Jacob and their parents had suffered, but added: 'We disagree with the solicitor's statement that the restraints used "failed to deliver any therapeutic benefit to the twins". In fact, it was the occupational therapy service which prescribed specialist chairs to Samuel and Jacob for therapeutic reasons, after reviewing their needs. It also prescribed various safety accessories, including lap and shoulder belts and lap trays. The school used the chairs only because they had been prescribed for the twins for therapeutic purposes. It did not intend to control the twins' behaviour... The use of these specialist chairs should always be agreed by a multi-disciplinary team in consultation with service users, their families and advocates, and recorded within an individual's care or education plan. Regrettably this did not happen in Samuel and Jacob's case.'[105]

Useful resources and further guidance

- The Challenging Behaviour Foundation is a UK charity which has campaigned against the use of mechanical restraints on children with special needs in school. The charity can be contacted at www.challengingbehaviour.org.uk/
- In 2013, the Department for Education published a fact sheet on 'Use of reasonable force: Advice for headteachers, staff and governing bodies'. It can be accessed at: https://assets.publishing.service.gov.uk/government/uploads/system/uploads/attachment_data/file/444051/Use_of_reasonable_force_advice_Reviewed_July_2015.pdf (accessed January 2024).
- Ten years later, in 2023, the Department for Education released a 'call for evidence' on 'Use of reasonable force and restrictive practices in schools'. This can be accessed at: https://consult.education.gov.uk/school-absence-and-exclusions-team/use-of-force-and-restrictive-practices-call-for-ev/supporting_documents/Call%20for%20evidence%20%20use%20of%20reasonable%20force%20and%20restrictive%20practices%20in%20schools%202023%20PUBLISHED.pdf

Masking at school: the legal implications

Much has been written about the ability of adult autistic women to camouflage or mask their condition, especially in the workplace, and the exhaustion and distress this masking process can provoke. But little attention has been paid to autistic children who behave very differently at school from at home and the horrendous situations this can produce.

One mother told me that her autistic son was refusing to attend school. 'When one of his other brothers started at another, larger primary school, we moved him there. The teachers were much more proactive. They supported him to get a referral to CAMHS and then with a referral to a residential paediatric centre for children with mental health challenges and their families. It was the home life that was challenging for our son. He masked at school – although that was a word I would not have known at the time. At

105 See www.localgovernmentlawyer.co.uk/litigation-and-enforcement/400-litigation-news/50062-twins-forced-into-mechanical-restraint-chairs-at-school-awarded-80k-compensation-by-council (Accessed March 2024).

home, his behaviour was incredibly challenging. We would say we couldn't cope and were overwhelmed, but everyone we spoke to just sent us for more and more training. So the problem was the parenting, in their eyes.'[106]

She said it got to the point 'where we knew more than the people delivering the training. Eventually, the school asked us to keep a log of our son's worst behaviour. When they saw it, they were shocked. Because he is high-functioning, he will investigate a topic thoroughly and talk about it very intently. He is very good at telling you things, but often he does not engage very effectively with instructions. Change and transition are very difficult for him. I suspect that he wasn't learning enough at his mainstream school. He was learning enough to do well at SATs, but we could not get an EHC Plan, because however bad things were at home, they would say there was no evidence of this at school. In fact, we were paying the price for the fact that he was coping so well at school, because he was utterly burnt-out when he got home.'[107]

The mother said it became harder and harder when her son moved up to secondary school: 'It was a battle to get him to go in every day. It got particularly rocky by the time we got to lockdown. He could never do his homework at home even before that and so he wasn't able to engage with online learning. In fact, he never really went back to school after the lockdown. We felt we were setting him up to be a failure by forcing him to go to school. He himself said it was a "hostile" environment.'[108]

The boy is now 15 years old and six-foot-six tall. His mother says that, although he has very thoughtful things to say about topics, 'he can appear to be closer to a three-year-old in the way that he experiences and processes things. We had a period when he was cutting himself, and binge-eating and we didn't know how to support him and get him through that... My husband could not even leave me alone with him and his two younger boys overnight. It was just too dangerous. We were actually looking at him having a criminal record because the social workers had told us to phone the police when things became really dangerous.'[109]

A specialist, residential school was recommended to the boy's parents 'but we weren't even allowed to visit unless we had an EHC Plan. We had endless meetings and we finally got referred. Then Wilds Lodge offered us a place. But after seeming to support us and our son through this long battle and all of the meetings with so many representatives from different agencies our social worker told us: "I hope you don't expect us to pay for it." It made us wonder what all the meetings were for. The lawyers told us that if we wanted to fight, it would cost £20,000 and would take a year. There was no legal aid available for a tribunal. I was totally overwrought. In the end, the County Council agreed to pay. All it needs is for them to believe parents and not to think they're inadequate. The whole family is in delayed shock!'[110]

106 Personal communication, March 12, 2024.

107 Ibid.

108 Ibid.

109 Ibid.

110 Ibid.

Research indicates that autistic individuals may develop masking behaviours during childhood, learning from reading fiction or observing social interactions on television. They might also mimic phrases from television or imitate socially accepted behaviour from their peers. As a result, they may appear 'less' autistic on the surface and resemble neurotypical children more closely. However, it is widely recognised that their presentation mechanisms are distinct and differ from those of neurotypical individuals.[111]

Sara Alston, an experienced SENCO and safeguarding lead who also works as a SEND, inclusion and safeguarding consultant and trainer, points out that children can often mask their special and other educational needs. At the same time, schools can struggle to support those with multiple needs and vulnerabilities, often focusing only on the 'visible' tip of the iceberg. Alston writes:

> 'At school, they "mask" their differences and anxieties to try and fit in with those around them. Often, they work hard, attain well and appear to have friends. The school sees no issues. Therefore, they are not able to provide SEND support, because from their point of view there is nothing to support. The child's needs in school, as they display them, are being met.
>
> 'However, once they get home, their behaviour changes. They have "meltdowns", display obsessive behaviours, a high level of anxiety and even self-harming. Some may engage in emotionally based school avoidance.'[112]

This discrepancy in behaviour at home and at school is common and very difficult to manage:

> 'It can often lead to conflict with, and frustration for, parents who cannot understand why the school is not able to offer them more support. At the same time, schools can end up questioning the parents' narrative and parenting skills. Conversely, there are many children in need, including those subject to a child protection plan, where the focus of the school and other services on ensuring the child's safety and well-being can mean that they miss their SEND needs. There can be an assumption that any lack of educational achievement is a feature of their safeguarding needs and as such it is not further investigated. One set of needs masks another, so they are not supported.
>
> 'These children's behaviour could have been a communication of their learning needs and difficulties with accessing learning, yet the school response 'was to focus solely on their behaviour needs, not the cause of them. At the heart of the complexity of understanding these children's behaviour is a difficulty in seeing the whole child.'[113]

---

111 See, for example, Hull *et al* (2017) "Putting on my best normal": social camouflaging in adults with autism spectrum condition. *Journal of Autism and Developmental Disorders* **47** 2519–2534.

112 Alston S (2022) *The tip of the iceberg: SEND masking and multiple needs* [online]. Available at: www.sec-ed.co.uk/best-practice/the-tip-of-the-iceberg-send-masking-and-multiple-needs-children-students-inclusion-wellbeing-ehcps/ (accessed January 2024)

113 Ibid.

When a child is experiencing academic difficulties, it may be relatively easy to recognise masking as an underlying factor. However, it is vital to acknowledge that there are children who may meet the expected performance standards at school, yet these standards fail to capture their untapped potential. Unfortunately, their progress is hindered because their special needs are not adequately addressed. This poses a significant challenge, particularly for children known as 'twice-exceptional' as they have both a disability and high learning potential. While these children may be making progress academically, their advances often come at a considerable personal cost, and their progress may not align with their true potential or their zone of proximal development.[114]

If the school does not fully grasp the challenges the child is facing and proves hesitant to offer the necessary help and support, seeking a social needs assessment can be beneficial since this allows for a comprehensive understanding of the child's life and behaviour across various settings. However, families might find it challenging to pursue this assessment due to concerns about involving social services. It is important to consider which procedure or assessment can provide a holistic view of the child, as different arrangements tend to focus on different aspects.[115]

Often, vital messages or expressions of needs can be inadvertently overlooked or dismissed as disruptive behaviour. Masking can arise as a coping mechanism, employed to conceal these underlying communications that may not align with societal expectations or norms.

Useful resources and further guidance

For useful information on masking, see Amy Pearson, Kieran Rose: *Autistic Masking: Understanding Identity Management and the Role of Stigma.* Shoreham-by-Sea: Pavilion Publishing, 2023.

A helpful fact sheet called Talking to your child's school about autistic masking is available at https://enquire.org.uk/3175/wp-content/uploads/2022/10/Talking-to-your-childs-school-about-autistic-masking.pdf (accessed January 2024)

Summary

Under UK law, it is compulsory for children to participate in education starting from the age of five. The law should protect children with special needs and smooth the transition into education. All too often, it does not, sometimes with tragic consequences. Families of autistic children and young people frequently obtain the educational support they require only after long fights and through expensive and stressful legal action. The Equality Act (2010) states that schools must provide all eligible children with free and appropriate public education that meets their unique needs. So, if your child does need extra support, then parents, teachers and the school special educational needs coordinator (SENCO) can work together to request an Education, Health and Care assessment. If successful, the child can then be given an EHC Plan, which documents

114 See https://axia-asd.co.uk/evidence-autistic-people-hiding-masking-difficulties-educational-settings/ (accessed March 2024).

115 Ibid.

exactly what resources and strategies need to be put in place to help the child with his or her learning. To ensure an appropriate learning environment for autistic learners, it is crucial for a school to demonstrate its understanding of autism. Unfortunately, however, exclusions of autistic pupils from schools have increased significantly in the UK over the past few years. If your child has been permanently excluded from school, you will be invited to a review meeting with the school's governors. This will happen within 15 school days. If you believe your child was excluded due to discrimination in relation to a protected characteristic, then you can make a claim to an appropriate court or tribunal. This must be done within six months of the exclusion taking place. Making a discrimination claim in relation to a school exclusion can be very challenging. Sadly, there have also been disturbing instances of the use of restraints on autistic children in UK schools. And there has also been a lack of understanding in schools of the ability of some autistic children to 'mask' their differences and anxieties in the educational setting (but not home) in order to try and fit in with those around them. This leads to an absence of help and support in the school environment.

Chapter 3: Mental capacity in autistic children and adults, deprivation of liberty and the law

This chapter will focus on:

- Mental capacity and deprivation of liberty.
- The alarming rise in numbers in the psychiatric system.
- The implications of reform.
- The differences between the Mental Health Act and the Mental Capacity Act.
- Mental capacity and the Court of Protection.
- The neglected area of fluctuating capacity.
- The right to vote.
- The right to drive.

Mental capacity and deprivation of liberty

There are two main procedures prescribed by law in England and Wales for deprivation of liberty in the context of mental health. These are:

1. Detaining patients under the Mental Health Act (1983). The criteria for detention under this Act are not contingent on an individual's mental capacity. Those in need of treatment for mental disorders are typically cared for under MHA (1983), which establishes the legal framework for their treatment, care, and, when necessary, compulsory detention. A person who is being treated in hospital may not be subject to deprivation of liberty if he or she meets the criteria for detention under the MHA (1983) (Section 28, MCA (2005)).
2. Authorising a deprivation of liberty under the Mental Capacity Act (2005). This Act considers 'impairment of, or a disturbance in the functioning of, the mind or brain' and aligns this with the individual's best interests.

It is crucial to bear in mind that these legislative Acts may have distinct applications in the various territories of the UK. What holds true for England and Wales might not necessarily apply in Wales or Scotland, and the other way around.

Yo Dunn, a leading British authority on the Mental Capacity Act, who is herself autistic, points out there is a fundamental legal difference between detention under the Mental Health Act and detention under the Mental Capacity Act (using the so-called Deprivation of Liberty Safeguards or DoLS): 'Detention under the MHA gives a licence to detain, in the same way as a criminal justice order does. DoLS is not a licence to detain. It merely renders lawful arrangements for care and support.'[116]

Since the 1960s, most autistic people and/or people with a learning disability in the UK's 'mental handicap hospitals' would have been there 'informally' – without the use of the MHA (1983), based on mid-century policies viewing 'compulsory powers' as unnecessary for these individuals, since they were seen as 'childlike' and tractable. Then, in 2004, came a landmark decision[117] (see below). It led to the European Court of Human Rights emphasising the necessity of following a legally prescribed procedure when caring for or treating a person with a mental disorder in conditions that amount to a deprivation of liberty. Following this case, several provisions were introduced into the MCA (2005) by the Mental Health Act (2007), becoming effective on April 1, 2009. Notably, the addition of Schedule 1A introduced what is now known as the Deprivation of Liberty Safeguards

116 Yo Dunn, personal communication, January 5, 2023.

117 *HL v United Kingdom [2004] All ER (D) 39 (Oct)*, commonly referred to as the 'Bournewood case'.

regime. The Mental Health Act (2007) gave the Court of Protection new powers and established the DoLS regime to afford appropriate legal safeguards for incapacitated individuals who may face a deprivation of liberty outside the framework of the MHA (1983). (While there is statutory guidance on the DoLS regime, it is advised to approach it with caution, because it has, in some respects, been superseded by case law, particularly concerning the definition of a deprivation of liberty.[118])

Deprivation of Liberty Safeguards

In 2004, the European Court of Human Rights ruled that a 49-year-old non-verbal autistic man, HL, had been unlawfully deprived of his liberty in Bournewood Hospital, Surrey, after clinicians had admitted him 'informally' in his best interests. Following a lengthy battle with HL's carers (Mr and Mrs E), with whom he had been living until his admission to Bournewood, the hospital Trust, supported by the UK Department of Health, appealed to the House of Lords over the ruling. The Mental Health Act Commission suggested that 22,000 people being detained informally would have to be detained formally under the Mental Health Act if the ruling were upheld. In 1998, the House of Lords overturned the ruling that HL's detention had been illegal. Mr and Mrs E proceeded to take the case to the European Court of Human Rights, which in October 2004 ruled in HL's favour.

As a result, the UK government introduced the new Deprivation of Liberty Safeguards (DoLS), which came into force in April 2009. The DoLS provide extra protection for the human rights of people who lack capacity and find themselves deprived of their liberty. As well as people with learning difficulties and mental health conditions, this could apply to older people in care homes. The safeguards provide a rigorous process by which health services have to prove that compulsory detention is the best solution for the individual concerned.[119]

The DoLS regime faced substantial criticism from the House of Lords Select Committee tasked with conducting post-legislative scrutiny of the MCA (2005). Additionally, in light of the Supreme Court's ruling in *Cheshire West and Chester Council v P*, it became evident that public authorities would need to seek authorisations for the deprivation of liberty in numerous other settings, notably in supported living arrangements.

In response to the Select Committee's report, the government commissioned the Law Commission in the summer of 2014 to embark on a project concerning the authorisation of deprivations of liberty in settings not covered by Schedule A1 of the MCA (2005). Moreover, the Commission was tasked with assessing the implications of that work on the existing DoLS regime. On March 13, 2017, the Law Commission released its report on Mental Capacity and Deprivation of Liberty, which proposed amendments to the MCA (2005), with a specific focus on issues related to the authorisation of deprivation of liberty. The resultant Mental Capacity (Amendment) Act (2019), while based on the Law Commission's draft Bill, incorporates some differences and received Royal Assent on May 16, 2019. This Act introduced amendments to the MCA (2005), replacing the

118 Ekaterina Harrison, personal communication.

119 For the full story of the HL case, see online resources: www.pavpub.com/autism-and-the-law-resources.

existing DoLS regime with a new framework, known as the Liberty Protection Safeguards (LPS). Originally scheduled to take effect in April 2022, the government announced in December 2021 that this timeline would not be met. Subsequently, in April 2023, it was communicated that the implementation of the LPS would be postponed beyond the life of the current Parliament, probably extending beyond the autumn of 2024.

In another landmark case in 2011[120], the UK's Court of Protection emphatically ruled that a local authority, Hillingdon, had unlawfully detained a young autistic man with learning difficulties, Steven Neary, for almost an entire year, breaching his right to respect for family life as a result (see **Case study 9** on p.63).

The judge in this case, Mr Justice Peter Jackson, had to determine whether a long, complicated series of events had constituted unlawful detention and breach of Steven's rights to private and family life. He had no difficulty in holding that it did, on the basis of both long-standing common-law principles and human rights grounds. Justice Jackson referred first to a 'basic legal principle found in an era long before the invention of local authorities as we know them' – Chapter 29 of Magna Carta (1297), which provides that 'no freeman shall be taken or imprisoned or disseised of his … liberties … but by lawful judgement of his peers or by the law of the land'.[121]

Justice Jackson went on to declare that this fundamental constitutional right: '…will certainly not lose its importance in the field of adult social care, with an ageing population increasing the responsibilities of families and the state. Decisions about incapacitated people must always be determined by their best interests, but the starting point is their right to respect for their family life, where it exists. The burden is always on the state to show that an incapacitated person's welfare cannot be sustained by living with, and being looked after by, his or her family, with or without outside support.'[122]

That said, Justice Jackson did set out three general issues that arose from this case:

1. The DoLS scheme is an important safeguard against arbitrary detention and is not to be used by a local authority to get its way. Any significant welfare issues that cannot be resolved by discussion should be taken before the Court of Protection.
2. Local authorities need to make sure they have clear decision-making processes in place – in this case, no one took ultimate responsibility.
3. There needs to be a separation between the managing authority and supervisory body in making DoL authorisations, and the supervisory body must conduct a full best-interest assessment, not a superficial one.[123]

Yo Dunn feels that the DoLS can sometimes be very helpful. She cited the case of an autistic man with quite serious health problems who had a massive phobia about all medical staff:

120 *London Borough of Hillingdon v Neary and another [2011] EWHC 1377 (COP)* (09 June 2011).

121 Henderson A (2011) *A young autistic man, Magna Carta, human rights and unlawful detention* [online]. Available at: https://ukhumanrightsblog.com/2011/06/16/a-young-autistic-man-magna-carta-human-rights-and-unlawful-detention/ (accessed January 2024)

122 Ibid.*I

123 Ibid. For more on Justice Jackson's ruling, see online resources: www.pavpub.com/autism-and-the-law-resources.

'He had been living in his own flat, with district nurses coming in intermittently. Because he had rejected medical treatment, it looked as though he would not survive. I helped him to write an "advance decision" saying that he did not want, in any circumstances, to be taken to into hospital. Then one day, his carers called an ambulance, which took him to hospital against his wishes, despite the signed and witnessed advanced decision. The man said that he had been "kidnapped". It was completely unlawful. The problem was that, although the man wished to leave the hospital, you cannot compel the ambulance service to provide transport. He was not physically capable of walking out of the hospital and getting a taxi. The ambulance service were unwilling to transport him. So he had no means of returning home.

'So he stayed in hospital, very depressed, for about a month. By then, even the doctors agreed that the most humane solution would be to send him home. At that point, someone belatedly applied for DoLS. This prompted the involvement of a Best Interests Assessor (BIA), who was able to make nuanced and informed decisions about his capacity and best interests, in consultation with those who knew him well, which moved the situation forward. We were just preparing to remove him from hospital when he died. He was going to die anyway. The question was whether this would happen with him traumatised in hospital or on his own terms at home, where he wanted to be. So, sometimes DoLs can be great. But it is massively under-funded.'[124]

Case study 9: Steven Neary

Since 2009, Steven Neary, who is autistic and has a severe learning disability, had lived with his father, Mark Neary, who looks after him with the help of an extensive care package provided by the local authority, Hillingdon. In December 2009, Steven became more difficult to handle than usual and his father was ill. It was therefore agreed on December 31, 2009, that Steven would go into a support unit for a few days so that his father could have some rest. It was at this point that the problems began.[125]

After experiencing problems looking after Steven, the staff at the support unit held a meeting on January 4, 2010, at which they decided that Steven should be kept at the unit for longer so that they could assess his needs. This was not fully explained to his father, Mark, who believed Steven would be returning home very shortly. Steven badly wanted to go home and, as a result, his behaviour deteriorated, which was taken by the staff as evidence that he posed a danger to himself or others and should be kept at the unit. Mark Neary made it very clear that he did not consent to Steven remaining at the support unit and asked that he be returned home, but his requests were not heeded. In April 2010, Steven attempted to leave the unit and broke the glasses of a passer-by in the process. As a result of this incident, Hillingdon local authority signed an urgent DoLS authorisation allowing Steven to be kept at the support unit for seven days without any outside activities. On April 21 that year, after a 'best interests' assessment, the local authority made a standard DoLS authorisation, which allowed Steven's detention for two months.

➔

124 Yo Dunn, personal communication, January 5, 2023.

125 See https://ukhumanrightsblog.com/2011/06/16/a-young-autistic-man-magna-carta-human-rights-and-unlawful-detention/ (accessed January 2024)

When Mark Neary was told about the DoLS order, he was understandably very upset, but he was not informed that Hillingdon were now planning to keep Steven in the support unit or a similar location indefinitely and not allow him to return home. Mark was still under the impression that there was a 'transition plan' to ensure that Steven returned home relatively soon. A second DoLS authorisation was made on June 21, 2010. Throughout all of this process, Steven had no independent representation and neither did Mark. On July 7, Mark was finally told, to his shock and alarm, that the local authority did not intend to return Steven home. His concern increased even further when it seemed that Hillingdon was considering a residential placement for Steven many miles away.[126]

Despite long letters of complaint being sent from Mark and Mrs Neary (Steven's mother), the local authority decided, in August 2010, that it would issue court proceedings to obtain permission to detain Steven for longer. These proceedings were not, in fact, issued until October 28, 2010, by which time Steven had been at the support unit for ten months. By December, Steven's case had been taken up by at least one blogger, who had some success in giving his predicament wider publicity. Mr Justice Mostyn heard the case on December 23, 2010. He promptly terminated the DoL authorisation and returned Steven to his home, almost 12 months after he had left 'for a few days'.[127]

Rising numbers in the psychiatric system

While the UK government's flagship Transforming Care for People with Learning Disabilities and Autism programme had a degree of success in moving autistic people and/or people with learning difficulties from hospital into the community, recent years have unfortunately seen a hidden trend: rising numbers of autistic children and young people entering the psychiatric system.

In 2011, young people made up 7.6% of all disabled people detained under the Mental Health Act (1983) in the UK but, by 2017, this figure had risen to 13%. Many of these are autistic people and/or people with learning difficulties who are admitted for short stays which then become long-stay placements. Young people end up in the psychiatric system because of local authorities' and clinical commissioning groups' systematic failure to fund well-coordinated education, health and care services.

According to NHS figures, more than 2,000 autistic people and/or people with learning disabilities were being held in mental health inpatient units in the UK as of 2022 for an average of around 5.5 years, and 350 had been detained for a decade or longer. Some of these are detained under part 3 of the MHA (patients involved in criminal proceedings). A further 1,095 people detained under part 2 (Sections 2 or 3) of the MHA will continue to be detained until they have suitable housing and care in the community. In other words, they are detained in hospitals for mental health treatment even though many – unless they have a mental illness – do not need actually need mental health treatment in a hospital. The NHS figures also revealed that, in the first six months of 2022, there were

126 Ibid.

127 Ibid.

nearly 26,000 reported uses of restrictive practices in the UK, such as people being kept in isolation or being restrained – either physically or with medication. And in some instances, mechanical restraints are employed – using objects such as handcuffs, belts or harnesses to restrict movement.

Oliver Lewis, a barrister from Doughty Street Chambers who has represented several autistic individuals and/or people with learning disabilities detained under the Mental Health Act (1983) as well as their families, points out that the MHA's definition of 'medical treatment' is very wide: if someone benefits from having nurses around, that counts as medical treatment. This is, in Lewis's words, a 'legal fiction' which 'may well be a breach of the person's right to liberty, given that "the validity of continued confinement depends upon the persistence of such a [mental] disorder"'.[128] The European Committee for the Prevention of Torture agrees: 'Involuntary placement in a psychiatric establishment should cease as soon as it is no longer required by the patient's mental state'.[129]

However, as Lewis correctly notes, the opposite of institutionalisation is not liberty; it is community. Achieving the right to live in the community, as set out in Article 19 of the United Nations Convention on the Rights of Persons with Disabilities, requires housing, specialist support services, access to leisure, sports, culture, transport and family. Article 19 calls on states to provide services to people with disabilities that 'prevent isolation or segregation from the community'. However, these support services are woefully inadequate in the UK, despite the fact that the UK government ratified the UN Convention in 2009. As Lewis puts it: '...people with learning disabilities and/or autism are regularly failed by local authorities by inadequate care planning and provision. The government's austerity approach has made social workers' jobs more difficult: often there simply isn't sufficient resource to meet needs.'[130]

Ironically, the Mental Health Act itself concedes that hospital is not the appropriate place for an autistic individual. Paragraph 20.20 of the MHA Code of Practice states that 'Compulsory treatment in a hospital setting is rarely likely to be helpful for a person with autism'. The fact is that, once in a hospital, an autistic individual's sensory differences or challenging behaviours often mean they experience escalating levels of restriction (seclusion, restraint or sedation). This is counterproductive and, in turn, leads to more restrictive practices.

128 Lewis O (2022) *Reducing mental health detention of people with autism and/or learning disabilities* [online]. Available at: https://insights.doughtystreet.co.uk/post/102hfgz/reducing-mental-health-detention-of-people-with-autism-and-or-learning-disabiliti (accessed January 2024).

129 See www.mentalcapacitylawandpolicy.org.uk/european-committee-for-the-prevention-of-torture-and-inhuman-or-degrading-treatment-or-punishment-and-mha-reform/ (accessed March 2024).

130 Ibid.

Case study 10: Hayden Remi

In 2022, Hayden Remi, a ten-year-old autistic boy with learning difficulties from Hertfordshire, was sectioned under the Mental Health Act (1983) in a general children's ward in hospital. He ended up there because his mother, Jaycee, had asked for help with his care, but a lack of facilities for people with his condition meant that Hayden spent four weeks in a room staring at bare walls with nothing but a plastic mattress on the floor. Jaycee told ITV News: 'When I'm showing family members or friends the photos, they will say it looks like a prison. We were met with a lot of staff saying that they weren't trained to deal with autism or learning disabilities. It just made us feel like he was a problem and not a human being. He wasn't dealt with any sort of compassion.'[131]

It was in this environment that Hayden was supposed to be assessed for what care he might need, but it was precisely the environment that made him worse: 'He was just really not himself,' said Jaycee. 'He didn't want to draw all of the things he would usually be interested in. He just didn't want to anymore. Just watching him decline basically on a daily basis and not having anything to do about it. Every day I asked: "Please can I take him out?" And I was told no. It was due to the weather or he's a bit upset today so we're not gonna take him. It's too dangerous. We've had to do a risk assessment. He's not allowed out so many days.'

Hayden also has severe allergies to dairy and his mother said she made that clear to carers but he was given food containing dairy, which triggered a severe reaction. Jaycee said she had agreed to have him sectioned for assessment, because she felt she had no other choice to get him help.[132]

Responsible clinicians

Unfortunately, it is difficult or impossible for a family – or the lawyers representing the family – to challenge the approach or decisions to use restrictive practices. This is because the MHA (1983) delegates all responsibility for Part 2 patients' care and treatment (including every part of the daily regime) to the 'Responsible Clinician' (RC), who is usually a consultant psychiatrist. Remarkably, the RC is not legally obliged to have any specific expertise in learning disabilities or autism, although the MHA Code of Practice mentions at para 36.3 that the RC should have 'the most appropriate expertise' to meet the patient's needs. Oliver Lewis cited the case of an RC treating an autistic person as if he had a mental illness. The RC kept talking about the patient's 'recovery,' as if someone can recover from a learning disability. 'Not only did the family find this bewildering, but it meant that the patient was treated potentially negligently. In what other field of medicine would we tolerate this?'[133]

The Responsible Clinician has enormous powers. He or she can change the person's medication without consultation or agreement with the individual or the family. Section 17 of the MHA (1983) permits a person to leave hospital to visit their family, but the RC can prevent this from happening. Lewis quotes the case of Lisa Perry, whose son is autistic and has a learning disability. The RC banned him from seeing his family because, after

131 See www.itv.com/news/2022-11-16/mum-pleads-for-help-with-autistic-son-10-in-broken-system (accessed January 2024).

132 Ibid.

133 Lewis O (2022) *Reducing mental health detention of people with autism and/or learning disabilities* [online]. Available at: https://insights.doughtystreet.co.uk/post/102hfgz/reducing-mental-health-detention-of-people-with-autism-and-or-learning-disabiliti (accessed January 2024).

returning to hospital from a trip out with them, he was noisy. Lisa believed her son was merely expressing the fact that he had a good time and did not want to be back in the seclusion room. To the hospital staff, however, he represented a noisy danger.[134]

Although a Second Opinion Appointed Doctor (SOAD) is supposed to review the care and treatment of patients who lack capacity to consent, the only way an individual or his or her family can challenge decisions by the RC is to use the hospital's complaint processes, but the hospital managers usually agree with the RC's point of view. The only remaining option in this horrendous process is to make an application for judicial review. However, not only do families require legal aid to protect them from adverse costs, but it is notoriously difficult to persuade the administrative court that the RC had acted in a way that was, in law, unreasonable or irrational.

Section 117 of the MHA (1983) acts as a disincentive for local authorities and clinical commissioning groups (CCGs), who can save enormous sums of money by keeping people in hospital. Once the person has been discharged, the authorities have to pay for the entirety of care, which can include housing. All they need to do is say that they are searching for a community placement and that a particular patient has 'complex needs'. There is no legal or financial sanction on local authorities or CCGs for failing to find or establish suitable community provision. This is in clear breach of Article 5 (the right to liberty) of the UN Convention on the Rights of Persons with Disabilities.

Oliver Lewis claims that keeping an individual in hospital may also violate Article 3 of the European Court of Human Rights (the prohibition on torture, inhuman or degrading treatment or punishment). The ECHR states that resource limitations cannot justify a breach of Article 3. As Lewis observes:

> 'People with learning disabilities and/or autism who have experienced and survived institutionalisation often carry the psychological scars for many years... In a similar way that victims of torture are provided with psychological, medical and legal rehabilitation, so too should people with disabilities and their families – often the champions of their rights – be offered these services, as an acknowledgement of the harm that the state has caused.'[135]

There is increasing concern about the over-use (and abuse) of so-called Assessment and Treatment Units (ATUs), which are essentially used for detentions in hospital under the MHA (1983).

The United Nations Convention on the Rights of Persons with Disabilities (UNCRPD) Disability Committee, in its guidance on how the government can achieve successful implementation of disabled people's rights to independent living (as set out in Article 19 of the Convention), proposed that the UK's Mental Health Act be amended to prevent ATUs becoming the only route of securing state-funded 'assistance' for disabled people with learning difficulties and autism. The Committee argued that, if disabled people had the support they needed from birth, there would be no reason ATUs to exist.

---

134 Ibid.

135 Ibid.

During 2016, the Justice Together Project held a family event to explore why their loved ones end up in ATUs. The authors found that the Special Education Needs Framework of the Children and Families Act (2014) came in for a high level of criticism. The whole system failed disabled children time and time again. In particular, children's educational needs were not being assessed properly, leading to schools failing to understand triggers of distress and being unable to support the children's behaviour at school or during secondary school transitions.[136] Richard Griffiths, the father of an adult autistic son, is vehemently opposed to the use of autism treatment units: 'ATUs are synonymous with the Berlin Wall, in that a person held cannot be released, otherwise all the others will have to be released from captivity...' [137]

Case study 11: Tony Hickmott

Tony Hickmott, 45, an autistic man with learning difficulties and epilepsy who had been held in a secure hospital for over two decades, was told in October 2022, that he could finally return home. Hickmott, who had been dubbed 'the loneliest man in the hospital', was sectioned after he had a mental health crisis in 2001. Yet despite a protracted legal battle fought by his family to have him released, he remained in a secure unit for 21 years. In 2022, Judge Hilder, Senior Judge of the Court of Protection, criticised Hickmott's detention, instructing authorities to find a home near to his parents' bungalow in Brighton. Tony's parents, Pam, 78, and Roy, 82, live over two hours' drive away from the short-term facility. 'He wants to go to the pub with me', said Roy. 'I'll have a pint and he'll have a half and he says he'll have a cheese roll. That's what he wants, a cheese roll. I can't wait. It'll be heaven.'[138]

Hickmott had been held in a secure Assessment and Treatment Unit (ATU) designed to be a short-term safe space for use in a crisis. In 2013, psychiatrists agreed he was 'fit for discharge' but the authorities failed to create a care package with appropriate support in the community. In December 2021, Pam and Roy took the case to the Court of Protection. This court was created under the Mental Capacity Act in 2005 and has jurisdiction over the welfare, financial affairs and assets of people who are deemed to lack the mental capacity to make decisions for themselves. Brighton & Hove City Council stated at the time that Tony had 'extremely complex needs', declaring: 'His current out-of-town accommodation is the nearest that offers the specialist care and very high staffing ratios required to care for him and manage his needs'.

Details of Hickmott's case emerged only after a whistleblower, Phil Devine, who worked in the private, low-secure hospital as a cleaner and a support worker between 2015 and 2017, came forward to the BBC. Devine described how Tony, had only his basic needs met 'like an animal' and spent all his time in segregation. He also said that Hickmott spoke to staff through a hatch, leaving the paint thin from his countless knocks and bangs. The hospital has not been named in order to protect Hickmott's well-being. However, in 2022, the Care Quality Commission (CQC) watchdog said the hospital was failing to meet patients' needs. Inspectors also ordered that further patient admissions be delayed because they believed 'people would or may be exposed to significant risk of harm'.[139]

---

136 See https://committees.parliament.uk/writtenevidence/25145/html/ (accessed January 2024).

137 Griffiths R, in written evidence to the UK Parliament: https://committees.parliament.uk/writtenevidence/99436/pdf/ (accessed January 2024).

138 See www.bbc.co.uk/news/uk-62819017 (accessed January 2024).

139 Ibid.

Detention under the Mental Health Act

Alison Rogers, from Worksop, Nottinghamshire, told ITV News that her autistic son, Adam Downs, who also has learning difficulties, had been detained in Rampton high-security hospital under the Mental Health Act, even though he was not suffering from a mental health illness. The definition of 'mental disorder' in the MHA (1983) includes autism, which makes possible the detention of autistic people who do not have a mental health condition. After Adam went missing at the age of 15, police found him and he was taken into the system. His mother was told he would be back home after six months, following assessments. Fifteen years later, after Adam was moved from secure unit to secure unit, his mother was still waiting for him to come home. 'He's got a mattress on the floor, they shut the toilets off, and they made him go to the toilet in front of the cameras', Rogers told ITV News. 'He can't be cured of his learning disabilities and autism, he has special requirements and needs proper care and support – he won't get that where he is. He's left alone for long periods of time. The environment is a trigger for him, so then they end up restraining him or secluding him and that makes him worse. It's a vicious cycle.' She claims that Adam is deteriorating mentally and physically and says he has been given medication for a mental illness that he does not have: 'He's a shadow of himself. He can't do anything now. He can't function properly, because he's on high doses of medication.'[140]

One senior nurse with two decades' experience working inside secure units, who spoke anonymously to ITV News, said that Adam's experience was symptomatic of a broken system. The nurse said she believed people with learning disabilities and autism should not be in mental health units:

> 'The system abuses them ... few will have any training. Staff just aren't trained to support them and often there just isn't the staff. Mental health wards are completely the wrong environment and are triggers for patients with autism and learning disabilities, who then end up being restrained or secluded for long periods of time when they don't need to be.[141]

'Seclusion has its place if it's used to make an area safe for an hour or two, but for days, weeks, months and years it's unacceptable', said the senior nurse. 'I've tried to raise concerns, but I'm just seen as a trouble-maker'. She added that she had regularly witnessed the misuse of restraints or medication: 'Patients are being given medication they don't need. It's being used as a chemical cosh, because staff just don't know what else to do. They're not trained so medication and seclusion become the only alternative for them. The system abuses them. We have staff shortages and few are trained in disabilities or autism.'[142] Jeremy Harris managed to save his daughter, Bethany, from following a similar path to that of Adam Downs. Bethany is autistic and has mild learning disabilities. She was held in ATUs for several years since she was a teenager. So desperate was he to get her out that he secretly filmed one of his visits while Bethany was kept in isolation for

140 Ibid.

141 ITV News (2022) *'Barbaric': Hundreds with learning disabilities kept locked up for years* [online]. Available at: www.itv.com/news/2022-11-02/barbaric-hundreds-with-learning-disabilities-kept-locked-up-for-years (accessed January 2024).

142 Ibid.

three years. They could communicate only through a hatch in the door: 'That was my contact with Beth for three years. She hated it, she just wanted a hug more than anything in the world and I couldn't do that,' her father told ITV News. 'Three years she was kept in isolation. Just a mattress on the floor. She was so broken that she would try and end her own life using her clothing, using her underwear. Groups of men would storm into the room and pin her to the floor to remove her clothing and restrain her. You don't treat animals like that, you shouldn't be doing that to human beings.'[143]

Following a review, Bethany was finally given a support package to help her live independently, which her father says has transformed her life. Her father says she is now happy and thriving:

> 'Where Beth is now, she goes out every day. She talks to friends, she goes shopping. She does what I do. There's no reason why she shouldn't have had that, instead of being placed in a hospital.' Jeremy says people like his daughter are being failed by the system: 'It's a case of out of sight out of mind. It's easier, it saves the local authority money and let's face it: they're all cash-strapped at the moment. It saves them having to provide the care, because the moment that a person is place in hospital, it's the NHS who picks up the bill.'[144]

Jeremy Harris now dedicates his time to helping prevent other families from facing a similar situation. He is on a panel advising organisations about the support which people like his daughter need. The charity, Mencap, is also campaigning to end the practice of detaining people with learning disabilities and/or autism under the Mental Health Act in secure units. Dan Scorer, Mencap's head of policy, told ITV News: 'It just shows that people with learning disabilities and autism just do not matter as much in the eyes of the government. To keep them locked up is Dickensian and barbaric.'[145]

Another mother in a similar situation to Bethany's father told ITV News:

> 'We wish we'd never asked for help, if help comes in the form of locking somebody up 24 hours a day with occasional leaves with no real meaningful life. No, no, I wouldn't ever have asked, had I known. The system has swallowed him up. He hasn't spent a single birthday or Christmas at home since he was locked away at 13. And his family say the system has failed him. He's a different person. He's at times suicidal. He's withdrawn, he's exhausted. He doesn't have a quality of life. It's been so detrimental too, to us as a family, having a family member go through this existence with real poor quality of human rights. The trauma, the abuse, the institutionalisation: when we hear of families at the start of this journey, it's soul-destroying.'[146]

In February 2020, the Equality and Human Rights Commission (EHRC) launched a legal challenge against the UK's Secretary of State for Health and Social Care over the repeated

143 Ibid.

144 Ibid.

145 Ibid.

146 Ibid.

failure to move autistic people and/or people with learning disabilities into appropriate accommodation. In its pre-action letter to the UK's then-Secretary of State for Health and Social Care, Matt Hancock, the EHRC declared:

> 'We have long-standing concerns about the rights of more than 2,000 people with learning disabilities and autism being detained in secure hospitals, often far away from home and for many years. These concerns increased significantly following the BBC's exposure of the shocking violation of patients' human rights at Whorlton Hall, where patients suffered horrific physical and psychological abuse. We... [are] arguing that the Department of Health and Social Care (DHSC) has breached the European Convention of Human Rights (ECHR) for failing to meet the targets set in the Transforming Care programme and the Building the Right Support programme. These targets included moving patients from inappropriate inpatient care to community-based settings and reducing the reliance on inpatient care for people with learning disabilities and autism.'[147]

Rebecca Hilsenrath, Chief Executive of the EHRC, said:

> 'We cannot afford to miss more deadlines. We cannot afford any more Winterbourne Views or Whorlton Halls. We cannot afford to risk further abuse being inflicted on even a single more person at the distressing and horrific levels we have seen. We need the DHSC to act now. These are people who deserve our support and compassion, not abuse and brutality. Inhumane and degrading treatment in place of adequate healthcare cannot be the hallmark of our society. One scandal should have been one too many... Alongside our discussions with the DHSC, the Care Quality Commission and NHS England, we have been calling for an enforceable right to independent living and the development of a legal model to incorporate it into domestic law. This would protect the right of disabled people to live independently and as part of the community, and it would also strengthen the law that puts a presumption in favour of living in the community and the views of individuals at the heart of decision-making.'[148]

147 See: www.localgovernmentlawyer.co.uk/adult-social-care/391-adult-care-news/42772-equalities-watchdog-in-legal-action-against-health-secretary-over-accommodation-for-people-with-learning-disabilities-and-autism (accessed January 2024).

148 See www.equalityhumanrights.com/health-secretary-faces-legal-challenge-failing-patients-learning-disabilities-and-autism (accessed January 2024).

Useful resources and further guidance

- Useful information can be found at the following websites:
  - Care and Treatment Reviews: www.england.nhs.uk/learning-disabilities/care/ctr/
  - Bringing Us Together: http://pbsacademy.org.uk/
  - Transforming Care: www.england.nhs.uk/learning-disabilities/care/
  - Mental Health Units (Use of Force) Act (2018): www.legislation.gov.uk/ukpga/2018/27/enacted
- The Independent Mental Capacity Advocate (IMCA), unlike the appropriate advocate used in the criminal justice system (see Chapter 6), is a role created under the Mental Capacity Act. An IMCA is required in certain specific situations, such as when there is a proposal for a person to be moved into residential care or a hospital and also when a serious medical treatment is being proposed, and where there is no appropriate family member to advocate for the person or where there might be a conflict of interests. Local authorities do also appoint IMCAs in a broader range of situations. Sometimes, if an autistic adult has behaved inappropriately, the police become involved and there is concern over whether the individual has the mental capacity to understand whether he or she would be criminally liable, the local authority could well appoint an IMCA to support that person. IMCAs have quite specific, high-level requirements for their training. They have to undergo refresher courses every year and a significant proportion are trained in non-instructive advocacy – advocacy on behalf of someone who is unable to tell them what he or she wants. (Appropriate adults do not need any training at all.) Most IMCAs are employed by voluntary sector organisations, who are then commissioned by local authorities. However, the IMCA has to be independent of the local authority.

The implications of reforming Britain's Mental Health Act (1983)

Reforms to the Mental Health Act (1983) were first promised in 2017, when the UK's then Prime Minister, Theresa May, commissioned a major review of the legislation, amid fears that it was 'outdated' and 'not fit for purpose.' However, the King's Speech in November 2023 shelved the reforms, making them very unlikely to be introduced in the life of the current Parliament.

The proposed reforms would have tightened the criteria for detention for assessment under Section 2 of the MHA (1983) by requiring that there would otherwise be serious harm to the patient or another person and that detaining the patient was necessary given the nature, degree and likelihood of that harm. Currently, individuals may be detained for assessment if they are suffering from a mental health disorder of a nature or degree that warrants detention and they ought to be detained for the purposes of their health or safety or the protection of others.

The reforms would have introduced equivalent changes in criteria for detention for treatment under Section 3 of the MHA (1983) and further tightened the criteria by requiring that a person be detained only if necessary treatment could not otherwise be provided and that treatment which had a reasonable prospect of alleviating their condition, or preventing it from deteriorating, were available.

Most relevantly, the proposed reforms would have prohibited a person from being detained for treatment simply on the basis of his or her being autistic or having a learning disability. Currently, people can be detained for treatment on the basis of autism, while a person with a learning disability can be detained if this is associated with 'abnormally aggressive or seriously irresponsible conduct'.

However, many people were opposed to the proposed reforms to the MHA (1983). These opponents feared that the changes would simply move long-term hospital placements on to a different legal footing, such as detention under the Mental Capacity Act (2005) (under the DoLS) or an increase in the use of mental health guardianship. The new mental health legislation could have the opposite effect since proposed changes to the law which are intended to prevent autistic people from being unfairly detained in hospital could lead to many of them ending up in prison instead. This is because if people no longer fall under the remit of the Mental Health Act (1983), they can be deprived of their liberty under the Mental Capacity Act (2005) instead under the DoLS or – in the future – the 'Liberty Protection Safeguards'. This is due to complicated rules at the 'interface' between the two laws – so complicated, in fact, that a senior judge described them as akin to putting your head in a washing machine and spin dryer.[149]

In October 2022, Alexis Quinn, who is autistic herself, told UK MPs and peers comprising the joint committee on the government's draft Mental Health Bill that she had been a teacher for eight years before she was detained as an inpatient in hospital and ended up in long-term segregation after her brother died at around the same time that she was having a baby. She spent three-and-a-half years detained in hospital before she managed to escape to Africa. She believes she would probably still be detained in the mental health system today if she had not fled.

The draft Bill included measures which would mean autistic individuals and people with learning difficulties would not be able to be detained under the Act unless they also had a diagnosed mental health condition or they were being assessed for one. But Quinn, manager of the Restraint Reduction Network, said that the changes could lead to those like her ending up in prison if they had an autistic meltdown because of how they were being treated in hospital while they were being assessed.

Quinn told MPs:

> 'I just don't think this is preferable to the Mental Health Act. So, although, yes, I think in principle [the measures relating to autistic people and those with learning difficulties] should be taken out [of the Mental Health Act], unless we can really know that people aren't going to be criminalised, I think that's more life-limiting. It's more life-limiting for me to have a criminal record as a law-abiding citizen. The [current] system is very inappropriate to detain autistic people. Having said that, I would really rather be in a hospital than in prison. With the right support and the right environment, this won't happen to people. But what I really want to make clear is that there isn't the right support and the

149 See https://thesmallplaces.wordpress.com/2019/01/03/psychiatric-detention-under-the-mental-capacity-act-2005/ (accessed March 2024).

> right environment in this country at the moment. It's not here. So we're setting people up to fail if we don't do something. I live in fear, to be quite honest, that I'll have a meltdown in the street and the whole process can start again.'[150]

Quinn told the committee that she was all for reducing the number of autistic people who are detained for no reason: 'But for that to work, for people not to then be detained in other settings or detained under the Mental Capacity Act, we have to change what we're doing in the community and how we support people, and we're not there yet'. She said the support structures were not in place even for autistic people experiencing moderate distress, while the current system was not 'responsive'.[151]

At an earlier meeting, in 2021, Quinn told MPs on the Commons Health and Social Care Committee that, 'any kind of autistic reaction to a stressful life event ... can, and too often does, result in sectioning because of the failure to provide any community-based support for autistic people in crisis'. She described her ordeal in Assessment and Treatment Units, including 'not being treated quite as a human, being told constantly that I need to get better, from what I don't know' and being 'rewarded with star charts and fresh air if I managed to look normal, [but] confined to the indoors if my "autisticness," my reaction to the environment, couldn't be adequately masked that day'.[152]

Quinn told the *Daily Mail* that her parents – a prison officer and a police officer who are both now retired – had always been wonderfully supportive. She achieved a first-class degree in education and had been working as a teacher in Tokyo, but when her brother died suddenly, she found it difficult to cope. She returned to the UK, changed jobs, and gave birth to a daughter. Seeking help from her GP, she eventually found herself in an ATU in the south of England and 'her nightmare began that very next day'. After six months of being restrained, her clothes being forcibly removed, and being drugged with medication 'so powerful that my brain felt as though it was filled with thick clouds', Alexis tried to kill herself and was transferred to an intensive care unit, then to an acute unit, and then to a rehabilitation centre. In the end, a retired GP friend helped Quinn to leave her rehab and she went to France and from there on to Lagos, Nigeria. She now lives back in the UK with her daughter.[153]

Quinn explained to me that:

> 'At the moment, we have a community that can't support people even when they are not in a crisis. I have an autistic daughter who is having a horrid time at school. I do not think that adequate resources, such as bespoke in-house support, occupational therapy, speech and language support and neurodivergent affirming

---

150 Pring J (2022) *Mental health reforms 'could have unintended consequences' for autistic people* [online]. Available at: www.disabilitynewsservice.com/mental-health-reforms-could-have-unintended-consequences-for-autistic-people/ (accessed January 2024).

151 Ibid.

152 Pring J (2021) *Autistic activist tells MPs of 'brutal... aggressive... sink or swim' support system* [online]. Available at: www.disabilitynewsservice.com/autistic-activist-tells-mps-of-brutal-aggressive-sink-or-swim-support-system/ (accessed January 2024).

153 Quinn's full story can be found at www.dailymail.co.uk/news/article-6349939/Mother-reveals-drugged-suicidal-diagnosed-autism.html; it makes for a harrowing but worthwhile read.

> therapy, will be commonly accessible in my lifetime. What we have been seeing, certainly in the past five years (since I escaped from hospital), is a government tinkering around the edges sufficiently, until the next government comes in and does the same thing. The Mental Health Act has become a safety net, so that when people do enter crisis and act in ways others perceive as out of the ordinary or dangerous, they are not being criminalised for that activity. Without the Mental Health Act, many with low support needs will end up dying by suicide or entering the prison system. Those with co-occurring learning disabilities might end up subject to DoLS. But in terms of my experience, there is a move to criminalise people in inpatient settings. This is happening in mental hospitals. I have a fluctuating ability to speak using big words. My behaviour was seen as volitional and criminal, rather than a disorder. Are you mad or bad?'[154]

She added:

> 'The other aspect is that autism will become a diagnosis for exclusion, like personality disorder. So you will not be admitted, because autism can't be treated. Therefore, you are just a bad person. Every time I hear about a school shooting in America, there's a murmuring about whether the killer may have Asperger's syndrome. Now, I am a great advocate for the neurodivergent movement, and the desire to see autism as a normal variation of humanity, but I am disabled. What is going to happen is that, if we say that autism is not an illness (and I don't believe it is), then it's just behaviour and for certain people, like me with low support needs, that behaviour is volitional. Take the case of Jonty Bravery.[155] What he did was heinous. But if you look at the case material, it was a complete breakdown in community care. People did not listen to his warning that he was going to do that kind of thing. I put in a petition a few years ago for autism to be removed from the Mental Health Act. What was I thinking? Autism is a condition, a way of being, which should definitely be included in the Act. all the while community provision is appalling. Perhaps autism requires a separate section in the Act. I fear they are going to remove it and feel thoroughly pleased with themselves. '[156]

As Dr Lucy Series, Senior Lecturer in the School for Policy Studies at Bristol University, has noted, removing people with learning disabilities and/or autism from mental health legislation has been a policy goal for organisations campaigning with and for these groups since at least the middle of the 20th century:

---

154 Alexis Quinn, personal communication, November 8, 2022.

155 Jonty Bravery, a 17-year-old autistic teenager, threw a young French tourist from the tenth-storey viewing platform of Tate Modern art gallery in London in 2019. The child survived but has undergone round-the-clock treatment since, while Bravery, who told onlookers that social services were to blame for the incident, is serving a 15-year minimum prison term for attempted murder. A serious case review into Bravery found that, while his case was characterised by 'appropriate efforts by professionals from across agencies to access assessment and treatment' for him, those efforts 'were stymied due to the lack of services, placements and provisions that were suitable for his needs as an autistic young person with a co-existing conduct disorder diagnosis.' The serious case review said Bravery was diagnosed with autism at the age of five, but that there was a clear 'lack of join-up between different elements of support that were being provided to [Bravery] and his family' and that he was not known to children's social care or child and adolescent mental health services (CAMHS) until more than a decade later.

156 Alexis Quinn, personal communication, November 8, 2022.

> 'It makes sense, because properly speaking, mental health legislation is not about this population, since "mental disorders" such as schizophrenia, bipolar disorder and depression, are not necessarily life-long conditions such as learning disability and autism. Moreover, the Mental Capacity Act (2005) frameworks for detention use exactly the same term and definition of "mental disorder" to define the populations who can lawfully be detained under the Deprivation of Liberty Safeguards (DoLS) and the Liberty Protection Safeguards (LPS).'[157]

Series points out that the belief that the MHA (1983) should not apply to people with long-term developmental disabilities (or, similarly, people with brain injury or dementia):

> '...is cultural, not legal... This has deep historical roots in how these different populations were parsed and treated in the late 19th and 20th century, with one group deemed curable and the other incurable but perhaps trainable. Arguably, removing some populations from the scope of the MHA because it is associated with stigma is simply reinforcing that stigma for others without addressing the core problem... I suspect many will argue that removing people with learning disabilities and autism from the scope of the MHA will mean they are less likely to be detained in hospital settings such as ATUs. While I absolutely support the intention here, I believe the opposite outcome might result. Odd as it might sound, removing people from the scope of the MHA will not actually prevent them from being detained in hospitals and ATUs, and might even make it easier to detain them where they or their families object. This is because, when you take people out of the scope of the MHA, they become "eligible" for detention under the MCA instead. The DoLS are a framework for detention within the MCA that apply in hospitals and care homes... If they are detained under the MCA, they and their families will have fewer opportunities to object to or challenge their detention and treatment.'[158]

Useful resources and further guidance

- Being stuck in an ATU: Belinda Schwehr CASCAIDr (specialist advice charity): www.cascaidr.org.uk/2018/11/06/being-stuck-in-an-atu/

The Mental Health Act versus the Mental Capacity Act

Dr Lucy Series – whose research and evidence have been cited by the House of Lords Committee on the Mental Capacity Act, and the Law Commission in their proposals for reforms to the DoLS – has pointed out that, historically, there has been a reluctance to use the Mental Health Act to authorise the detention of people with learning disabilities. This is why the MHA's definition of 'mental disorder' was amended in 2007 to include a specific provision stating that 'a person with learning disability shall not be considered

157 Series L (2021) *Perils of mental health law reform* [online]. Available at: https://communitylivingmagazine.com/perils-of-mental-health-law-reform/ (accessed January 2024).

158 Ibid.

by reason of that disability' to have a mental disorder in the meaning of the MHA 'unless that disability is associated with abnormally aggressive or seriously irresponsible conduct on his part'. During the independent review of the MHA, there was debate as to whether autistic individuals should also be included in this exemption:

> 'The difficulty is that being excluded from the provisions of the MHA does not prevent a person from being detained in an Assessment and Treatment Unit. Rather, it means that the person may be admitted informally and de facto detained without any legal safeguards at all, or that they may be detained under the MCA. Currently, that would be under the DoLS; once the 2019 amendments to the MCA are in force, that would be under the Liberty Protection Safeguards (LPS). The DoLS, and in particular the LPS, generally offer far weaker protection of human rights than the MHA, and make it much harder for the detained person or their family to challenge the detention.'[159]

The MCA is essentially a legal overflow system for populations who, for various reasons, have been ousted from the MHA. A person who has been detained under the MHA, and then discharged by a mental health tribunal because he or she does not meet the MHA's criteria for detention, cannot then be re-detained under the MHA. However, it seems that the individual can then become eligible for detention under the MCA DoLS instead. So, perversely, the same person could be detained again in the same place, just under a different law.

Table 3.1: Comparison of the MHA (1983) and the MCA (2005)

Rights and powers of friends and relatives	
Detention under the Mental Health Act (1983)	Detention under the Mental Capacity Act (2005) Deprivation of Liberty Safeguards and the Liberty Protection Safeguards
When a person is detained for treatment under the MHA, their 'nearest relative' has certain rights that can be used to secure their release from an ATU. They can exercise powers of discharge, or they can object to an application for admission for treatment under Section 3 of the MHA. The hospital can seek to override this by issuing a 'barring order' or applying to the county court to displace the nearest relative. However, the nearest relative would retain the right to trigger a tribunal hearing.	The equivalent role for a person's family under the DoLS (the 'relevant person's representative') and the LPS (the 'appropriate person') does not include any power to object to admission or powers of discharge. They have a right to be consulted, but cannot prevent the detention. It is possible that family members may not be regarded as 'appropriate' to hold this role, although the policy intention appears to be that, generally, they will be. Their duties are to support and represent the person, but their rights of challenge are limited to requesting a review or initiating an appeal to the Court of Protection (see below). ➔

159 See Dr Lucy Series' written evidence the UK Parliament, https://committees.parliament.uk/writtenevidence/102426/pdf/

Assessments and independent oversight	
Detention under the Mental Health Act (1983)	**Detention under the Mental Capacity Act (2005) Deprivation of Liberty Safeguards and the Liberty Protection Safeguards**
Detention under s2 or s3 of the MHA requires two medical opinions and an application from an Approved Mental Health Professional, AMHP (unless the nearest relatives themselves apply, which is extremely rare). An AMHP is a specially trained professional, often a social worker, who is employed by the local authority, and who has to give an independent view on whether the criteria for detention are met.	Under the DoLS, a person will have assessments from both an independent Best Interests Assessor and a Mental Health Assessor. Under the LPS, there is no explicit statutory requirement for an assessment by a medical professional (although the regulations are still being drafted, but it appears that an assessment from other professionals such as psychologists might be accepted). On the Bill's face, it appears that all of the core LPS assessments could be carried out by one person who is employed by the hospital. For those detained in independent hospitals, the application will be reviewed by an Approved Mental Capacity Professional (AMCP) before the detention is authorised. These are independent specially trained professionals, with powers to consult with the person and take appropriate steps to determine whether the arrangements should be authorised. The 'responsible body' that must decide whether or not to authorise the arrangements will be the local authority where the detention is in an independent hospital, providing a degree of independence. For those detained in independent hospitals, the application will be reviewed by an Approved Mental Capacity Professional (AMCP) before the detention is authorised. These are independent specially trained professionals, with powers to consult with the person and take appropriate steps to determine whether the arrangements should be authorised. The 'responsible body' that must decide whether or not to authorise the arrangements will be the local authority where the detention is in an independent hospital, providing a degree of independence. However, for those detained in NHS hospitals, the responsible body reviewing the application will be the hospital itself. There will not be an independent review by an AMCP unless the person is objecting, which will be unlikely because of the rules on the interface between the MHA and the MCA. This means the only independent scrutiny of the assessments will be a desktop review by somebody employed by the hospital itself, who must be independent of the person's care. Relatives who are concerned can request a review by an AMCP, but this 'whistleblower' provision is not a cast-iron right to an independent review and it depends on whether the AMCP accepts the invitation. ➔

Rights of appeal	
Detention under the Mental Health Act (1983)	**Detention under the Mental Capacity Act (2005) Deprivation of Liberty Safeguards and the Liberty Protection Safeguards**
A person who is detained for treatment under the MHA will have a tribunal hearing within six months of the initial detention – and sooner if they, their nearest relative or the hospital managers request an earlier hearing. The appeal should be heard within a matter of weeks. The detained person will participate in the hearing, which will usually be held in the hospital. Under the MHA, the annual number of tribunal referrals is more than half the number of recorded detentions.	Appeals under the DoLS and the LPS goes to the Court of Protection. There is no automatic referral – an appeal must be initiated either by the detained person themselves, the 'appropriate person', those responsible for the detention or some other interested party. The court application process is complicated and will usually require legal assistance. Only the cared-for person and the appropriate person will qualify for legal aid in this costly litigation, however. Appeals can take several months. The person may participate in the hearing – which will be in a traditional courtroom – but this is not guaranteed. The rate of appeal under the DoLS is 1% and the government projects that this will fall to 0.5% under the LPS. The reality is that it is extremely difficult for detained persons, or those close to them, to trigger rights of appeal under the MCA.
Treatment safeguards	
Detention under the Mental Health Act (1983)	**Detention under the Mental Capacity Act (2005) Deprivation of Liberty Safeguards and the Liberty Protection Safeguards**
A person who is detained under the MHA and treated without consent (either because they refuse consent or because they lack the capacity to consent) is entitled to additional safeguards under Part IV of the MHA. These include an independent review of medical treatment by a Second Opinion Appointed Doctor (SOAD) for medical treatments lasting longer than three months. In 2017-18, 27% of SOAD reviews resulted in changes to the treatment plan.	There is no analogous second opinion scheme under the MCA, the DoLS or the LPS. Treatment might be considered as part of the DoLS or LPS authorisation process, particularly if it amounts to chemical restraint, but this is a grey area. If the person lacks the capacity to consent to treatment, the person's family should be consulted about their best interests and if there is nobody appropriate to consult, an Independent Mental Capacity Advocate should be appointed. Neither the family nor the advocate has a right to 'object' to treatment, however, unless they hold the authority to make these decisions via a Lasting Power of Attorney or Deputyship. ➔

Aftercare	
Detention under the Mental Health Act (1983)	**Detention under the Mental Capacity Act (2005) Deprivation of Liberty Safeguards and the Liberty Protection Safeguards**
A person who has been admitted for treatment under s3 of the MHA is entitled to free aftercare to facilitate their discharge into the community.	There is no entitlement to aftercare attached to the DoLS or the LPS. This means that any aftercare that is needed is subject to the usual adult social care charging rules.

(Reproduced with the kind permission of Dr Lucy Series)

A key test case of whether the Mental Health Act or the Mental Capacity Act should be applied was *Manchester University Hospitals NHS Foundation Trust v JS & Anor* (see **Case study 12** on p.81). Lucy Series, commenting on this case, explained to me that:

> 'The person was deprived of her liberty in hospital, so the question was whether DoLS or the MHA should be used. The hospital (unlawfully) detained her without any legal authority, once Section 2 of MHA had elapsed. For some reason, the hospital then applied to court, thinking they would use the MCA instead of Section 3 of the MHA.'[160]

The 'ineligibility' section is basically about whether the hospital could/should use the MCA or the MHA. It turns on a set of rules that can be summarised as follows:

- A person cannot be detained in hospital for treatment for a mental disorder under the MCA (DoLS/LPS) if:
  - they are 'within scope' of the MHA; that is, they 'could be' detained for assessment or treatment if an application were made under the MHA.
  - they are objecting either to 'being accommodated in a hospital for that purpose' or 'to being given some or all of that treatment'.

This is more complicated than it sounds, as Dr Series readily concedes:

> 'Essentially, the rule is set up so that it gives a kind of priority to the MHA, because it is viewed (by many) as offering more rigorous safeguards. But it has got an "escape" outlet for people who either aren't actually being treated for mental disorder or who aren't objecting. For various reasons, there's a culture of thinking that people with learning disability/autism should not be under the MHA, because people (wrongly) think that the MCA would be more empowering for them. But, as the judge points out in this case, the MHA contains mechanisms (including s117 aftercare and requirements for discharge care planning in the Code) that are supposed to facilitate discharge, plus tribunals to challenge confinement, plus mechanisms to oversee medical treatment, and use of restraint/seclusion. The MCA contains none of that...'[161]

160 Lucy Series, personal communication, August 8, 2023.

161 Ibid.

Case study 12: Manchester University Hospitals NHS Foundation Trust v JS & Anor

JS is a 17-year-old autistic teenager with attention deficit hyperactivity disorder, a learning disability and an attachment disorder. She had complex mental health needs and was vulnerable to self-harm. In December 2022, JS was admitted as an informal psychiatric inpatient to a specialist hospital and was discharged home in January 2023. She was subsequently detained under Section 136 of the Mental Health Act on two occasions in quick succession. On the second of those occasions, she was detained under Section 2 of the MHA to a general adult acute hospital ward, to be treated for the physical consequences of an overdose. When her s.2 MHA detention expired in February 2023, JS was physically fit for discharge, but remained in hospital in the absence of a safe discharge destination, in circumstances which amounted to a deprivation of her liberty. The Trust made the application to the Court of Protection to authorise JS's deprivation of liberty in hospital under the Mental Capacity Act, having refused to detain her under Section 3 of the MHA. The issue was whether the Court of Protection had the authority to detain JS, if she ought to be detained under the MHA.[162]

The judge, HHJ Burrows, accepted that JS lacked capacity to make decisions regarding her residence and care. Similarly, he accepted that, despite its not being the best environment for her, remaining where she was represented the best available option while professionals developed a robust care package to facilitate JS's return to her mother's care. He was, however, concerned that JS may fall into Case E of Schedule 1A of the MCA, and thus be ineligible to be deprived of her liberty under the MCA.[163]

For someone to be ineligible under Case E, the relevant person has to be within the scope of the MHA and Paragraph 5, Schedule 1A of the MCA must be satisfied (i.e. the patient must object to some, or all, of the mental health treatment). The relevant person is 'within the scope of the MHA' if an application in respect of the person could be made under Section 2 or Section 3 of the MHA and the person could be detained in a hospital in pursuance of such an application, were one made.

Ultimately, the court found that JS was within the scope of the MHA and was thus ineligible for detention under the MCA. The judge disagreed with the argument that JS did not need inpatient medical treatment after her overdose because she was no longer physically harmed. The judge stated that JS needed to be safely nursed and medicated for her mental disorder, which made her a danger to herself and others. The argument that JS's mental disorder did not require medical treatment in a hospital was rejected by the judge. He argued that medical treatment JS was receiving was necessary to keep her safe and prevent her from harming herself, and there was no other alternative available at the time.[164]

The judge disagreed with the argument that inpatient care was not necessary for JS's condition and that she could be treated in the community. The judge stated that until a suitable package of care was available for the patient, she could not safely leave the hospital. The judge held that patients detained under the MHA could be discharged into the community only with a suitable package of care. However, it can take weeks or months to put together such a package, and until then, patients remain detained. ➔

162 See www.localgovernmentlawyer.co.uk/adult-social-care/307-adult-care-features/54654-court-of-protection-case-update-2 (accessed March 2024)..

163 Ibid.

164 Ibid.

The Section 117 process is designed to accelerate the process of providing aftercare to ensure that patients are discharged from the hospital and do not return. The judge rejected the hospital's argument that detaining the patient under the MHA would harm her mental health and that keeping her in the hospital for a day longer than necessary was invalid. The judge stated that the label given to the care plan was irrelevant and that JS was detained for treatment regardless of the jurisdictional label.[165]

The judge stated that good clinical practice and the operation of Article 5 of the European Convention on Human Rights required a patient to be detained only for as long as necessary, and the MHA did not prolong detention. Proper use of s. 117 should reduce the overall time a patient spends in the hospital because professionals should work together to put together an effective discharge plan quickly.

The judge also declared that the decision to use the MHA should not be viewed in isolation from what was available elsewhere at the time the decision was taken. If a patient needed to be detained for treatment for their mental disorder, and there was no alternative outside the hospital setting, and no other treatment plan available, JS should not be detained under the MCA, but rather under the MHA.[166]

Mental capacity and the Court of Protection

The Court of Protection was created under the Mental Capacity Act in 2005 and has jurisdiction over the welfare, financial affairs and assets of people who are deemed to lack the mental capacity to make decisions for themselves. Alex Ruck Keene, a barrister who specialises in mental capacity law, says that the Court of Protection 'is a vital process in ensuring that people around those who cannot make decisions for themselves are always acting in their best interests.'[167]

Some autistic children and young adults with associated learning difficulties may need a degree of care after they reach 18 and one way to ensure that your son or daughter receives the care and provision they need as they enter adult life, is for parents and/or guardians to obtain a Deputyship Order for their child's property and financial affairs and/or their health and personal welfare. The Deputyship Order is obtained by making an application to the Court of Protection.

Obtaining a Deputyship Order is not an automatic process. On the contrary, it involves a series of steps which culminate in Deputyship Orders being granted to parents or other nominated individuals, giving them authority to make decisions on behalf of the young person.

When seeking to obtain a Deputyship Order, it is important to think through the following issues so you can make the best possible plan for your child:

- Education: Will your child be pursuing education later in life, or are they already doing so?

165 Ibid.

166 Ibid.

167 Clegg R (2023) *Teens locked out of Child Trust Funds also risk benefits cut* [online]. Available at: www.bbc.co.uk/news/education-65880559 (accessed January 2024).

- Medical services: Knowing the range of medical services available to your child/young person and making sure he or she continues to receive the correct treatments.
- Income and finances: Figuring out how to support a young person who lacks capacity once they become an adult is a concern for parents who may wish to maintain a degree of control over the young person's finances and income.
- Living arrangements: Being involved in decisions about where a young person will live and what type of accommodation is suitable for them is another issue which parents and guardians may wish to be involved in.
- Safety: Many young people lacking capacity, are vulnerable and cannot look out for themselves, so it's important that parents/guardians are involved in the planning of safety strategies and safeguarding procedures for these vulnerable young people. Unfortunately, individuals who lack capacity and also young autistic people are much more likely to be taken advantage of, and need protecting, especially when they are living away from the parental home.
- Decision-making: A young person may be able to make some decisions themselves, or they may not. This will depend on their mental capacity and abilities, their history and how comfortable you feel with allowing them a degree of control over their own choices.

You can apply to become someone's deputy if they 'lack mental capacity'. This means they cannot make a decision for themselves at the time it needs to be made. They may still be able to make decisions for themselves at certain times.

People may lack mental capacity because, for example:

- they have had a serious brain injury or illness.
- they have dementia.
- they have severe learning disabilities.

As a deputy, you will be authorised by the Court of Protection to make decisions on their behalf. There are two types of deputy.

Property and financial affairs deputy: You will be responsible for tasks such as paying the person's bills or organising his or her pension.

Personal (health and welfare) deputy: You will make decisions about medical treatment and how someone is looked after.

You cannot become someone's personal welfare deputy if he or she is under 16 years of age. The Court of Protection will usually appoint a personal welfare deputy only if:

- There is a doubt over whether decisions will be made in someone's best interests, for example because the family disagree about care.
- Someone needs to be appointed to make decisions about a specific issue over time, for example where someone will live.

You can apply to be just one type of deputy or both. If you are appointed, you will receive a court order saying what you can and cannot do. When you become a deputy, you must send an annual deputy report to the Office of the Public Guardian (OPG) each year explaining the decisions you have made.

How to apply

The application process is different depending on whether you are applying to be a personal welfare deputy or a property and financial affairs deputy. You do not need to be a deputy if you are simply looking after someone's benefits. In that instance, apply to become an appointee instead.

The Court of Protection will check:

- Whether the person needs a deputy or some other kind of help.
- There are no objections to your appointment.

If you are appointed, the Office of the Public Guardian will help you carry out your responsibilities. You will continue to be a deputy until your court order is changed, cancelled or it expires.

If you want to make a single important decision, you can apply to the Court of Protection for a one-off order.

If the person already has a Lasting Power of Attorney (LPA) or enduring power of attorney (EPA), they do not usually need a deputy. Check if they have an LPA or EPA before you apply.

Property and financial affairs deputyships

Short-term help: You can be appointed to make decisions about a person's money or property for a limited time – for example, while they are on holiday.

Long-term help: You can be appointed with a Lasting Power of Attorney to help someone make ongoing decisions about either or both:

- Money and property – starting at any time, or when they do not have mental capacity.
- Health and welfare – starting when they do not have mental capacity.

Case study 13: Ryan Catherall

Claire Catherall has paid £25 a month into the account of her 16-year-old son Ryan, who is autistic and has learning disabilities, since he was born. There is now £8,500 in the pot but she feels she is being 'penalised' for having savings. When Ryan turns 18, he will be eligible for universal credit, which is a benefit for people who are unable to work. But he will receive about £43 less a month as a result of having more than £6,000 in savings. Most universal credit claimants would stop receiving payments if their savings or capital reached £16,000.[168]

Catherall, who has three other children, says she cannot face taking legal action to get access to Ryan's savings because she has a full-time job and is already fighting on many fronts to ensure that Ryan receives the appropriate education and support. She stopped topping up Ryan's trust fund a few months ago when she realised she would have to go through the Court of Protection to access it. 'I actually cried when I stopped the direct debit', she told the BBC. 'He is so loving, so caring, but because of his autism he can also find the world very difficult and have challenging behaviours. He will...always rely on benefits... so the importance of having those savings is massive.'[169]

Millions of children born between 2002 and 2011 received between £250 and £500 through the then-Labour government's Child Trust Fund scheme. In June 2023, however, a BBC News investigation revealed that some 80,000 young people who lacked the mental capacity to manage their finances were unable to access their Child Trust Funds without their families going through the Court of Protection. The process can take months and cost hundreds of pounds, leaving many unable to access their money. Using data from two trust fund providers, BBC News calculated that around 9% (about 7,000) of those disabled young people had more than £6,000 in their accounts. Of these, more than half would be eligible for universal credit, according to government figures on the population as a whole – and will see reductions to their monthly payments.[170]

Teddy Nyahasha, the chief executive officer of the Child Trust Fund provider, One Family, believes that making families go to court to access their child's savings infringes his duty to the consumer. Nyahasha's company has chosen to release £3.6m from 1,000 accounts, without involving the Court of Protection. Around 92 of those will have savings of £6,000 or more. Nyahasha insists that doing so is not in breach of the Mental Capacity Act. He says if a parent is trusted by the government to handle their child's benefits, then they can be trusted to access their child's savings account. 'In most of these cases, these families are already receiving benefits from the government,' he said. 'If you just follow that paper trail, you can establish the link between the parent who is looking after the young adult, and the owner of the money.' Nyahasha says failure to help disabled people's families to access the Child Trust Funds constituted 'discriminating on the grounds of disability.'[171]

---

168 See https://a.bbc.co.uk/news/education-65880559 (accessed March 2024)/

169 Ibid.

170 Ibid.

171 Clegg R (2023) *Teens locked out of Child Trust Funds also risk benefits cut* [online]. Available at: www.bbc.co.uk/news/education-65880559 (accessed January 2024).

However, Alex Ruck Keene, the previously quoted barrister who specialises in mental capacity law, warned that One Family's stance set a 'dangerous precedent' which risks 'infantilising' disabled people and left them open to financial abuse.[172]

Health and welfare deputyships

On the whole, NHS healthcare is generally very good and most people do not experience any difficulties. But occasionally things can go wrong. If you are the next of kin of someone who has died because of negligent clinical care or who cannot take legal action themselves because they do not have capacity, you may be able to take legal action for compensation on their behalf.

Making a claim can be an expensive, stressful and potentially lengthy process. When considering the reason for your claim, it is important to note that the process of taking legal action is only about claiming compensation: the court cannot discipline healthcare practitioners, force a hospital or individual healthcare practitioner to change how they work or oblige a healthcare practitioner to apologise.

If the treatment you received fell below a minimum standard of competence and you suffered an injury as a result, and it is more likely than not that the injury could have been avoided or been less severe with proper treatment, then you may be able to take legal action for compensation. In order to receive compensation, you will need to be able to prove that both 'breach of duty of care' and 'causation' has taken place. The health practitioner must have acted in a way which fell short of acceptable professional standards. In 1957, the Bolam Test stipulated that no doctor can be found guilty of negligence if he or she is deemed to have acted 'in accordance with a responsible body of medical opinion'. The Bolam principle is not about what 'could have been done' that other health professionals might have done something differently, but whether it '*should* have been done' – in other words, would a 'responsible body' of health professionals support the action taken?[173]

An amendment to the Bolam Test, the so-called Bolitho Test (resulting from the 1996 court case of *Bolitho v City and Hackney HA*), helped to clarify what was meant by 'a responsible body', defining it as one whose opinion had a 'logical basis'. Combined, the Bolam Test and the Bolitho Test make up the twin pillars of all assessments of medical negligence. They state that a doctor is not negligent if he or she acts in accordance with a responsible body of medical opinion, provided that the court finds such an opinion to be logical. This means that the court should not accept a defence argument as being 'reasonable', 'respectable' or 'responsible' without first assessing whether such opinion is susceptible to logical analysis. [174]

172 Ibid.

173 See: https://resolution.nhs.uk/services/claims-management/advice-for-claimants/ (accessed March 2024).

174 Ibid.

The harm suffered must be shown, on the balance of probabilities, to be directly linked with the failure of the health professional to meet appropriate standards. If, for example, there was a good chance that the harm would have taken place even if the health professional had acted differently, then a claim is unlikely to succeed.

You will need to establish both a breach of duty of care and causation to be entitled to receive compensation. Compensation is aimed at putting you back, as close as possible, to the position you were in before the negligent care.

Remember that compensation claims for personal injury are generally subject to a 'limitation period' of three years. A claimant must issue their claim at court within three years of the alleged negligence taking place or within three years of becoming aware that something went wrong. However, individuals who lack 'capacity' (under 18 years of age or without the mental ability to make the necessary decisions) are not subject to this limitation period.[175]

Depending on the nature of your claim and the consequences of the injury sustained, you may be entitled to claim compensation for:

- General damages, that include compensation for both the pain suffered and loss of amenity you have incurred.
- Special damages that include any additional losses you may have incurred such as loss of earnings, additional care requirements, medical expenses, funeral expenses (in cases of bereavement) and other expenditure – where appropriate, a claim for special damages will need to be supported by appropriate receipts.

The compensation awarded for general damages takes into account the nature and extent of the injury sustained and the likely prognosis for resolution of any such pain and suffering experienced. This will also be based on guidelines provided by the Judicial Studies Board and previous awards by the courts in similar cases. To assess accurately the amount of compensation you are entitled to receive, it is likely that you will need to undergo an examination by an appropriate expert instructed either by you, on your behalf, or by the defendant NHS Trust. This is known as a 'condition and prognosis report'.[176]

Claims for personal injury are required to be reported to the Compensation Recovery Unit (CRU) at the Department for Works and Pensions. This is so that any compensation you receive takes into account (deducts) any government-awarded benefits you have received as a result of the injury you have sustained. This is why your date of birth, address and National Insurance Number are required.[177]

175 Ibid.

176 Ibid.

177 Ibid.

Case study 14: Adam Penfold

Adam Penfold, 23, who is autistic and has severe learning disabilities, and epilepsy, frequently becomes constipated and, when he lived at home, his parents were told to give him laxatives, as required. According to his father, Ian, Adam would sometimes go two weeks without passing solids, even with the laxatives, and would then suffer severe diarrhoea to clear his system. He even developed stretch marks on each side of his stomach.

Adam's GP refused to examine him because he had previously been slapped by Adam in his surgery. The GP would come no closer than six feet or so from Adam, even during home visits. Adam's mother has Crohn's disease and Ian has an underactive thyroid, which can also cause stomach problems. As Ian puts it: 'I would have thought that the family history would have been enough for them to agree to testing and examination. I think they are maybe more worried about getting sued for infringing his rights than providing proper care.' Adam has now moved into NHS-funded residential care (because there were no local day services that could take him). 'The wonderful staff have tried to get him diagnosed and treated, without much success either. His doctor does visit the home and offers guidance and assistance but seems to have the view that she cannot do much, because Adam won't let her examine him,' says Ian.[178]

Ian successfully applied to the Court of Protection to be appointed Adam's Health and Welfare Deputy for a period of six months. This meant that Ian could provide consent to treatment as necessary and within strict guidelines written in the court order. 'Thanks to the intervention of NHS Hampshire senior management as a result of the court order, and practical help from the Head of Learning Disabilities and Physical Disabilities for NHS Hampshire, we set up a multi-disciplinary team to take things forward. Adam finally had a much-needed blood test, CT scan and gastroscopy. The scan revealed a faecal compaction in his bowel over 12 centimetres in diameter.'[179]

Following the scan, the consultant prescribed a course of two strong laxatives for Adam. 'He spent over two months on these uncomfortable drugs, after which we took him for an abdominal X-ray, which showed that the blockage was still there and even worse than before,' says Ian. As a result, the consultant agreed to arrange a manual evacuation under general anaesthetic as a matter of urgency. Before the due date, however, Adam's condition deteriorated worryingly and he was then taken into hospital as an emergency admission. He had the procedure carried out and afterwards the surgeon confirmed that his bowel was clear. She didn't actually have to remove the blockage; we deduced that the laxatives finally did their job just before his admission. The good thing was that Adam had a full bowel check with a camera, biopsies taken and all the results were clear.'

According to his father, Adam is still displaying pain and discomfort symptoms, bending at the waist, pressing his groin and groaning occasionally. This could be habitual or might be due to something else, such as irritable bowel syndrome or inflammatory bowel disease. Ian's temporary Deputyship was extended. As he noted: 'Keeping me as his Deputy is very sensible, in the circumstances... I am furious at the length of time Adam had to suffer because no one would do anything, and feel that the NHS has been responsible for sustained and substantial abuse as a result of their neglect. Also, the majority of hospital staff didn't seem to understand our needs or make reasonable adjustments, although a few wonderful staff, when faced with the situation, did their best to help. I continue to fight for Adam and am delighted that the court has renewed my Deputyship. I think my involvement will be essential for the long term.'[180]

---

178 See https://committees.parliament.uk/writtenevidence/99394/pdf/ (accessed March 2024).

179 Ibid.

180 Ibid.

Case study 15: 'Molly'

'Molly' (not her real name) was born by emergency caesarean during a family holiday at 29 months. She weighed just 3 lb 1 oz. Once back in the local hospital in the UK, the nurses wanted her mother to express milk for her daughter. 'It was really hard. I was stressed and my body just wasn't producing a lot.' A few days later, her parents found Molly in a different room by herself and they had to wait outside in the corridor. 'We could see a nurse sitting really close to her, rubbing her hand,' her mother recalled. 'It looked as though Molly had hiccoughs and she was jerking weirdly. Suddenly, we heard them shout for help... A nurse told us that they were putting a long line in to give Molly some nutrition, but she was "misbehaving". We were left alone in that room, with a box of tissues, for ages. When we did finally see Molly, she looked dreadful and was choking and gasping for air.'[181]

The parents went back home but had to return to hospital because Molly was having a fit. 'She had a tube in her mouth and was all limp and grey. We were in complete shock and didn't know what to do.' The next morning, they were told by a consultant at the specialist hospital discussing her case that Molly was breathing by herself but that she had suffered severe brain damage. They learned that Molly's blood sugar 'had been off the end of the scale, almost too high to read. The consultant told us that the only time he'd seen something like this was when a child had been given a glucose overdose.'[182]

Over the next few weeks, Molly seemed fairly alert, but she would look only at lights and would not focus on faces. An EEG revealed that she had a type of epilepsy known as infantile spasms. She was put on epilim just before her first Christmas. The dose was gradually increased to the maximum by the time she reached two years of age. Although the spasms had stopped, she was still suffering partial seizures.

'Molly was supposed to have lots of different people involved in her case as she grew up, because of her special needs, but accessing them was a nightmare,' her mother said. 'We spent months battling for Molly to have physiotherapy, speech and language therapy and occupational therapy.'[183]

At the age of three, Molly was diagnosed as autistic. She is now 20. 'We spent the first ten years of her life finding a medical negligence case against our local hospital, said her mother. It was a case they eventually won. 'Luckily, because of the court case, we know Molly has the funds to be looked after for the rest of her life... Doctors told us Molly would have no quality of life, that she would be wheelchair-bound and wouldn't be able to learn. But she's proving them wrong. She's happy and learning to communicate. Molly loves going for long walks with us, listening to music, playing the piano and spending time on her iPad. She's always laughing and joking. We wish the mistake hadn't happened. But she is our Molly, all the same.'[184]

181 This case was reported by Felicity Ockelford in *Learning from Paediatric Patient Journeys: What children and their families can tell us*, CRC Press, pp. 70-73.

182 Ibid.

183 Ibid

184 Ibid

Useful resources and further guidance

- For more advice on how to apply to be a deputy, see www.gov.uk/become-deputy
- Contact details for The Office of the Public Guardian can be found at www.gov.uk/government/organisations/office-of-the-public-guardian
- In pursuing a claim for medical negligence, it is strongly recommended that you consider seeking independent legal advice to assist you in the process. The following organisations can help you locate a legal firm in your area with appropriate experience in dealing with these types of claims:
  - Your local Citizen's Advice Bureau www.citizensadvice.org.uk/
  - Action Against Medical Accidents (AvMa): www.avma.org.uk/
  - The Law Society: www.lawsociety.org.uk/

Fluctuating capacity

A crucial aspect in all this which has largely been ignored is the fluctuating capacity of many autistic people. One woman with Asperger's syndrome, Caroline Hearst, prefers to speak of an autism 'constellation' rather than a spectrum, because an autistic individual's spiky profile may mean that he or she (like a twinkling star) may shine more brightly one day than the next.[185]

In 2023, a Court of Protection decision addressed the complex issues arising precisely from this fluctuating capacity. The case of *A Local Authority v H [2023]* related to H, a young adult 'natal male' who identified as a woman and preferred to be known by female pronouns. In her life so far, H had experienced significant trauma and abuse. H has diagnoses of global developmental delay, attention deficit hyperactivity disorder, executive dysfunction, developmental trauma disorder and possibly emotionally unstable personality disorder. H has also displayed 'traits of autism spectrum condition, extremely disordered attachment, and highly disrupted emotional regulation'. H has been assessed as being at 'a real risk of [causing] sexual harm to children, both in contact with them and online'. At H's current placement, she seemed to settle well and felt supported by staff.

The Court of Protection was asked to consider whether H had capacity to make decisions regarding where she lived, her care and support, her contact with others (adults and children) and her use of the internet and social media. H's solicitor informed the court that H does not like to be perceived as lacking capacity. H herself expressed views on the issues in question and she consented to the restrictions put in place over her daily life. However, it was the view of H's psychiatrist that H had not yet achieved capacity, although she did believe that H was progressing towards it.[186]

185 Ibid

186 See Pilcher K (2023) *Fluctuating capacity: another Court of Protection decision* [online]. Available at: www.mills-reeve.com/insights/blogs/health-and-care/february-2023/fluctuating-capacity-another-court-of-protection-d (accessed January 2024).

Mr Justice Hayden presented a brief review of the relevant case law on capacity and commented that in the cases of vulnerable adults, 'the danger of elevating the instinctive need to protect a vulnerable adult to such a degree that it corrupts the integrity of an objective assessment of capacity, is an ever-present danger in this sphere of work'. The emphasis must always be on protecting the autonomy of the individual.

The court found that when H's emotions were 'dysregulated', she did not have capacity. Ultimately, it was Mr Justice Hayden's view that 'H ... has some insights into her behaviour, but that it remains incomplete'. An optimistic view was taken of H's capacity in the future, primarily based on her cooperation with her care plan and H's psychiatrist's opinion that H was 'progressing towards [capacity]'. However, at the time of this judgement, Mr Justice Hayden concurred with the view of H's psychiatrist, and the presumption of H's capacity was rebutted.[187]

This decision highlighted the fact that the court's role is a balancing act between protecting the individual's right to make decisions and protecting the individual's best interests.

Yo Dunn has importantly emphasised that disabled children are often excluded from the freedoms and structured learning opportunities commonly available to non-disabled children. She has noted that 'lack of opportunity to experience taking risks and making mistakes is often then assumed to be a lack of decision-making capacity in adult life...'[188]

Dunn explained that special schools 'are a nightmare' in this context:

> 'They never allow children to make any decisions for themselves. It's built into the system. They assume the child has no autonomy, no capacity. We should focus more on rights, on autonomy, on control over one's own life. There's a lot of talk in social care about 'person-centredness' and choices, but it's all very superficial and totemistic. You learn quickly how easy it is for your autonomy to disappear when you are dependent on other people. We are not a set of problems to be solved or a collection of behaviours to be modified. The trouble is that a lot of well-meaning people, including those working in health and social care have no idea what it feels like to have your autonomy compromised. It does not occur to them that this is a harm, an infringement of a person's rights.
>
> 'Autonomy is not the same thing as independence. If I were independent, I would not have much autonomy because I wouldn't be able to do much. But I get to steer the ship. I just need a lot of help getting there. Legally speaking, this makes a lot of sense. Duty of care and safeguarding are badly misunderstood concepts. A lot of people working in health and social care believe that their duty of care requires them to keep everyone perfectly safe all the time. Actually, that is complete nonsense. What the law requires is proportionality. And proportionality is all about balancing human rights.'[189]

---

187 Ibid

188 See Yo Dunn: *Social Work with Autistic People: Essential Knowledge, Skills and the Law for Working with Children and Adults*. London: Jessica Kingsley, 2020.

189 Yo Dunn, personal communication, January 5, 2023.

The right to vote

A lack of mental capacity is not a legal incapacity to vote. Individuals who meet the other registration qualifications are eligible for registration regardless of their mental capacity. While electors with any level or no level of mental capacity may be registered to vote, the decision as to whether and how to vote at an election must be made by the electors themselves and not by any other person on their behalf. Those who care for or who otherwise make decisions on behalf of a person may not make decisions on voting.

Yo Dunn, who is involved in working for a major British care provider in the autism world, asked one of the staff, a senior manager: 'How many people autistic people whom you support in residential supported living are registered to vote?' Her reply was: 'Oh, well, none of them has asked'. Dunn said this was just one illustration of how autistic individuals are 'disabled by the system, by the assumption of incapacity.'[190]

On February 28, 2023, the 'My Vote, My Voice' campaign was launched in the UK Parliament. This campaign is designed to encourage people with learning disabilities and autism to vote in the 2024 general election and onwards. The event was sponsored by Alex Norris MP, Shadow Minister for Levelling Up, Housing, Communities and Local Government, and was attended by learning-disabled and autistic self-advocates, as well as representatives from provider organisations and charities, democracy campaigners, MPs and peers. Guests heard from autistic individuals and people with learning disabilities leading the campaign about their previous experiences of voting and what they want to change.

A number of principles were emphasised:

- Everybody who is eligible to vote should be registered, irrespective of any illness or disability they may have.
- There should be a presumption that a person has capacity to register to vote.
- Only the applicant, or a person to whom they have given power of attorney, can make the required declaration as part of an application for registration.

The 2023 meeting highlighted the profound challenges faced by autistic people and people with learning disabilities when it comes to voting. People with learning disabilities and autistic people face greater challenges when exercising their right to vote. Dr Mark Brookes, MBE, Gáibhin McGranaghan, and Ismail Kaji stressed the systemic challenges currently inherent in the voting system, including excessively complex forms and a lack of privacy. Autistic individuals and/or those with learning disabilities are forced to exert greater effort than the general public in order to exercise their right to vote. Voting locations can be overstimulating and poll workers often do not have the training to offer effective help to someone with additional needs. Voters can face extreme social anxiety, making public transport and voting locations challenging to navigate. The impaired executive function of people with autism and learning disabilities means that planning to vote and executing those plans can be even more difficult.[191]

---

190 Ibid.

191 See https://lgiu.org/blog-article/my-vote-my-voice-launch/ (accessed March 2024).

In addition to these issues, voting is set to become even more difficult for autistic people and people with learning disabilities. The Elections Act (2002), which came into effect on May 4, 2023, requires voters to present a valid photo ID when voting in person this coming election season. As Hannah Molloy, from the charity Ambitious About Autism, has pointed out, this presents additional hurdles for autistic voters. While many of the UK population lack a passport or driver's licence, which are both accepted forms of voter ID, even fewer autistic people and/or those with learning disabilities are likely to have them, making the process increasingly challenging.[192]

The 2023 meeting proposed a number of measures designed to help autistic voters, including colour-coding reading materials, more Easy Read and braille material online and in print, voting reminders via text and email, and online access to voting.

James, 24, from Hull, is classed as having profound and multiple learning disabilities. He says one polling station suggested he vote in the disabled toilet. He cannot talk but uses eye gaze technology to communicate, has a support team, and relies on his mother to help him vote.

'Since I turned 18, my mum said I should cast a vote and have my own say on who runs the country,' James told the *Sunday Mirror*. 'I need Easy Read manifestos in advance to know their policies but some parties don't bother to create them so they lose my vote. Unfortunately, my polling station is a health centre with nowhere quiet for me to speak my choice aloud to my carers so they can mark my vote. I was once offered the disabled toilet to cast my vote. I think there should be a quiet room separate for people who have learning difficulties so we can have privacy. It worries me that people with learning disabilities do not vote because it is too difficult for them without reasonable adjustments.'[193]

Labour's Alex Norris, the Shadow Levelling up Minister, hosted a meeting in Parliament of My Vote My Voice in March 2023 to launch their campaign. 'Listening to people with lived experiences, I am shocked and saddened to hear of cases where people with learning disabilities have been unable to cast their vote,' he said. 'The point is simple, if we want a democracy to be proud of then must ensure we listen to those most vulnerable in society.'[194]

Speaking at the event, the Local Government Minister Lee Rowley said it was a 'very important issue' and promised to 'continue to work with disability charities and local leaders across the elections sector to ensure everyone can exercise their democratic right to vote'.[195]

---

192 Ibid

193 Smith M (2023) *Parties 'missing out on a million votes' by failing to make elections accessible* [online]. Available at: www.mirror.co.uk/news/politics/parties-missing-out-million-votes-29374333 (accessed January 2024).

194 My Voice, My Vote. *MPs sign up to support accessible voting with disability coalition* [online]. Available at: www.myvotemyvoice.org.uk/news-item/mps-sign-up-to-support-accessible-voting-with-disability-coalition/ (accessed January 2024).

195 Ibid.

Useful resources and further guidance

- United Response has produced some useful booklets, which can be accessed online: www.unitedresponse.org.uk/get-involved/campaign/raising-awareness/accessible-voting-day/
- See also: www.everyvotecounts.org.uk/

The right to drive

Having a car can give you easier access to a job, a work scheme, college, training or a day centre. It can also save you from having to rely on friends or family for lifts or using taxis and public transport. Once you've got used to having your own car and become accustomed to driving it whenever you want, it could even boost your confidence in other areas of your life.

Julia says driving is enormously helpful if you are autistic because it boosts sense of self. She explains: 'We need confidence and ability to achieve more than typical people do. That is because our self-esteem is naturally weak because of our communication difficulties. Driving does help to resolve that kind of thing by giving us the ability to believe in ourselves.'[196]

The situation on the right to drive, however – as with so many others in the legal minefield where autism is concerned – is complicated. The general understanding was that autistic people had the same rights to drive as anyone else in the UK. You can apply for a provisional driving licence when you are 15 years and nine months old and you can start driving a car when you are 17. However, if you obtain, or have applied for, the enhanced rate of the mobility component of Personal Independence Payment (PIP), then you can learn to drive a car when you are 16. If you receive the higher-rate mobility component of PIP, you are eligible to join the Motability scheme. This will mean that the higher-rate mobility component of your PIP will be paid directly to Motability and you can lease or purchase a vehicle through the scheme in return. You may also be able to obtain help with the cost of driving lessons through a Motability Charitable Grant. You can get free road tax if you receive the enhanced mobility element of PIP. A car insurance company should be notified of a disability. Under the Equality Act (2010), insurers can charge disabled people higher premiums only if the extra charge is based on factual or statistical data, or if there are other factors which mean that a disabled person is a higher risk.[197]

Now for the confusing part. You should disclose your autism to the DVLA only if it could somehow affect your ability to drive safely. If being autistic does affect your ability to drive safely, and you do not disclose it when you apply for your provisional licence, you could be fined up to £1,000 and be prosecuted if you are involved in an accident. Initially, the

---

196 Marcus L (2020) *Can I drive with autism?* [online]. Available at: https://news.motability.co.uk/everyday-tips/can-i-drive-with-autism/ (accessed January 2024).

197 National Autistic Society. *Driving – a guide for autistic adults in England* [online]. Available at: www.autism.org.uk/advice-and-guidance/topics/transport/driving/england (accessed January 2024).

first person to discuss this with is your GP, who will have access to the DVLA guidelines for people with a disability and will be able to go through these with you to find out whether you can take the next steps.

Barriers to holding a driving licence for autistic individuals might include a history of:

- Epilepsy.
- Perceptual problems.
- Difficulties with multitasking.
- Poor motor control or dyspraxia.
- Problems with sequencing.[198]

However, writing in *The Independent* in 2019, one father, James Moore, said the country's insistence that autistic drivers declare their condition is 'another slice of breath-taking ignorance. Surely if people have issues that could compromise their ability to drive, the test ought to be able to pick those up regardless of whether they are autistic or not? My wife and I have known for a while that our son was likely autistic. We went through the lengthy and somewhat tortuous process of securing a formal diagnosis (which confirmed it) with the aim of securing for him the support he needs to thrive as he moves into secondary education. Just days after receiving it, I've been left in the horrible position of questioning whether we did the right thing.'[199]

Moore said the DVLA's website now indicated that drivers must disclose their diagnosed autism. 'The previous instruction said only that they must inform the agency if their condition could affect their driving. In the case of many autistic people, it doesn't. The change – described to me by the DVLA as "recently updated advice" – is a subtle one. But it is important and seems to be one of those things that government agencies and departments quietly shuffle out in the hope that no one notices until someone does. It does rather look as if whoever made the decision had watched *Rain Man* on Netflix, or something, and thought: "Oo-er, we'd better find out if some of these scary people are out and about on the roads."

'We have been told that the UK driving test has been made harder than the one I took a couple of decades ago. If people have issues that could compromise their ability to drive, and their safety on the roads, surely it ought to be able to pick those up regardless of whether they are autistic or not? ... A person within the autistic population with the capacity to pass a UK driving test will be as safe on the road as anyone else. They might be safer than some. Part of the way the condition manifests itself in the case of my son is through his absolute determination to adhere to rules. I'm sure that would include the Highway Code, were he to learn to drive, a document that is regularly ignored by, what, 60 per cent of the motorists in London? Eighty per cent? Ninety per cent?'[200]

---

198 Marcus L (2020) *Can I drive with autism?* [online]. Available at: https://news.motability.co.uk/everyday-tips/can-i-drive-with-autism/ (accessed January 2024).

199 Moore J (2019) *Britain's insistence that autistic drivers declare their condition is another slice of breathtaking ignorance* [online]. Available at: www.independent.co.uk/voices/autism-dvla-driving-jess-phillips-a8807096.html (accessed January 2024).

200 Ibid.

Useful resources and further guidance

- When you're learning to drive with autism, there is lots of support out there for you. There are driving instructors who specialise in teaching people with disabilities.
- The Motability scheme offers an all-inclusive package. If you receive a qualifying mobility allowance you can use it to lease a car, scooter, powered wheelchair or wheelchair accessible vehicle.

Summary

According to NHS figures, more than 2,000 autistic people and/or people with learning disabilities were being held in mental health inpatient units in the UK under the Mental Health Act (1983) as of 2022 for an average of around 5.5 years, and 350 had been detained for a decade or longer. There is increasing concern about the over-use (and abuse) of so-called Assessment and Treatment Units (ATUs), which are essentially used for detentions in hospital under the MHA. There are two legally different procedures prescribed by law in England and Wales for deprivation of liberty in the context of mental health. Detention under the MHA gives a licence to detain, in the same way as a criminal justice order does, whereas the use of Deprivation of Liberty Safeguards or DoLS under the Mental Capacity Act (2005) renders lawful arrangements for care and support. The complex interface between the two laws means that an individual can be discharged by a mental health tribunal because he or she does not meet the MHA's criteria for detention (and cannot then be re-detained under the MHA) but can then become eligible for detention under the MCA DoLS, instead. So, perversely, the same person could be detained again in the same place, under a different law. Parents or guardians can apply to the Court of Protection for a Deputyship Order for their child's property and financial affairs and/or their health and personal welfare if the child is deemed to lack the mental capacity to make decisions for him- or herself. Although there should be no legal barriers to autistic people engaging in many activities open to adults in the UK, such as driving a car or voting in elections, practical obstacles do still exist.

Chapter 4: Social care and the law

This chapter will focus on:

- The crisis in social care.
- The Care Act (2014) and the Health and Care Act (2022).
- Judicial reviews.
- The Care Act, the Mental Capacity Act, advocacy and the Court of Protection.

The Care Act (2014) and the Health and Care Act (2022)

Social care is in crisis in the UK. That seems to be the consensus among professionals working in this sector. A leading lawyer in this area, Alex Rook, told me: 'The Care Act (2014) is, broadly speaking, a good piece of legislation. The problem is that there is a complete disconnect between what the law says *should* be happening and what is actually happening'.[201] This disconnect could be said to be a central theme of this book in general. Namely, that even when legislation exists which, at least in theory, protects the rights of autistic individuals, a severe lack of money makes it very hard to implement or enforce this legislation.

According to one of the foremost authorities in the field, Yo Dunn, the problem is a lack of resources, rather than legal inadequacies. She argues that the Care Act (2014) 'does not need fixing, except for more money to implement it'.[202] Lack of funding, she says, means that 'every local authority in the country is behaving unlawfully under the Care Act. They are ignoring their statutory duties, because the law both requires them to meet needs and to balance their budgets. With current levels of massive cuts to funding from central government, achieving both is simply impossible. So local authorities have no choice but to fail to fulfil their Care Act duties to meet needs'[203] At the same time, legal aid has been gutted to such an extent that there are few lawyers currently working in adult social care judicial reviews. 'It's a Wild West out there!' says Dunn. 'Because social care is delegated to the local authorities, governments give all the duties to the local authorities and then do not give them the money to fulfil those duties. Then they turn round and blame the local authorities.'[204] In some cases, like those of Sammy Alban (see Chapters 1 and 3) and Stefan Kluibenschadl (see **Case study 16** on p.109), the consequences are tragic. According to another leading authority in this area, Belinda Schwehr, the problem is that there are two

201 Alex Rook, personal communication, December 7, 2023.

202 Yo Dunn, personal communication, January 5, 2023.

203 bid.

204 bid.

radically different legal frameworks that were just pulled together in the Health and Care Act (2022): 'It is the NHS framework and culture of target duties only which will come to dominate, and which suits any government which does not want to spend more money'.[205]

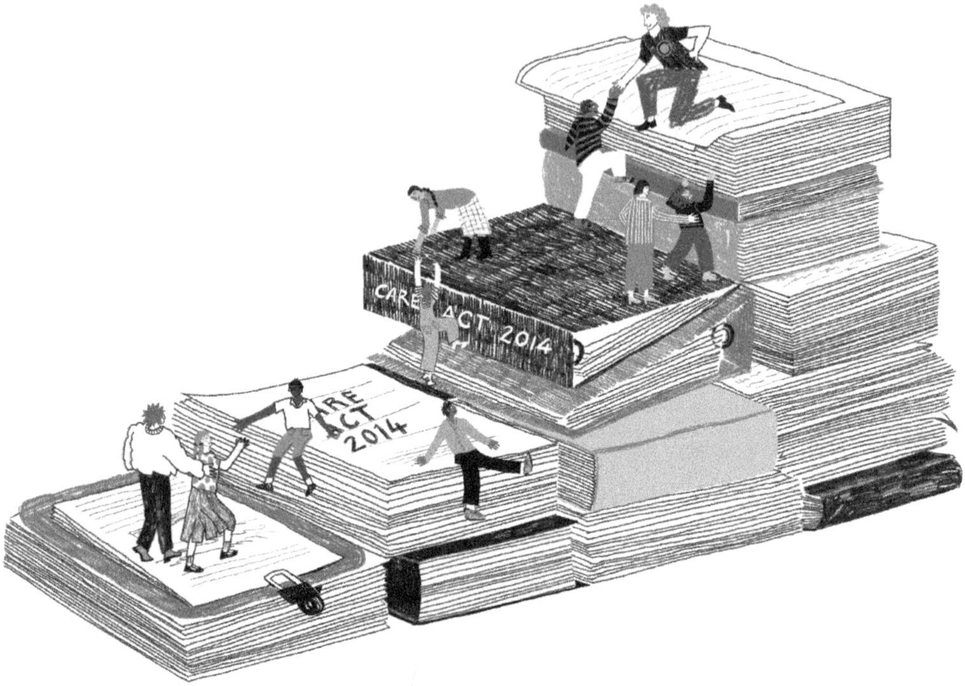

The conflict between health and social care

Ekaterina Harrison has highlighted a significant conflict lying at the heart of the provision of care in the UK – the interplay between two systems, namely health and social care.[206] Established in 1948, the National Health Service (NHS) strives to deliver free healthcare to all UK residents at the point of need. Predominantly overseen by the NHS, with a few exceptions, healthcare covers both physical and mental health treatments. Conversely, social care, encompassing personal care and practical assistance, is solely under the statutory jurisdiction of local authorities. As Harrison explains, this approach is rooted in the belief:

> '...that central government is better equipped to grasp the needs of the entire national population and offer comprehensive guidance on public health issues that are applicable across all local authority areas. In contrast, local government is adept at addressing the broader factors that influence health and well-being within their specific geographical areas. Because of this delineation of responsibilities, there is a clear and important difference between health services and social care services.'[207]

205 Belinda Schwehr, personal communication, November 21, 2023.

206 Ekaterina Harrison, personal communication, December 17, 2023.

207 Ibid.

The responsibilities of local authorities are also part of this difference. Health services are mostly free at the point of use and follow the NHS rules. Social care services, on the other hand, have a different set of rules for assessment. As Harrison notes:

> 'Overall, for healthcare to work well, social care needs to work well too. This explains why there is an ongoing effort to bring together health and social care services, as outlined in the Health and Care Act (2022). Social care is care and support for people who need extra help to live safe, independent and fulfilling lives. It can include residential care support with personal care such as eating, washing, or getting dressed, personal assistants or carers to support when going out shopping or socialising or specialist recreational services.'[208]

The Care Act (2014) was intended to strengthen the rights of people with learning disabilities and/or autism and their family carers. It promoted fairer, more personalised care – and shifted the focus of local authorities from providing services for specific groups to supporting individuals to achieve the outcomes that matter to them. Local authorities must promote a person's well-being when making any decision about that person. This means that the local authority must consider the impact of any decision they make on the individual's well-being. This is the driving force behind the Care Act and it applies equally to family carers.

Put simply, the Act aims to make care and support clearer and fairer for people to access. The Care Act:

- Outlines a single national eligibility threshold for care and support.
- Requires local authorities to provide all local people with information and advice, related to care and support, to help them understand their rights and responsibilities, and plan for their future needs.
- Includes protections so that people do not go without care if their provider fails, regardless of who pays for their care.
- Clarifies local responsibilities for people in prison who have needs for care and support so that they can access the care they need.[209]

Under the Act, local authorities must promote well-being when carrying out any of their care and support functions in respect of a person. This may sometimes be referred to as 'the well-being principle,' because it is a guiding principle that puts well-being at the heart of care and support. Well-being is a broad concept, and the statutory guidance defines it as relating to the following nine areas in particular

- Personal dignity (including treatment of the individual with respect).
- Physical and mental health and emotional well-being.
- Protection from abuse and neglect.
- Control by the individual over day-to-day life (including over care and support provided and the way it is provided).

208 Ibid.

209 See www.local.gov.uk/sites/default/files/documents/self-study-pack-669.pdf (accessed March 2024)

- Participation in work, education, training or recreation.
- Social and economic well-being.
- Domestic, family and personal relationships.
- Suitability of living accommodation.
- The individual's contribution to society.[210]

Under Section 4 of the Care Act, local authorities must provide information and advice to help all local people understand the care and support system, access services and plan for the future, including enabling people to access independent financial advice to help steer them through the complexities of care funding. Information and advice on all care and support matters must be accessible to all, so it cannot be simply online, and must be 'proportionate' to an individual's needs – for example, a simple, short answer to a simple question or more intensive and more personalised information and advice if a person has more complex issues.[211]

Determining eligible needs

The Care Act introduced a national framework to determine whether a person has eligible needs, meaning that, regardless of where you live in England, the same criteria are applied. For the first time in law, family carers have the same rights to assessment and support as the people for whom they care.

Richard Griffiths, for one, is sceptical. In written evidence to the UK Parliament, Griffiths, the father of an adult autistic son, declared:

> 'Transforming Care is in the Care Act 2014, under Section 26 (direct budgets) and Section 31 (direct payments). Local Authorities are responsible for meeting these needs in this way under the Care Act, but they fetter their discretion of every section of the Act in every conceivable way that you wouldn't believe possible. The current government has reduced the funding to the local authorities, making it financially uncomfortable for them to meet these needs. So a local authority will seek to find ways to unload a prospective high-budget, vulnerable person from their responsibility to somewhere else: the NHS. The local authorities do this by offering the vulnerable person a temporary respite at a respite centre. It is at these centres that vulnerable persons are inappropriately mishandled to overload and aggravate their vulnerabilities, which frightens them out of control. They are then assessed as having complex needs requiring complex measures only available at an Assessment and Treatment Unit.' [212]

---

210 Ibid.

211 Ibid.

212 Griffiths R, in written evidence to the UK Parliament: https://committees.parliament.uk/writtenevidence/99436/pdf/ (accessed January 2024).

Ekaterina Harrison told me that she found the sentiment expressed by Richard Griffiths 'deeply troubling.' She explains:

> 'It is troubling to think that this might be intentional (directing someone to a place where their condition worsens before determining the need for complex measures). In my experience, I repeatedly encounter the mindset within local authorities that individuals must "fail enough" to receive help, and it is an incredibly distressing approach to problem-solving. The example above vividly illustrates how such a system might operate.'[213]

For his part, Richard Griffiths added:

> 'I had to spend six years getting my law degree in order for my wife and I to concurrently advocate for our son, uphold the Law and ensure that the Care Act 2014 was enforced through three upheld LGO decisions over the same six years. Our son now has his personal budget, direct payments, his own housing association house with a lifetime tenancy for his independent living and 24-hour support in the village he grew up in, with close proximity to family and friends, and he is at liberty to lead a life of his choosing at a fraction of the ATU figure of the finger in the pie costs.'[214]

Harrison noted that the ultimately positive outcome for Griffiths' son 'suggests that opting for the right approach (providing social care, rather than exploiting the health system) is not only ethical but also cost-effective. There is a pressing need to investigate why the system is not operating as intended.'[215]

During a Carer's Assessment, a local authority must not make any assumptions about what a family carer is willing and able to do for their relative. Needs met by a family carer can be considered only after the eligible needs of their relative have been determined. The local authority does not have to meet needs that a carer is willing and able to meet, but it is important to ensure that all eligible needs are identified during the assessment to protect against any potential breakdown in the caring relationship. If needs are already identified as eligible, the local authority must take steps to meet them without further assessment.

People with care and support needs and family carers have a right to a Care Act Independent Advocate if they would otherwise find it too difficult to participate in Care Act processes and have no appropriate person to support them.

Local authorities have a legal duty to prevent, reduce and delay people's needs from worsening. The aim is to have responsive local authorities that can support people at an early stage, to prevent and reduce the likelihood of people ending up in crises. Yo Dunn explained:

> 'The 2014 Care Act is fantastic. It was extremely well-written by the Law Commission, a brilliantly thought-through piece of legislation. It doesn't need fixing, except for more money. The core problem with the Care Act is that local authorities do not have the money to implement it. So every local authority in

213 Ekaterina Harrison, personal communication, December 17, 2023.

214 Griffiths R, in written evidence to the UK Parliament: https://committees.parliament.uk/writtenevidence/99436/pdf/ (accessed March 2024).

215 Ekaterina Harrison, personal communication, December 17, 2023.

the country is behaving unlawfully under the Care Act. They are unable to fulfil their statutory duties. They are fudging the eligibility criteria and failing to provide social care, when the face of the law requires them to do so. How does this go unchallenged? Well, the people who need care and support are vulnerable and, emotionally speaking, are not in any position to challenge. They do not know what the rules are, either. Moreover, legal aid has been gutted to such an extent that there are few lawyers working in adult social care judicial reviews. It is almost impossible to find a lawyer, even if you have an incredibly strong case.'[216]

Access to legal aid

Nearly a hundred years ago, one judge, Sir James Mathew, quipped that, 'in England, justice is open to all – like the Ritz Hotel'. These days, fears are growing that budget cuts may mean access to legal aid becomes an inaccessible luxury for many. Legal aid was first introduced in 1949, as a principal pillar of the welfare state. Originally, its reach was almost universal with 80% of the UK population eligible. But as the years have gone by, legal aid went the way of free dentistry, with eligibility dropping steadily. Rounds of cuts in 2004, 2007 and 2010 introduced fixed fees for certain types of cases and led to many providers pulling out of more complex legally aided areas like immigration and asylum. However, the 2013 Legal Aid, Sentencing and Punishment of Offenders Act (LASPO) was far more far-reaching. It recommended hefty cuts to the system that would slash the yearly legal aid budget by £320 million from 2014. LASPO was part of the Conservative government's plans to cut the national deficit.[217]

One often-cited argument for reform is that the UK's £2 billion legal aid system is one of the most expensive in the world. However, opponents to the cuts argue that this is partly because other European countries (or those in the European Union, which the UK left in 2016), use an inquisitorial system, instead of the UK's common law, meaning that their outlay is skewed towards courts and prosecutors and fewer cases come to trial. The proponents of the cuts point to barristers earning six-figure salaries, but legal aid lawyers were keen to emphasise that, in 2014, for example, the average salary in the sector was £25,000, compared with a nurse's average salary of £29,500, a GP's £56,000 and an MP's £65,000.[218]

Under the government's proposals, members of households with disposable incomes of over £3,000 a month would no longer be eligible for legal aid, on the grounds that they should be able to fund their own cases. Huge areas of civil law have been removed from the scope of legal aid. All family law cases that do not involve domestic violence are no longer covered, although payments may be made to help with mediation. Immigration cases are covered only if they involve claims for asylum, human rights issues or domestic

216 Yo Dunn, personal communication, January 5, 2023.

217 See www.lawsociety.org.uk/topics/legal-aid/laspo-act (accessed March 2024).

218 Chambers (2013) *Thanks to the latest wave of sweeping budget cuts access to the law looks set to become an inaccessible luxury for many* [online]. Available at: www.chambersstudent.co.uk/where-to-start/newsletter/legal-aid-cuts-and-reforms (accessed January 2024).

violence. Benefits, debt and housing cases are also ineligible unless there is a direct threat of homelessness. Criminal cases remain in scope, subject to means testing, and LASPO's original proposal to remove client choice from solicitor allocation has been overturned.[219]

Since the beginning of April 2013, legal aid has been administered by the Legal Aid Agency (LAA), which forms part of the Ministry of Justice and is under close government control. The LAA replaced the Legal Services Commission (LSC), which had more independence thanks to its status as a non-departmental public body (or quango). Legal aid is administered on the basis of a means test, which looks at a client's income and capital, and a merit test, which examines their chances of winning in civil cases, and weighs up the seriousness of the charges in criminal cases. Clients in civil areas including housing and immigration come directly to firms, which then apply for funding on a case-by-case basis. Clients looking for support in special educational needs, debt and discrimination cases must use a new Ministry of Justice telephone gateway, and then find a legal aid solicitor if they gain approval. Criminal clients are entitled to free legal advice from duty solicitors while they are being held at police stations, before choosing their own solicitor if they are eligible for further legal aid.[220]

Writing in 2023, a decade after the government's decision to introduce severe cuts to legal aid, The Law Society declared:

> 'Justice is increasingly out of reach for those in most need... The number of legal aid cases to help people get the early advice they need dropped from almost a million in 2009/10 to just 130,000 in 2021/22. Over the same period, the number of people having to go to court without representation trebled. The number of advice agencies and law centres doing this work has fallen by 59 per cent. Law centres across the country closed down. Firms were forced to close their legal aid departments. This resulted in large advice deserts. Millions of people now live in areas where they can no longer access the help and advice that Parliament has said they are entitled to.'[221]

Lubna Shuja. the president of The Law Society of England and Wales, said:

> 'Legal aid can help a child with disabilities get the education and support they need. For rights to be real, everyone who qualifies for state-funded legal advice must be able to get that advice when they need it so that they can uphold and enforce their rights... A decade on from LASPO, civil legal aid is facing an existential crisis. The survival of these services is in the balance. People can't get the legal support they need when they need it.'[222]

According to Yo Dunn, most autistic people are, in fact, eligible for social care, if the statutory eligibility criteria are fully and knowledgeably applied and thorough assessments are carried out. 'and yet, over 50% of requests for adult social care by people

---

219 Ibid.

220 Ibid.

221 The Law Society (2023) *A decade of cuts: Legal aid in tatters* [online]. Available at: www.lawsociety.org.uk/contact-or-visit-us/press-office/press-releases/a-decade-of-cuts-legal-aid-in-tatters (accessed January 2024).

222 Ibid.

generally – not just autistic individuals – are turned down (according to a BBC report). So it has turned into a postcode lottery and many people who should get support, never get an assessment, let alone the full application of the eligibility criteria to their needs. Most social workers do not go into the profession to make money or to be popular: they want to fix things. Of course, you do get a few managerialist thinkers who seem content with the status quo, but you also find people leaving the profession in tears at being forced to withdraw care and support from people who really need them.'[223]

Alex Rook says the 2014 Act itself:

> '...is fairly clear-cut, in terms of having an eligible need. but once you have been assessed as having an eligible need, the question is how to meet those needs? My experience is that there is a disconnect between the eligibility for needs and how a local authority proposes to meet them. The law states that, if there are two ways to meet a need, and one costs much less than the other, the authorities can lawfully decide to choose the cheaper way, so long as it meets the need. That leaves the obvious question as to whether it can in fact meet the need, and this is why we need an independent tribunal to review care plans – in other words, to review how a local authority proposes to meet these needs.
>
> 'How do parents proceed if they disagree with the local authorities? Exactly. The answer is, through a complaint leading to the ombudsman or through judicial review, but neither is very satisfactory. Those are the only two options. There should be a third way: a tribunal.'[224]

How the Care Act works in practice

Social care is delegated to the local authorities in the UK. Dunn says the central government grant to local authorities has dropped 'to a shameful degree' over the past decade. 'Governments always play the same game: they give all the duties to the local authorities and then do not give them the money to fulfil those duties. Then they turn round and blame the local authorities.'[225]

Dunn feels that, although the Care Act is a good piece of legislation, assessments are often 'superficial and cursory' and are treated as some sort of triage prior to assessment, despite the legal reality that they are all assessments, because the Care Act threshold for assessment is very low. As she told me: 'Believe it or not, it is common, in adult social care, for local authorities to assess by phoning up and asking: "OK, so what is it you think you need from us?" This is totally unlawful, because it is not a professional assessment of what the person's needs actually are, but people do not challenge it because they do not know. And the advocates do not receive adequate training to challenge such practice – and they are not lawyers. This style of "assessment" particularly disadvantages autistic people, because the telephone is a massive obstacle for many autistic people.'[226]

---

223 Yo Dunn, personal communication, January 5, 2023.

224 Alex Rook, personal communication, December 7, 2023.

225 Yo Dunn, personal communication, January 5, 2023.

226 Ibid.

Ekaterina Harrison agrees:

> 'There is, indeed, a concern about social services heavily relying on telephone communication. It is important for autistic individuals to be encouraged to self-advocate and express their communication preferences, such as through email, to ensure more accommodating interactions.'[227]

Dunn is adamant that autistic people:

> '...need to know what the law actually says, so that they can challenge the local authorities on an individual level. But even then, it depends on which part of the country you live in. The number of judicial reviews since the Care Act was introduced in 2014 is suspiciously low – just five or six, which is ridiculous [see following section]. Why? One factor is that many local authorities are quietly settling a few individual cases to avoid going to court, because they don't want other people to know and also challenge. But also, things are now so bad, that we have desperate local authorities arguing to the Supreme Court that they should not be required to actually fulfil their statutory duties, because they don't have the resources (even though the Supreme Court confirmed that a duty is a duty and that lack of money is not a defence).'[228]

Alex Rook (*see his comments below*) does not believe that individuals have much chance of success in challenging a local authority in a judicial review on their own (in other words, without strong legal backing). Ekaterina Harrison agrees:

> 'As a lawyer, I would feel uneasy about advising individuals to confront a system with brute force, especially when it is evident that the system is stacked up against them. Promoting awareness is essential, and it is equally important to advocate for systemic changes.'[229]

However, Rook concurs with Dunn that there is nothing intrinsically wrong with the Care Act (2014):

> 'It is, generally speaking, a good piece of legislation... The difficulty is the way you challenge any decision. You can make a complaint to the local authority, which is usually a toothless and slow process. You can go to the ombudsman, but again that is a long, arduous process. Or you bring judicial review proceedings, which are expensive and complex. The ombudsman serves a purpose, and so does the judicial review. But where do all those people go who are in the middle? There are not enough social workers doing the assessments.'[230]

Section 72 of the Care Act (2014) grants the Secretary of State for Health and Social Care the authority to create regulations for an appeals process regarding decisions made by local authorities under Part 1 of the Act. In the Department of Health and Social Care's 2021 Policy Paper entitled *People at the Heart of Care: Adult Social Care Reform*, the government

227 Ekaterina Harrison, personal communication, December 17, 2023.

228 Yo Dunn, personal communication, January 5, 2023.

229 Ekaterina Harrison, personal communication, December 17, 2023.

230 Alex Rook, personal communication, December 7, 2023.

stated its decision not to put the appeals system into action. However, it emphasised that the matter would be continually assessed, and the government would persist in collecting evidence to shape future considerations.

In the case of *R (HL) v Secretary of State for Health and Social Care [2023] EWHC 866 (Admin)*, the High Court dismissed a claim asserting that the government's decision not to implement Section 72 for the foreseeable future was unlawful. According to the judgement overview, the Secretary of State had not compromised HL's access to justice or her ability to access a court or tribunal. Furthermore, the Secretary of State had not violated her procedural rights under Article 8 of the European Convention on Human Rights; the 2021 white paper was considered a political judgement, especially given the broad discretionary powers in the socio-economic context. As noted by the court, an individual dissatisfied with a local authority's decision on care and support can voice concerns through the authority's internal complaints procedure, approach the Local Government Social Care Ombudsman (LGSCO) or initiate judicial review proceedings. HL highlighted the limitations of these channels for challenge and presented evidence to suggest that her experience was not unique.[231]

Belinda Schwehr, chief executive of Centre for Adults' Social Care – Advice, Information and Dispute Resolution (CASCAIDr) – a charity she launched to provide free and chargeable legal advice about people's rights to care funding, and which has now closed – told me:

> 'One of the things the 2014 Care Act did was to make many more people technically eligible but then to facilitate making what they ultimately received as a result of this eligibility as small and "residual" as possible. The means by which the concept of eligibility was actually broadened was by making it clear that one is supposed to assess a person's needs, without regard to whatever good things they actually have available to them from other human beings and apply the eligibility test to that picture. It is the person's total, global need arising from his or her condition which must be recorded and the impact arising: it is not the life they lead but the life they would lead if they had no one to look after them or visit them, that matters. On paper, that makes many more people eligible. But at the care planning stage, all the good things they do have access to or are available are offset against their needs or ticked off, making the unmet needs left over ever smaller. That is why I believe that, despite more people being eligible, in theory, it is hard to get a decent care package after what may well be a dodgy assessment, a dodgy eligibility decision, an indefensible "indicative" budget and a final care planning process with nobody knowing the law. Defects in those four stages accumulate and people receive an inadequate care package, which they tend to accept because it is better than nothing. Very few people challenge the care plan.'[232]

Ekaterina Harrison observed:

> 'This leads me to wonder whether the Care Act (2014) was perhaps deliberately crafted to encompass a multitude of situations, intending to be broad. However, it appears that this breadth has resulted in a lack of precision, leaving many without

231 My thanks to Ekaterina Harrison for highlighting this important case.

232 Belinda Schwehr, personal communication, November 21, 2023.

support. The absence of established court practices further complicates matters, as we lack insights into how courts might interpret the Act's provisions.'[233]

Serious failings

A BBC investigation in September 2023 reported that dozens of young autistic people had died after serious failings in their care, despite repeated warnings from coroners. We already featured the case of Sammy Alban-Stanley (see Chapters 1 and 2), a boy with both autism and Prader-Willi syndrome, who died at the age of 13 after falling from a cliff near his home in Ramsgate in April 2020. Witnesses reported that his last words were: 'I'm autistic'. His mother, Patricia, says, 'He meant: "Please help me"'. Patricia had repeatedly asked for help to keep Sammy safe. After six years, she was finally granted two hours of after-school care in January 2020. But it was not enough – Sammy died just three months later. Without extra help, his mother could not prevent him from leaving the house. Blind to the danger the nearby cliff posed, he fell. He died four days later in intensive care, in his mother's arms.

After Sammy's death, the coroner criticised NHS Kent and Medway for 'inadequate support' and warned that a similar incident might happen if this continued. Two years later, a second autistic teenager, Stefan Kluibenschad, 15, died under the care of the same local authority (see **Case study 16** on p.109). The same coroner found that had Stefan received the recommended level of care, he might have been given the therapy he needed.

In the first piece of research of its kind, the BBC analysed more than 4,000 Prevention of Future Death (PFD) notices delivered in England and Wales over the past ten years, to look for autism-related deaths. Coroners are legally required to issue such warnings at inquests if they believe there is a risk that future deaths will occur unless action is taken by the authorities responsible. But there is currently no legal duty for these local authorities to act.

In 2023, the BBC identified 51 cases where PFDs described serious failings in the care of autistic people, and health and social care bodies were urged to take action to prevent future deaths. The majority of those who died were under 30, and nearly a third were children.[234]

Britain's former Justice Secretary, Sir Robert Buckland, described the BBC's findings as 'deeply disturbing' and called on the government to investigate the matter urgently: 'Lessons are not being learned. Fifty-one [deaths] is a lot. It suggests a systemic problem.' Sir Robert added: 'What is the point of PFDs if there is no accountability? Autistic people carry on having to put up with poorer life outcomes.'[235]

In a statement to the BBC, the chief nursing officer at NHS Kent and Medway, Allison Cannon, apologised on behalf of the NHS for the 'tragic loss' of both Sammy and Stefan. Many changes had been made, she said, including enhancing its community support and key worker programme to improve services. Nevertheless, the families feel that NHS Kent and Medway's responses to the PFD do not address the coroner's concerns.

233 Ekaterina Harrison, personal communication, December 17, 2023.

234 Clegg R *et al* (2023) *Young autistic people still dying despite coroner warnings over care* [online]. Available at: www.bbc.co.uk/news/uk-66731265 (accessed January 2024).

235 Ibid.

In 2022, the government introduced the Health and Care Act. This Act introduced significant changes to the National Health Service Act (2006) (NHSA (2006)) and the Health and Social Care Act (2012) (HSCA (2012)). Its goal is to reform the delivery of health services and foster integration between health and care in England. The HCA (2022) puts into effect the policies outlined in the NHS's recommendations for legislative reform, aligning with the 2019 NHS Long-Term Plan, as detailed in the February 2021 white paper titled *Integration and Innovation: Working together to improve Health and Social Care for all*. Making the NHS Long-Term Plan a part of legislation was a commitment outlined in the government manifesto during the 2019 general election. To provide more insight into the measures outlined in the HCA (2022), the Department of Health and Social Care released a series of factsheets. These documents explain why these measures were deemed necessary and outline their expected impact.

Belinda Schwehr, for one, does not see the Health and Care Act (2022) as an improvement:

> 'The 2022 Act provides for a form of integration that goes beyond what I feel we already tried and failed at: namely, local authorities working in parallel with health for seamless outcomes. It goes beyond cross-delegation of functions and pooled budgets. As far as I know, the 2022 Act operates through the architecture of joint decision-making about strategic issues: for instance, the state of the market for affordable services for people with autism and learning disabilities, or just autism, who absolutely need housing. The 2022 Act has been "sexed-up" to make existing mechanisms sound new. Integration is structurally much more deeply embedded, without collapsing the distinctions between health and social care, the legal frameworks being very different in nature.'[236]

Schwehr said the biggest conflict between the 2014 and 2022 Acts was:

> '...the different legal frameworks which have entirely different degrees of enforceability through public law. This is a terrible basis for a partnership! If one of your partners with only target duties in place can say: "We've run out of money and we have no obligation to find any more" and the other partner can't say that, because the public law idea behind individually enforceable duties is that a statutory duty is still a duty, you're going to fall out of love very quickly with your strategic partner.'[237]

She goes even further:

> 'One of the first things they did after the lockdown was announced was to suspend most of the duties in the 2014 Care Act and then tell local authorities not to treat it as if it were suspended, unless, or until, it was absolutely essential to do so. Then they could claim the benefit of "the easements". Only eight councils did that. So the clarity of the Care Act was damaged, In fact it is now, rather than during Covid, that councils need the easements, because most councils cannot do their legal duty for want of staff, money or businesses to be paid to meet needs. So we already

236 Belinda Schwehr, personal communication, November 21, 2023.

237 Ibid

have local councils knowingly not doing their duty, and yet nobody is suing them. No one is suing them (apart from the odd, brave parent), perhaps because there is, at the heart of British people, some kind of common sense that says: "What can a judge actually do about this, if in fact, the sector itself is unravelling and the real costs are unimaginably impossible to resource? What is the point of going to court?" A judge might say it is non-justiciable or that no mandatory order should be given, even though the council is in breach In other words, duty is no longer a duty. No lawyer or barrister will want to be the one who brings down 25 years of that principle by picking the wrong case.'[238]

Case study 16: Stefan Kluibenschadl

Stefan Kluibenschadl was diagnosed as autistic at the age of six. He was bullied for many years while his family tried to get the help he desperately needed. Despite their GP's making referrals, the family's pleas for help were rejected by the local authority, NHS Kent and Medway.

In March 2022, just over a month after their final application for autism-specific counselling was turned down, Stefan's father found him ligatured in his bedroom in Margate. He died four days later in intensive care, at the age of just 15. The coroner, Catherine Wood, said Stefan had died as a consequence of his own actions but determined that there was insufficient evidence of intention for a suicide conclusion. She addressed her concerns to NHS Kent and Medway – highlighting that the Trust had not been following NICE guidelines, which state that every autistic child should have access to a designated key worker. With such a health professional overseeing his care, Wood said, Stefan might have received the therapy he needed. Stefan 'didn't get any care – never mind coordinated care. Our lives have been destroyed.'[239]

The family's lawyer, Aimee Brackfield from Simpson Millar, said there appeared to be a 'lack of autism spectrum condition-appropriate support for young people in crisis' and 'little to no assistance for their families who find themselves passed from pillar to post desperately looking for help'.

Stefan attended Laleham Gap, a Special Educational Needs School in Kent. He became disillusioned with school during the Covid pandemic and the one-to-one support he was receiving was reduced to remote contact. In 2020, Stefan started working at a butcher' shop at the weekends and during holidays. He loved this job as he felt he could just be himself and not be judged. However, towards the end of 2021, the inquest heard that Stefan told his parents and his school that some individuals at his work had begun bullying him after discovering that he was attending a Special school. The bullying caused low mood and anxiety and Stefan felt he had no choice but to leave the job he once loved.

In February 2022, his parents had a private counselling assessment which identified that Stefan scored highly for depression and low mood. They were offered only short-term counselling, which the family declined to instigate, since they felt such counselling was unable to meet Stefan's needs. As Stefan's low mood worsened, his parents turned to the GP but were warned that there was no specialist Child and Adolescent Mental Health Services (CAMHS) provision or counselling in the local area for autistic children. The GP submitted an application for autism-specific counselling or CBT to a specialist provider (SCAAND) commissioned by NHS England, which was declined as he was not on the local CAMHS radar. A referral to CAMHS was never made and therefore no therapeutic intervention was provided. ➔

238 Ibid.

239 See www.inquest.org.uk/stefan-kluibenschadl-inquest (accessed January 2024).

Stefan's family said:

> 'Stefan was a beautiful boy in every way. He was kind, clever, caring and funny and would always look out for other people. We, as a family, are devasted at the loss of the life we all had together and the life that he and we would have had. Stefan touched so many lives for the better and has left an indescribable hole in all our hearts and our lives. We miss him terribly. Stefan was bullied by those who are ignorant and who do not wish to understand or accept neurodiversity. Then, when he needed help, he was let down by lack of services for autistic children by the very authorities who should have been there to support him and who fail vulnerable children and adults time and time again. Mental Health provision has to change to stop our children dying.'[240]

Useful resources and further guidance

- Access Social Care provides free legal advice and information for people with social care needs. They work with communities to increase knowledge of the law and people's rights. They highlight the gap left by cuts to legal aid and provide advice for those who cannot afford it. They collaborate with social services while ensuring that legal obligations are met. Find out more at: www.accesscharity.org.uk/what-we-do (accessed January 2024).
- The Autism Alliance has produced a report, 'Breaking Point: Closing the gap in care and support for autistic adults in England'. It can be accessed at www.autism-alliance.org.uk/breaking-point

Judicial reviews

Judicial Review is a remedy of the 'last' resort to challenge a local authority for unlawfully infringing the Care Act. Permission to pursue a claim for judicial review might be denied, where alternative remedies are available, particularly when the alternative remedy is statutory, such as through an appeal. Yo Dunn and others have confirmed that the severe cuts in legal aid (see Chapter 3) and the shortage of lawyers willing to take on judicial reviews are making life extremely difficult for aggrieved families.

Alex Rook believes the problems start earlier:

> 'Judicial review is when you go to the highest first-instance court in the land and you claim that your local authority has acted unlawfully. What that court does not do is look at the actual facts on the ground and make new decisions on what the care should be. You cannot go the judicial review and say: "You said I needed ten hours a week when I need 25". The court is not interested in that. The court is interested only in whether an assessment was lawful or not. What we need in this country, which was envisaged in the Care Act but which has not been enacted, is some kind of tribunal where you do not need a High Court judge but you go before a magistrate or equivalent – a Tribunal Chair (as you have in special educational needs tribunals) – where you can claim: "My care requires an hour, not 30 minutes". Or you can argue that a person is not suitably qualified because he or she

240 Ibid.

does not understand autism. Or you can argue against the local authority's claim that you can take public transport. There is currently no court or tribunal in the country that will hear those issues. That, to me, is the biggest problem. There is no mechanism with which you can easily enforce your rights under the Care Act and request an actual outcome.' [241]

Rook agrees that lack of money is another reason why it is difficult to enforce your legal rights. He added:

'I think there may be a cynical reason for that, which is that if everyone received the support to which they were entitled under the Care Act, there simply wouldn't be enough money in the system. So if there were a fully functioning tribunal, it would cost hundreds of millions of pounds, which the local authorities do not have. I still argue strongly that such a tribunal should exist, but it would need to be properly funded by central government.'[242]

Belinda Schwehr's view of the future of the judicial review process is extremely bleak:

'There are very few lawyers doing this kind of work. My prediction is that it will be dead within five years, that the integration between health and social care will always mean that the poor relation will give way to the better resourced partner. According to the NHS framework, nobody is owed a really solid duty which can be enforced in court, by individuals using public law. Whereas in Care Act law, rights are enforceable if one selects the right remedy, the right lawyers and if one qualifies for legal aid and can find a lawyer interested in offering it. As the Care Act gets sucked into the NHS culture, and the legal aid fraternity shows little interest in using judicial review, because they can make far more money in the Court of Protection, the bottom line is that the notion of enforceable individual public law rights will disappear into fondly remembered legal history.'[243]

Schwehr says that, in the early 2000s, there were 60 or so cases a year of judicial review:

'...so there was a legal framework which was growing and changing every week and it was exciting, and people needed training to keep up. Now, there are about two or three cases a year coming out of the Administrative Court which do generally tend to uphold the old legal principles, but local councils know that they can get away with failing to abide by these principles 95 per cent of the time. I would call this a Machiavellian route to getting rid of a whole area of law. You don't need to remove legal aid from community care. You do not have to do anything controversial, such as declaring that judicial review does not apply. All you have to do is turn the tap off from professionals being able to earn a living from a field of law, and then it disappears. No journalist is interested in this. Journalists are interested in blood, bullying and bruises. And in people being confined in cell-like seclusion rooms. I have asked people at the Ministry of Justice whether this situation is a cock-up or

241 Alex Rook in conversation with the author, December 7, 2023.

242 Ibid.

243 Belinda Schwehr, personal communication, November 21, 2023.

> a conspiracy. They assured me that it was not a conspiracy – and then went quiet on the alternative! You have unjoined-up government as between the Ministry of Justice and the Departments of Levelling Up and Health and Social Care so the two spheres are unravelling in parallel but coming together in what someone will no doubt call a "singularity", in which there is regard for the rule of law but there are also no practicable means for anyone who cares to do anything about it.'[244]

Schwehr fears that organisations like hers (CASCAIDr), as well as Access Social Care and the Disability Law Service, 'will go on talking about what the law is, but there won't be anyone to make referrals to, in order to take a case to judicial review. This will stop anyone getting costs protection through legal aid, and so it will be like housing law, which has operated in a completely a-legal way with officers who are not legally *au fait* with what they are supposed to be doing. They are simply given tick boxes and instructions. I believe this is what Covid and the introduction of the 2022 Health and Care Act have done to the rule of law in adults' social services. I am very gloomy about it'.[245]

Some local authorities back down before a case comes to judicial review. Alex Rook explained that this happened in the 'vast majority' of his cases. 'This is good news. But you must ask: are they backing down because we are right (ie. because they are making unlawful decisions), or because, if you have a thousand people in your area and only five have lawyers, you give up on those five and keep going on the remaining 995?'[246]

Several cases have led to successful outcomes for the claimants, as in the precedent-setting *JF versus London Borough of Merton* (see **Case study 17** on p.115). JF versus Merton Council was the first successfully to challenge a local authority's care assessment under the newly introduced Care Act (2014). JF's family were of the view that the residential college where he had been living since 2012 was suitable and was adequately meeting his needs. This provision included an on-site multi-disciplinary team (MDT) and total communication environment (TCE), which was an approach the claimant had also received at previous placements for a considerable period of time. The defendant (Merton Council) undertook a needs assessment, pursuant to its duties under Section 9 of the Care Act, which was finalised on July 17, 2016. The council also proposed to transfer the JF from his residential college to an alternative residential care setting, which it contended could also meet his needs on a more affordable basis. In his claim for judicial review, JF claimed that the assessment of his needs by the defendant (Ground 1) and the defendant's decision to transfer him to an alternative care home (Ground 2), were unlawful. The defendant disputed this and further contended that it had not yet made any decision about the proposed change of residential provider.[247]

The claim under Ground 1 succeeded on the basis that the assessment report was silent about whether there was a need for an on-site MDT and total communication environment (in relation to which there was a significant body of evidence available),

---

244 Ibid.

245 Ibid.

246 Ibid.

247 For more information, see www.outertemple.com/wp-content/uploads/2017/08/LexisPSL.pdf (accessed March 2024).

and was therefore unlawful and in breach of the Care Act (2014), Sections 1(1), (3) and 9(4). In particular, at para 54, the court noted:

> 'The absence of information about the decision [of the defendant that there was no need for MDT] is contrasted with the information contained in various reports preceding and post-dating the assessment which suggest an arguable need for both an on-site MDT and a TCE and a definite requirement to consider whether JF has such needs. It also sits alongside the clearly-stated views of JF's parents, who speak for their son because he cannot speak for himself...'[248]

The claim under Ground 2 also succeeded. The court rejected the defendant's argument that it had not yet made a decision that was capable of public law challenge, The court further found that the defendant had taken a decision to terminate JF's placement at his residential college and that the claimant should be transferred to another residential provision. The court then went on to hold that the defendant's decision to terminate the existing placement was unlawful because it was taken at a point before the assessment and planning process had been completed. The court found:

> 'No reasonable local authority would terminate the placement of someone with JF's complex needs without having conducted a lawful assessment of those needs and without having lawfully decided that suitable alternative accommodation was available that would enable them to meet his needs. I have found that the assessment was not lawful for the reasons given above. The decision to terminate can therefore not stand, regardless of the date on which it was taken.'[249]

Analysing this case, Alexander Line, a barrister practising from Outer Temple Chambers specialising in the areas of public law (in particular, education and social welfare) and employment law, who was counsel for JF, drew attention to para 47 of the court judgement. This para declared that:

> '...the needs assessment must specify what JF's needs are and it must do so on a rational basis. If the assessment failed to assess the impact of JF's needs for care and support upon the factors of well-being listed in Section 1(2) of the Act, then it is an unlawful assessment. Likewise, if it failed to assess the outcomes that JF's wishes to achieve in day-to-day life, and whether, and if so to what extent, the provision of care and support could contribute to the achievement of those outcomes, it is unlawful... This judgement will not address all of JF's needs, merely those referred to in the statement of facts and grounds in order to determine whether they were lawfully considered applying these principles.'[250]

Line also pointed to para 32 of the judgement, which stated: 'There is a clear statutory theme placing the individual at the heart and centre of the process so that he or she is full involved in decision-making. This is emphasised by the duty to have regard to the wishes and preferences of the individual.' He added that JF versus Merton Council was therefore

---

248 Ibid.

249 Ibid.

250 Ibid.

an important case because it demonstrated 'the development of the court's interpretation of the well-being principle. It also stands as a successful challenge to a community care decision applying this principle.'[251]

Line said that, following the JF versus Merton Council case, local authorities:

> '...will need to exercise caution at both the assessment and planning stages of the Care Act (2014) to ensure that the well-being principle, as defined in Section, has been in all respects complied with... The predominant implication of this judgement is that it serves as a successful example of a challenge to a care assessment using CA 2014, Section 1, as a litigation tool... For those advising claimants, JF demonstrates the importance of carefully pleading breaches of the CA 2014 with detailed reference to particular facets of the well-being principle. It also shows that tactical consideration should be given to the timing of a challenge, because for some clients there may be benefit obtained from challenging at the assessment stage, as opposed to awaiting a challenge to the care plan. For those advising defendants, the importance of properly assessing well-being is obvious from the judgement, and the assessment process can be undermined by such failures leading to wasted time and cost for local authorities.'[252]

Rook is not as pessimistic as Schwehr about the future of judicial reviews. Still, he highlights other problems:

> 'There is a massive problem with funding the initial legal work, which comes under the Legal Help Scheme. To oversimply, there are two stages to legal aid. The first provides for initial work, including writing pre-action letters to the local authority to see whether they may back down. That first stage is normally done under the Legal Help Scheme. That stage pays absolutely terribly – certainly it is loss-making work, in my experience, which unsurprisingly means it can be almost impossible to find lawyers who will be willing to work under that scheme. This a huge issue in the sector. The second stage comes after the local authority replies their action is considered unlawful. We can then apply for a full Legal Aid Certificate. That second bit of work is still paid very poorly, but nowhere near as terribly as the first stage! The lawyers are the same, but the funding mechanism is different. The nub is that, to get to the second stage, you have to get past the first, terribly paid first stage. That is often the problem. Lawyers sometimes do the first stage pro bono, because the pay is so bad and it is far less hassle. My firm is also able to offer a Social Justice Fund, which we use to try and help families who cannot get legal aid or where families are unable to provide all the financial details required in order to get legal aid. It is funded by an anonymous donor.'[253]

251 Ibid.

252 Ibid.

253 Alex Rook in conversation with the author, December 7, 2023.

Once again, Rook feels that an independent tribunal would be enormously helpful in these circumstances:

> 'If there were a tribunal, everyone would benefit from a lawyer to assist them. In fact, if there were a tribunal, families might even be able to handle the case themselves. It would certainly be much easier. There is no way families could bring a judicial review themselves: it is too complicated and the costs risks are too great. In special educational needs tribunals, you have a much better chance of succeeding if you have a lawyer, but families can, and often do, represent themselves. If there were a social care tribunal, it would just be a much cheaper, more efficient way of arguing for more social care. Contrast that with judicial review, where the loser normally has to pay the winner's costs. That alone is enough to prevent most people from bringing a case without lawyers. Whereas you do not ordinarily have to pay costs in the special educational tribunal, whether you win or lose. I would advise anyone not to go solo on judicial review. I am sure that some people do try. But it is very complicated: you are trying to argue that someone acted unlawfully and that is very hard to achieve without detailed legal knowledge and experience.'[254]

Ekaterina Harrison agrees that the costs issue is a critical one.

Case study 17: JF versus London Borough of Merton

A judge in 2017 quashed a London council's decision to terminate a specialist residential care placement for a man with autism and severe learning disabilities. In a precedent-setting ruling, Deputy High Court judge Anne Whyte QC found that Merton Council's plan to move the 'very vulnerable' 24-year-old autistic man, JF, to a cheaper placement was based on a Care Act needs assessment which was 'not lawful'. JF cannot communicate verbally and requires a high level of constant and specialist care. Since 2012, he has lived in an excellent specialist centre in Cheshire, where he receives on-site support from a multi-disciplinary team, including speech therapists, physiotherapists and occupational therapists.[255]

The council had funded this on-site care for 15 years. In 2016, however, it proposed moving JF to a service in Sussex where this would not be provided. In evidence, lawyers for the council said cheaper placement options were explored because the council deemed that JF no longer needed this extra on-site support. The judge found that the council had failed to justify that decision and that its Care Act needs assessment had failed to show that JF's need for the on-site team had been properly considered.

JF's parents, who acted as his health and welfare deputies and told the council the placement move posed a risk to his progress, had also made their opposition clear, the judge added. She ruled that the council had failed to comply with statutory duties under Section 1 of the Care Act 2014 (to promote an individual's well-being) and Section 9 (assessment of an adult's needs for care and support). 'Accordingly, the assessment was not lawful. ➔

254 Ibid.

255 See www.communitycare.co.uk/2017/07/03/court-quashes-unlawful-care-act-assessment-disabled-man/#:~:text=In%20a%20ruling%20published%20this,that%20was%20%E2%80%9Cnot%20lawful%E2%80%9D. (accessed March 2024).

Any re-assessment of JF's needs must be based on his current situation and not conducted (as I find it was) from the position that his placement is no longer available to him,' the judge said. 'It should be noted that this finding is entirely fact-specific in a case where there is a dispute about which decisions were actually made, with virtually no evidence in support from the defendant [the council] to assist the court one way or another.'

The council denied it had decided to terminate JF's placement and claimed that the Sussex move had merely been an option 'on the table'. But the judge rejected this. She said the council had 'simply deferred the implementation of its decision' and it seemed 'inevitable' that JF would have been moved if he had not launched a legal challenge.

The judge allowed JF's claim and quashed the Care Act assessment. She also quashed the council's decisions to terminate his placement and assess the Sussex unit as a suitable alternative. The council was ordered to undertake a further assessment of JF's needs in line with the Care Act.

The Care Act, the Mental Capacity Act, advocacy and the Court of Protection

How do the Care Act (2014) and the Mental Capacity Act (2005) (MCA) inter-relate in practice? References to the MCA's core concepts of mental capacity and best interests can be found throughout the Care Act. The principles of the Care Act have a strong affinity to the principles of the MCA: for example, under the Care Act, local authorities must begin with 'the assumption that the individual is best-placed to judge questions of their own well-being', just as under the MCA they must assume that a person has mental capacity unless it is shown otherwise.[256]

Both Acts also emphasise the importance of:

- The individual's views, wishes, feelings and beliefs.
- Not jumping to conclusions about a person based on their age, appearance, any condition they have or an aspect of their behaviour which might lead others to make unjustified assumptions about them.
- The individual participating as fully as possible in decisions which are about them.
- Involving others in helping a person to make decisions for themselves, or in making decisions which affect them.
- Minimising restrictions on a person's rights or freedom of action.[257]

During assessment and care planning, questions of mental capacity and best interests may arise for a variety of different reasons. For example, authorities may need to assess a person's mental capacity to refuse a needs assessment or to involve others in care planning or reviews and to make financial decisions around paying for care or requesting direct payments.[258]

256 See www.local.gov.uk/sites/default/files/documents/self-study-pack-669.pdf (accessed January 2024).

257 Ibid.

258 Ibid.

Independent mental capacity advocates (IMCAs)

Mental capacity issues can also often arise during safeguarding. (Safeguarding means protecting a citizen's health, well-being and human rights; enabling him or her to live free from harm, abuse and neglect. It is an integral part of providing high-quality healthcare.) Mental capacity advocates may be involved in supporting people whose mental capacity is being assessed, or about whom best interests decisions may be made, in relation to local authority functions under the Care Act. Advocates can play an important role in ensuring that people are appropriately supported and represented during this process, and help them to understand and assert their rights. Advocates must help individuals to understand their rights and the local authorities' duties in relation to the Care Act. Where issues around mental capacity and best interests arise in connection with care planning and assessment, advocates may also need to help a person to understand their rights and the authority's duties regarding the MCA. Advocates have a general duty to 'make such representations as are necessary' to secure a person's rights in relation to the Care Act. Where assessment and care planning raise questions of mental capacity or best interests, this duty to make representations may extend to securing a person's rights under the MCA. For example, advocates may consider it appropriate to remind authorities of the key principles of the MCA.[259]

Yo Dunn explained the essential difference between the independent mental capacity advocate (IMCA) and the appropriate adult used in the criminal justice system (see Chapter 6):

> 'The IMCA is a role created in the Mental Capacity Act. An IMCA is required in certain specific situations, such as when there is a proposal for a person to be moved into residential care or a hospital and also when a serious medical treatment is being proposed, where there is no appropriate family member to advocate for the person or where there might be a conflict of interests. Local authorities do also appoint IMCAs in a broader range of situations.
>
> 'Sometimes, if an autistic adult has behaved in an inappropriate way, the police become involved and there is concern over whether the individual has the mental capacity to understand whether he or she would be criminally liable. The local authority could well appoint an IMCA to support that person. But this is completely separate from the criminal justice process.'[260]

IMCAs are not usually commissioned to provide services within the criminal justice system. IMCAs have quite specific, high-level requirements for their training. They have to undergo refresher courses every year and a significant proportion are trained in non-instructive advocacy – advocacy on behalf of someone who is unable to tell them what he or she wants. Appropriate adults do not need any training at all.

Most IMCAs are employed by voluntary sector organisations, who are then commissioned by local authorities because local authorities are legally required to instruct an IMCA:

---

259 Ibid.

260 Yo Dunn, personal communication, January 5, 2023.

> 'But the IMCA has to be independent of the local authority. Because advocacy agencies are mostly third-sector organisations, they are utterly dependent on being commissioned by local authorities and how much they are paid by local authorities. This will determine how much training they can offer the IMCAs. This is a problem. Lack of adequate training is due to lack of money, not lack of will.' [261]

Belinda Schwehr says that she has seen an 'overlaying' of the Care Act (2014) with the Mental Capacity Act in an increasing number of cases over the past five years, and she insists that the MCA is being misused or misapplied to suit a local authority agenda of denying services:

> 'Local authorities are either overdoing it, considering every decision as a best-interest decision, regardless of the person's capacity, or underdoing it and letting what comes out of a person's mouth be the determinant of capacity. Neither of these approaches is appropriate. There will be autistic people who are very eloquent and they will be treated as refusing services. But they might be displaying Pathological Demand Avoidance. They may be so volatile and entrenched that people will take against them personally. And because low-calibre professionals marginalise them, the local authority will just turn away or claim that the person is … refusing treatment. So the Mental Capacity Act is being misapplied, usually ignorantly but also sometimes deliberately, every day of the week. Not everywhere, but in most places.' [262]

For his part, Alex Rook does around half of his work under the MCA:

> 'There is definitely a big overlap. The Court of Protection is a much more flexible jurisdiction. A judge will actually listen to what is happening on the ground. You do not have to prove that something is unlawful. But the Court of Protection has no jurisdiction if a local authority refuses to pay for specific provision. The Court of Protection exists to decide between available options. But if a local authority refuses to pay for services, this is not an issue for the Court of Protection. The judge cannot make a decision to order the authority to pay 18 pounds an hour for a therapist, for example, because this is not an available option. The only remedy, then, is judicial review. It becomes an issue for the Court of Protection when the local authority is willing to fund two different agencies, for example. Or whether it is the choice between going into a care institution or living at home, but both are available, in the sense that the local authority is willing to pay for them. I would say it would be better to go to the Court of Protection, if you can, because it is more flexible, but if the issue is a council's refusal to pay money, then there is no role for the Court of Protection. It is probably easier to access the Court of Protection than judicial review because generally there is no risk involved – if you don't get the outcome you want, only in very extreme circumstances would you face a costs order. In judicial review, if you lose, you are likely to have to pay the local authorities' costs, as well as your own, albeit legal aid does provide protection against that scenario' [263]

261 Ibid.

262 Belinda Schwehr, personal communication, November 21, 2023.

263 Alex Rook, personal communication, December 7, 2023.

Summary

Social care is in crisis in the UK. There is a general consensus that the Care Act (2014) – which was intended to strengthen the rights of people with learning disabilities and/or autism and their family and carers – is, broadly speaking, a good piece of legislation. But there is a disconnect between what the law says *should* be happening and what is actually happening. The problem is largely a lack of resources, rather than legal inadequacies. Most autistic people are, in fact, eligible for social care, if the statutory eligibility criteria are fully and knowledgeably applied and thorough assessments are carried out. Yet many people who should get support, never even obtain an assessment, let alone the full application of the eligibility criteria to their needs. The slashing of legal aid has made it very difficult for families to challenge a local authority for unlawfully infringing the Care Act. Their chief options are via a complaint leading to the ombudsman or through judicial review. Although several judicial review cases have led to successful outcomes for the claimants, there are fewer lawyers than ever willing to take on such cases, because the Court of Protection is far more lucrative. Fortunately, many local authorities back down before a case comes to judicial review. Nevertheless it has been argued that there is a pressing need for an independent tribunal which would review care plans – in other words, review how a local authority proposes to meet an autistic individual's needs. In the meantime, mental capacity advocates can play an important role in ensuring that people are appropriately supported and represented during the process of assessing an individual's mental capacity, or about whom best interests decisions may be made in relation to local authority functions under the Care Act. These mental capacity advocates can help families to understand and assert their rights.

Chapter 5: Autism and employment law

This chapter will focus on:

- The life-changing transition into employment.
- Whether, when and how to disclose your autism.
- Reasonable adjustments under the Equality Act.
- Disability discrimination in the workplace.
- Harassment (or bullying) in the workplace.
- The role of mediation.

Employment law – an overview of how it affects autistic adults

When they leave school, too few autistic young people carry on into further education, employment or training. The National Children's Group recently issued a statement declaring that 'All too often, provision up until age 18 is reasonable but the transition from education to employment, from childhood to adulthood and from children's service to adult services can be much like falling off a cliff edge'.[264] It went on to highlight that 'Only 15% of adults with autism are in full-time paid employment. The National Children's Group feel it is time for government, charities, employers and families to collaborate to change this gross inequality.'

The transition from secondary school can be one of the most life-changing events a young person and their family faces, and the process is often difficult and confusing. Decisions made as we prepare to leave school can have an impact on the rest of our lives. A successful transition plan should involve everyone in a young person's life who knows them well. Planning should be person-centred, focusing on what the young person wants for their future and what matters to them. Motivation is crucial here. As this chapter makes clear, despite the considerable skills of many autistic individuals, this community remains a largely untapped pool of human potential in the UK workplace. For those who do find employment, some may not be offered the 'reasonable adjustments' stipulated by the Equality Act (2010). And, as the various case studies illustrate, bullying, harassment and discrimination remain a threat for autistic employees, despite the legal protection supposedly enshrined in the Act.[265]

---

264 See www.achieveability.org.uk/main/policy/barry-sheerman-president-sets-up-the-autism-commission (accessed January 2024).

265 Further examples of bullying, harassment and discrimination in the workplace can be found in Chapter 18 of the author's book, *Autism Works: A guide to successful employment across the entire spectrum*, Routledge, 2018, pp294-209.

As I pointed out in my book *Autism Works: A Guide to Successful Employment Across the Entire Spectrum,*[266] there is a huge disparity in employment for people with disabilities. So it is scarcely surprising that people with autism (and others with disabilities) consistently fail to achieve the same degree of life satisfaction as people without disabilities. The prevalence of autism is reported to be as high as one in 36 by the US-based Centers for Disease Control

266 Op. cit.

and Prevention.[267] That would mean there are more than 600,000 autistic individuals in the UK. However, only around 25% of autistic people progress to further or higher education in the UK. Just 15% of individuals with autism have full-time jobs, as mentioned. As Dame Stephanie Shirley put it in 2009, this is 'a shockingly low figure for a group whose main impairment is in social interaction'. It compares with around 31% for all disabled people and 57% for non-disabled people of working age in Britain. Recent research found that only 10% of adults diagnosed with autism currently received support to find employment, yet 79% of people with autism on unemployment benefits want to work.

According to the social model of disability, people are disabled by barriers in society, not by their impairment or difference. The Equality Act (2010) sets out when someone is considered to be disabled. The law states that someone is disabled if both of these apply:

- They have a 'physical or mental impairment'.
- The impairment 'has a substantial and long-term adverse effect on their ability to carry out normal day-to-day activities'.

Speaking on World Autism Day in 2023, Professor Sir Simon Baron-Cohen, director of Cambridge University's Autism Research Centre, urged bosses to end the discrimination against talented people with the condition. He said many had the unique skills needed to become scientists, technicians and engineers. They were an 'extraordinary resource' that was being wasted because too few companies made them feel 'welcome.' He added:

> 'Autistic people are not defined by their disability – they are simply different and their brains are wired differently... If we are serious about treating people equally, we should be offering opportunities to work, irrespective of whether people are autistic. I want to encourage employers to reach out to them and make job adverts welcoming to neurodivergent people, encouraging them to apply, because there has been some discrimination, perhaps inadvertent, to this group.'[268]

Up to 85% of the population with Asperger's syndrome are without full-time employment, despite the fact that many have above-average intelligence – and Asperger's syndrome comes with no learning disability. (It is, nevertheless, totally misleading to call it 'mild autism', since it can be associated with serious social and sensory problems and severe depression). At present, of this more able group, many of those in work do not have jobs that match their intellectual abilities. Despite graduate level skills, they fail to get or keep jobs – even ones (typically in retail, care or administration) that do not represent their formal qualifications.

Research has shown that between 20% and 30% of autistic children are classified as minimally verbal, presenting with a range of expressive abilities from no use of oral language to use of few oral words or phrases[269]. Whereas some of these children go on

---

267 CDC (2023) *Data and Statistics on Autism Spectrum Disorder* [online]. Available at: www.cdc.gov/ncbddd/autism/data.html (accessed January 2024).

268 See: www.independent.co.uk/news/uk/home-news/world-autism-day-discrimination-b2312443.html (accessed January 2024).

269 Tager-Flusberg H & Kasari C (2013) Minimally verbal school-aged children with autism spectrum disorder: the neglected end of the spectrum. *Autism Research* **6** (6) 468-78 doi: 10.1002/aur.1329

to develop additional verbal skills, many remain minimally verbal into adulthood. Young adults with more advanced skills, including conversational abilities, are more likely to obtain employment. The 20% to 30% have more significant challenges in obtaining and retaining jobs, due to the frequent need for specialised support, such as augmentative and alternative communication (AAC). However, approximately 20% of the participants in one study lacking conversational skills were still able to find work[270]. This specific conclusion supports the notion that paid employment is attainable for autistic across levels of functioning and communicative abilities. Indeed, so convinced am I that many non-verbal or non-speaking autistic individuals may be able to find meaningful employment that I am in the process of setting up an organisation designed to help such individuals find jobs.

Increasing employers' awareness about autism

In 2023, the Buckland Review was launched as part of the UK government's national strategy (The National Strategy for Autistic Children, Young People and Adults, 2021 to 2026, released in 2021). The Review focuses on assisting employers in recruiting and retaining autistic individuals. Its aim is to reduce the employment gap by increasing employers' awareness about autism, enabling them to grasp the advantages of employing autistic individuals and facilitating the necessary adjustments for effective recruitment and support. The Secretary of State for Work and Pensions, Mel Stride, appointed Sir Robert Buckland, KC, MP, to lead the review. It will ask 'businesses, employment organisations, specialist support groups and autistic people to help identify the barriers to securing and retaining work and progressing with their careers'. Issues to be considered include how employers identify and better support autistic staff already in their workforce, what more could be done to prepare autistic people effectively for beginning or returning to a career, and working practices or initiatives to reduce stigma and improve the productivity of autistic employees.

As part of the review, it is recognised that many of the adjustments and initiatives that would benefit autistic people could also benefit a wider group of people who think differently, including those with other neurodivergence, such as ADHD, dyslexia and dyspraxia. Under the Equality Act (2010), employers have a duty to make reasonable adjustments to enable neurodivergent employees to do their work and feel supported in the workplace.

It is true, of course, that autism incorporates a broad range of abilities. Many autistic people are very successful at work. Other people may have difficulties in the workplace and some people may remain unemployed. Because of this 'spiky' profile, the hierarchical structure of the workplace may suit some and hamper others. However, lack of skills, enthusiasm or motivation to acquire a job are not the barriers for autistic (and other neurodiverse) workers once they do find employment. These obstacles include failure to introduce reasonable adjustments in the workplace, discrimination, bullying and harassment. In 2022, 102 UK employment tribunals included claims of neurodiversity

270 Roux et al (2013) Postsecondary employment experiences among young adults with an autism spectrum disorder. *Journal of the American Academy of Child and Adolescent Psychiatry* **52** (9) 931-9. doi: 10.1016/j.jaac.2013.05.019

discrimination, according to employment law firm, Fox & Partners. This is a continuation in the upward trend from 70 cases in 2020 to 93 cases in 2021.[271]

Ivor Adair, a partner at Fox & Partners, told HR magazine:

> 'Whereas many employers have become more aware of neurodiversity within their workforce, that is not yet translating into strategies that are working, as disputes of this type are still making their way to employment tribunals.' He added that employers could avoid discrimination claims against them by training managers in how to discuss adjustments with employees proactively: 'Employers will need to be astute to recognise in what way neurodivergent employees are disadvantaged by the workplace set-up, be ready to discuss accommodations and ensure managers are trained so not to mishandle the situation. Reasonable adjustments might include clear and specific instructions, a quiet workspace, longer core hours with break, or a mentor. Much will depend on identifying what it is about the job the employee finds challenging, while maintaining their trust.'[272]

According to a recent study from the consultancy firm INvolve UK, more than two-thirds (67%) of employees with 'invisible' disabilities such as autism, dyslexia and ADHD say they currently have to source support and reasonable adjustments at work alone.

By law, employers must:

- Make reasonable adjustments when they know, or could reasonably be expected to know, someone is disabled.
- Do all they reasonably can to support disabled staff and job applicants and protect them from discrimination.
- Take steps to prevent disability discrimination – this includes recognising the benefits of having an inclusive and diverse workforce that does not exclude disabled people.

It is also the employer's responsibility to ensure that other people do what is needed for a reasonable adjustment to work well. For example, if someone needs information presented in a certain format, the employer must make sure other people do the same.

Employers could be liable under the law if they do not do these things. For example, an employee or job applicant could make a disability discrimination claim to an employment tribunal.

Under the Equality Act (2010), the following actions by an employer are considered unlawful:

- **Direct discrimination:**
  Employers are prohibited from engaging in direct discrimination, which involves treating disabled individuals less favourably than others. An illustrative case is *Fabian v City Plumbing Supplies Holdings*. In this instance, the employer was found not to have

271 Machell M (2023) *Neurodiversity tribunals continue to rise* [online]. Available at: www.hrmagazine.co.uk/content/news/neurodiversity-tribunals-continue-to-rise/ (accessed January 2024).

272 Ibid.

directly discriminated against the claimant due to his autism. This verdict was reached as the employer was unaware of the condition and the employer could not reasonably be expected to have known about it.

- **Indirect discrimination:**
  Employers are prohibited from indirectly discriminating against disabled individuals. This means that they cannot implement a policy or practice that puts those with a disability at a disadvantage compared to those without, and this disadvantage cannot be justified as a reasonable means of achieving a legitimate aim. In the case of *Fabian v City Plumbing Supplies Holdings*, the employer, who employed the claimant as a 'picker' in a warehouse, was deemed not to have committed indirect discrimination. This determination was based on the fact that autistic individuals, including the claimant, were not significantly disadvantaged by the specific policy in question. This policy entailed using the one-man Low Level Order Picker with a high degree of accuracy.
- **Discrimination arising from disability:**
  Employers are prohibited from treating disabled individuals unfavourably due to something that arises from, or as a consequence of, their disability. For instance, in the employment tribunal case in *Lonsdale v The Barn Childcare*, the claimant was determined to have been terminated due to sickness absence, which stemmed from the claimant's autism, anxiety and depression.
- **Duty to make reasonable adjustments:**
  Employers are required to implement reasonable adjustments for disabled individuals if they experience significant disadvantages compared to those without disabilities.
- **Harassment:**
  Employers are prohibited from subjecting disabled individuals to harassment through unwanted conduct related to their disability. This prohibition extends to situations where the conduct aims to, or results in, a breach of the victim's dignity or the creation of an environment that is intimidating (such as bullying), hostile, degrading, humiliating, or offensive. For instance, in the case of *Morgan v Buckinghamshire Council* (see **Case study 22** on p.138), the council was found to have harassed its employee. This occurred when, in the letter dismissing the claimant's appeal against her dismissal, the council implied that she had deliberately chosen to mask her autism, rather than having learned behaviours that led to this masking. This implication had the effect of violating her dignity.
- **Victimisation:**
  Employers must not subject disabled individuals to victimisation for engaging in a protected act, such as, for example, initiating employment tribunal proceedings. This also applies if the employer believes the individual has taken or may take such an action. In the case of *Holland v A & A Coach Travel*, which involved an autistic claimant, the employer was found to have victimised the bus driver (see **Case study 23** on p.141). They initiated an unsupported civil claim for alleged bus damage, contacted the DVLA and the claimant's new employer attempted to obstruct future employment prospects and tried to pressure the claimant into withdrawing his employment tribunal claim.

In addition, the Equality Act (2010) places distinct responsibilities on public sector employers to alleviate disadvantages experienced by disabled workers, address their requirements, and promote their active participation in public life or any other activity where their involvement is notably limited. This obligation is known as the public sector equality duty.

To disclose or not to disclose?

The tricky decision about whether, when and how an employee should disclose his or her autism is discussed in detail in my book, *Autism Works*. The late Dinah Murray believed it was a bad idea to reveal your condition, because the sadly still prevalent deficit-based medical model of autism automatically sets up negative expectations. However, advocates of disclosure point out that this is the only way to obtain the necessary 'reasonable adjustments' to the work environment from employers, as stipulated in the Equality Act. This is questionable. As Ekaterina Harrison has observed, the Equality and Human Rights Commission's Statutory Code of Practice regarding employment discrimination emphasises that an employer has to make reasonable efforts to determine whether a worker has a disability. In such cases, the employer should assess whether an individual may have a disability, even if it has not been disclosed.[273]

No one is obliged to inform his or her employer – or potential employer – of a disability. Reasons for withholding this information could include:

- You do not realise your condition is considered a disability by law.
- You do not think of yourself as disabled.
- You are worried about how your employer might react.
- You do not want anyone to know.

Employees are still protected from discrimination if their employer could reasonably be expected to know they have a disability. From a legal point of view, it is important for employers to understand that an employee's neurodiversity could qualify as a disability under the Equality Act (2010). However, not all neurodivergent employees will consider themselves to have a disability. Under the law, employees have the right to identify as having a disability or not to identify. But the legal definition of 'disability' under the Equality Act means that neurodivergent workers are likely to meet the conditions. UK government guidance states: 'A disability can arise from a wide range of impairments which can be … developmental, such as autistic spectrum disorders (ASD), dyslexia and dyspraxia.'[274]

Matters can be complicated where employees are unwilling to disclose their neurodiversity or do not see themselves as disabled, because employers can still be liable if they have 'constructive knowledge' of a disability. In the recent (2020) case of Fabian v City Plumbing Supplies, Viktor Fabian had ticked 'no' to having a medical condition or a disability in his medical questionnaire and was later unsuccessful in pursuing complaints of disability

273 Ekaterina Harrison, personal communication.

274 See www.gov.uk/government/publications/equality-act-guidance/disability-equality-act-2010-guidance-on-matters-to-be-taken-into-account-in-determining-questions-relating-to-the-definition-of-disability-html (accessed January 2024).

discrimination before an employment tribunal. He claimed that, while he had provided these responses on starting work, he had since notified his manager that he had autism and a personality development disorder. In fact, Fabian claimed that he had likened himself to Greta Thunberg (the well-known environmental campaigner with Asperger's syndrome) in the course of conversation, and that this meant he had officially made his employer aware of his condition. The employment tribunal found that such a reference was 'oblique, unclear and insufficient' to successfully alert his employer to him having a disability (see **Case study 18** on below).

Paragraph 5.15 of the Employment Statutory Code of Practice states that: 'An employer must do all they can reasonably be expected to do to find out if a worker has a disability. What is reasonable will depend on the circumstances. This is an objective assessment. When making enquiries about disability, employers should consider issues of dignity and privacy and ensure that personal information is dealt with confidentially'.[275]

As Ekaterina Harrison has pointed out, this entire process is not straightforward: 'The employer must engage in reasonable inquiries concerning the employee's mental and physical health. They would be deemed to have constructive knowledge of the disability only if these inquiries would have reasonably led them to discover it.'[276]

A study from Birkbeck's Research Centre for Neurodiversity at Work, commissioned by the charity Neurodiversity in Business (NiB), found significant barriers to neurodivergent employees disclosing their neurodivergence to employers. Led by Birkbeck Professors Almuth McDowall and Nancy Doyle, the research team surveyed 1,117 people, 127 employers and 990 neurodivergent employees, asking about how work is adjusted, as employers need to accommodate requests, barriers and opportunities, and neurodiverse careers. The researchers identified stark barriers to neurodivergent employees disclosing their conditions to employers: 65% of employees feared discrimination from management, 55% from colleagues, and 40% said that there are not enough knowledgeable staff to help. The Birkbeck researchers produced an accessible report with clear recommendations which was launched at the first Neurodiversity in Business Annual Conference at ExCel London in March 2023.

Case study 18: Viktor Fabian v City Plumbing Supplies

Viktor Fabian, an employee of Hungarian origin, lost his claim of unfair discrimination against City Plumbing Supplies, under Section 15 of the Equality Act (2010). He also claimed he had been subject to indirect discrimination under Section 19 of the Act, that the company had failed to make reasonable adjustments under Sections 20 and 21 of the Act and that he had been subject to harassment related to disability under Section 26 of the Act.[277]

The case rested on whether Fabian had made his employers aware of his autism. The employment tribunal, held in Cambridge in August 2020, heard that an autism Diagnostic Report dated August 12, 2019, had concluded that Fabian was ➔

275 EHRC (2011) Employment Statutory Code of Practice [online]. Available at: www.equalityhumanrights.com/sites/default/files/employercode.pdf (accessed January 2024).

276 Ekaterina Harrison, personal communication.

277 See https://assets.publishing.service.gov.uk/media/5f85720fd3bf7f6ba4f45094/Mr_V_Fabian_-v_-_City_Plumbing_Supplies_Holdings_Ltd_-_3326133-2019_-_Judgment.pdf (accessed March 2024).

a confident individual who was passionate about his interests, but that he was rigid in his thinking and displayed some difficulties in social communication. In addition, he had on many occasions made inappropriate comments in the workplace which had resulted in his being asked to leave his place of work. The opinion of the ASC Diagnostic Service was that Fabian met the criteria for a diagnosis of autism.

On the basis of this evidence, before the hearing, the respondent conceded that Fabian was a disabled person within Section 6 of the Equality Act on the basis of his autism.[278]

Fabian began working for City Plumbing Supplies in a warehouse on an agency basis from October 2017. Before his Lift Truck Operators training, he completed a medical questionnaire and was asked to disclose 'any medical condition you feel is relevant'. The tribunal heard that Fabian did not disclose anything. The form also asked if he had a disability, and he ticked the box 'no'. Fabian said that he did not regard himself as having a disability but that, at some point after starting his employment, he spoke to Peter Warriner, a frontline manager of operations, about his autism and personality development disorder, and further said that he found it hard to concentrate and that he struggled with complex tasks that required a lot of instructions. Warriner categorically denied this conversation had ever taken place. At one point, Fabian said he had told Warriner about his condition in the context of a conversation about veganism, about which Fabian is passionate. At another point, he said that, in the context of a conversation about plastics in the ocean, he had likened himself to Greta Thunberg [the Swedish environmentalist with Asperger's syndrome], saying he had her condition. Warriner said he had no memory of Fabian mentioning Greta Thunberg and that he did not know who she was.

In April 2019, Warriner invited Fabian to attend a probationary review meeting to discuss his work performance and timekeeping, and stated that a possible outcome could be the termination of his employment. At the meeting, Fabian stated that, when his performance was being discussed, he had informed Warriner that he found it hard to concentrate and follow detailed instructions because of his autism and that he became anxious and upset that nobody was taking his disability into account. In response, Warriner again denied that Fabian had referred to any disability or condition. Warriner said he had adjourned the meeting to consider his decision and when he reconvened it ten minutes later, he informed Fabian that he was being dismissed because he had failed to meet the standards of the six-month probation period. In response to Fabian's claims of disability-related discrimination and failure to make reasonable adjustments, Warriner submitted that he did not know, and could not have been reasonably expected to know, that Fabian had autism or any disability (which is a defence to such claims under, respectively Sections 15(2) and paragraph 20 of part 3 of schedule 8 of the Equality Act).[279]

The tribunal found that Fabian had not informed Warriner that he had autism or any disability either shortly after being taken on as an employee in October 2018, or in December 2018, or at the probationary review meeting in March 2019, or at any time until after he had been dismissed on April 18, 2019. 'We further accept that if he [Warriner] had been told the claimant had the disability of an autism spectrum condition, he would have responded appropriately... Finally, we note that the claimant did not receive his diagnosis from the ASC Diagnostic Service until August 2019, after he had left the respondent's employment'.[280]

Accordingly, the complaint of indirect discrimination against Fabian was dismissed.

278 Ibid.

279 Ibid.

280 Ibid.

Reasonable adjustments under the Equality Act

Under the Equality Act (2010), if an employee identifies as having a disability, he or she must be provided with certain rights and protections under the law. Employers must make reasonable adjustments to allow them to perform their best work and protect them from discrimination, harassment and victimisation.

Many reasonable adjustments may be required to help neurodivergent workers perform at their best. Typically, these may include accommodations related to focus, attentiveness and distraction – for example, allowing the worker to take short breaks throughout the day, providing them with a space free from distraction or enabling them to work from home and support with social interaction in the workplace. Support for neurodivergent workers should be assessed on a case-by-case basis.

In the interview process, some autistic candidates may not feel comfortable in a traditional interview situation. **There are many ways to make interviews more accessible:**

- Provide questions before the interview for all candidates, to stop bias and encourage candidates to answer more cohesively.
- Minimise sensory overload – reducing bright lights and/or conducting the interview in a quiet place can help candidates who might have sensory needs.
- Give the candidate more than the usual set interview time – this will allow candidates enough processing time to understand the questions and to give their answers.
- Make questions clear. Provide appropriate context to questions so candidates can relate to the questions more easily, and use literal, rather than metaphorical, language.
- Allowing a job coach or employment adviser to attend interviews with the candidate to help relax and prompt him or her when needed.

As for the work environment, there are adjustments that employers can make to provide continuing support to their autistic employees:

- Create a weekly timetable (using visuals, if required).
- Introduce a buddy system and assign an experienced member of staff to a new employee.
- Provide written instructions for all tasks.
- Advise an employee in advance of any changes to normal routine to help them prepare.
- Provide a quiet space, without fluorescent lighting, if appropriate.
- Permit an employee to listen to music via headphones, or to wear noise-cancelling headphones, so they can control their sensory input.
- Allow an employee extra time for to process instructions and other information.

Employers should consider that autistic employees might not be aware of the available or most beneficial adjustments for them. Therefore, it is helpful to provide a list of potential adjustments. **Some examples of measures employers can implement to create a more autism-friendly work environment include:**

- Providing dedicated workspaces to minimise disruption caused by moving around.
- Establishing designated quiet areas for employees to use as a safe haven.
- Minimising visual stimuli by limiting information and bright artwork displayed on walls.
- Allocating workspaces with ample natural light for those sensitive to office lighting, or permitting the use of daylight lamps.
- Installing dividers in appropriate areas to block and reduce noise.
- Allowing, when appropriate, the use of equipment like noise-cancelling headphones or voice-to-text software.
- Regularly reminding staff to be considerate of their colleagues and maintain a quiet environment.
- Providing clear instructions next to office equipment and machinery, such as photocopiers.
- Supplying organisers, lockers, cabinets and name labels to assist with organisation and retention of work and equipment.
- Issuing written instructions in addition to verbal ones for tasks.
- Presenting information in various formats, including audio, video, diagrams, flowcharts, and checklists.
- Allowing more time for completing specific tasks.
- Permitting the booking of meeting rooms for tasks that require high levels of concentration.
- Conducting meetings at suitable times, with an agenda, keeping them concise, and recording action points.
- Allowing participation in meetings through alternative means, such as providing written input.
- Permitting the use of digital recording devices during meetings.
- Designating a point of contact, in person or over the phone, for each neurodivergent individual to address concerns.
- Establishing a private internal network for individuals with similar challenges to exchange tips and resources.
- Granting access to an occupational health professional.
- Offering fixed hours rather than variable shifts to establish a routine.
- Providing flexible work arrangements, such as part-week homeworking or allowing to start earlier or finish later.

Ekaterina Harrison has highlighted the significance of remote work:

> 'This arrangement, whether full-time or part-time, can be a crucial adjustment for an autistic individual, as it alleviates the stress of commuting and allows for creation of a customised work environment tailored to his or her specific needs at home. Additionally, the presence of supportive family members who understand the autistic person's needs can be invaluable. It is essential to acknowledge, though, that remote work comes with its own set of challenges, such as potential difficulties in maintaining a structured and consistent schedule. In these situations, providing support in establishing and managing a work schedule, or assigning a work coach, can prove to be highly beneficial. Employers may also need to provide the necessary technology and ergonomic workstation furniture to ensure that autistic individuals have a comfortable and conducive working environment at home.'[281]

Kliemt.Arbeitsrecht, a leading German law company and a member of Ius Laboris – the global alliance of top employment law firms – says that it is generally advisable, when an employee explains that he or she has any disability, to talk to them and discuss referring them for an occupational health appointment:

> 'An occupational health report can support an understanding of what adjustments may be needed and if it is reasonable to make these adjustments. Further occupational health assessments might be needed, especially when an employee's disability is subject to fluctuation, for example, in times of stress or if their medication changes. It can also be useful for managers to have training on neurodiversity and how it can present in individuals within the work environment. All staff should be reminded that even one-off comments can constitute harassment and that they have an obligation to be considerate towards colleagues.'[282]

Kliemt emphasised the importance of appreciating the effect the employee's condition, or the medication he or she is taking, may have on them and how this might have played a role in the purported 'misconduct'. It is particularly difficult when a neuroatypical employee behaves inappropriately:

> '...and then makes the case that this was linked to neurodiversity... In our experience, cases of this nature are becoming more common. It may still be appropriate to dismiss, but it requires more consideration and care than a situation which does not involve a disability... If, even with reasonable adjustments, there is a strong likelihood that serious misbehaviour could be repeated (for example, because the employee does not accept that there has been misconduct or understand why) dismissal is likely to be lawful. As always, dismissal should be a last resort and other options such as giving a final warning, moving the employee to a different team and/or working from home should be considered first.'[283]

Kliemt lists the following key factors in deciding which approach to adopt in situations of misconduct where an individual relies on his or her neurodivergence as an explanation:

281 Ekaterina Harrison, personal communication.

282 See: https://kliemt.blog/2022/11/25/neurodiversity-harassment-and-misconduct/ (accessed January 2024).

283 Ibid.

- How the neurodivergence and/or medication affects the employee.
- What the likelihood is that the behaviour will be repeated.
- Whether any reasonable adjustments would assist with reducing the risk.
- Whether there are any other sanctions which would be appropriate in the scenario.[284]

There is a risk of a vicious cycle here. If employees do not feel comfortable disclosing their needs for fear of discrimination, how can companies really get to grips with what those needs are and implement changes that make the workplace more inclusive in the first place?

As the Tom Sherbourne case study illustrates (see **Case study 19** below), even when an employer takes measures to identify an employee with neurodiversity and suggests adjustments, proper management training is crucial for successful implementation.

As Ekaterina Harrison pointed out to me:

> 'Just as with any employee, managers should ensure fair treatment for autistic employees if conduct-related issues arise. Employers should be particularly mindful of the potential for claims of unfavourable treatment stemming from something related to a person's disability. Employers who are aware of an employee's neurodivergent status should consider whether the employee's behaviour may be influenced by their condition and/or any medication they may be taking as a result. Otherwise, the treatment of an employee might give rise to a claim that they were treated in a certain way because of their disability.'[285]

Case study 19: Tom Sherbourne

Tom Sherbourne, an autistic senior analyst, won a claim for indirect disability discrimination, after his employer failed to make reasonable adjustments for his condition. Judge Jeremy Shulman ruled in 2019 that the energy supplier, npower, had suffered a 'continuous management failure' after it failed to take reasonable steps to understand Sherbourne's disability and failed to implement two sets of reasonable adjustments, one of which was recommended by the company's own in-house doctor.[286]

Sherbourne joined npower in October 2017. He worked in an open-plan setting with a busy walkway behind him and the tribunal heard it was not very long before he felt overwhelmed. Debra Glancy, operations manager at npower, told the tribunal she had felt compelled to hold an informal discussion with Sherbourne about his 'disruptive and loud behaviour' on just his second day. She spoke with him again a week later, on October 10, where she reportedly told him: 'We're not here to wipe arse'. By November, Sherbourne had become distressed about changes to his working environment and different people sitting near him due to the flexible working policy. He 'felt subject to distraction' and the 'noise and smells' at work caused him distress. ➔

284 Ibid.

285 Ekaterina Harrison, personal communication.

286 See www.peoplemanagement.co.uk/article/1742388/analyst-autism-wins-discrimination-claim-overwhelmed-office-environment#: ~ :text = Judge % 20Jeremy % 20Shulman % 20ruled % 20that,its % 20own % 20in % 2Dhouse % 2-0doctor. (accesses

On February 2, 2018, Sherbourne suffered what he described as a 'breakdown' at work and said he had suicidal thoughts. He went off sick and was diagnosed by his GP with an anxiety disorder. Sherbourne underwent an autism assessment and was referred to npower's occupational health team on April 11. His employment was terminated with effect from September 30. He complained to the Leeds employment tribunal, claiming that npower had indirectly discriminated against him on the grounds of his disability and failed to make reasonable adjustments for his autism. Judge Shulman ruled in favour of Sherbourne, saying npower had failed to implement reasonable adjustments, inappropriately used its capability procedure and used 'dismissal as a tool to rid themselves of a disabled employee'.

Recruitment procedures have been considered in a number of claims filed with the employment tribunal by autistic individuals. In the case of *The Government Legal Service v Brookes*, the Employment Appeals Tribunal (EAT) affirmed an employment tribunal's decision. It found that the autistic claimant had faced discrimination when required to take a multiple-choice 'Situational Judgement Test' as the initial stage of a competitive recruitment process for lawyers aspiring to join the respondent. (The claimant had asked for permission to submit short written answers to questions instead of completing multiple-choice options. The respondent's refusal of this accommodation resulted in the subsequent legal proceedings.) In this case, the tribunal determined that the claimant had been placed at a specific disadvantage compared to non-disabled candidates, and this requirement could not be justified.

In contrast, another autistic job candidate, Jonathan Rackham (see **Case study 20** below), lost his claim against the Judicial Appointments Commission for the use of online application forms and multiple-choice situational qualifying tests. In this case, the judge decided that the adjustments Rackham had requested were 'far too onerous'.

Case study 20: Jonathan Rackham

An autistic candidate for the Bench (UK judiciary), Jonathan Rackham, lost an employment tribunal claim against the Judicial Appointments Commission (JAC) over reasonable adjustments.

In a judgement published in July 2023, Judge Postle ruled that Rackham's claims under the Equality Act (2010) were not well-founded. The JAC accepted that the online application forms and multiple-choice situational qualifying tests would have put Rackham, who was diagnosed with Asperger's syndrome, at a substantial disadvantage compared with a non-disabled candidate, but argued that the measures it took were a proportionate means of achieving a legitimate aim. The tribunal agreed.

Judge Postle declared: 'Clearly, courts and tribunals deal with complex and abstract cases with time constraints. The whole purpose of the selection process is to test candidates' ability and it clearly would not be appropriate to adjust the process to such an extent that it undermines the process itself to select those who can perform in the role.'[287]

➔

287 See www.lawgazette.co.uk/news/neurodiverse-judicial-candidate-fails-in-tribunal-claim-/5116693.article#:~:text=Rackham%20argued%20the%20commission%20should,on%20the%20commission%2C%20Postle%20said (accessed March 2024)

Rackham had argued that adjustments which the Commission should have made include simplified questions on the application form. However, Judge Postle said the questions were 'no more complex than the legal questions the tribunal would have to answer at a hearing'. The judge found that reasonable adjustments had been afforded to Rackham, such as submitting the application form offline and being helped by someone to complete it. Certain adjustments that Rackham wanted were 'simply not realistic'.

Rackham had been given extra time to complete the test, with the assistance of someone he knew and allowed to submit his answers offline or by email. It was deemed not reasonable to require the employer to provide a trained autism facilitator to assist, as the employer had been entitled to rely on National Autistic Society advice that it was better to have someone known to Rackham to assist him. The tribunal stated that seeking best practice advice from a relevant charity or expert body obviously was prudent, particularly where an employer was proposing a different adjustment from that sought by the individual. The tribunal also noted that the test had been reviewed by the employer's Diversity and Engagement Team to ensure it was effective and did not disadvantage individuals in society.

Rackham had also argued that the Commission should have set up a mock scenario to assess how he reacted and responded, using scenarios set out in the qualifying tests. While a mock scenario was a 'legitimate aid' that an applicant would face in a tribunal, setting up live ones was 'far too onerous' on the Commission, Judge Postle said. 'The qualifying test that simply involves 20 questions would have to be scripted, the form loaded and have to be done in a time frame which would be a significant burden on the respondents. It was simply not reasonable or realistic to turn it into a live video.'[288]

Disability discrimination in the workplace

At work, the law protects the following people against discrimination:

- Employees and workers.
- Contractors and self-employed people hired personally to do the work.
- Job applicants.
- Former employees – usually around providing references.

Someone could experience disability discrimination from anyone they come into contact through their job. This includes other people at work, customers and members of the public.

Employers are becoming increasingly aware of neurodiversity and the benefits of more inclusive hiring strategies. At the same time, neurodiversity-based discrimination claims are on the rise. The previously mentioned study by Birkbeck's Research Centre for Neurodiversity at Work found that 65% of neurodivergent employees feared discrimination at work, despite the fact that companies increasingly recognised the need for inclusivity and the advantages that diversity brings to the workforce.

Disability is one of nine 'protected characteristics' covered by the Equality Act. Disability discrimination includes direct and indirect discrimination, harassment and victimisation. Disability discrimination can happen in any aspect of work. It can result from decisions

288 Ibid.

made at work or from how people behave towards each other. It could be a regular pattern of behaviour or a one-off incident. It can happen in the workplace, at work social events or when people are working remotely. Harassment and victimisation are specific prohibited behaviours, distinct from forms of discrimination. Harassment involves prohibited conduct linked to a protected characteristic (e.g, disability), which aims to, or results in, a breach of the victim's dignity or creates an environment that is intimidating, hostile, degrading, humiliating or offensive.

Case study 21: Chris Tyerman

An autistic man, Chris Tyerman, who also has several long-term health conditions as a result of treatment for lymphoma as a child, was due to receive £20,000 in compensation after a 'discriminatory' refusal to make the reasonable adjustments he requested for a job interview with the government agency responsible for NHS digital technology.[289]

In August 2021, Tyerman, from Barnsley, in Yorkshire, applied for posts in cyber-security with NHS Digital but, after being shortlisted, he was informed that some of the adjustments he needed to be made ahead of an interview were not possible. Tyerman, who struggles with communication, had requested to be able to see the questions he would be asked in advance, and also asked for his interviewers to avoid open-ended questions. However, NHS Digital – which became part of NHS England earlier in 2023, but described itself at the time as a Disability Confident employer – rejected these requests, arguing that all applicants had to be treated in the same way, a clear breach of the Equality Act (2010). Tyerman's request to have a skills assessment or work trial was also rejected.[290]

Tyerman has a Masters degree in computing information security and forensics. When NHS Digital rejected his requests, he decided not to attend the interview, because he felt its efforts were paying 'lip service' to his need (and the legally enshrined obligation) to make adjustments. He also decided that, if NHS Digital was not willing to offer reasonable adjustments in the interview, it would not provide the adjustments he would require to do the job.

NHS Digital later claimed that employment and security checks meant a work trial would be 'prohibitive', while providing questions three days before the interview would not be a reasonable adjustment and avoiding open-ended questions would also be 'unreasonable'.

In October 2021, Tyerman applied for a second time for a position, this time as a cyber-security adviser. On this occasion, a telephone interview took place, but there were further problems with securing the reasonable adjustments he needed, including a refusal to avoid asking open-ended questions, which led to his being unsuccessful with his application. When he finally received feedback on his failure to secure the position, he was told his answers to the open-ended questions 'were not strong/in depth enough'.

Tyerman believes NHS Digital's actions were discriminatory under the Equality Act, and that they also breached the NHS Constitution for England and the United Nations Convention on the Rights of Persons with Disabilities. ➔

289 See www.disabilitynewsservice.com/autistic-man-to-receive-20000-from-nhs-after-refusal-of-job-interview-adjustments/ (accessed March 2024).

290 Ibid.

After NHS Digital failed to provide a 'positive response' to his complaint about his treatment, he took his case to an employment tribunal. During the tribunal process, NHS Digital requested a medical report to confirm his autism diagnosis, despite having seen a report from a clinical psychologist who had already diagnosed him and in spite of the fact that Tyerman was receiving support from an autism service funded by his local council.

A settlement in the case was reached after a conciliation process led by the conciliation service, ACAS. But it was only after a 16-month legal battle that NHS England offered Tyerman a £20,000 payment as compensation for injury to feelings. It failed to admit liability. It has also agreed to accept Tyerman's feedback as part of its review of how it deals with reasonable adjustments for disabled staff members and job applicants.[291]

Tyerman welcomed the settlement by NHS England and said he felt 'vindicated'. However, he described the initial 'aggressive' defence by NHS Digital as 'destructive, inappropriate and a waste of NHS resources'. He added: 'The adjustments I asked for were reasonable and I hope that the outcome will encourage a more positive attitude to recruiting neurodiverse people.'[292]

The landmark 2022 case of *Morgan v Buckinghamshire Council* raised a number of interesting questions, particularly in relation to the experiences of neurodiverse employees. Ms Morgan was a social worker who lost her case against unfair dismissal for giving gifts of a bottle of shampoo, a necklace and a voucher to a child without seeking permission but won her case for harassment (see **Case study 22** on p.138). Lyse Hurd, representing Ms Morgan, declared:

> 'This case is not about safeguarding and it never has been. This child was never at risk of harm from MM and she never will be. This case is not about boundaries. There is actually no evidence in this bundle, or from any of the witnesses, that MM had done anything to try and infiltrate SH's life in any way other than as a family finder...
>
> 'Treating children equally does not mean treating them the same. If you treat them the same, you lose sight of the individual child. I don't know very many good social workers who have not had at least one child who seemed to be the "underdog" of their caseload – in this case, SH was technically the only child on MM's caseload. You do what you can to make that child feel special. You tell them things like "I care for you unconditionally." ... A social worker has the power and ability to make a child feel loved and cared for, yet still maintain professional boundaries. If that ability is not used by every social worker who works with children, then maybe they need to consider a different profession...
>
> 'The mistake is, as MM said in her evidence, she should have written up a detailed good-bye plan, shared it and tweaked it with her line manager and then got the funding for any agreed gifts from management. That is a learning point, not gross misconduct.'[293]

291 Ibid.

292 Ibid.

293 For the full verdict, see https://assets.publishing.service.gov.uk/media/5fdb8011d3bf7f3a2ecdb7cf/Ms_M_Morgan_v_Buckinghamshire_Council_3303876-2019___Others_FMH_Judgment.pdf (accessed January 2024).

Case study 22: Morgan v Buckinghamshire Council

Ms M. Morgan was an autistic and dyslexic social worker in Buckinghamshire Council's fostering team. The council's code of conduct outlines the circumstances under which gifts can be given to children, emphasising the risk that gift giving can be 'misinterpreted by others as being a gesture either to bribe or groom'. Following a disciplinary process, Ms Morgan's employment was terminated. Her dismissal was primarily (the tribunal later found) for giving gifts to a child for whom she was responsible, without the authority of her manager, and for writing a case note in inappropriate terms consisting largely of her own thoughts and feelings. Ms Morgan unsuccessfully appealed her dismissal. In the appeal decision, the appeal officer stated that it was a matter of serious concern that Ms Morgan had chosen to withhold her autism by 'masking' throughout much of her employment, potentially putting vulnerable children at risk.[294]

In the employment tribunal, Ms Morgan claimed that she had been unfairly dismissed. She asserted that her conduct had been influenced by her autism and she asserted that, in dismissing her for her conduct, the council had subjected her to discrimination arising from her disability. Ms Morgan also claimed that the appeal officer's criticism of her for masking her autism was an act of harassment.

The employment tribunal found that Ms Morgan had not been unfairly dismissed. It also found that she had not been subjected to discrimination arising from her disability, because the council had justified her dismissal. However, the tribunal held that she had been subjected to harassment, in that the appeal officer had suggested that Ms Morgan had chosen to act deceitfully in concealing her autism when she had in fact simply learned behaviours which led to her masking her autism, and it was offensive of the appeal officer to suggest that she had acted deceitfully in doing so. She reasonably felt her dignity had been violated, it was ruled.

Ms Morgan appealed to the Employment Appeal Tribunal (EAT) and the council cross-appealed the harassment decision. The appeal and the cross-appeal were unsuccessful in October 2022. The keypoints in the tribunal's and the EAT's judgements were:

- The council had reasonably formed the view that Ms Morgan had breached professional boundaries and that the council could not be confident that she would not do so again if, instead of being dismissed, she were to be given a written warning.
- Ms Morgan knew that she needed proper authority for gift giving, and she also knew that such a breach was a potentially serious matter for which she could be dismissed.
- Although there was evidence that another employee had given an unauthorised gift and was not subjected to disciplinary action, this did not necessarily mean that Ms Morgan's dismissal had to be unfair.
- Although the appeal officer made a single comment, it was a considered observation in a formal letter, and it could potentially reach the high threshold required of a harassment claim.

This decision was not a departure from existing case law. However, it offered a useful reminder to employers that employees' disabilities (particularly hidden health conditions) may have an impact on their conduct and their performance. In considering what action to take in relation to performance and conduct issues, the employer must take the impact of the disability into account and justify any disciplinary action or dismissal, by showing they are pursuing a legitimate aim proportionately. Employers must also be careful not to harass individuals who are neurodiverse by criticising them for adopting strategies to help them cope with their conditions.

294 See: https://www.dacbeachcroft.com/en/What-we-think/Disability-discrimination-Dismissal-of-an-employee-whose-autism-influenced-their-conduct-was-neither

Ekaterina Harrison, who analysed this case in some detail, pointed out that:

> 'MM was dismissed from her position due to misconduct. The reasons for her dismissal included giving gifts to a child without obtaining permission from her manager and writing an inappropriate case note. MM argued that her dismissal was unfair and discriminatory, primarily because her autism had affected her judgement and understanding of the gift-giving policy and the appropriateness of the case note. The tribunal acknowledged that the conduct leading to MM's dismissal likely resulted from her autism. However, they also found that the employer was justified in dismissing her, as it was seen as a reasonable way to achieve a legitimate goal.
>
> 'A significant aspect of this case is that MM declined to undergo an occupational health assessment. As a result, her employer did not receive advice on whether her behaviour was likely to recur or the level of risk associated with continuing her employment. However, MM did succeed in her claim for disability-related harassment.'[295]

Harrison added that the guidance provided on gift-giving in this case did not seem to be very clear and left room for interpretation. For instance, the meaning of the term 'gifts of insignificant value' was not explicitly defined:

> 'In general, autistic individuals often encounter difficulties when faced with unclear instructions or guidelines. Ambiguous or vague wording can pose challenges for them, as they may struggle to interpret and fully understand the intended meaning. This can result in confusion and difficulties in accurately following directions. However, in this case, the tribunal found the evidence regarding MM's autism and its likely impact on her actions inconclusive. It was noted that MM had significant experience in her role, and it appeared that she intentionally chose to give gifts in violation of the guidance and policy.'[296]

Ms Morgan's manager identified the ability (or otherwise) to set boundaries as a potential issue affecting her capacity to maintain a fully professional relationship with the child. The employment tribunal did not consider this aspect in any great detail, but it appears that Ms Morgan went to some lengths to support the child. It was explained in the tribunal that Ms Morgan had wanted the child to understand that she was worthy of receiving gifts. She believed that every child, looked after or not, needed a 'golden thread' though their lives. In Ekaterina Harrison's view, this simply means 'that children should have good memories from their childhood that they can then reach for when times are tough, or even if it is just to tell their children about it someday'. Interestingly, Harrison speculated that Ms Morgan's 'hyper-empathy' towards the child in social care might have made it difficult for her to maintain appropriate professional boundaries: 'It would have been important to recognise this and provide her with the necessary support and training. However, this understanding and assistance should ideally have come from someone knowledgeable about autism. It is unfortunate that this avenue was not explored in this case.'[297]

295 Ekaterina Harrison, personal communication, October 20, 2023.

296 Ibid.

297 Ibid.

Useful resources and further guidance

- The Disability Law Service is a charity offering free legal advice: https://dls.org.uk/about-us/
- The Citizens' Advice Bureau can help you check whether you are protected from disability discrimination: www.citizensadvice.org.uk/law-and-courts/discrimination/check-if-youre-protected-from-discrimination/what-counts-as-disability/ (accessed January 2024).

Harassment (or bullying) in the workplace

Employers are mandated, to the extent reasonably practicable, to ensure the health, safety, and well-being of their employees, a principle enshrined in Section 2 of the Health and Safety at Work Act (1974). This duty naturally extends to include autistic employees who may have specific needs for their health, safety, and well-being at work. For instance, an autistic employee might require adjustments to their physical environment to reduce sensory stimuli like excessive light and noise. Employers should, to the extent reasonably practicable, address these needs to fulfil their duty.

Neurodivergent or neuroatypical people may have a disability for the purposes of the Equality Act (2010) even if they do not have a formal diagnosis. It is unlawful to treat someone unfavourably because of something arising as a consequence of their disability, unless the treatment is a proportionate means of achieving a legitimate aim. Disability-related harassment is also unlawful, which can cover making offensive remarks about neurodivergence.

With specific reference to Ms Morgan's legal victory in her claim against Buckingham Council, that she had been subject to disability-related harassment, Ekaterina Harrison has pointed out that the tribunal had found offensive a suggestion made by the appeal officer that Ms Morgan had chosen to withhold her autism by masking throughout much of her employment, 'potentially putting at risk the vulnerable children with whom you were working'. The implication of the appeal officer's statement, Harrison noted, was that Ms Morgan had intentionally acted deceitfully by hiding her autism, 'whereas in reality, she was engaging in a coping mechanism called "masking"... The fact that this statement was carefully considered and included in a formal letter provided additional evidence to classify it as harassment.'[298]

298 Ekaterina Harrison, in communication with the author.

Case study 23: Tom Holland

A coach firm, A&A Coach Travel Ltd, was ordered in 2023 to pay £30,000 to an autistic driver who had been called an 'imbecile' by work colleagues. A Leeds employment tribunal found that Tom Holland, 35, who has Asperger's syndrome, was subjected to frequent name-calling and abuse related to his disability and was threatened with dismissal from his job. Mr Holland was told: 'Just do what you are told to do, you special needs waste of space'. He was also called an 'imbecile', an 'illiterate cretin' and referred to as 'Mr Bean' (after the hapless TV character).

A&A Coach Travel Ltd took to social media to declare:

> 'As a responsible and caring company, we would like to reassure our employees and clients that we do not tolerate any forms of discrimination in the workplace. Disrespectful behaviour has no place in our working environment. While we are disappointed and taking it extremely seriously, an employment tribunal has ruled against us. This is a complex case. We are looking to appeal this decision, as this is not who we are.'

The tribunal in Leeds heard that, in the end, Mr Holland was constructively dismissed and, after he'd left the firm, he was reported to the Driver and Vehicle Licensing Agency (DVLA) and his former employer wrote to a new employer, putting his new job in jeopardy. The panel heard that Mr Holland would cry himself to sleep, dreading going into work every day and hoping the behaviour would stop.

The panel awarded Mr Holland £29,000 for injury to feelings plus £1,500 costs. Mr Holland, who has been a bus driver for more than seven years, said he is now 'much happier in life' working for a company near Doncaster:

> 'I was in a really dark place at the time. I didn't have anyone to talk to about what was going on and the fact that it carried on even after I left, with them contacting my new employer, meant I couldn't get away from it. Now I just want my award. The tribunal have found in my favour and I just want what's owed to me.'

Useful resources and further guidance

- If you think you are being bullied, try to talk to someone about what has been happening. This could be someone you trust at work or someone you see outside work.
- If you feel comfortable doing so, talk to other colleagues at work to see if anyone else feels they are being bullied or if they have seen you being bullied. It may be that the bully is targeting other people as well.
- Keep a detailed written record, if possible, as evidence.
- If you are a member of a union and there is a union safety representative where you work, you could arrange a confidential meeting to tell them what is happening.
- Visit National Bullying Helpline at: www.nationalbullyinghelpline.co.uk/
- Visit ACAS (Advisory, Conciliation and Arbitration Service): www.acas.org.uk/

Mediation

Not so long ago, if problems arose between an employer and a staff member, the issue was handled internally. Today, a company may be willing to instigate (and pay for) an independent mediation process between the aggrieved parties.

There are many different types of mediation: commercial, civil, marital and relationship, neighbourhood, special educational needs (SEN), and the type that was used in Northern Ireland and conflict zones. Each has its own characteristics and protocols. Many types of mediation involve two rooms: one for the joint mediation and one that remains empty, except when it is used as a break-out room for the mediator and one or other of the parties for private discussion, before resuming the joint process.

An episode of Radio 4's business programme, *The Bottom Line*, stated:

> 'Organisations have policies for investigating grievances, but they don't tend to have mechanisms for resolving disputes.' George Andruszkiewicz, who has many years' experience as an independent mediator in employment disputes, explains: 'Mediation is a dispute resolution process. It is not a quick fix, but neither is it overly time-consuming or expensive. It usually takes a day in total and can be split into half-days, if needed. It can be conducted face-to-face, or online via Zoom or Teams. Some people in dispute prefer the online option for a variety of reasons. Mediation involves a neutral person, a mediator, who is external to your organisation and who is less likely to be identified as part of management and more likely to build a rapport with both parties involved in the dispute. The mediation process is voluntary. It works best if the people involved want to give it a try, rather than being made to do it.'[299]

The mediation process usually involves two stages:

- **Pre-mediation**: Where there is a confidential online or face-to-face meeting with the mediator. This usually takes 60 to 90 minutes for each person. Confidentiality is a big factor: the mediator will not say anything to anyone else without express permission. People use the pre-meeting with the mediator as an opportunity to discuss their feelings, explore options, or to 'try out' what they would like to say to the other person.
- **Joint mediation**: This is also confidential. Both people sign up and agree that the discussion between them cannot be shared without the permission of both of them. This is joint pact that can help them to explore a gradual process of being honest with one another. The mediator is there to help guide them through this process safely and step by step.[300]

Mediation is flexible, with no set procedure. The process is managed by the mediator to suit the parties and in consultation with them. Rather than three people being together in a room all day, there are breaks and opportunities for reflection, as well as one-to-one sessions with the mediator.

299 George Andruszkiewicz, personal communication, December 14, 2023.

300 Ibid.

Mediation enables the parties to create solutions which may not be possible in formal processes, such as conduct or grievance procedures, or legal processes such as litigation or tribunals. It may be particularly useful if there is the possibility of a continuing relationship between the parties. The people engaging in mediation are open to the possibility that some of the issues may be resolved between themselves. If the mediation is successful, the end result is some form of agreement. This is usually written down and the two parties jointly decide who, if anyone else, gets to have sight of their agreement – or some form of short joint statement, should they prefer to keep the details private.[301]

Mediation can be used whether or not other formal dispute processes have commenced. In some organisations, a disciplinary or grievance is put on hold pending the mediation, and this may recommence or not, depending on the outcome of mediation.[302] As Andruszkiewicz points out, 'mediation can help people to begin to heal the rift between them on the day, but more often it is the start of a renegotiated working relationship. The two parties devise steps in consultation with one another, which can be built on in the weeks and months to come.'[303]

If the employee is a member of a trade union, he or she can ask a union representative to step in and assist. But this trade union representative will not normally be present at the actual meeting between the two parties to the dispute.

Andruszkiewicz explained that an employee may have chosen to disclose his or her autism, but this is by no means always the case. Some workplaces, such as universities, local authorities and NHS establishments appear to be more aware of the need to respect people with cognitive differences, or what Andruszkiewicz calls 'neuro-inclusion'. Andruszkiewicz says that, although these employers do not always specifically cite the Equality Act and its stipulated obligation to introduce 'reasonable adjustments', they do seem to be conscious of their duties in this area.[304]

Andruszkiewicz adds that, despite the anxiety often associated with autism, the autistic employees he has dealt with tend to stay fairly calm during the encounter and welcome his calm, fact-based approach.[305]

Sometimes, it is the line manager himself who is autistic, rather than the employee. Andruszkiewicz recalled one line manager at a university who was upset at constant interruptions from his colleagues. They came up with a solution: coloured Post-it notes placed on the corner of his computer to indicate to his colleagues that he was not to be disturbed at that time.[306]

301 Ibid.
302 Ibid.
303 Ibid.
304 Ibid.
305 Ibid.
306 Ibid.

Useful resources and further guidance

- George Andruszkiewicz, a registered, London-based Workplace Mediator and Training Facilitator, can be contacted via email at: georgeandrus9@gmail.com
- UK Mediation are a company based in Belper, Derbyshire, but operating throughout most of the UK. Over the decades, they have built up a reputation as a mediation service provider as well as a training organisation.
  - Website: admin@ukmediation.net

Summary

Autistic individuals represent an extraordinary untapped resource in the workplace. Many have special skills which make them better qualified for a particular role than their non-autistic counterparts. Yet very few are even in part-time employment in the UK. The recently published Buckland Review aims to reduce the employment gap by increasing employers' awareness about autism, enabling them to grasp the advantages of employing autistic individuals and facilitating the necessary adjustments for effective recruitment and support. In the meantime, despite the protection theoretically afforded by the Equality Act (2010), autistic employees continue to be subjected to unlawful treatment. These cases include direct discrimination (treating disabled individuals less favourably than others); indirect discrimination (implementing a policy or practice that puts those with a disability at a disadvantage compared to those without); discrimination arising from disability (treating disabled individuals unfavourably due to something that arises from their disability; duty to make reasonable adjustments in the workplace; harassment (subjecting disabled individuals to harassment through unwanted conduct related to their disability), and victimisation: employers (subjecting disabled individuals to victimisation for engaging in a protected act, such as, for example, initiating employment tribunal proceedings). In this context, whether, when or how to disclose your autism might seem to be a highly pertinent issue. However, no one is obliged to inform his or her employer – or potential employer – of a disability. The Equality and Human Rights Commission's Statutory Code of Practice regarding employment discrimination emphasises that an employer has to make reasonable efforts to determine whether a worker has a disability. In such cases, the employer should assess whether an individual may have a disability, even if it has not been disclosed. In legal disputes, mediation may be an option. Mediation enables the parties to the dispute to create solutions which may not be possible in formal processes, such as conduct or grievance procedures, or legal processes such as litigation or tribunals. This may be particularly useful if there is the possibility of a continuing relationship between the parties. Mediation can be used whether or not other formal dispute processes have commenced. If the employee is a member of a trade union, he or she can ask a union representative to step in and assist. But this trade union representative will not normally be present at the actual meeting between the two parties to the dispute.

Chapter 6: Autism and the criminal justice system

This chapter will focus on:

- Support for autistic suspects or witnesses.
- The rules of 'stop and search'.
- Your rights in police custody.
- Appropriate adults versus intermediaries.
- The police interview.
- Autism in the courtroom.
- The 'double-edged sword' of the autism defence.
- The injustice of joint enterprise.
- Autistic individuals in prison.
- Problems after prison.

As Ian Freckelton has noted, while criminal offending by autistic individuals is rare, the symptoms of such disorders have the potential to be relevant to almost every aspect of the criminal justice process, from police interviews with suspects, to accused persons' fitness to stand trial, a variety of defences to which accused persons may be entitled, especially self-defence, mental impairment/insanity, provocation and diminished responsibility, and to the sentencing process.[307]

Everyone wants to avoid autistic people coming into contact with the criminal justice system (CJS). However, as for the neurotypical (non-autistic) population, this can be a complex issue. There needs to be better support available at the earliest opportunity for autistic individuals, their families and those working with them to avoid what Laura Crane et al at the University of Bath call the 'potential negative spiral' which can lead to their getting into trouble.[308]

---

307 Freckelton I (2011) 'Autism Spectrum Disorders and the Criminal Law'. In: *A Comprehensive Book on Autism Spectrum Disorders* (2011), ed. Mohammad-Reza Mohammad, p249.

308 Laura Crane, Katie Maras, et al (2016) Experiences of Autism Spectrum Disorder and Policing in England and Wales: Surveying Police and the Autism Community. *J. Autism Dev. Disord.* **46** 2028–2041.

I have had only one personal, autism-related encounter with the police (so far). When my autistic son, Johnny, was still living at home, I took him to the park at the end of the road. He was around eight years old but already quite tall. Night began to fall and the cold was setting in. But Johnny didn't seem bothered at all. Indeed, he was more worried by the sensory discomfort caused by his clothing. This led him to start stripping off. By now, I was shivering and started to shout, as calmly as possibly, to Johnny that we had to go back home right away. There was no one else left in the playground. At this point, Johnny was practically naked. I began chasing him around the playground to catch him, while Johnny giggled at the fun of it all. That was precisely the moment a police car pulled up and a police officer climbed out and entered the playground. I suddenly realised, to my horror, what it must look like for an adult to be chasing a giggling, naked youth around a playground. I could imagine the prison bars already! I tried, in vain, to persuade the policeman that my son was autistic and often disrobed when he found his clothes uncomfortable. The policeman, however, had clearly received not a single moment of training in autism and did not believe my version of events.

It took quite a while to convince the officer of the truth – after moments of increasing terror. It is funny looking back now, but it certainly wasn't at the time. And if it was uncomfortable for me, a non-autistic adult, to come into contact with the police, imagine what it must be like for a person on the spectrum.

If autistic individuals come into contact with the police or other CJS professionals, there are a number of adaptations which can be made to improve their experiences and to facilitate equal access to justice. The problem is that many of these adaptations are precluded if the individual does not disclose his or her autism diagnosis in the first instance.

Initial contact with the criminal justice system

The study of offending in autistic individuals is a politically and emotionally charged area due to the nature of the condition and the long history of poor treatment of those affected by it, be they individuals, families or service providers. Moreover, it is challenging to obtain sufficient autistic participants they are often, due to the very nature of their condition, reluctant to engage with strangers.

There is a growing interest within clinical, prison and forensic settings as to what makes one autistic individual more prone to offending than another. The characteristics of autism have often been associated with offending. However, there is little more than anecdotal evidence to support this association. Furthermore, autistic features in offenders are not necessarily the determining factors in the perpetration of a crime. It would therefore be erroneous to generalise such a philosophy to all people with autism, a condition which, in any case, is extremely heterogeneous.

Professor Glynis Murphy, Professor of Clinical Psychology and Disability at the University of Kent's Tizard Centre, believes that the academic papers claiming that autistic individuals are over-represented in the criminal justice system are of very poor quality. She told me:

> 'The methodology of their papers is terrible. There is no good evidence for this purported over-representation. What usually happens is that they have a very biased sample. So, for instance, they might look at the proportion of people with autism in the secure services. But the fact that that number is high does not mean anything, because you need a total sample of everyone who has been diagnosed with autism, then you need to compare their rates of appearance in the criminal justice system with people who do not have autism who are of the same age and come from the same socio-economic background (because we all know that you are more likely to appear in the criminal justice system if you are socially deprived). The few good studies out there have found that autistic people are not over-represented in the criminal justice system.' [309]

One 2014 report stated that general factors which may make an autistic individual vulnerable to offending include 'poor school achievement, truancy, aggressive behaviour' and factors directly linked to autistic characteristics such as 'poor social understanding

309 Professor Glynis Murphy, personal communication, March 13, 2023.

or circumscribed interests; difficulties in adjusting to the diagnosis; and the impact of social exclusion. Considering that autistic individuals often rely on regimented routines, [a]ggressive behaviour may arise from a disruption of routines or stress from change in daily circumstances. Criminal acts might also stem from obsessions or special interests.' The factor, for example, that often links criminal offending and Asperger's syndrome is 'the pursuit of circumscribed interests, such as theft of electronics for the purpose of disassembling them'. On the other hand, however, autistic individuals might be less likely to commit crimes, considering 'the very rigid way' in which many of these individuals 'tend to keep to rules and regulations'[310].

Although there is no direct link between autism and sex crimes, the above-cited 2014 report indicated that an individual with a pervasive developmental disorder 'may have difficulty indicating his or her interest toward another person in a socially acceptable way, which may lead to touching or kissing a stranger.'[311] Autistic individuals may struggle to distinguish boundaries. For example, an individual with Asperger's may look at indecent images of children/or images of sexual abuse of children but have no sense of the harm it is causing the child.

There are a number of reasons why autistic individuals come into contact with the criminal justice system. Unfortunately, people with autism experience higher rates of victimisation and exploitation. This can precipitate contact with the CJS as either victims or witnesses. Behavioural differences may also lead to an autistic person experiencing arrest and questioning as an innocent suspect. This could occur, for instance, when behaviours such as 'stimming' (self-stimulating behaviours) are interpreted as intoxication or as an act of aggression.

Criminal responsibility

The age of criminal responsibility in England, Wales and Northern Ireland is ten years and in Scotland it is 12 years. This means that children under ten (or 12 in Scotland) cannot be arrested or charged with a crime, making the age of criminal responsibility (ACR) among the lowest in the whole of Europe. It is certainly out of step with what is currently known about brain maturation. In fact, the United Nations Committee on the Rights of the Child has criticised the UK situation. The UN Committee advocates a minimum ACR of no lower than 14 years of age.[312]

In the UK, children between the minimum ACR and 17 can be arrested and taken to court if they commit a crime. However, the CJS treats children differently from adults, and significant weight is attached to the age of the suspect if he or she is aged under 18.

Anecdotally, and unsurprisingly, the most successful interactions between police officers, police staff and autistic children occur when the police have a personal understanding of autism and adjust their behaviour accordingly. Unfortunately, autism-specific training is not currently provided by the UK College of Policing, and it is therefore left to individual

310 Cea CN (2014) Autism and the Criminal Defendant, *St. John's Law Review* **88** (2).

311 Ibid.

312 For more information, see https://researchbriefings.files.parliament.uk/documents/CBP-7687/CBP-7687.pdf (accessed March 2024).

police forces to develop and maintain autism-specific training. It is frequently the police officer's failure to recognise and understand the key facts of autism that leads to the rapid deterioration of the situation, resulting in adverse incidents which can affect autistic individuals for a long time afterwards. One of these key facts is communication difficulties, particularly when the police first arrive on the scene. This is very often a moment of heightened stress for everyone involved. Research has shown that when the police attempt to determine what has occurred, the ability of autistic individuals to communicate under the stress of interaction with the police is impaired. The police may misinterpret these communication difficulties as non-compliance and respond accordingly.

A solution, or at least a considerable benefit, may lie in the introduction of autism alert card schemes. Many police services now offer autism-specific card schemes such as the Metropolitan Police Autism Passport scheme or more generic schemes such as Safe Places. These not only allow the police to understand that they are dealing with an autistic individual but also inform them as to how best to communicate with that individual. As Dr Katie Maras, Senior Lecturer in Psychology and Deputy Director of the Centre for Applied Autism Research at the University of Bath, and her colleagues have pointed out, this is especially important for those who may become non-verbal under stress.[313]

As for the use of force, each police officer or staff member has to justify such use. The Police Code of Ethics stipulates the policing principles which members of the police service are expected to uphold.

Dr Richard Mills, who works a great deal with training the police, says that autism is not the blank canvas it used to be:

> 'The word "autism" is pretty well known, whereas it wasn't a few years ago. Not long ago, the police would not know what you were talking about or else they would have a Rain Man[314] idea of the condition. But most police officers simply do not have the time to digest the over-convoluted material which is often put out about autism. Most of the police officers I have met in this context who do not have a personal connection with autism (many do – they may have autistic children or they may be autistic themselves) are generally pretty decent and want to do the right thing, if they feel someone is vulnerable. In my experience, they are not under pressure to obtain a conviction. They really want to know how to conduct themselves so that the process is fair.'[315]

Further statistics

Two years after an Equality and Human Rights Commission report warned that the UK criminal justice system was failing those with learning disabilities and autistic people, a 2022 survey by Slavney-Cross *et al* in Cambridge of 93 defence lawyers found that an overwhelming majority of their clients were not provided with adequate support or

313 Maras K (2022) *Police interviewing of autistic people* [online]. Available at: www.autism.org.uk/advice-and-guidance/professional-practice/police-interviews (accessed March 2024).

314 The 1988 film starring Dustin Hoffman and Tom Cruise, for which Hoffman won an Academy Award for his portrayal of the autistic savant Raymond Babbit.

315 Dr Richard Mills, personal communication, November 8, 2022.

adjustments within the CJS. The study found that only half of autistic people (52%) were considered by the police to be vulnerable adults, even though the law recognises all autistic people as vulnerable. Over a third (35%) of autistic defendants were not given an 'appropriate adult' during police investigations, even though their diagnosis was known to police, and despite all autistic people being entitled under the law to have an appropriate adult present when being interviewed by the police. A further 18% did not have an 'appropriate adult' present because their diagnosis was not known to the police.[316] Appropriate adults act to safeguard the interests and rights of vulnerable defendants by ensuring that they are treated in a just manner and are able to participate effectively during an investigation.

According to the 2022 survey, a quarter (25%) of autistic people were given 'reasonable adjustments', with 38% not given any, even though lawyers stated that this would have been beneficial. This is despite the fact that all autistic people are entitled to reasonable adjustments under the law. A further 33% did not receive any adjustments, because their autism diagnosis was unknown at the time. Of the autistic people whose cases went to trial, more than one in five (22%) were not given any reasonable adjustments, even though their lawyers stated that this would have been helpful. Reasonable adjustments, such as using visual aids to assist with communication and allowing extra time to process information, can be made by the police to assist the detainee.[317]

In just under half of the cases that included a trial by jury (47%), the jury was not informed that the defendant was autistic. A total of 59% of prosecution barristers and 46% of judges or magistrates said or did something during the trial that made them concerned that they did not have an adequate understanding of autism.[318]

The 2022 study also found that lawyers were more likely to be concerned that their autistic clients would engage in self-harm behaviours compared with their non-autistic clients, and were more likely to report that their autistic clients experienced 'meltdowns' as a result of their involvement in the CJS. The research showed that those working within the CJS may be unaware that an individual is autistic, or of the implications of an autism diagnosis. They found that many autistic people do not disclose their diagnosis at the point of police contact or are themselves unaware they are autistic. However, as the study shows, even autistic defendants who disclose their diagnosis fail to receive reasonable adjustments.[319]

Dr Rachel Slavny-Cross, who led the study, said: 'Our research shows quite clearly that autistic adults are not receiving fair treatment within the criminal justice system. Without reasonable adjustments or support, this could place them at a significant disadvantage.' Another member of the research team, Dr Carrie Allison, declared: 'It's vital that jurors are provided with information about a defendant's autism and its implications,

316 Slavny-Cross R, Allison C, Griffiths S & Baron-Cohen S (2022) Autism and the criminal justice system: An analysis of 93 cases. *Autism Research* **15** (5) 904-914.

317 Ibid.

318 Ibid.

319 Ibid.

otherwise they are likely to misinterpret atypical behaviour exhibited by the defendant in court. Similarly, judges may fail to take into consideration mitigating factors that might otherwise influence sentencing.'[320]

One positive finding was that, in cases where their client was found to have committed a crime, 60% of judges saw the defendant's autism as a mitigating factor, and in these cases the majority of autistic people were given a suspended or reduced sentence.[321] However, the use of autism as a legal defence can sometimes prove to be a 'double-edged sword' (see Section 6.9)

Professor Sir Simon Baron-Cohen observed: 'There's an urgent need across the criminal justice system for increased awareness about autism. The police, lawyers, judges and jurors should be given mandatory training to be aware of how autism affects an individual's behaviour so that autistic defendants are treated fairly within the criminal justice system.'[322]

Dr Richard Mills, another of the UK's foremost autism researchers, agreed: 'We should be focusing on the lawyers. If there is a vulnerable person in a police station, he or she is entitled to legal representation. So the first stage is the lawyers. The second stage is to focus on the judges. The lawyers are often clueless and the parents have come to me for help.'[323]

'Stop and search'

It is unquestionably the case that there are likely to be times when autistic people will need the help of the police service. Building and maintaining trust between the police and the community is of paramount importance, particularly when considering those who have additional vulnerabilities.

Under Section 1 of the Police and Criminal Evidence Act (1984), UK police officers, or constables, are permitted to search people in public for offensive weapons or articles for use in connection with certain offences, including:

- Theft.
- Burglary.
- Fraud.
- Taking a vehicle without the owner's consent.
- Destroying or damaging property, for example, a spray paint can, which they intend to use in producing graffiti.
- Prohibited fireworks.
- Offences involving bladed or sharp-pointed articles such as knives.

320 Ibid.

321 Ibid.

322 Ibid.

323 Dr Richard Mills, personal communication, November 8, 2022.

Section 60 of the Criminal Justice and Public Order Act (1994) gives the police the power to search people in a defined area during a specific time-period for dangerous instruments or offensive weapons. Section 23(2) of the Misuse of Drugs Act (1971) allows a constable to search a person suspected of being in possession of a controlled drug and detain that individual for the purpose of the search.

When police officers are trained, they are often taught the mnemonic **GOWISELY** to help them remember the steps to be followed before a stop and search takes place. This stands for:

G – Grounds. A police officer cannot simply carry out a stop and search on a whim. There must be reasonable grounds for suspicion. What this means in practice is that:

- The officer must genuinely suspect that they will find the item searched for (not the likelihood that the person being searched is committing an offence).
- It must be objectively reasonable for them to suspect the items will be found, given the information available to them.

O – Object. Officers must give a clear explanation of the object for which the individual is being searched and the purpose of the search.

W – Warrant card. A warrant card is proof of identification and confirmation of position, which police officers carry. If a police officer carrying out a stop and search is not in uniform, they must show the person being searched their warrant card. Even if the officers are in uniform, they should show their warrant card if asked to do so.

I – Identity. The officer or officers conducting the search are required to give their name and number, which is unique to them.

S – Station. The officer or officers conducting the search are required to give the name of the police station to which they are attached.

E – Entitlement. The person being searched should be told that he or she is entitled to a copy of the written record of the search when it is finished. They should also be informed that they can get a copy of the record within three months of the search by making a request at any police station.

L – Legal Power Used. The person being searched should, in this case, be told that the power being used is contained in Section 1 of the Police and Criminal Evidence Act (1984).

Y – You are being detained. The person being searched must be told that he or she is being detained for the purpose of the search. This means that the person is not free to walk away until informed that the detention is over. Police officers do not need to obtain consent to conduct a lawful search.

When in public, police officers are restricted to searching outer clothing only. When being trained, officers are often taught the mnemonic 'JOG,' which stands for:

- Jacket.
- Outer coat.
- Gloves.

These are the only items which an officer can ask a person to remove during a search if in a public place. If officers believe a more thorough search is needed, this must not be done in public and may even need to take place at a police station. It is important to remember that the person being searched is not obliged to give his or her name and address. Police officers may also use reasonable force to carry out a lawful search. A person being searched can be handcuffed, but the use of handcuffs by police officers is certainly not routine.

Brown and Kennedy report

As noted in *Stop and Search – Guidance for Autistic People and Police Officers*, by Metropolitan Police Superintendent Dion Brown and barrister Sean Kennedy[324], stop and search:

> '...is a practice which arouses strong debate... On the one hand, there are those who think it should be abolished, as it does more harm than good. Others think its use should be more limited. The police, on the other hand, think that when used professionally, intelligently, and lawfully, it provides them with an essential tool to protect the public, tackle crime and keep the streets safe. A good example of where stop and search can be employed to promote public safety is in tackling knife crime. The news often contains tragic and heart-rending stories of serious injuries and deaths of people who are stabbed. Stop and search is an indispensable practice in the fight to get knives off our streets. It is no exaggeration to say that the list of victims of knife crime is far too long – but it would be even longer if the police did not use stop and search...'[325]

Brown, who has an autistic son, and Kennedy, who is autistic himself and has autistic children, note:

> 'The police are aware of people's concerns and are fully committed to getting better at stop and search. This is why police officers are now required to video stop and search... All the police services fully appreciate that being stopped and searched can be unwanted. It can cause annoyance and even anxiety and stress. Therefore, they make it very clear that this power must never be misused. For autistic people, stop and search can be especially problematic. If they are not aware of what is happening, such contact with police officers can be very uncomfortable. It can sometimes cause them to react in a way that can be misinterpreted as being uncooperative, but it is important to remember that this behaviour is likely to arise in consequence of their disability.'[326]

In their 2022 report, Brown and Kennedy offer two scenarios based on a number of real-life experiences of when an autistic person was approached by two police officers. The two scenarios illustrate how the same situation can have two very different outcomes.

---

324 Brown D & Kennedy S (2002) *Stop and Search – Guidance for Autistic People and Police Officers* [online]. Available at: www.met.police.uk/SysSiteAssets/foi-media/metropolitan-police/priorities_and_how_we_are_doing/corporate/stop-search-guidance-autistic-people-police-officers-large-print.pdf (accessed March 2024).

325 Ibid.

326 Ibid.

In Scenario 1

PC Mick O'Brien and PC Amritpal Grewal were in a response car and took a call about a recent burglary in a nearby street. They were told that the suspect was a white European male in his early 20s who was wearing a red top, jeans, and black trainers, and was approximately six feet tall. The officers were also informed that the suspect had stolen some high-value jewellery and had damaged property. Five minutes later, they came across Adrien, an 18-year-old who had been diagnosed with Asperger's syndrome at the age of ten. As usual when he was stressed, to reduce sensory input, Adrien was wearing his hood on and was listening to loud music through headphones on his smartphone. Given Adrien's visual similarity to the suspect, PCs O'Brien and Grewal stopped the car. They got out, greeted him, and asked him how he was and whether he would mind telling them where he was going. On seeing the officers, Adrien started to panic. He had decided that he did not trust the police. Having become stressed and anxious, Adrien decided that the best thing to do was run away. PCs O'Brien and Grewal called for assistance and then pursued Adrien. They followed him into an alleyway with no exit. Thinking he was trapped, Adrien lashed out at the officers. The situation had now deteriorated even though Adrien had done nothing wrong when the officers initially addressed him.[327]

In Scenario 2

When PCs O'Brien and Grewal stopped to greet Adrien, his response was different. Rather than being wholly influenced by the one-sided views he had heard about the police, Adrien had decided to do his own research. He had heard about the many challenges faced by police officers when trying to fight crime. He also found the Autism Alert Card and decided to carry one with him wherever he went. This time, when Adrien was stopped, and even though he was not in the best of moods, he responded by pulling down his hood, turning off his music and greeting the officers. He introduced himself and told them he was going home after attending a gamers' club. He then asked the officers whether he could reach into his pocket to retrieve his Autism Alert Card. After quickly ensuring that no members of the public were nearby, Mick and Amritpal told Adrien that this was perfectly acceptable. As Brown and Kennedy state: 'If people had been observing, they would have handled things differently as all officers are aware of the need to treat sensitive personal information with the utmost confidence.'[328]

Adrien handed over his alert card. Nevertheless, although the officers now knew Adrien was autistic, they still had a duty to try and find the burglar. PC Grewal pointed out that her nephews and nieces were all into computer games. PC O'Brien then chimed in by saying that he could not play computer games well, even if he was paid. They invited Adrien to talk about his gaming activities. PCs O'Brien and Grewal concluded that Adrien had no connection with the burglary, but their opinion may have been different if his attitude had been confrontational, evasive or uncompliant. Adrien knew about 'stop and search'. This is something he had wanted to avoid because he did not like being touched by anyone he did not know, even if it was a police officer. He also knew that police officers could not simply stop and search anyone without good reason. He had even taken the

327 Ibid.

328 Ibid.

time to learn the steps that, in most cases, police officers had to go through to make such a search lawful. In any case, Adrien knew he had done nothing wrong and took the view that working productively with police officers was a positive approach. The officers were very conscious of the need to pursue the suspect, so PCs O'Brien and Grewal apologised for not being able to talk but asked Adrien whether he would update them on his progress at the gamers' club should he see them again.[329]

According to the 2022 report, Scenario 2 illustrates an important point: ensuring a positive outcome for an autistic person innocently involved in the criminal justice system is a two-way process. The police must first be aware that the person they have approached is autistic and be trained in how to handle an autistic individual, given these individuals' particular behavioural and cognitive traits. At the same time, autistic people must have the confidence to interact with police officers in a way that avoids unnecessary conflict and misunderstandings.[330]

Unfortunately, police training in autism remains extremely patchy across the UK. I spoke to one policeman at Bishopsgate Police Station in London who had recently undergone a neurodiversity course. But such courses remain the exception. Dr Chloe Holloway-George, an assistant professor in criminal law and criminal justice at the University of Nottingham, said that awareness had increased: 'There has been a big drive over the past few years, which has actually been led by the police. But there is no centrally delivered training. The police are doing the best they can with the tools they have.'[331]

It is my firm conviction that autism training should be mandatory for *all* police officers *throughout* the UK, and that this training should be introduced by the British Ministry of Justice as soon as possible.

Nigel Archer, a retired police inspector working for the charity Autism West Midlands as Criminal Justice System Development Coordinator, says police officers need to be able to identify the behavioural clues that may indicate an autistic individual so that appropriate measures can be taken to ensure they are treated as vulnerable persons by the system:

> 'When responding to a call that involves [an autistic person], officers may face a situation that will challenge the training, instincts and professional conduct of even the most experienced. Whilst officers may approach what they perceive to be a 'run of the mill' incident in a manner they have developed to ensure their own safety and that of others, their mere presence may cause what they perceive as inappropriate response by a person with an autism spectrum condition (ASC). A person with an ASC may not understand the implications of their behaviour or the consequences of their actions, especially if their actions appear aggressive. They may run, failing to respond to an order to stop or drop to the floor and begin rocking back and forth or avoid eye contact with the officer. Officers should not misinterpret these actions as a reason for increased use of force, as an ASC person may escalate into tantrum-like behaviour from fear, frustration or confusion. The

329 Ibid.

330 Ibid.

331 Dr Chloe Holloway-George, personal communication, September 12, 2022.

individual with an ASC cannot conceptualise meanness or acts of purposeful injury to others. They just want the circumstances to change and become less frightening, but may not have the ability to formulate a way to implement such a change.'[332]

Useful resources and guidance

- *Stop and Search – Guidance for Autistic People and Police Officers*, by Detective Chief Inspector Dion Brown and Sean Kennedy, 2002: www.met.police.uk/SysSiteAssets/foi-media/metropolitan-police/priorities_and_how_we_are_doing/corporate/stop-search-guidance-autistic-people-police-officers-large-print.pdf (accessed March 2024).
- *Autism: A guide for police officers and staff* – First published by the National Autistic Society in 2005. Revised in 2008, 2011 and 2017. Contains useful information on how to recognise autism, how to handle arrests, managing an autistic suspect in custody and interviewing autistic victims, witnesses or suspects. Available at: www.safeguardingadultsinbexley.com/wp-content/uploads/Autism-Booklet-for-Police-Officers.pdf (accessed March 2024).
- 'Alert Card Schemes', by the National Police Autism Association – a useful guide to autism alert card schemes right across the UK: www.npaa.org.uk/alert-card-schemes/ (accessed March 2024). For autistic individuals, an autism alert card or passport is a document you can carry to help communicate your needs as an autistic/neurodivergent individual to police officers or other officials when you are away from home. The card typically contains your details and advice for the officer to whom you are speaking. Alert card schemes are run in most police areas across the UK.
- Some British police forces have similar initiatives:
  - Safe Places, as used by Avon & Somerset Police, assists the cardholder to get in touch with police, if needed, and links to a network of local safe locations such as police stations and council offices.
  - The Pegasus system, used by Nottinghamshire Police and a number of other forces, features a database shared with other 999 emergency services and a card with a unique PIN to allow emergency calls to be made quickly. Pegasus was developed by the Paralympian Chris Channon.

The rights of autistic individuals in police custody

Dr Chloe Holloway-George at the University of Nottingham has conducted research aimed at improving the support of autistic individuals in detention settings through changes to practice, policy and the custody environment and has helped to co-produce an improved autism training package and toolkit for custody staff.[333] She has also identified the use of non-specific questions during the booking-in process as problematic.

332 Archer N (undated) *When Two Different Worlds Collide (Autism Spectrum Conditions and The Criminal Justice System)* [online]. https://livingautism.com/two-different-worlds-collide-autism-spectrum-conditions-criminal-justice-system/ (accessed March 2024).

333 See www.nottingham.ac.uk/news/autism-awareness-training-for-police (accessed March 2024).

For instance, autistic detainees have noted that social communication difficulties are intensified when ambiguous language is used. (For example, 'Where do you live?' rather than 'What's your address?')[334]

> 'We focused on what needed to change to improve the situation for autistic people in custody all the way up to the interview,' Dr Holloway-George told me. 'We found there needed to be changes to practice, environment and policy or legislation. Since there is no custody-specific training, we thought we might as well use the findings we had already obtained to identify what would make the biggest difference. We produced visual resources for autistic people so that custody staff could inform those individuals about the process. We also produced a training video. We launched this in 2022, just before the Covid pandemic, and started rolling it out on an ad hoc basis, whenever we received a request. When I did an evaluation in March 2022 to see whether forces had been using it, I found there was understandable disruption due to Covid. We would now like to feed our material into discussions with the Ministry of Justice.'[335]

She said her toolkit had been very well received. 'But supported implementation is still an issue. A lot of this is not statutory. It is still down to individual police forces as to whether they adhere to it or enforce it. Our next stage is to try to bring about policy change. Many forces have produced useful information, but they do not share it. Good practice must be shared, in order to standardise it. That's our goal.'[336]

Nigel Archer, the above-quoted retired police officer, has written:

> 'If officers take a person into custody and even remotely suspect [autism], to reduce the risk they must be treated as vulnerable in line with the requirements of the Police and Criminal Evidence Act (PACE) (1984) and will require constant watch during their stay. Advance notice to the Custody Unit to ensure the desk and entrance area is clear of all other persons on arrival would be advisable to keep the person calm. A doctor should always be called and the suspicion of ASC made clear to them. An appropriate adult who knows them and understands their behaviours should be sought immediately in order to help reduce their anxiety and assist officers with their processes to have any hope of achieving any progress'[337]

Police custody suites can be noisy and frightening places for any detainee, whether autistic or not. Nevertheless, there are specific features which can be particularly challenging for autistic detainees. Some have reported finding the lighting or loud sounds distressing. For many, the unpredictability of the process is disturbing: it is not uncommon for detainees to be kept waiting for some time before they are 'booked in'

---

334 Holloway-George C, Munro N, Jackson J, Phillips S & Ropar D (2022) Exploring the autistic and police perspectives of the custody process through a participative walkthrough. *Res Dev Disabil*, Feb: 97: 103545.

335 Dr Chloe Holloway-George, personal communication, September 12, 2022.

336 Ibid.

337 Archer N (undated) *When Two Different Worlds Collide (Autism Spectrum Conditions and The Criminal Justice System)* [online]. https://livingautism.com/two-different-worlds-collide-autism-spectrum-conditions-criminal-justice-system/ (accessed March 2024).

and even then are kept waiting, sometimes in police cells, for several hours before the interview takes place. To reduce the stress levels, the detainee should be kept clearly informed at all times about the length of the wait.

At the start of the process, the arresting officer is required by law to explain to the custody staff why a detainee has been arrested and is in custody in the first place. When the officer explains this to the autistic detainee, he or she may disagree with the narrative or even the allegation offered, and this can understandably increase anxiety levels. It is essential that the officer emphasises that no decision has yet been taken as to what is to happen.

Unsurprisingly, the most positive outcomes usually rely on a custody staff member having a specific understanding of autism from personal experience. The obvious risk for an autistic detainee is that failure to identify him or her as vulnerable during the booking-in process can result in their being denied access to an appropriate adult or additional well-being support.

A 2020 report by Britain's National Appropriate Adult Network (NAAN) found almost four out of ten suspects in police custody (39%) had a 'mental disorder'; but the need for an appropriate adult was recorded in just six per cent of these cases. Of course, autism is not a 'mental disorder' but the picture is similarly bleak here: a major study by three criminal justice inspectorates published in 2021 estimated that as many as half of all people going into prison could be neurodivergent. 'We were struck by the number of times the word "difficult" was used in evidence,' wrote Charlie Taylor, Justin Russell and Sir Thomas Winsor, chief inspectors of prisons, probation and constabulary, respectively.[338]

Case study 24: Louis De Zoysa

A 26-year-old autistic man, Louis De Zoysa, was sentenced to a whole-life order (meaning he will spend the rest of his life in prison) for the murder of Sergeant Matt Ratana, whom he shot at point-black range with a gun he had smuggled into a custody centre in Croydon, south London, in September 2020, while handcuffed.

De Zoysa's lawyers had argued a defence of diminished responsibility and claimed he had suffered 'an autistic meltdown' caused by the stress of the arrest and confined space, but after a three-week trial at Northampton crown court, a jury convicted him of murder. Passing sentence in July 2023, Mr Justice Johnson said: 'You did not have an autistic meltdown. Your actions were voluntary, they were controlled, they were deliberate, you acted in cold blood. The video footage shows you were treated with conspicuous compassion and kindness. None of the officers gave any reason for you to feel at risk of harm. You deliberately concealed the gun from the police. You made strenuous efforts to retrieve the gun while your hands were handcuffed behind your back. You had time and space to consider what to do. Autism is not to blame for your decision to murder Sgt Ratana; you are to blame for that.'[339]

The court heard that De Zoysa had suffered 'vicious bullying' at school and was beaten by his father at home. He had not received a formal autism diagnosis until he was nearly 14. At the time of the shooting, he was living independently in Banstead, Surrey, had worked successfully ➔

338 Bath C & Dehaghani R (2020) *There to Help 3* [online]. Available at: www.appropriateadult.org.uk/phocadownload/Research/2020_There_To_Help_3.pdf (accessed March 2024).

339 See www.theguardian.com/uk-news/2023/jul/27/killer-met-police-officer-sgt-matt-ratana-jailed-louis-de-zoysa (accessed March 2024).

as a tax analyst at HMRC, and was in a long-term relationship. A stash of weapons, including a shortened infantry rifle, numerous types of ammunition, a pipe gun and a dummy launcher, were found at De Zoysa's home after the killing. A search of his digital devices confirmed his interest in weapons and uncovered material relating to ideologies, including Right-wing extremism, Islamic extremism and homophobia, in all of which he later denied being interested.

Ratana, 54, was the first police officer to be killed inside a British police station. Originally from New Zealand, he worked as the custody sergeant at the Windmill Road custody centre in Croydon, where De Zoysa was brought in the early hours of September 25, 2020, after being arrested for possession of cannabis and ammunition. A gun concealed in a holster around De Zoysa's chest was missed during an initial search by officers, and he managed to retrieve the weapon while travelling in a police van to the centre, despite his hands being handcuffed behind his back. De Zoysa received a self-inflicted gunshot wound to the neck during the incident, and a subsequent blood clot has left him with brain damage and physical disability. His lawyer, Imran Khan KC, said communication problems caused by his injuries meant it 'may never be possible to know exactly what was going through his mind' at the time of the shooting. 'The precise motive for why he shot Sgt Ratana may never be known. We may never know why he had a loaded revolver on him. There was no evidence he went out to shoot a police officer, or anyone in particular.'[340]

De Zoysa, who is now serving his sentence at HMP Belmarsh in south-east London, showed no obvious emotion as he was told he would spend the rest of his life in prison.

Appropriate adults versus intermediaries

When a person is booked into police custody, he or she is entitled, under certain circumstances, to be accompanied and represented by another person of adult age. These circumstances are based on vulnerability, most commonly due to age – the Police and Criminal Evidence Act (PACE) (1984) states that all juvenile detainees (that is, under the age of 18) must have an appropriate adult (AA) in custody. The AA's role is to facilitate communication with the detainee and ensure that his or her best interests are represented. The AA does not have to remain with the detainee during the entire stay in custody, but must be present at certain key times, including the moment the detainee is read his or her legal rights after being booked in, during a strip search (usually required if the detainee is believed to be concealing drugs), and when the detainee is interviewed. An AA is usually a parent or carer for a child detainee, or a friend or other family member not connected with the matter being investigated. The AA may also be a social work professional or a trained volunteer.

Codes of Practice

Before July 2018, when the revised Codes of Practice took effect, PACE Code C referred to detainees who were 'mentally disordered' or otherwise 'mentally vulnerable' as requiring an AA. The term 'mental disorder' is a throwback to a less enlightened age. Most autistic people would rightly feel that a condition which is part of their identity is not a mental disorder and would probably hesitate to describe themselves as 'mentally vulnerable'. Nevertheless, there are practical reasons why an autistic person of any standing in life

340 Ibid.

would need an AA in police custody. No matter how intelligent, independent or successful that autistic individual may be, or how well-trained the officers dealing with them, the difficulties with social communication inherent in the condition may lead to a detainee missing the nuance of a question, or feeling obliged to make disclosures which could have far-reaching consequences.

Following representations made by stakeholders and members of the public, the revised Codes of Practice introduced a new description of 'vulnerable', linking to the Mental Health Act, which in turn lists conditions, including autism, which may cause a person to require support in a custody setting. The new Codes of Practice acknowledge that there are many reasons outside diagnosed conditions or illnesses that may require a person in custody to have an AA. These reasons include: the behaviour of the detainee, the mental health and capacity of the detainee, what the detainee says about himself or herself, information supplied by relatives or friends of the detainee, information gathered from police officers and staff and from police records, and information from health and social care professionals, including liaison and diversion services, and other professionals who know, or have had previous contact with, the detainee.

Dr Richard Mills told the author that 'it is at this stage that you run into a lot of problems. Many people I have seen in the past were not seen as vulnerable at the time of their arrest. They present perfectly "normally" at first.'[341] .

According to the National Appropriate Adult Network (NAAN), hundreds of thousands of 'vulnerable people' are going unidentified when detained or questioned by police in England and Wales. This means that people with learning disabilities, mental health conditions, and autistic people do not get the support required by law, including an appropriate adult. The law defines a category of 'vulnerable people' as those who may:

- Be highly suggestible or eager to please.
- Become confused.
- Have difficulty understanding the implications of police procedures and processes.
- Have difficulty understanding the significance of what they are told, of questions they are asked, or of their replies.
- Not understand or be able to exercise their rights and entitlements.

This does not mean that people are not capable of providing evidence. It means that, if their needs are not met:

- Their rights may not be fully respected.
- Their welfare may be harmed.
- Their ability to participate effectively may be limited.

This can lead to unreliable information being obtained, including false confessions.

341 Dr Richard Mills, personal communication, November 8, 2022.

The appropriate adult is a mandatory procedural safeguard for suspects who may be mentally vulnerable. There are many tasks that police may not carry out without an appropriate adult being present. These include interviews, identity procedures and some forms of search.

Failure to secure an AA may result in:

- A miscarriage of justice.
- Evidence being ruled inadmissible in court.

NAAN research

Research conducted by the NAAN has shown that, while recorded need for AAs is improving, progress is slow. In 2012/13, UK police forces recorded the need for an AA in only 2.7% of adult detentions. By 2021, this had risen to 6.9%. However, most 'vulnerable people' are not identified as needing an appropriate adult. The recorded rate of need for appropriate adults (in adult detentions) varies hugely across police forces. Compared to custody officers, investigating officers may be less familiar with how to identify vulnerable people and the relevant safeguards.[342]

In 2002, the NAAN began working on a joint project with Cardiff University to create three ten-minute videos on PACE vulnerability for police officers, custody nurses and liaison and diversion teams. According to these videos, once it has been decided that a client should be assessed, and their consent has been carefully obtained, it is important to find a psychologist who has experience of assessing adults and, in the case of women, understands the female autism phenotype (the particular way in which autistic women can present – this is a very new area in which research is still very much in its infancy).[343]

Ultimately, the decision as to whether to provide an AA for a detainee lies with the custody sergeant. The good news is that, in addition to providing training to custody staff, several UK police forces, such as Avon & Somerset Police, now explicitly ask detainees whether they are autistic as part of the booking-in process. These measures will help to ensure that all autistic people held in police custody are treated fairly and given the support they need.

In England, Wales and Northern Ireland, police are required to make contact with an AA 'as soon as practicable' when detaining, voluntarily interviewing or issuing out-of-court disposals (where an offender has to admit he or she is guilty in order to be issued with out-of-court resolution) to anyone under 18 years of age. The police must start by asking a parent or legal guardian to undertake the AA role. If this is not possible, an AA will be provided. The use of a family member as an AA is double-edged. The family member may not understand the nature of the AA role, but he or she is likely to be knowledgeable about the young person's needs and style of communication and the mere presence of a family member may bring comforting familiarity.

342 See www.appropriateadult.org.uk/policy/research/there-to-help-2?view=article&id=268:provision&catid=9#:~:text=Our%20research%20has%20shown%20that,only%202.7%25%20of%20adult%20detentions. (accessed March 2024).

343 Ibid.

The Appropriate Adult Service

The provision of Appropriate Adult services is a bit of a postcode lottery - although the Police and Criminal Evidence Act (1984) determines that all juveniles and vulnerable adults should be provided with an AA in order to safeguard their rights, entitlements and welfare whilst in custody. Each Police Force interprets and provides differently. The Met use two main providers, the Appropriate Adult Service and AA UK, although some Custody Suites also have regular volunteers who provide support.

To take on an appropriate adult, a person has to be assessed as vulnerable. Sarah Doyle, a vastly experienced London-based appropriate adult, described the booking-in procedure at the custody desk:

> 'The detainee is brought in by the arresting officers, generally in handcuffs. They are booked in by a custody sergeant. The custody sergeant asks a series of questions after the arresting officer has detailed arrest justification: These include: "Do you want to see the healthcare professional for any reason? Do you have, or have you ever been told you have, any mental health condition or vulnerability? Do you have, or have you ever been told you have, autism, Asperger's or ADHD?" It is surprising how forthcoming the detainees are. These are the most deprived, disadvantaged, downtrodden members of society. Many have criminal records already.
>
> The Police and Criminal Evidence Act (1986) ensures that an appropriate adult is provided for any Juvenile (under 18) or Vulnerable Adult brought into Custody. Most Juveniles have a parent/family member to act as their appropriate adult. The AA is primarily someone who can look after their emotional well-being/ facilitate communication and observe that officers follow the correct procedures. Approximately 80 per cent of under-aged people who are arrested do actually have a parent (or a social worker) as their appropriate adult. I am called in when the juvenile does not have anyone available. Once you declare your vulnerability, the police have to call an appropriate adult, or whoever their provider is. They must do this. When I get to the police station, they give me the "front sheet". Then I fill in the true picture from my own observations of the detainee. My role, as an AA, is to speak to the detainee privately and go through the series of questions, and hopefully alleviate their concerns. Very occasionally; a detainee will refuse to engage with me, because they feel affronted at the suggestion that they have vulnerabilities.'[344]

Doyle said the appropriate adult is left alone with the detainee:

> 'The appropriate adult meets privately with the detainee before they go into interview. I am there to support the detainee. I ask them whether they have been treated respectfully by custody staff. They invariably confirm that they have. I then ask several welfare questions to ensure they are being well cared for. I will check they understand the legal process and are prepared for their meeting with a solicitor. I make it clear that I am not their solicitor. I do not talk to them about the alleged

344 Sarah Doyle, personal communication, November 14, 2022.

> offence. I just want to know that they are satisfied with the way they have been treated and that they understand what is happening. My conversation with the detainee is not being recorded: it is entirely confidential.' '[345]

Some detainees are extremely anxious. If they indicate or express any self-harm intentions they will be placed on "Constant Watch" to ensure their well-being.

> Doyle emphasised that, for some people on the autism spectrum who come from 'disadvantaged backgrounds,' the police station can actually represent a temporary refuge. 'Three nights ago, an autistic detainee's alleged crime was being evicted from his bedsit. The landlord called the police and said there had been a break-in. He was arrested at 4pm. I arrived at around 11pm. By that time, he had been given several meals. Although he had a significant criminal record; he had never broken bail before and was being instructed to leave the station on bail and to return several weeks later. He refused to leave, because he had nowhere to go. The police said that he was bailed and had to leave. In the end, it took about an hour and a half to persuade him to leave. It was 2am. He said he refused to leave until 8 the following morning. It was pitiful, shocking. The contrast between the haves and the have-nots is appalling. I know of cases of people who are released from custody and immediately smash up a car outside so they can get re-arrested. There is no support for them whatsoever in the outside community.'[346]

> Doyle stays until the detainee is released or charged. Within 24 hours, they have to be either released, charged and bailed, or charged and detained. 'The solicitor could be called within hours. I may be called in to prepare them for the interview. It is very rare that I am concerned about treatment. My view of custody staff has dramatically improved.'[347]

Dr Katie Maras explained that the problem with appropriate adults is that their quality varies and their remit is different from the so-called intermediaries:

> 'If someone is a victim or a witness and is vulnerable, they should have a registered intermediary, If they are a suspect, they should have an appropriate adult – but they don't always. Suspects have been eligible for non-registered intermediaries, but they never get used. There have been changes within the past year to try to extend the provision of intermediaries to vulnerable suspects and defendants.' [348]

Intermediaries are independent communication specialists, introduced in England and Wales in 2004 as a result of the Youth Justice and Criminal Evidence Act (1999). A Registered Intermediary is an impartial, trained professional who facilitates communication between vulnerable victims/witnesses and members of the justice system. Assistance may be provided at various stages, from before trial at the investigative interview through to court. They may recommend adaptations and directly facilitate communication during cross-examination (whether pre-recorded or live during the trial). Although intermediaries

345 Ibid.

346 Ibid.

347 Ibid.

348 Dr Katie Maras, personal communication, September 9, 2022.

can also facilitate evidence provided by defendants, there is currently no statutory framework for this (as is the case for vulnerable victims/witnesses). At present, such assistance – if approved by a trial judge – can only be provided in the form of a 'non-registered intermediary' (although recent proposals by the Ministry of Justice indicate that the provision of intermediaries for defendants, as well as all other parties in non-criminal courts, is in the process of being formalised and regulated). Instead, the provision of an AA is required for all vulnerable suspects in England and Wales, whose role it is to safeguard the interests and rights of vulnerable defendants by ensuring that they are treated in a just manner and are able to participate effectively during an investigation.

'The role of the appropriate adult is basically to look after the rights of the suspect, whereas the role of the intermediary is to facilitate communication,' said Dr Maras. 'They have slightly different roles, and this is extremely important. Suspects have been eligible for non-registered intermediaries, but they never get used. They tend to get, if anything, an appropriate adult. There have been changes within the past year to try to extend the provision of intermediaries to vulnerable suspects and defendants. So I think there is a recognition that appropriate adults and intermediaries have different roles.'[349]

Sarah Doyle feels that the distinction between the roles of the AA and the intermediary (the former's supposedly being solely to ensure the well-being of the detainee and the latter's being to help communication) may be over-simplistic: 'It's a combination. A lot of detainees are autistic, but they are not necessarily cognitively impaired.'[350]

Anyone can be an AA. No qualification is required. 'Appropriate adults do have their uses, but I think it's vital to support the communication aspect, which is not the role of the appropriate adult, or to a lesser extent,' Dr Maras explains. 'People should be informed that they are entitled to an intermediary to help facilitate communication and two-way understanding. But they do not always know this.'[351]

Registered Intermediaries

Once the client has received a diagnosis of autism and the psychologist has said that an intermediary assessment would be beneficial, what next? Registered Intermediaries are only available to prosecution witnesses and are allocated via the Witness Intermediary Service. Thus, intermediaries for defence witnesses/defendants are all 'unregistered' but not necessarily less competent or less qualified. They can be instructed via one of at least two private companies that cover England and Wales.

After the report has been acquired and the intermediary has made his or her recommendations, it may be appropriate to make an application to the court. This is done on the basis of the court's inherent powers, as per C v Sevenoaks Youth Court [2009] EWHC 3088. Rule 18.27 of the Criminal Procedure Rules 2020 also applies. It is

349 Ibid.

350 Ibid.

351 Ibid.

extremely rare for the court to grant a defence application for an intermediary to attend on the defendant throughout the whole trial. If the intermediary is permitted to assist the defendant at all, it is ordinarily allowed only while the defendant gives evidence.

There are two kinds of intermediary. The registered intermediary scheme is run by the Ministry of Justice. To be registered, you have to do your training with them, pass the assessments and complete a minimum of 24 days of RI work in a year, including 12 days of face-to-face casework.

Under the other scheme, you can become an HMCTS-approved supplier (His Majesty's Courts and Tribunal Service). The training is not apparently as intense. It is far more regulated than before. They handle defendants, rather than witnesses or victims. They are paid not by the Ministry of Justice but by police or the Crown Prosecution Service.[352]

The police interview: suspects, witnesses and victims

When suspects are interviewed in England and Wales, the PEACE (Preparation and Planning; Engage and explain; Account, clarify and challenge; Closure; Evaluation) model of investigative interviewing is employed. The emphasis is on information gathering and hypothesis and hypothesis testing. The use of very open questions is the 'gold standard', since this avoids leading an interviewee or constraining his or her recall. The problem is that standard police interview techniques have been developed on the basis of neurotypical models of communication and memory. For an autistic person, the open-ended interview structure can be problematic. It requires 'theory of mind' processes (allowing the detainee to infer which details would be of interest to the interviewer and how much to recall). Many autistic individuals find this hugely challenging.

Dr Dermot Bowler, a leading world authority on memory in autism, explained:

> 'The cognitive interview they [criminal justice professionals] use actually increases the risk that autistic people confabulate more. You have to contrast real life with the way memory is examined in the lab. Autistic people tend to report things inaccurately. They describe accurately what they see, but they also describe things that have not happened but which might have happened. There is no malice involved. Is this imagination? I'm not sure. You will have certain scripts in your mind. If you have witnessed a row in a pub car park, for example, there are certain perfectly reasonable scenarios. In a sense, you cannot remember the details. There are plausible things, which just require script knowledge. Autistic people watch films and pick up ideas, as we all do. An autistic person's episodic memory tends to be rather ritualised and script-focused. Most of us [non-autistic people] go over the whole scene in our minds and do a lot of editing. Whereas an autistic person will just think of the script with much less editing.'[353]

352 Ibid.

353 Dr Dermot Bowler, personal communication, June 23, 2023.

Dr Bowler added, 'Judges and lawyers seem to be very naïve when it comes to memory, in my experience. You don't just rewind the tape. If a person is autistic, just asking the person what they saw is probably the best way. But you need to be aware that the person is likely to tell you scheme-congruent things that didn't actually happen. At the extreme, this may end in a wrongful conviction or self-incrimination.'[354]

Providing support

Conditions in the interview room can often be very unpleasant for autistic detainees. Sarah Doyle said: 'There are appalling echoes in the older police stations with high ceilings. The newer ones are better. They do try, but it's difficult.'[355]

In a 2022 study, Dr Katie Maras noted: 'Police environments are often loud, brightly lit (for example, with florescent strip lighting) and strong-smelling environments... A discussion between the individual, relevant support person(s) and police regarding particular sensitivities, triggers and other stressors should take place and where possible adaptations should be made.'[356] She highlighted a number of possible adaptations, including:

- Removing a ticking clock from the wall of the interview room.
- Conducting the interview in a familiar environment such as the interviewee's own home.
- Allowing stimming and other self-stimulatory behaviours (these are often used as a soothing mechanism and a way of regulating sensory input) including the use of a calming object (for example, a fidget spinner).[357]

How much does an autistic person lie to escape the discomfort, or even distress, of the interview room? 'They are not incapable of such calculations,' says Dr Bowler. 'They may well say a mish-mash of rather contradictory ideas which the police officer will try to untangle. But remember: everything is recorded now.'[358]

Dr Richard Mills agrees that autistic people will often 'go along' with police suggestions in order to shorten the time they are in custody.[359]

It is critical that the police hold discussions with the AA or intermediary about what an autistic detainee's particular sensory sensitivities are and, where possible, the timing and the location of the interview should be organised around these. Sometimes, the interview can be conducted in the interviewee's own home, for example. The police should also be told not to prevent any stimming that the detainee may be using to regulate his or her sensory arousal levels and that the detainee should be allowed to retain an object which clearly helps calm him or her down.

354 bid.

355 Sarah Doyle, personal communication, November 14, 2022.

356 Maras K (2022) *Police interviewing of autistic people* [online]. Available at: www.autism.org.uk/advice-and-guidance/professional-practice/police-interviews (accessed March 2024).

357 Ibid.

358 Dr Dermot Bowler, personal communication, June 23, 2023.

359 Dr Richard Mills, personal communication, November 8, 2922.

Autistic people also have difficulties freely recalling specific past events (which they have personally experienced) in such open-ended situations. With this in mind, Dr Katie Maras and her colleagues at the University of Bath have developed the 'Witnessed-Aimed First Account' (WAFA) interview technique. As Dr Maras explained:

> 'Saying to an autistic person "Tell me everything you know and don't leave anything out" is problematic for different reasons, one of which is that you still need to have an understanding of where the parameters are. There are cognitive aspects like executive functioning. Because you have to keep the whole event in mind and then recall it in a great big splurge all at once. That is actually quite cognitively demanding. Whereas if you break it down into smaller segments, as in our WAFA, that minimises the cognitive demands, because it is rather more piecemeal. The police cannot go in with a focus that is too directed. That is leading. What you do instead is tell the witness: "We are going to break the incident up into several parts. In a few words, tell me the main thing that happened." So the witness says: "There was a stabbing." The police interviewer will write that down on a Post-it note on the wall. Then the interviewer asks: "Tell me something else that happened after the stabbing." Answer: "Two cars pulled into the car park." The interviewer writes that down on another Post-it note. And so on, until they feel they have segmented the event. It comes from the witness, rather than being generated by the police officer. The witness has generated his or her discrete little chunks which they can focus on one at a time.' [360]

Intriguingly, this is the method that Ben Miller uses to solve crimes in his role as the detective, Richard Poole, in the hit TV series, *Death in Paradise*. Miller has told me that he believes Poole is autistic.[361]

Useful resources and guidance

Dr Katie Maras et al (2020): The Witness-Aimed First Account (WAFA): A new technique for interviewing autistic witnesses and victims. Autism 24 (6). https://journals.sagepub.com/doi/10.1177/1362361320908986

Autistic individuals in court

Research has demonstrated that autistic individuals often feel unhappy with their experiences in the courtroom, especially with the way in which they are questioned. It is not hard to see why. The objective of cross-examination is to discredit the witness. The use of suggestive questions is widespread. For example, 'He was wearing a red hat, wasn't he?' or complex questions such as 'Did you leave the house and was this before or after you received the phone call?' or 'Is it not the case that when you saw John, his demeanour was shifty, which led you to believe that he must have done something untoward?' Some questions are grammatically confusing, with double negatives ('Is it not the case that he did not go outside?'

360 Dr Katie Maras, personal communication, September 9, 2022.

361 Ben Miller, personal communication, January 6, 2022.

The appointment of an intermediary can prove crucial in facilitating communication between the court and an autistic defendant. The above-mentioned Youth Justice and Criminal Evidence Act (1999) allows English and Welsh courts to introduce a range of 'special measures' to assist the provision of testimony from vulnerable witnesses and victims. These include the use of screens in court (so that the witness cannot see the defendant), evidence via video link to the courtroom, the use of the previously video-recorded investigative interview, if appropriate, the use of a registered intermediary and communication aids. Witnesses may also be permitted to visit the court ahead of their trial, to aid familiarisation. It has been argued that these special measures could be extended to vulnerable suspects and, under a recent development in England and Wales, defendants will now be eligible for the provision of an intermediary to support them in giving evidence in court. (In Northern Ireland, registered intermediaries are fortunately available for vulnerable young defendants. In Scotland, 'special measures' are employed for vulnerable individuals, but so far this has not involved the use of intermediaries.)

If a vulnerable defendant is accompanied by an intermediary in court, jurors' perceptions of that defendant are often improved, contrary to some lay beliefs. Evidently, a critical factor is whether jurors are aware of an individual's autism diagnosis. A fascinating 2019 study led by Dr Katie Maras involved mock jurors who were presented with a written vignette about a hypothetical 27-year-old male defendant who had been arrested and appeared in court on a charge of assault and battery of a police officer. The mock jurors were informed that the defendant had been behaving aggressively at a train station and, when police officers tried to restrain him with handcuffs, he became violent and struck an officer. During the police interview, it reportedly emerged that the defendant was trainspotting and was upset because his train had been cancelled. The defendant's crime and behaviour in court were portrayed in a manner consistent with autistic symptomatology and with previous research on offending in autism. This included aggressive behaviours that were reactive to high stress, invasion of personal space and disruption to routine and brought about following the defendant's pursuit of his circumscribed interest in trains. The defendant also displayed high levels of anxiety and intolerance of uncertainty, together with impaired social communication, poor eye contact, sensory sensitivities, restrictive and repetitive behaviours and a need for sameness. Half the mock jurors were informed of the defendant's diagnosis of autism. These jurors rated him as significantly more honest and likeable, and less culpable for his or her actions than the jurors who had received no diagnostic information about the defendant.[362]

The 'double-edged sword' of the autism defence

When an autistic individual is charged with a crime, a key issue which arises is whether autism is a defence to that crime. A positive diagnosis has been used by defence lawyers to persuade the court to show leniency during criminal proceedings. However, the risk is that it could, paradoxically, increase the risk of stigmatising autism, either by suggesting that you are more likely to be perpetrator of a crime if you are autistic – whereas the evidence

362 Maras K, Marshall I & Sands C (2019) Mock juror perceptions of credibility and culpability in an autistic defendant. *J Autism Dev Disord* **49** (3) 996-1010.

appears to suggest that you are more likely to be a victim of crime – or that you deserve specific leniency because your autism made it impossible for you to distinguish between right and wrong (again, the evidence indicates that most autistic people are well aware of the difference).

The issue was highlighted by two well-known cases of British computer hackers with a diagnosis of Asperger's syndrome – Gary McKinnon (see **Case study 25** on p.170) and Lauri Love – both of whom won their battles against being extradited to the United States for trial on the basis that their condition made it likely that they would attempt suicide in the US. In the case of McKinnon, Dr Richard Mills told me that he (Mills) needed a Home Office forensic psychiatrist:

> '...because the prosecution had some Home Office psychiatrists who were not au fait with autism. We were arguing that depression represents a higher risk of suicide in autistic individuals. We weren't saying that McKinnon should not be extradited because he was autistic. We were saying he shouldn't be extradited because he would not receive the right kind of help in the US. I did a lot of work with Gary Mesibov[363] looking at the facilities to which McKinnon would have been going to in the US and they had no adequate psychiatric services or support at all. So we argued that he would basically be extradited to a prison where he would be kept in solitary confinement for 24 hours a day without any suitable medical facilities and that he would kill himself. We were not using autism as a mitigation for the crime. But we were bringing in autism indirectly as a "defence" because it put McKinnon at higher risk of suicide. We had meetings with the then Home Secretary, Theresa May, who was very sympathetic. She went along with the line we were putting forward.'[364]

Professor Glynis Murphy told me about the case of a young man with autism in south-east London who was involved in setting fire to a building, together with a group of other men. He was just the guy who drove the car. The only reason he could drive was that his mother realised that he was so autistic that he would not be able to cope with public transport:

> 'He wanted a job and the only way he could get to and from this job was by driving. So she made sure that he learned to drive. But then he was approached by these unscrupulous guys who wanted him to do this job. He didn't ask what it was about and he was totally taken in by them. He obviously had a problem with theory of mind, because he was not asking himself what these chaps were doing. He was cleared because he had an autism diagnosis. But he did not receive this diagnosis until after he became involved in the criminal justice system. However, it is not always a "get out of jail free" defence. It depends on each individual case.'[365]

363 Dr Mesibov was a professor of psychology at the University of North Carolina (UNC) at Chapel Hill for 35 years. For all but four of those 35 years, he was on the UNC Treatment and Education of Autistic and Related Communication Handicapped Children (TEACCH) faculty. From 1992 to 2012, he was director of TEACCH, founded by UNC psychiatry and psychology professor Eric Schopler. Dr Mesibov has had an enormous influence worldwide on introducing enlightened approaches to educating autistic children.

364 Richard Mills, personal communication, November 8, 2002.

365 Professor Glynis Murphy, personal communication, March 13, 2023.

Case study 25: Gary McKinnon

In 2012, the then British Home Secretary, Theresa May, announced that a computer hacker with Asperger's syndrome, Gary McKinnon, would not be extradited to the United States. McKinnon, 46, who admitted accessing US government computers but claimed he was looking for evidence of UFOs, had been fighting extradition since 2002. The US authorities described Glasgow-born McKinnon's actions as the 'biggest military computer hack of all time and demanded he face justice in America. The Americans said his actions had caused $800,000 worth of damage to military computer systems.[366]

The Home Secretary told MPs there was no doubt McKinnon was 'seriously ill' and the extradition warrant against him should be withdrawn: 'He has Asperger's syndrome and suffers from depressive illness. The legal question before me is now whether the extent of that illness is sufficient to preclude extradition. After careful consideration of all of the relevant material, I have concluded that Mr McKinnon's extradition would give rise to such a high risk of him ending his life that a decision to extradite would be incompatible with Mr McKinnon's human rights.' McKinnon faced 60 years in jail if convicted in the US.

The BBC's legal correspondent, Clive Coleman, said it was a dramatic decision – the first time a Home Secretary had stepped in to block an extradition under the current treaty with the US. Mark Lever, then chief executive of Britain's National Autistic Society, said he was 'delighted that the years of waiting are finally over for Gary and his family.' But the Labour Party's former Home Secretary, Alan Johnson, criticised the decision: 'Gary McKinnon is accused of very serious offences. The US was perfectly within its rights and it was extremely reasonable of them to seek his extradition.'

Dr Katie Maras feels that 'it very much depends on the individual case. In some cases, it is appropriate to take the autism into account.'[367] For his part, Dr Richard Mills said that many autistic people he knew were not happy about autism being used as a legal 'defence':

> 'It stigmatises people, whenever there's an association. I have been involved in quite a few cases where extreme crimes are mentioned and the perpetrator happens to be autistic. People draw a link. But what we are talking about is whether these cases are over-represented. The evidence is that they are under-represented in autistic people. Statistically, there are far more non-autistic people committing these offences than there are autistic people. We are not saying that autistic people do not commit crimes. They do. But there is no over-representation.'[368]

Are autistic people more likely to be victims of crime? 'The evidence for that is quite old', said Dr Mills:

> 'There are certain crimes where they could be at greater risk and others where they are at less risk. A lot of the research relating to such vulnerabilities dates back quite a few years. You might expect autistic people to be at greater risk of crimes of exploitation. But I am not sure what the evidence for that is. In a lot of the research we have done, the majority of people who were regarded as autistic when they were arrested turned out not to be autistic at all. They had a higher number

366 See: https://www.bbc.co.uk/news/uk-19957138

367 Dr Katie Maras, personal communication, September 9, 2022.

368 Dr Richard Mills, personal communication, November 8, 2022.

> of autistic traits, but they didn't qualify for a diagnosis of autism. When Rebecca Ledingham and I did a study on cybercrime back in 2015,[369] several international law enforcement agencies, in the wake of the McKinnon case, were running away with the idea that just about every cyber offender was autistic. The follow-up study we did with Marl Brosnan in Bath[370] showed that, in fact, very few were autistic.'[371]

If an individual has autistic traits but does not qualify for a diagnosis of autism, where does the law come in, in terms of protection? 'It doesn't,' said Dr Mills:

> 'The world is full of unusual or odd people who do strange things. They may have personality traits, even personality disorders. These may be exacerbated by alcohol and drugs. I am currently doing a lot of work with the police relating to counter-terrorism offences [see Chapter 8]. They are often very unusual people and you would probably classify them as neurodivergent, but it is really hard to tell how many of them are autistic.'[372]

Case study 26: Brianna Ghey

The horrific murder of Brianna Ghey on February 11, 2023, was a rare case in which the victim was autistic and her two killers were also autistic or had autistic traits. Scarlett Jenkinson and Eddie Ratcliffe, both 16, were sentenced to a minimum of 22 years and 20 years in prison, respectively, on February 2, 2024, for fatally stabbing the 16-year-old transgender Brianna 28 times in a park.

Brianna was lured to Culcheth Linear Park near Warrington, Cheshire, by Jenkinson, then 15, whom she believed was her friend. Brianna had no idea Jenkinson had secretly been plotting to kill her, with her friend Ratcliffe, also then 15. Judge Mrs Justice Yip identified Jenkinson and Ratcliffe, who had been subject to anonymity throughout their four-week trial in 2023.

Speaking directly to Jenkinson, Justice Yip said: 'Scarlett, you make up stories. You blur the lines between fantasy and real life... The messages show you wanted to make a real victim feel pain and fear.' The judge told Ratcliffe: 'You knew very well that what you were doing was terribly wrong, and that you were capable of saying no to Scarlett. Your autism cannot provide any real excuse for the offence.' She told the pair: 'This was a murder involving sadistic conduct. You both took part in a brutal and planned murder which was sadistic in nature, and where a secondary motive was hostility towards Brianna because of her transgender identity.'[373]

Emma Mills, head teacher of Birchwood Community High School, said that Brianna had come out as trans shortly after joining Birchwood in year 8, first changing her trousers for a skirt and then wearing a wig before switching to hair extensions and starting hormone treatment. 'She was very out and proud as a trans girl', said Mills, adding that Brianna's gender identity was accepted by her peers.

➔

369 Ledingham R & Mills R (2015) A preliminary study of autism and cybercrime in the context of international law enforcement. *Advances in Autism* **1** (1).

370 Payne, KL., Russell, A., Mills, R. et al (2019):. Is There a Relationship Between Cyber-Dependent Crime, Autistic-Like Traits and Autism?. *J Autism Dev Disord* **49**, 4159–4169.

371 Dr Richard Mills, personal communication, November 8, 2022.

372 Ibid.

373 See www.judiciary.uk/wp-content/uploads/2024/02/Sentencing-Remarks-FINAL-2.2.24.pdf (accessed March 2024).

Brianna had been treated in hospital for a time with an eating disorder, and found the return from Covid very difficult, Mills recalled. 'She really, really struggled after the lockdown. She didn't like going out on to the corridors or to the canteen. So our special needs coordinator would take her down to the canteen and get a lunch with her and take her back to the inclusion building.' Brianna did not take part in many normal classes, having one-to-one tuition in the school's 'inclusion room' after diagnoses of attention deficit hyperactivity disorder (ADHD) and anxiety.[374]

Her mother, Esther Ghey, said in her victim impact statement: 'Brianna was an extremely vulnerable teenager. As Brianna's mother. I was constantly worried that she was putting herself in risky situations. With these conditions [ADHD and autism], she found it extremely difficult to identify dangerous situations. Although, in this case, no one could have predicted that it was a dangerous situation for Brianna.'[375]

Detectives found the murder weapon with Brianna's blood on the knife blade in Ratcliffe's bedroom, along with heavily blood-stained clothing and trainers. At Jenkinson's home, they found a handwritten note detailing the murder plan and naming Brianna as the victim. Messages on their phones detailed their fascination with murder, torture and death, plans to kill other children and an earlier attempt to give Brianna an overdose.

It was only after they were charged with murdering Brianna that Ratcliffe was diagnosed with anxiety and autism, and Jenkinson with 'traits' of ADHD and autism. A psychiatrist who assessed Jenkinson for a second time after her conviction modified his view, saying he now believed she actually suffered from a 'form of anti-social personality disorder, rather than a mental illness.'[376]

The unjust joint enterprise common law doctrine

Joint enterprise is a common law doctrine in the UK under which, if one or more people commit an offence (the main offenders) and another or others (secondary offenders) intended to encourage or assist them to commit the offence, the secondary offender(s) can be prosecuted as if they were a main offender. This has resulted in bystanders, or people involved in much lesser criminal offences, being convicted of murder or manslaughter.

Thousands of people are estimated to have been prosecuted under the joint enterprise doctrine. But we know that people are often convicted under joint enterprise based on prejudicial evidence, information that could be inaccurate, or racial stereotypes. And a large proportion of those arrested and prosecuted are autistic.

Why do autistic people so often become victims of this unjust law? Barry Sheerman, MP, chairman of the All-Party Parliamentary Group on Miscarriages of Justice, explained: 'They are very easily led. They follow along, thinking it will be a night of fun. But everyone in the group goes to prison. It's hard to say how many of the thousand young men currently in prison on this law are autistic.'[377]

374 See www.theguardian.com/uk-news/2024/feb/02/scarlett-jenkinson-eddie-ratcliffe-teenagers-planned-murder-of-brianna-ghey (accessed March 2024).

375 Ibid.

376 Ibid.

377 Barry Sheerman, personal communication, September 7, 2022.

One of the most prominent cases is that of Alex Henry (see **Case study 27** on p.174). Alex's sister, Charlotte, who is acting as his legal advocate, said:

> 'We have always maintained that Alex's autism means that he is not guilty (or very unlikely to be guilty), as to be guilty under joint enterprise, Alex must have known that Cameron Ferguson possessed the requisite intent to cause the victim serious injury and predict that he would act on that intent by stabbing the victim. Alex's autism and lack of theory of mind (cognitive empathy) renders him unlikely to be capable of knowing what would happen. This is in the context of a spontaneous, fast-moving, 47-second affray between strangers. There was no evidence that Alex knew Cameron had a knife with him, but the prosecution told the jury that "friends tell each other everything" and, subsequently, that Alex would have been told earlier on in the shopping trip that his friend possessed a knife and would therefore believe Cameron Ferguson would use it with the requisite intent to seriously injure the victim (a stranger) once the spontaneous fight began. Despite the fact that Professor Sir Simon Baron-Cohen gave evidence to the Court of Appeal about Alex's autism and explained the significance of his lack of theory of mind, the Court said that his autism was irrelevant. The Court of Appeal did not explain why his autism was irrelevant and, although Dr Woodbury-Smith has provided a report concurring with Simon Baron-Cohen, this has been rejected by the Criminal Cases Review Commission (CCRC) as adding nothing new.'[378]

Henry said her next options were either to take the CCRC's decision to judicial review or proceed with a so-called Mercy Petition. A Mercy Petition is a very old avenue to 'appeal' (albeit not an appeal in the way the term is usually employed) which existed from the time before the existence of an appeal court or the CCRC. It is a political exercise whereby the government can show mercy by erasing the sentence of someone it believes has been convicted unjustly, either because that person is innocent and the jury/courts made an error, or because the individual is guilty but there are justice issues which mean that mercy should be shown.

Mercy petitions

Unlike the CCRC application (in which the CCRC considers new arguments but is bound by the previous decisions of the court and jury), when considering a Mercy Petition, the deciding body can review all the facts afresh and come to a new conclusion on the evidence. Another advantage is that a Mercy Petition is a political exercise, in which the opinions of society, politicians and experts lending their voice can be considered. A pitfall, however, as Charlotte Henry noted, is that the evidence must show that Alex is innocent or likely to be innocent, which is a higher test than the standard CCRC application, which is only whether the new fact might make Alex innocent. 'I believe Baron-Cohen and Woodbury-Smith, in their previous reports, have concluded that Alex is likely to be innocent so, if the decision-maker agrees, this shouldn't be a problem.'[379]

---

378 Charlotte Henry, personal communication, October 19, 2022.

379 Ibid.

Royal pardons are rare. In fact, before a full Royal Pardon was granted to Michael Shields in September 2009, none had been granted since 1996. Shields, a Liverpool FC supporter, was arrested and convicted of the attempted murder of a Bulgarian, Martin Georgiev, in May 2005 with a paving slab in the Black Sea resort of Golden Sands. Shields launched two appeals against his conviction in 2005 and 2006, which both failed. Nevertheless, in September 2009, the then British Justice Secretary, Jack Straw, granted Shields a full Royal Pardon, citing evidence that had only recently been brought to his attention. However, Straw refused to reveal details about the new evidence.

Unfortunately, Alex Henry's Mercy Petition was rejected in April 2023. Charlotte Henry explained that the reason for the rejection was that, following the Shields case, the Royal Prerogative of Mercy (RPM) could not be given if the Court of Appeal had already heard and rejected the case.

> 'Previously, the RPM could be used where the decision-maker believes the Court of Appeal or jury have come to a wrong decision. Following Shields, the RPM can now be used only in very limited circumstances where the Court of Appeal has not already considered the case, as the evidence is inadmissible or the conviction was obtained abroad.'[380]

Henry added that her lawyers had advised her that she should appeal to the United Nations: 'While we appeal to the UN, I'm also going to campaign for Alex to be given a lie detector test, which we can use for a new Mercy Petition, as lie detectors are inadmissible evidence in court but are being trialled for parole decisions.'[381]

Case study 27: Alex Henry

In 2013, Alex Henry's mother, Sally Halsall, received a phone call from Croydon Police in south London to say that they had arrested her son for murder. She said that on the afternoon of August 6, Alex and his three friends – Younis Tayyib, Janhelle Grant-Murray and Cameron Ferguson – were shopping in Ealing Broadway. In west London. 'From a distance, Alex spotted Janhelle, who appeared to be in trouble and was surrounded by four older men. The groups were strangers to each other and Younis was trying to act as a peacemaker. One of the assailants had removed his belt to use as a weapon and Janhelle had taken a bottle of wine from the local Costcutter and was holding it down by his side. Alex ran to Janhelle's defence, with Cameron behind him, and threw one punch. Janhelle didn't punch anyone. The bottle was put down intact. But in those few seconds, Cameron had put his hand inside his JD Sports bag. Inside was a knife. He never took the knife out of the bag and it was concealed at all times, but he stabbed both Taqui and Bourhane through the bag before fleeing the scene. Tragically, Taqui later died from his stab wound.'[382]

Alex's trial began in February 2014 at the Old Bailey in London and lasted six weeks. In spite of the fact there was no evidence against Alex except for his presence at the scene of the stabbing, the judge sentenced Alex to 19 years in jail. ➔

380 Charlotte Henry, personal communication, May 16, 2023.

381 Ibid.

382 See www.itv.com/news/london/2016-02-18/campaigner-i-had-to-google-joint-enterprise-after-a-police-sergeant-told-me-my-son-had-been-charged-with-murder (accessed March 2024).

Under the centuries-old common law practice of joint enterprise, his presence alone resulted in his being given the minimum mandatory life sentence, which means he is due to serve every single one of those 19 years before he gets parole – and then only if he shows remorse for a crime he did not commit.

At the time of his arrest, Alex's girlfriend was pregnant with their baby – Alex's daughter has only ever seen her father in prison. The first leave to appeal was turned down in December 2014, followed by the wait for what many had hoped would be a landmark case, the Supreme Court's judgement in the case of R v Jogee (see below)

In the meantime, however, Alex had been diagnosed as autistic and Professor Sir Simon Baron-Cohen, of the University of Cambridge, agreed to act pro bono as an expert witness at Alex's appeal on the grounds of autism, specifically Alex's mental vulnerability and the absurdity of his being able to predict the actions of another person. In June 2017, the Court of Appeal heard Alex's Leave (permission) to Appeal and when the prosecution failed to call their own expert witness, the family's hopes were lifted. However, the Court of Appeal upheld the prosecution's case on all counts, effectively slamming the door shut on further appeals, Nevertheless, Alex's legal team, together with his sister, Charlotte. remain determined to continue their fight for justice.[383]

Joint enterprise law

Until 2016, UK courts interpreted the joint enterprise law to mean that if two people set out to commit an offence, and in the course of doing so, one of them commits a different offence, the other person will also be guilty of that offence if they had foreseen the possibility that it might be committed. For example, if two people set out to commit a robbery, but in the course of the robbery one of them pulls out a knife and commits a murder, the other party will be guilty of murder on a joint enterprise basis if he foresaw this as a possibility, but did not himself intend it.

In 2016, the Supreme Court, in a judgement in the case of R v Jogee, appeared to raise the burden of proof from mere association with the actual killer or simply presence at the scene. The Supreme Court reconsidered the joint enterprise doctrine and said that the law had taken a 'wrong turn' and been misinterpreted. Instead, it said that a person would be guilty of a joint enterprise offence only if they intended to encourage or assist the person who committed the offence to do it. This judgement effectively reversed the law of joint enterprise, signalling hope for thousands of prisoners, some convicted as children, who hoped to appeal their life sentences. However, the Supreme Court ruled that the change in the law could not apply retrospectively, and the cases of all those who had been serving sentences under the joint enterprise law for the previous 30 years were denied the right to appeal. The first 13 test cases applied for permission to appeal in November 2016, but all 13 were dismissed by the appeal court.

The way that the law is used continues to be problematic. At present, neither the Crown Prosecution Service nor the Ministry of Justice records or monitors data about joint enterprise prosecutions – meaning there is no official record of the ethnicity or age of those prosecuted under joint enterprise or the outcomes of those prosecutions. The civil rights organisation Liberty has threatened legal action against the Crown Prosecution

383 See https://autisminjustice.org/alexs-story/ (accessed March 2024).

Service and the Ministry of Justice on behalf of the grassroots campaign group, JENGbA (Joint Enterprise Not Guilty by Association), for failing to record these data. This failure breaches their duties under the Equality Act (2010) to have due regard to eliminating race discrimination.

Campaigners maintain that joint enterprise is disproportionately targeted against black or minority ethnic young men, as well as individuals who are autistic. Barry Sheerman MP is determined that autistic suspects wrongly falling into this legal trap also find justice. He argues that the treatment of autistic people in joint enterprise cases has 'been nothing short of a travesty.'[384] In 2022, Sheerman introduced the Criminal Appeal (Amendment) Bill. This would amend the Criminal Appeal Act (1968) to enable appeals in the wake of the landmark ruling of the Supreme Court in 2016. Charlotte Henry, the brother of Alex Henry, explained that this new Bill would abolish what is known as the substantial injustice test, which has effectively prevented appeals. 'It's a really small amendment that enables thousands of people to have justice,' she told me.[385]

Andrea Coomber KC, director of the Howard League for Penal Reform, said:

> 'The disproportionality and the way it is applied isn't just shocking and a disgrace; there is a bigger question beside the sadness and the injustice of it all: it is creating a generation of people for whom the law has become illegitimate and that is really damaging for the rule of law and our system of government.'[386]

Autistic individuals in prison

Many autistic individuals remain undiagnosed, especially in forensic environments such as prisons. The UK Autism Act (2009) stressed the importance of identification, diagnosis and support of autistic adults in the community and other environments. Following this, the Department of Health developed statutory guidelines making public and private services accountable for addressing the human rights and equality of autistic individuals in accessing adequate support in all areas of life, including secure mental health facilities and prisons. The identification and treatment of autistic offenders is therefore not only essential in managing the risk of re-offending, but also in meeting the requirements of the law.

UK prisons are responsible, by law, for staff failures to screen and assess prisoners with special needs and make reasonable adaptations to provision. The social, communication and sensory impairments with which autistic prisoners often present pose particular problems for understanding and managing their risk and addressing issues effectively in rehabilitative programmes. For example, their behaviour may seem inappropriate, disrespectful or antagonistic to staff and other prisoners. The noise levels and specific lighting in a prison environment may exacerbate this behaviour, resulting in staff believing the individual to be intentionally hostile, aggressive and anti-social.

---

384 Barry Sheerman, personal communication, September 7, 2022.

385 Charlotte Henry, personal communication, October 12, 2022.

386 See: www.thejusticegap.com/mps-to-debate-bill-seeking-to-bring-justice-to-those-wrongly-convicted-under-joint-enterprise/ (accessed March 2024).

Loucks[387] described the difficulties autistic people may experience in coping with the transition from community to prison, but this is also the case when returning back to the community. Autistic individuals often have difficulty adopting generalisable skills. Those learned in the prison environment, therefore, may not be transferred effectively to other environments, such as the community. An understanding of the capacity to empathise and the nature of attachment is essential in supporting individuals through offender behaviour programmes and also, when leaving prison, to build stable and supportive relationships in managing their risk of re-offending.

The American film director Joseph Losey, who made the magnificent prison drama *The Criminal* in 1960, once declared that all criminals feel more comfortable behind bars than in the world outside:

> 'People have written a great deal about the fact that most people who come out of jail need a long period of rehabilitation and some of them never manage it at all. Sometimes, they try to get re-arrested for a new crime to regain the security of prison. It's a place where codes are applied without restrictions. The only marginal people are the prison guards.'[388]

It has frequently been suggested that the prison environment might actually prove conducive to autistic individuals, because of the carefully structured days and the routines. The late Dr Lorna Wing used to say that she knew of a number of autistic people who would re-offend because they liked the predictability of the prison environment.

However, this view ignores the fact that the rules and routines of prison life are constantly changing and indeed can be altered at a moment's notice. Many autistic prisoners feel distressed by lack of control over their world. A prisoner in one research study attempted to achieve 'sameness' in an unpredictable environment by cleaning his jail cell every day at the expense of participating in programmes.

Professor Glynis Murphy explained:

> 'It is more common for someone with autism to be bullied and beaten up in prison. Just occasionally, people find prisons comforting places to be because of the clear structure and the clear set of rules. But mostly people with autism find prisons very scary. Some do re-offend, but not many (and that is because they are getting so little support in the community).' [389]

Dr Dermot Bowler agreed about the risk of bullying: 'A lot of non-autistic prisoners are very clued-in and can spot differences quickly.' And there were other issues. He described a visit to Brixton Prison in south London: 'From the sensory point of view, it must have been horrible for an autistic inmate. There is fluorescent lighting and all that loud clinking of prison bars. Not to mention the relentless din of prisoners and staff shouting at each other.'[390]

387 Loucks N (2007) *Prisoners with learning difficulties and learning disabilities – review of prevalence and associated needs*. London: Prison Reform Trust.

388 Ciment M (1979) *Le livre de Losey*. Paris: Editions Stock, 1979, p235. (English translation by Adam Feinstein.)

389 Professor Glynis Murphy, personal communication, March 13, 2023.

390 Dr Dermot Bowler, personal communication, June 23, 2023.

Dr Richard Mills has seen many autistic prisoners. He says it is not at all his experience that they tend to re-offend:

> 'There are a lot of myths in this area. If you go to most prisons, the routines are more than offset by the hellish conditions. And one thing you can guarantee in prison is sensory overload. Most of the autistic people have really struggled with this in prison: the banging and the screaming. It stinks, the lighting is terrible. Anyone who thinks that they would engineer a situation to return to that is wrong. The routine aspect is also over-estimated, because the routines change from day to day, depending on staffing contingencies – unless you are in a high-security environment such as Broadmoor Hospital, where things are generally pretty calm, structured and safe, even though the patients are more "dangerous" on paper. Whereas in prisons, inmates may be there for relatively insignificant offences, but they are often very violent in prison. They might be young, impulsive, influenced by drugs, bored, angry. To put an autistic individual in this pressure cooker environment is very difficult.'[391]

Dr Mills said that awareness and knowledge of autism among prison officers was 'patchy', in his experience. The hierarchy was the problem:

'Prison officers are often interested in learning more. But the level above them has shown little interest. That is the obstacle for the people I have come across, I did some work at Jersey Prison, for example. Two or three of the prison officers asked to see me after the session and it turned out they all had autistic children. But their concerns were more about the physical conditions in jail. So you have this balancing act between keeping people safe and doing what could be regarded as therapeutic.'[392]

After prison: autism and the probation services

In Hugo Fregonese's excellent 1952 psychological film set in a prison, *My Six Convicts*, Carleton Young (who plays the jail's chief disciplinary officer), tells the psychologist (John Beal): 'It's good to be a little scared in a prison. Of course, outside the scare's bigger: you're scared you can't pay the rent, scared you can't pay for the groceries, scared you might lose your practice. Yes, outside there are a thousand fears. Here, only one: the fear of violence. I like working in a prison: life's much simpler.'

The situation facing autistic individuals when they emerge from prison can be as daunting as their time behind bars. Professor Glynis Murphy explained:

> 'Prisons are supposed to be for both punishment and rehabilitation, but in reality, the amount of rehabilitation for people with learning disabilities and autism is very little, on the whole. And we did a research project looking at what happens when they come out of prison. It was shocking. They get so little help. Quite often they are said to be ineligible for help from local community teams, and they were

391 Dr Richard Mills, personal communication, November 8, 2022.

392 Ibid.

> frequently going back into prison. The problem is that they are generally people with mild learning disabilities, because you do not get into the criminal justice system, on the whole, if you have severe learning disabilities.
>
> 'Apart from that, as resources for learning disability teams have shrunk, the teams have got stricter and stricter about whom they will help. I strongly disapprove of this situation, because I believe the people who are often left out are the people with mild learning disabilities, who can fend for themselves, to some degree: they can wash, they can dress, they can engage in conversation, but there are other things which they really cannot do, and this makes them incredibly vulnerable, as a result. Like understanding budgeting, like understanding when someone is taking advantage of them. Where are they supposed to get their support, if the team is saying they are not eligible?'[393]

Astonishingly, only two local authorities across the UK – Cumbria and Hampshire – employ an autism expert to assist probation officers. This has led to appalling situations, like the case of Rob (see also **Case study 30** on p.213). Rob (not his real name), 35, was convicted in 2019 of harassment by a magistrates' court. Because of his autism, combined with mild mental illness, he had a faulty understanding of why he had been found guilty and was now being punished with a community sentence: unpaid work, probation and a restraining order. During the several months that a burglary charge was awaiting court, Rob's already poor relationship with his probation officer hit bottom. This officer had heard of autism, but (by his own admission) had only a sketchy understanding of the condition. Rob's father, Andrew Robertson (also not his own name), says the officer was confrontational at times, and at others disapproving. 'The officer implied that, because Rob's autism diagnosis had been paid for privately, his family had, in effect, purchased him an excuse. Rob dreaded the meetings because he thought they were a ploy to trick him into admitting the (unknown) offence.'[394]

After Rob had missed appointments and failed to engage, this probation officer prosecuted him for breach. Pending the court hearing, his solicitor, by way of defence, commissioned a psychiatric report from an autism expert. It concluded that probation had failed him and noted that a private autism expert would not prejudice their reputation by delivering a diagnosis unless justified. Rob failed to attend court and was therefore arrested and remanded in custody for breaching his supervision order and because he was awaiting trial for burglary. According to his father, on his first night in prison, Rob should have been placed in the vulnerable prisoners' wing. Instead, he was put on a regular wing to share with a violent individual. There was a disagreement. Rob was beaten up by his cellmate, aided by others in nearby cells.[395]

After Rob's second term in prison, he was given a new probation officer. Robertson said she was in a different class from the earlier one, understanding that to make progress she needed to support, not confront, while also being firm. 'Rob's anger, paranoia and

393 Professor Glynis Murphy in conversation with the author, March 13, 2023.

394 www.transformjustice.org.uk/news-insight/a-different-understanding-how-the-cjs-discriminates-against-those-with-autism/ (accessed March 2024).

395 Ibid.

drug use began to wane, slowly... However: Rob remains scarred by his arrests and spells inside, displaying many of the features of post-traumatic stress disorder (PTSD). Lapses are all too possible'[396]

Robertson proposes two ways of reforming a system which he says treats Rob and his like 'as villains requiring punitive restraint, rather than minimal restraint combined with treatment.' The first of Robertson's suggestions is the provision of annexes to mental health units or, better still, he says, self-contained 'safe houses' where people suffering short-term psychotic and/or drug induced episodes can be held securely until they calm down. Robertson's second suggestion is for an autism expert to be appointed to work with every local probation service in the country. [397]

Summary

Autistic people are entitled to support (appropriate adults, intermediaries and reasonable adjustments) throughout their contact with the criminal justice system. All too often, unfortunately, the vulnerability of these individuals is not recognised and they are consequently not offered the support which is their legal right. In police interviews, the specific nature of memory in autistic witnesses should be acknowledged in the phrasing of questions and in courtrooms, every effort should be taken to provide assistance to vulnerable witnesses and victims. This assistance might include the use of screens in court (so that the witness cannot see the defendant), evidence via video link to the courtroom, the use of the previously video-recorded investigative interview, if appropriate, the use of a registered intermediary and communication aids. Prison can be a very harsh environment for autistic people due to sensory bombardment, the potential for bullying and disruptions in routines. This chapter has outlined how crucial it is to build and maintain trust between the police and the autistic community, and how this is a two-way process. A huge improvement would be for the police, lawyers, judges and jurors to be given mandatory training in order to be aware of how autism affects an individual's behaviour so that autistic defendants are treated fairly, and for local authorities to employ an autism expert to assist probation officers.

396 Ibid.

397 Ibid.

Chapter 7: Autistic individuals, family law and the civil justice system

This chapter will focus on:

- Disputes with neighbours.
- The family justice system.
- Autism and divorce – the mediation process.

Disputes with neighbours

There has been a great deal written about autism and the criminal justice system but very little about *civil* justice issues, which generally seem less important to most of us but to an autistic individual can become a source of overwhelming distress. Such issues can include minor disputes with neighbours over noise, overhanging trees, or the much more upsetting divorce battles.

The law does not appear to be anywhere near as robust when resolving civil disputes as it does in cases involving the criminal justice system. This state of affairs may apply to all individuals, not exclusively to those who are autistic, but it remains the case that many autistic people and their families have fallen victim to this legislative vagueness or inadequacy.

Jon Adams, a talented artist with Asperger's syndrome, dyslexia and synaesthesia, told me:

> 'We may have a complaint against a neighbour and we won't drop it. Because we believe an injustice has been done, and we hate injustice. Autistic people have an innate sense of justice. It's funny: you'd expect lawyers, of all people, to respect that!'[398] Ekaterina Harrison, a finance lawyer who is autistic herself and who is the mother of three autistic children, says that, from her understanding, autistic individuals 'may sometimes persist in escalating any dispute, regardless of its significance, potentially due to difficulties in communication or conflict resolution skills. This does not necessarily indicate a superior sense of justice, but might be attributed to challenges in handling conflicts without involving authorities or to a preference for self-help solutions.'[399]

398 Jon Adams, personal communication, November 24, 2022.

399 Ekaterina Harrison, personal communication, November 25, 2023.

Autistic people frequently turn to the internet in their desperation to air their grievances. Mark, a 50-year-old autistic man with dyslexia living with his partner – a nurse – and two children, in Wigan, said he had been subjected to 'sporadic bullying' and harassment from three of his neighbours for more than a decade. However, this harassment took a new turn in 2020 when he was physically assaulted by one of them and two other neighbours joined in:

> 'Then we also had a change of occupancy of two other households. These new neighbours appear to have been recruited by the original protagonists. This brings the total of harassing group households up to seven.
>
> 'The incidents have become more frequent in the last few months and the threats have become more violent in nature. Every incident was reported to the police, but since the police are unwilling to prosecute, the protagonists seem to be getting emboldened by this apparent impunity. Some of the attacks we are subject to appear to be coordinated and the police and local council appear to have very little interest (or powers). They keep just saying there is no evidence (I have supplied them with what I consider reasonable evidence)... The incidents I have been subjected to include: physical assault, causing actual bodily harm, threats of violence ("Don't go to sleep, I am going to rip your head off"); abuse about my autism and name-calling; criminal damage, including pulling up plants in our garden and chopping the heads off trees in our garden; trespassing; fly-tipping; parking vehicles to prevent the use of our drive; untrue stories about my bad character being passed to other neighbours; openly accusing me of being a pervert and a paedo (all baseless); foul language and threats to my partner and myself in the presence of my son.'[400]

Mark is university-educated but works as a handyman (he says he has been unable to sustain his previous career in fund management):

> 'I appear to be socially subordinate when the police deal with me. But the reverse is true in terms of my ability to cognitively understand the issues. However, the

---

400 See: https://community.autism.org.uk/f/miscellaneous-and-chat/21602/harrassment-by-neighbours-group-hate-crime (accessed February 2024)

> neighbours involved just lie and I am left trying to justify my peaceful, law-abiding activities against a set of lies perpetrated on me to cover the protagonists' horrid behaviour. The police have stated to me that because of the number of people saying the same things about me, it does appear I am to blame! These statements leave me sick to my stomach with a huge and ever-increasing burden of anxiety. The other neighbours who know me also speak of the behaviour of these households as disgusting and say they all appear to have a vendetta against myself and my family just because we are different. But the neighbours who remain supportive don't want to become involved or publicly show support for us as they (understandably) don't want to be subject to any of the disgusting behaviour we receive.'

Mark later included an online update, saying that two local councillors had become involved in his case. The Deputy Mayor of Greater Manchester wrote to the police for a full explanation of the action (or lack of action) taken so far. The local Citizens' Advice Bureau gave Mark contacts for *pro bono* advice via the university on legal matters. Mark also wrote to the 'right to review' police department requesting a judgement from them about opening the case of physical assault against the neighbours. And most recently, his MP wrote to Manchester Police to ask for a report.

Touchingly, Mark expressed his immense gratitude to all those who had offered him online support:

> 'Thank you so much for all your kind words... I just needed a hand-up off my knees, and you all collectively did that! Being autistic is ace and I love what it brings me in terms of creativity and the amazing way it lets us live, but sometimes being without a large circle of friends and wider family, is hard in times like this! I never needed friends. as I love the pink clouds in my world. But sometimes, a stranger's hand is more powerful than a friend's embrace!'[401]

Commenting on this case, Ekaterina Harrison observed:

> 'What catches my attention is Mark's choice to address the matter online, prompting me to wonder whether he sought legal counsel in navigating this situation. The mention of the Citizens' Advice Bureau indicates their involvement in providing assistance, which is a positive note. However, it is concerning that Mark's online expressions could potentially include misleading and defamatory statements, particularly if specific individuals were named. This underscores the importance of individuals approaching such matters with sensitivity and seeking guidance through appropriate channels. It is crucial to encourage a thoughtful approach rather than relying on online forums, which may inadvertently lead to unintended repercussions.'[402]

401 Ibid.

402 Ekaterina Harrison, personal communication, November 25, 2023.

Self-help solutions

It is not always easy to solve civil disputes civilly. Take the example of Shay Kirkham, a six-year-old autistic boy whose mother was ordered to take down the fence she built in North Shields, north-east England, to keep him safe. Like my own autistic son, Johnny, Shay is a Houdini-like 'escape artist' with no awareness of physical danger. One of the neighbours had apparently complained to the local authority that the new gate was obstructing access to her property. But the fence was the only way Hayley could allow Shay to play in the back garden in safety. Hayley Kirkham, a single mother, said:

> 'Shay has autism. He doesn't understand the dangers of running into the street or talking to strangers. This fence and gate, which I put up, not only protect him from these dangers, but also from a very busy road and bus route. There are no locks on the gate, so the neighbours can easily get through. Shay also thinks everyone is his friend and he doesn't understand about strangers, but you can't reason with him and explain the dangers. I have explained the reasons for it to my neighbours but they don't understand.'[403]

In this case, the local council, North Tyneside Council, which originally told her the fence would have to come down, said staff would try and find a solution. A spokeswoman said: 'We are aware there is an issue of a fence and gate being erected at this property without our consent, which is obstructing the access of a neighbouring property. We are arranging to visit the two properties to see if we can find a solution agreeable to both parties.'[404]

Ekaterina Harrison said that, based on the facts of the case, Hayley Kirkham had chosen not to pursue legal channels to address the situation but had opted instead for what is commonly known as a self-help solution:

> 'We should consider the impact on other people whose access to the property is now obstructed. Do their rights matter in this context? Self-help measures have the potential to escalate conflicts. Without access to proper legal channels, disputes may intensify, causing more harm and impeding the possibility of a peaceful resolution. Taking matters into one's own hands may expose individuals to personal risks, especially in emotionally charged situations.'[405]

Harrison cited the case of an autistic farmer who had been jailed for three months for unauthorised work on a site of special scientific interest in Herefordshire between 2020 and 2021. He claimed the work was necessary to prevent flooding in the area and mentioned his ongoing efforts to clean up the river, citing his autism and aversion to a messy river. The charges against him included discharging silt into the river and destroying 71 trees. Although dredging has historically been used to combat flooding, the Environment Agency now considers it less effective and potentially harmful to the environment. The prosecution argued that the farmer's actions increased flood risks downstream, with no evidence of reduced local flooding impact. Following the verdict,

---

403 See www.chroniclelive.co.uk/news/north-east-news/north-shields-autistic-six-year-old-boy-3874668 (accessed January 2024).

404 Ibid.

405 Ekaterina Harrison, personal communication, November 25, 2023.

Natural England, the UK government's adviser for the natural environment in England, expressed concern about the devastating impact on species in the river, emphasising the importance of upholding environmental laws and sending a strong message against disrespecting them.[406] It is unclear whether the authorities communicated their messages to residents before the judgement to discourage the use of traditional dredging methods.

Harrison added that the farmer's story prompted her to reflect on wildlife conservation efforts in the area where she lived. Whenever changes were made, like fencing or construction work, there was a helpful leaflet provided with explanations. While people might initially disagree with certain actions, such as the removal of favourite trees, having the reasoning explained to them, like the tree being sick and a threat to other trees, prevented them from taking matters into their own hands:

> 'I recall an incident at the pond where a boy and his mom were feeding ducks, despite a clear sign not to,' Harrison told me, 'When I explained that leftover bread attracts rats, which can harm duck chicks, they became more understanding and accepted the rule. The key is communication and providing clear explanations for actions taken or rules in place. This is crucial for everyone, especially autistic individuals, as it helps them better comprehend the situation. Authorities should prioritise such clear communication to avoid misunderstandings and foster cooperation.'[407]

Why might autistic individuals favour self-help measures over legal processes in certain situations? Harrison says:

> 'For example, autistic individuals may find formal legal processes daunting, due to challenges in communication and understanding social nuances. In contrast, self-help measures offer a more direct and personally manageable approach. The preference for routine and familiarity, common among autistic individuals, aligns well with self-help actions, providing comfort and a sense of control. Moreover, legal environments, characterised by formality, noise, and unpredictability, may be distressing for those with sensory sensitivities related to autism, prompting a preference for familiar and controllable self-help strategies. Also, the difficulty in trusting authority figures or navigating complex bureaucratic systems may contribute to opting for self-help methods perceived as more straightforward and immediate.'[408]

In another case, very similar to the Kirkham case cited above, the local authorities appear to have taken a harder line, although they also claim to want to seek an amicable solution. Tiona-Jay Baker, 10, is autistic, has learning difficulties and is one of only two people in the world with a rare chromosome depletion which leaves her behaviour hard to predict. Her father, Cliff, said he would happily face arrest after their local council, Newark and Sherwood District Council in Nottinghamshire, ordered him and his wife, Dawn, to take down a fence they had installed when Tiona-Jai kept escaping and running out onto the road (see **Case study 28** on p.186). The local planning laws, in this case, were of little help to Tiona-Jay and her family. It is unclear what legal avenues the family

406 Ibid.

407 Ibid.

408 Ibid.

could have explored, given that the putative interests of the wider community appear to have been placed before the very specific interests (and needs) of a vulnerable young autistic individual.

However, Ekaterina Harrison observed:

> 'It is not necessarily true that the planning restrictions demonstrate that the interests of the wider community take precedence over the interests of a vulnerable person. What if one of the neighbours uses a wheelchair and the gate or fence restricts their access? Without a formal process to assess the suitability of the gate or fence, it is difficult to determine whether it was the only or most effective solution available. I have not personally experienced such a situation, so I am unable to draw from direct experience. However, potential solutions could involve social care interventions, such as having a social carer supervising the child during the specific hours. If appropriate, the use of GPS technology could help track the child's location if they wander off. Collaborating with neighbours to establish a neighbourhood watch or support network could offer additional supervision and assistance in ensuring the child's safety.'[409]

Case study 28: Tiona-Jai Baker

Cliff and Dawn Baker, from Edwinstowe, Nottinghamshire, who had received permission from their landlord to build a 6-foot fence to keep their autistic daughter, Tiona-Jai, safe, have now been ordered by the local council to take the fence down. Tiona-Jai,10, has learning difficulties and is one of only two people in the world with a rare chromosome depletion which leaves her behaviour hard to predict. Her father says he will happily face arrest as his daughter's safety 'comes first'.[410]

Cliff and Dawn installed the fence, at a cost of more than £1,000, after Tiona-Jai kept escaping and running out on to the road. However, a neighbour complained about the fence and Newark and Sherwood District Council ordered them to take it down.

Speaking to BBC Radio Nottingham, Cliff said: 'We were given nine months to remove the fence, otherwise it would be court action... If they do come to take it down, it is not going to happen – I'm standing my ground. My daughter's safety comes first. I'll get arrested for it, I'm not bothered. I've never had a criminal record but if it comes to that, so be it. I'm getting one for a good reason.'

Cliff added that the fence was 'purely for safety reasons' and that it was put up to give Tiona-Jai a place to play.[411]

Local planning inspectors initially informed them that the fence was a road safety hazard, but when this was proved not to be the case, the parents claim it was then said to be a 'street scene' issue instead. Cliff and Dawn paid more than £400 to appeal the decision. A children's consultant at King's Mill Hospital, Dr Jeanette Derbyshire, supported their appeal, according to a letter seen by the BBC. Dr Derbyshire said that Tiona-Jai had a 'tendency to climb', adding that an outdoor space suitable for an autistic child's needs was 'important' in order to keep that child safe. The couple said they had also provided a paediatrician's letter and medical records that proved the need for the fence for the youngster's own safety. Nevertheless, their appeal was also rejected by Newark and Sherwood District Council.[412]

---

409 Ekaterina Harrison, personal communication, February 8, 2024.

410 See www.bbc.co.uk/news/uk-england-nottinghamshire-67438457 (accessed March 2024).

411 Ibid,

412 Ibid,

Cliff and Dawn have now urged Michael Gove, the UK's Levelling Up Secretary, to make the planning laws more flexible when relating to children with disabilities.

The council claimed that it sent an enforcement letter to the couple which told them to lower the fence to one metre (3.2 feet). Lisa Hughes, business manager for planning at Newark and Sherwood District Council told the BBC: 'This is obviously a difficult and emotional case. We wanted to help the applicant and have offered alternative solutions, which have been supported by the Planning Inspector, but unfortunately these have thus far been turned down by the applicant. We're sorry to hear the applicant is frustrated by this decision, but we are still open to working with them to find an alternative if possible.'[413]

Hughes added that the local authority had a 'duty to investigate' the complaint and it had been ruled that the fence was too high: 'We followed the appropriate planning rules and law when investigating this case. We found the height of the fence contradicted national legislation and was negatively impacting upon local amenities. Therefore, a notice was issued, requiring the fence to be reduced to one metre, the maximum height permitted adjacent to a highway.'[414]

Useful resources and further guidance

- It is essential in cases like Mark's that everything is carefully documented. A diary should be kept of every incident, noting the down the place, time, person and circumstances, Photos should be taken of any damage. The neighbours may be violating the Protection from Harassment Act (1997). You can apply to the county court for an injunction, even if the police do not believe the neighbours are guilty of harassment. You can also consult your local Citizens' Advice Bureau. If you are entitled to legal aid, they can advise on how to apply for it and where to find a solicitor. However, autistic people often need someone to advocate for them.
- If you feel comfortable, you should approach your neighbour to discuss the problem. However, you should not approach your neighbour if he or she has acted with threats, violence or harassment. Instead, you should contact your local council or call the police.
- According to the Citizens' Advice Bureau, to resolve a dispute, you can:
  - Speak to your neighbour – take a note of the time and date you spoke to them in case you need it for evidence later.
  - Write your neighbour a letter if you have not been able to speak to them.
  - Describe the problem and the action you would like them to take. If appropriate, you should also explain when you would like them to resolve the problem by and what you'll do to help.
  - If your neighbour is a tenant, you can talk to their landlord. This could be the local council, a housing association or a private landlord.
  - If there is a residents' or tenants' association where you live, you could get their support. To find your local residents' or tenants' association, contact your local council.
  - Seek help from a mediation service (mediators are independent and will listen to both sides to help you reach an agreement). You might have to pay for mediation, depending on the provider. If you are on a low income, you might be eligible for a reduced rate.
  - Contact your local council. ➔

413 Ibid,

414 Ibid,

- You can contact a local councillor or MP if you have been unable to resolve your dispute by speaking to your neighbour or the local council.
- Contact the police if a criminal offence is being committed – for example, if your neighbour is being violent or harassing you. If you are not sure whether what your neighbour is doing is a crime, contact your local council, phone 101 or contact your local police station for advice.
- Consult a lawyer. You can send your neighbour a letter from a solicitor to show that you are serious about your complaint. A letter from a solicitor might help to explain the legal position in a dispute, for example, if neighbours cannot agree about the position of a boundary. However, it can be expensive to seek legal advice.
- Take legal action. Legal action should be a last resort after you have tried speaking to your neighbour and taking action through your local council. Going to court might resolve the dispute but damage your relationship with your neighbours. It is also expensive unless you are eligible for legal aid.
- If you are considering taking court action for a neighbour dispute, you should consult an experienced adviser, for example at a Citizens' Advice Bureau. An adviser cannot give you legal advice but can provide information on how to find legal advice and help you to determine whether you are eligible for legal aid.

- Stop Hate UK: www.stophateuk.org/
- Hourglass: www.wearehourglass.org/physical-abuse
- www.facebook.com/groups/disabilityhatecrimenetwork/about/
- Victim support: www.victimsupport.org.uk

The family justice system

In a sense, family law occupies a place mid-way between the civil justice and criminal justice systems. Family law deals with legal issues that involve both private relationships and potential societal interests. Like civil law, it addresses disputes between private parties (family members) and seeks fair resolutions. But as Ekaterina Harrison rightly points out, family law also shares characteristics with the criminal justice system, especially in cases involving domestic violence or child abuse, where the state may intervene to protect individuals and uphold societal interests. Yet, family law has unique attributes, such as its emphasis on preserving family relationships and the well-being of children, setting it apart from both civil and criminal justice.[415]

The family justice system exists to help families resolve disputes arising in respect of family matters quickly and with the minimum of disruption to those involved. In most cases, the parties are encouraged to resolve their family disputes out of court, for example through mediation, unless this is not a safe course. This approach is taken because outcomes are more likely to be successful if the parties themselves have had a role in planning and agreeing that outcome. Where agreement is not possible, the court still works to make the family dispute less adversarial, even if the case needs to go to court for the judge to decide the proper outcome.

415 Ekaterina Harrison, personal communication, November 25, 2023.

The role of the intermediary

The family court process is inherently adversarial. Nevertheless, family courts increasingly encourage alternative dispute resolution methods, such as mediation, to mitigate the adversarial nature of proceedings. These approaches aim to promote cooperation, communication and amicable resolutions, especially in cases involving children. Family and civil procedure law are very similar. The difference is that, in family law, the court is mainly closed. Members of the public are not normally allowed in, not even friends.

The role of the intermediary was created by the Youth Justice and Criminal Evidence Act (1999) to help 'vulnerable' witnesses in criminal cases. However, the use of intermediaries has since spread to be included in family court proceedings. This is because many people involved in these types of cases often have needs and vulnerabilities and they may need the support of someone else (an intermediary) to help explain the processes, especially if they have to give evidence.

There is no specific definition for a 'vulnerable' person, but this can be a person who:

- Has a learning difficulty.
- Has a mental health condition which affects their ability to communicate under pressure and stress.
- Is a child under the age of 18.
- Has a physical disability which affects the way they communicate effectively, for example speech and hearing difficulties.
- Has previously been a victim of domestic or sexual abuse.
- Has gender or sexuality issues.

A family court is under a duty to vulnerable witnesses or parties to the proceedings to make sure that they can fully take part in court proceedings when they may need to communicate in court and may need help to understand the court process. Article 6 of the European Convention on Human Rights ensures that people who need an intermediary remain part of the decision-making process and have a fair hearing.

When a person might need an intermediary, an application is usually made to the family court to allow the assessment to be undertaken. Usually, a specialist organisation such as Communicourt or Triangle will come to meet the person and assess him or her to determine whether they consider that an intermediary is required for the rest of the court process. The cost of this assessment is funded by the court.

Intermediaries are communication specialists who work on behalf of His Majesty's Courts and Tribunals Service (HMCTS) to support people participating in a court or tribunal hearing. They provide impartial recommendations to HMCTS about a person's specific communication needs and outline the steps needed to achieve them.

This could include:

- The types of questions that are likely to get the best response.
- The types of questions that should not be asked.

- How long the person will need to answer a question.
- When the person may need a break.

There are two types of HMCTS-approved intermediary services:

- Managed and approved service providers (MASPs) are larger organisations, with intermediary services available nationally.
- Approved service providers (ASPs) are self-employed individuals who provide specialist intermediary services.

In some cases, autistic litigants have been refused the use of an intermediary in a family court. Ekaterina Harrison cited a family case from 2022,[416] in which it was determined that appointing an intermediary in family proceedings for an autistic father with learning difficulties was deemed unnecessary, even though one had been appointed for him in criminal proceedings. This decision was influenced by the differences in formality, questioning style, and the judge's level of intervention in family proceedings. The judge was confident in implementing protective measures to ensure a fair hearing for the father.

The right to reasonable assistance

Any litigant who is not legally represented has the right to reasonable assistance from a layperson. This person is sometimes known as a McKenzie Friend, which derives from a 1970 divorce case, McKenzie v McKenzie. Because the husband was unable to afford to continue using solicitors, those solicitors, for free, sent someone (a Mr Hangar) to represent him in court. Mr Hangar was not there to take part in the proceedings but to prompt and to make suggestions to the husband in the conduct of his case, the calling of his witnesses and, perhaps more importantly, on the very critical and difficult questions of fact in this case, to assist him by making suggestions as to the cross-examination of the wife and her witnesses. In subsequent years, the practice of using a McKenzie Friend has become more widespread – especially after the drastic stripping down of legal aid.

McKenzie Friends have no independent right to provide assistance. They are not advocates and cannot carry out litigation. McKenzie Friends do not have to be legally qualified and can be a family member or friend. There are also various charities which provide McKenzie Friends for free. Some McKenzie Friends will offer their services for a fee. The activities of McKenzie Friends are not regulated, even where they charge a fee.

A McKenzie Friend can:

- Provide moral support.
- Take notes.
- Help with case papers.
- Quietly give advice, including on points of law or procedure, issues that the litigant in person may want to raise to the court, or questions that the litigant in person may wish to ask witnesses

416 MacDougall v KE [2022] EWHC 2479 (Fam)

A McKenzie Friend cannot:

- Act on behalf of the litigant in person.
- Manage the case outside of court (for example, signing court documents).
- Address the court, make submissions or question witnesses.
- Attend a closed court unless the litigant in person has received permission from the court.

A judge has the discretion to refuse to allow a McKenzie Friend to assist a litigant in person. However, in open court there is a presumption in favour of allowing a McKenzie Friend. If a judge does refuse, they should give the litigant in person the reasons for refusal. A litigant may be denied the assistance of a McKenzie Friend because its provision might undermine, or has undermined, the efficient administration of justice. Examples of circumstances where this might arise are: the assistance is being provided for an improper purpose; the assistance is unreasonable in nature or degree; the McKenzie Friend is subject to a civil proceedings order or a civil restraint order; the McKenzie Friend is using the litigant as a puppet; the McKenzie Friend is directly or indirectly conducting the litigation; the court is not satisfied that the McKenzie Friend fully understands the duty of confidentiality.[417]

In closed court, where the hearing is in chambers, in private, or when the proceedings relate to a child, there is still a presumption in favour of allowing a McKenzie Friend. However, the litigant in person must justify their presence in court and receive permission.

The court must often understand the lived reality of parents and children before making final decisions, having heard from parents with competing views. In cases where parents cannot agree a way forward, then evidence by way of witness statements and cross-examination is an integral feature of the court process. In such circumstances, the stakes are high and parents are under pressure, often being cross-examined by experienced barristers about their position and proposals for the child or children.

Family Procedure Rules for those who are vulnerable

Neurodivergence is an area of vulnerability which can go unaddressed within family proceedings. If someone has a matter within the family court, this can be a very stressful and foreign experience for them. This is true regardless of whether the individual is neurodivergent or not. However, there are particular challenges one might face at each stage of proceedings if the person is in fact neurodivergent, and very probably if he or she is autistic.

Specific Family Procedure Rules on vulnerable persons' participation in proceedings and evidence came into force in November 2017. Integral to this framework are essential obligations imposed on both the court representatives and the involved parties. They are mandated to cooperate, ensuring that parties and witnesses can engage fairly in proceedings.

417 See www.judiciary.uk/wp-content/uploads/2022/07/pfd-guidance-mckenzie-friends.pdf (accessed March 2024).

The objective is to preserve the quality of their evidence without subjecting them to fear or distress arising from their vulnerability.[418]

The *Equal Treatment Bench Book* is issued to every judge in all procedures.[419] It aims to increase awareness and understanding of the different circumstances of people appearing in courts and tribunals. It helps to enable effective communication and suggests steps which should increase participation by all parties. Chapter 2 of the *Bench Book* deals with special measures for children and young vulnerable adults. Nadine Finch, a former family barrister, explained:

> 'What used to happen before special measures became formalised in the Family Procedure Rules was that the advocate would have to ask to see the judge beforehand. Most of the judges would then make accommodations. Provided the barrister was aware and took the initiative, it could work well. The good thing today, with the introduction of special measures, is that the court is obliged to take the initiative. The problem, of course, is that many individuals do not have a formal diagnosis of autism.'[420]

Finch said that the *Equal Treatment Bench Book* was comprehensive and looked at the vulnerability of those appearing before the courts, 'but it is difficult to know how it is implemented on a case-by-case basis'. But she went on:

> 'Many appearing in court will not be represented and may not raise issues addressed in the Bench Book The outcomes of family proceedings often depend on evidence, as opposed to law, and many of those appearing in family courts will have little grasp of the relevance of some evidence or lack of it. They are often the least able to give cogent evidence. In some cases, it is because they are so upset. In other cases, it is because their education and knowledge are limited. Quite often, they get incredibly angry, even if they are not autistic. I have seen violence in the family court, whereas I have never seen such violence in the criminal court. I have seen people punch each other. I have even seen a woman wielding a knife at a judge because her children were being taken away. So the emotional level in the family court is extremely high. Most experienced judges will realise they have to be very careful when they assess what is said to them, because they know the emotions at play.'[421]

Delays in the diagnosis of autism can create problems right across the court system but are arguably most acute in family courts, which deal with pressing considerations such as the well-being of children and how divorcing couples might divide their assets. In 2022, there

418 See www.justice.gov.uk/courts/procedure-rules/family/parts/part-3a-vulnerable-persons-participation-in-proceedings-and-giving-evidence (accessed March 2024).

419 The February 2021 edition is available at: www.judiciary.uk/wp-content/uploads/2023/06/Equal-Treatment-Bench-Book-April-2023-revision.pdf (accessed February 2024).

420 Nadine Finch, personal communication, December 8, 2023.

421 Ibid.

was a 40% increase in delays in autism diagnoses compared with 2021.[422] Information released by the UK's Ministry of Justice indicates that family courts are already handling growing backlogs.[423]

Family court welfare service

Part of the reason why family cases now take so long to conclude is because of the strain experienced by the family court welfare service, Cafcass. (Cafcass is a government body that works with children and young people in family court cases and is charged with ensuring their safety and welfare during court proceedings.) This service has highlighted the fact that its workload has increased over the past five years and, as a consequence, proceedings now take far longer.[424] This can be a challenge for people – adults and children alike – who have not been diagnosed with a condition such as autism, but the inherent anxiety can be even greater for those who have been diagnosed as autistic.

The pressures confronted by Cafcass have another practical implication. Its volume of work means that it might only have a very limited time to meet and discuss the matters at hand with the adults and children involved. This can limit the contribution that those with neurodiverse conditions are able to make and, in turn, risks Cafcass submitting reports which are not wholly reflective of the circumstances under scrutiny.[425]

Autism is experienced differently by each individual. If children or parents tell their solicitor that they are autistic at the outset, then their solicitor can support them and ensure that the court makes sensible adjustments and truly understands them. It is essential that the court (and indeed solicitors) understand how the autistic litigant is likely to communicate and respond in a court setting, especially if he or she gives evidence in person to the court. There must be an acceptance that autistic litigants may interact with the court during the evidence process in a manner that is different. If the court is unaware of this, there could easily be misunderstandings.

It should also be noted that parents' responses to examination must not be misconstrued. For example, they may struggle to make effective eye contact throughout examination and/or make noises or have quick changes of body language. Behaviour like this is not a sign that a litigant is providing inaccurate information to the court or that they are not trustworthy. Instead, it may indicate that they are struggling with the process and/or self-regulating a response to a very difficult dynamic. If a litigant and solicitor have a transparent and open conversation early on in the process, this can be invaluable and ensure that the litigant is supported effectively. Autistic litigants must have access to clear, considered advice and, crucially, be confident that they are understood.

---

422 NHS England (2023) *Autism Statistics, January to December 2022* [online]. Available at: https://digital.nhs.uk/data-and-information/publications/statistical/autism-statistics/january-to-december-2022 (accessed February 2024).

423 Ministry of Justice (2023) *Family Court Statistics Quarterly: October to December 2022* [online]. Available at: www.gov.uk/government/statistics/family-court-statistics-quarterly-october-to-december-2022/family-court-statistics-quarterly-october-to-december-2022 (accessed February 2024).

424 Cafcass (undated) *Our Data* [online]. Available at: www.cafcass.gov.uk/about-cafcass/our-data/ (accessed February 2024).

425 Hubbard E (2023) *Autism, Family Courts and Fairness* [online]. Available at: https://hallbrown.co.uk/autism-family-courts-and-fairness/ (accessed February 2024).

Alia Lewis, a solicitor and director in the family department at the legal firm Duncan Lewis, represents numerous autistic children and adults and is also the mother of an eight-year-old autistic child. She says that 'great strides' have been made in understanding autism and helping families to navigate the legal system but much more work is needed to help families properly access justice:

> 'At the age of three and a half, my son could easily navigate the London Transport network without prompting from my husband and me, yet he has faced numerous challenges in his development. In my experience, there is much work to do to improve knowledge amongst professionals and to improve access to the services autistic people and those with other hidden disabilities require and are entitled to. I am concerned by the lack of understanding amongst legal, social care, health and education professionals of autism, and the need to adjust how we work, to accommodate autistic people and their needs. It is surprising to think that a significant proportion of professionals within the legal sector and social services, who deal with care proceedings cases, do not have specific training in autism or a true understanding of what this means about the way in which we should conduct ourselves when dealing with children and families where autism is present. Over the past few years, I have spoken to countless professionals who agree that awareness and training needs to be increased in our professions, and that what we are doing now is just not good enough. In a recent judgement, HHJ Middleton Roy highlighted the difficulties autistic parents involved in court proceedings may experience and adjustments that can be made in order to facilitate their full participation.[426]
>
> 'Whilst this is an extremely helpful starting point, such guidance must be underpinned by training across the professional sectors involved in such cases. Many cases come to court where local authorities are issuing proceedings in respect of children with hidden disabilities such as autism and ADHD. Quite often in these cases, the children are beyond parental control because they are not receiving the support and services they need from the wider system, yet the cases brought to court place the blame on the parents. This is not to say there are never any concerns with the parents' ability to care for the child, but the problematic aspect that I and so many other professionals struggle with is the parental blame element in relation to aspects of the child's hidden disability which manifest in behaviour that the parent (and professionals) struggle to manage.'[427]

Lewis says that the increase in this type of case has prompted important research by the University of Birmingham with West Midlands ADASS (Association of Directors of Adult Social Services), funded by NHS England, on parental blame in relation to

426 See: D and E (Parent with Autism) [2020] EWFC B18 (11 May 2020).

427 Lewis A (2023) *The Family Justice System and Autism – Room for improvement* [online]. Available at: www.duncanlewis.co.uk/family_news/The_Family_Justice_System_and_Autism_%E2%80%93_Room_for_Improvement_(29_March_2023).html (accessed February 2024).

autism. A questionnaire includes identifying parents who have ended up with social services involvement and facing care proceedings because of a lack of understanding by professionals:[428]

> 'That the research is being funded by an already cash-strapped NHS indicates how endemic the problem is. I am hopeful that the results will assist to drive change moving forward. So many children subject to care proceedings slip through the net of different services and remain without much-needed diagnoses, or even if they do have a diagnosis, without much-needed support and services... The Autism Act 2009 requires the Secretary of State to publish a document setting out a strategy for meeting the needs of adults in England with autism by improving the provision of relevant services to such adults by local authorities, NHS bodies and NHS foundations. The government's national strategy for autistic children, young people and adults: 2021 to 2026, is the first time the autism strategy has been extended to children and young people. Unfortunately, the strategy falls far short of where we need to be. It sets highly ambitious targets that are way off being fulfilled ... and the funding for what it sets out to achieve just isn't there. It presents an idealised view of what is possible in health, education, social care, employment, society and the justice system...
>
> 'It sets out plans for reform of the adult and youth criminal justice system but not the family court system... The HMCTS[429] vulnerability action plan confirmed in October 2022 that all courts and tribunals would, by summer 2023, be signed up to the Hidden Disabilities Sunflower Scheme where people wear a sunflower to indicate subtly to staff, colleagues and health professionals that they need additional support, help or a little more time. This is progress, but what of training amongst all staff within the court system, including those in call centres and admin staff at the coalface of dealing with many autistic court users each day? Will the government fund this?'[430]

The autistic experience in family courts

A ground-breaking 2020 qualitative study from University College London (UCL) was the first to explore the experiences of autistic individuals in the family courts.[431] While participants related some positive elements to their experiences, in particular about the willingness of professionals to try to learn more about their clients' needs, the overall picture showed significant concerns. The reports given showed considerable misunderstandings about autism and a system that struggled to make appropriate adjustments which would allow autistic court users to have access to justice on an

---

428 For more, see www.wm-adass.org.uk/networks/equality-diversity-and-inclusion/autism-and-parental-blame-research/ (accessed February 2024).

429 His Majesty's Courts and Tribunal Service, an executive agency of Britain's Ministry of Justice.

430 Lewis A (2023) *The Family Justice System and Autism – Room for improvement* [online]. Available at: www.duncanlewis.co.uk/family_news/The_Family_Justice_System_and_Autism_%E2%80%93_Room_for_Improvement_(29_March_2023).html (accessed February 2024).

431 George R, Crane L & Remington A (2020) 'Our normal is different': autistic adults' experiences of the family court. *Journal of Social Welfare and Family Law* **42** (2).

equivalent basis to non-autistic litigants. This situation stands in contrast to the position regarding other disabilities in the family justice system, but also to the relatively greater level of provision for autistic people within the criminal justice system.[432]

Currently, it is accepted that access to the family courts is more challenging for particular minority groups, for example those with disabilities. Not only do legal aid cuts disproportionately affect this group but, as the authors of the UCL study noted, 'this is compounded by persisting stereotypes and stigma surrounding disability whereby impairments are presumed to equate to inadequate parenting'[433].

Although there has been very little research on autistic people's experiences as users of the family justice system, the nature of the condition suggests that accessing the family courts may be particularly challenging for autistic individuals. The UCL study highlighted three aspects, in particular.

Firstly, altered communication (such as difficulty in understanding non-literal language or decoding non-verbal cues such as intonation, emphasis and facial expressions) may undermine a person's ability effectively to give instructions to a legal representative, give evidence in court or respond appropriately to questions. Autistic people also often show reduced affect (e.g. monotone voice, subdued emotional reactions) which is frequently incongruous with the emotions actually being felt and can be misinterpreted as apathy or insensitivity. As the study authors rightly point out, although these characteristics of autism may affect all areas of the law, they are particularly noticeable in areas like family law, where emotion and interpersonal relationships are a focus of the law's interests and may lead to behaviours or language being misunderstood or misinterpreted, for example by social workers, Cafcass or family court judges.

Secondly, a preference for sameness, rule-based systems and certainty might make deviating from daily routines to attend family court (with the inherent unpredictability) extremely distressing. Again, while these may affect any area of law, the potential impact may be higher in family law, particularly in regard to public law proceedings involving children, for example.

Thirdly, the physical environment at court or in other places where a family court litigant is required to go (such as a solicitors' office, local authority office, Cafcass meeting room, etc) may be a source of difficulty. As we have seen in previous chapters, autistic individuals experience altered sensory experiences compared to non-autistic people – indeed, sensory 'differences' were included for the first time as a criterion for the definition of autism in DSM-5 (2013). These sensory differences may manifest as increased sensitivity to lights, sounds and smells. As the authors of the University College London study rightly noted: 'In the family courts, where future-oriented assessments of issues like parenting capacity are a central focus, and a judge's ability to assess the personality of

432 See Eekelaar, J. (2011). 'Not of the highest importance': Family justice under threat. *Journal of Social Welfare and Family Law*, **33**: 311-317; Cobb, S. (2018). Do the vulnerable have effective access to justice? Family Law, January (PAGE),Maclean, M. and Eekelaar, J. (2019). *After the Act: Access to Family Justice After LASPO*. Oxford: Hart Publishing.

433 George R, Crane L & Remington A (2020), op. cit.

individuals is key, the potential impact on an autistic person's ability to operate effectively has potential to impact on case outcomes to a significant degree.'[434]

George *et al*, the authors of the landmark 2020 UCL study[435], go on to make the important point that, quite apart from the challenges linked to autistic traits:

> '...it is also possible that stigma and negative stereotypes held by legal professionals may prove a further barrier to access to justice. For example, persisting myths about autism include the (incorrect) presumption that autistic people do not wish to form personal relationships, have diminished empathy and a lack of ability to care for others. Likewise, it is untrue that autistic people have an increased tendency to perpetrate interpersonal violence, or are more suggestible (e.g. easily led when giving evidence) than non-autistic people. Yet, concerningly, both these statements were endorsed by many family lawyers and judges who participated in our previous research (George et al, 2018). These incorrect assumptions may bias the expectations of, assessments, processes and outcomes for autistic people in the family justice system.'

In the criminal justice system, efforts have been made to meet the needs of autistic witnesses and suspects/defendants. The Youth Justice and Criminal Evidence Act (1999) introduced a range of 'special measures' to support vulnerable and intimidated witnesses (including autistic witnesses) in the CJS. These include the provision of 'registered intermediaries' and, in court specifically, the use of screens, live links, and the removal of wigs and gowns. These initiatives were prompted, in part, by a number of high-profile cases of unacceptable encounters between autistic individuals and the CJS[436]

In the case of the ten autistic adults with direct experience of the family justice system (all of whose experiences had involved at least two court hearings) who were interviewed in the UCL study, communication issues were frequently cited by study participants. One of them, Abigail spoke about a difficulty for her arising from the fact that legal professionals 'don't ask direct questions, which means I don't give them the answers they might be looking for'. Other participants noted a particular challenge with verbal communication. Nancy noted that when she was 'asked questions that weren't written down or I hadn't thought about, that was a bit of a problem'. Zoey similarly explained that 'verbal communication is too difficult', and thought that 'using physical movement and sign language would have made it easier to communicate'. Leo said that he believed his communication style had led to his being misunderstood in the court process. He was particularly concerned that, at times when he considered that he was 'just venting my frustration' about the process, it would look 'from one perspective like I'm an aggressive male', and that assessment would then be used to determine the outcome of his application to spend time with his children. Leo recalled that judges had responded to him in 'a stronger tone'. Although he attempted to explain that his reaction was a result of his autism, Leo felt that no adjustments were introduced as a result.

---

434 Ibid.

435 Ibid..

436 For example, The Commissioner of Police for the Metropolis v ZH [2013] EWCA Civ 69).

Margaret told the researchers that a judge had become 'irate' and started 'making unfair comments and shouting at me later' as a consequence, in her view, of her staring at the judge too much or, conversely, listening while looking away. She found this particularly difficult: '...because nobody told me! I was only told to tell the truth in court. And I did!' Margaret added:

> 'Because they hear the word "autism", they see me stim [make repetitive movements like hand-flapping as self-stimulation], cry, talk very fast, get angry … and people instantly take that as evidence of me being "simple" and having "mental health problems". They think that I don't understand but I do. It is very frustrating, especially when it's actually often the opposite.'[437]

The ten study participants also mentioned their high levels of anxiety in the family court environment. Donna said she 'just became a nervous wreck'. Claudia said, '...in order to control myself in the [court] room, I needed to look to my solicitor before I responded to anything'. This created a specific problem at one hearing, where her regular solicitor was unable to attend and another lawyer was there in her place: 'I couldn't process what's being said to me because I was in such a state of panic'.[438]

Some of the study participants said that their experiences within the family justice system had exacerbated the manifestations of some autistic traits. Claudia, for example, noted that she was 'not the sort of person who has meltdowns … [or] who is violent or shouty, but if you put somebody in an extremely stressful situation that sort of thing can happen'. Margaret, reflecting a strong difficulty with what she perceived to be factual inaccuracies, referred to 'having a breakdown because the lawyer got the facts wrong', and noted that she could not sleep the night before a hearing because of her level of anxiety.[439]

In their study, George *et al* also raised the crucial issue of whether autistic individuals involved in the family justice system should disclose their diagnosis and, if so, when. (This issue was discussed in Chapter 5 on employment law, but here the context is distinctly different.) Leo said he had decided to disclose his autism upfront. Abigail, in contrast, said it had not occurred to her to reveal her condition. Others approached it as a tactical decision based on the fear that knowledge of their diagnosis would disadvantage them. Some participants reported that their diagnosis had been disclosed within the proceedings by their former partner, without their being consulted about that decision. Samuel said his ex-wife had received a copy of his assessment by email before their separation, 'and then she did mention [it] in the first-ever court hearing'. Claudia had decided to tell her own legal team about her autism and had discussed the pros and cons of making a disclosure. Apparently, her lawyer had put pressure on her not to disclose her condition. But then, in Claudia's words, her ex-husband began 'using the autism card in court, he was saying that I was autistic and therefore I was a rubbish person … so he was playing to stereotype'.[440]

---

437 George R, Crane L & Remington A (2020) 'Our normal is different': autistic adults' experiences of the family court, op. cit.

438 Ibid.

439 Ibid.

440 Ibid.

Significantly, although the study participants often had positive things to say about their own lawyers, they universally reported an almost total lack of prior knowledge or understanding about autism or its potential relevance to the proceedings. Toby, for example, found any knowledge that the legal professionals did have was 'dated and hugely inaccurate'. Several participants had to change lawyers mid-way through proceedings. While this is of course not uncommon, the consequences for autistic participants can be serious. They were often described as being 'pretty tough'. Some family justice professionals doubted that their client had autism at all because he or she had degree-level qualifications.

Participants mentioned assumptions about whether they were safe to see their children unaccompanied, whether they were likely to be aggressive, and their level of intellectual functioning as well as gendered expectations that autism was a condition which affected only men and boys, and not women or girls. Several also raised the perception that autism was treated differently – invariably, taken less seriously and given less respect – than other forms of disability, particularly physical disabilities. Josh, for example, was astounded that the question of which adjustments would be provided appeared to be at the discretion of the individual judge:

> 'You wouldn't expect the judge to make the decision as to whether you provide court papers in braille, or an induction loop for a deaf person, or an interpreter for someone who speaks a foreign language, so why should it be that a judge makes the determination "yes" or "no" about an appropriate adult? It should be very simple: you show evidence that you've got autism, the court service provides an appropriate adult.'[441]

(For more on the role of 'appropriate adults', see Chapter 6 on the criminal justice system.)

Some of the UCL study participants' stories included positive elements about how the family justice system had responded to their needs. Samuel was able to secure an intermediary. Claudia brought a counsellor from her local autism service to meetings with her solicitors and with the local authority in relation to the care proceedings. Margaret's experience of the one hearing where a support worker attended with her was that the support worker enabled her to access a separate waiting room, which was otherwise inaccessible to her throughout the proceedings. Nevertheless, these positive examples were relatively rare A particular concern was that some participants felt that asking for support or adjustments would be viewed negatively and consequently impact on their cases. Although some participants did sometimes manage to have an appropriate adult with them for court hearings, the provision of it was 'inconsistent', in Samuel's description.[442]

For a couple of the study participants, the case was at least in part about their being autistic – they were involved in care proceedings which had partly arisen because of the local authority's concern about their parenting. George *et al* emphasise that it is questionable whether these concerns were in themselves based on stereotypes and assumptions. Abigail, whose child was also autistic, was concerned that her parenting and her son's development were being judged through a non-autistic lens, whereas for herself and her son, 'our normal

441 Ibid.

442 Ibid.

is quite different from other people's normal'. Zoey commented that the outcome of her proceedings was that, because of her autism, 'it gave social services grounds to say I am too expensive to support'.[443]

George *et al* concluded:

> 'While family court litigation is inherently stressful for all involved, it is known that there is a higher prevalence of anxiety disorders in the autistic population compared to non-autistic people. Another recurring theme centred on the difficulty with situations where information or events were presented in such a way that was perceived to be inaccurate or deliberately untrue. This is in keeping with the fact that many autistic individuals rely on adherence to rule-based processes when navigating communication and social interaction, and therefore can find it distressing when faced with a violation of their knowledge or expectations. Taken together, some participants felt that all these factors impacted on the outcome of their case, even if autism was not – or should not have been – the focus of the proceedings. Interestingly, some participants also felt that the nature of the court process itself exacerbated their autistic traits leading to challenges (for example, meltdowns or extreme anxiety) that they did not usually encounter in daily life. This highlights the importance of considering an autistic individual's developing needs as the court process proceeds... While caution should be taken when generalising results from a small sample, the findings showed that though half the justice professionals were satisfied with experiences of professional encounters with autistic people, many autistic people expressed dissatisfaction... The individuals we spoke to had a number of recommendations for ways in which autistic people could be supported within the family courts. First, an emphasis was placed on the need for court staff and legal professionals to understand the unique needs and experiences of autistic litigants. Second, they suggested having a dedicated, trained, member of court staff to meet and guide those on the autistic spectrum through the process. Lastly, the need for a specific mode of communication was highlighted. This should be direct but respectful, and overtly address any misunderstandings that arise... Legal professionals should also be encouraged to consult their autistic clients, or those who appear before them, in order to understand any specific support needs or necessary adjustments.'[444]

Useful resources and guidance

- The Judicial College, which organises training for judges and magistrates in England and Wales produces the *Equal Treatment Bench Book*, a publication which 'aims to increase awareness and understanding of the different circumstances of people appearing in courts and tribunals'. It is available here: www.judiciary.uk/wp-content/uploads/2023/04/Equal-Treatment-Bench-Book-April-2023-revision-2.pdf (accessed February 2024).

443 Ibid.

444 Ibid.

- There are many family lawyers around the UK. One which has received recognition from the National Autistic Society is the Milton Keynes-based Rainscourt Family Law Solicitors. They claims that their approach includes: demystifying legal language by striving to present complex legal concepts and jargon in simple, straightforward language, so that clients fully understand the nuances of the case and the implications of each decision; providing a buffer in formal court settings by communicating on the clients' behalf and ensuring their views are clearly presented and taken into account; aiming to maintain a consistent approach throughout the legal proceedings (given that changes in routine can be particularly distressing for individuals with autism); addressing sensory sensitivities and arranging for an intermediary assessment to take place. An intermediary can help identify whether any special measures should be put in place during court proceedings to ensure that the client's needs are met, particularly regarding communication. They also assist in managing the significant changes that come with divorce or separation. This includes helping to negotiate changes in living arrangements, restructuring financial responsibilities and creating sensitive child arrangement plans. For families with children with autism, they provide specific guidance to ensure the child's best interests are safeguarded. This includes understanding the child's unique needs and crafting a bespoke child arrangement plan that ensures their well-being. For more information, see www.rainscourt.com/assisting-clients-with-autism-in-navigating-the-family-court/ (accessed February 2024).

Autism and divorce – the mediation process

Most parents of children with autism are acutely aware of the issues that come with the diagnosis and particularly, how stress affects their marriage. One study published by Hartley *et al* showed that parents who had a child with autism had a higher divorce rate than parents without a child with autism.[445] However, another study presented in 2010 found there was no increase in divorce rates. According to their research, 64% of children with autism lived with their real or adoptive parents, compared to a rate of 65% for children with no autism diagnosis.[446]

Kymberly Grosso, the mother of an autistic child, wonders whether, despite the fact that there are strong emotions resulting from a diagnosis of autism and there can be significant stress involved with raising an autistic child, it is necessarily true that parents who subsequently get divorced primarily do so because of the autism:

> 'I believe that a diagnosis of autism is similar to any other great life stressor. However, in addition to stress, the autism diagnosis frequently is a life-changing event for the parents of the child, as well as for the entire family unit. Therefore, if a marriage is strong, the couple may weather the storm over time and possibly come out stronger. But for couples who are already having difficulties in their marriage,

445 Hartley SL, Barker ET, Seltzer MM *et al* (2010: The relative risk and timing of divorce in families of children with an autism spectrum disorder. *Journal of Family Psychology* **24** (4) 449-457.

446 Freedman BH, Kalb L, Zablotsky B and Stuart E (2010) *Relationship Status Among Parents of Children with Autism Spectrum Disorders: A Population-Based Study, International Meeting for Autism Research* [online]. Available at: www.kennedykrieger.org/kki_news.jsp?pid = 8851 (accessed February 2024).

> autism is a stressor that can become the proverbial straw that breaks the camel's back. And for those couples, autism becomes yet another reason to divorce.'[447]

Grosso surveyed other divorced parents who have a child with autism, asking: 'Do parents believe that autism was the primary reason for their divorce? Specifically, how does the diagnosis of autism contribute as a reason for divorce? Of the 52 divorced parents with an autistic child who responded to the survey, 78% said they had divorced after their child was diagnosed, and, overwhelmingly, 76% of the respondents said that autism was not the primary cause of their divorce. Nevertheless, 50% did consider autism to be a contributing factor.[448]

Mediation

Autistic individuals involved in a divorce will understandably find the experience especially distressing. Obviously, it is preferable to reach an agreement out of court. To do this, mediation is essential. This is never a 'one-size-fits-all' approach. There may be a number of family matters and considerations to be made throughout the mediation process, especially regarding navigating relationships, adjustments and scheduling.

While there is no 'standard' for adjusting the mediation process, the central theme is always to create the most fruitful discussions by ensuring or facilitating communication between all involved parties. For autistic people, mediation may seem like a daunting task and a step into uncharted territory.

The first stage is the Mediation Information and Assessment Meeting (MIAM). This will give you the opportunity to understand how mediation can work best for you (and your family, if you have one). This session can last from 45 minutes to one hour and you will discuss the mediation process, what format of dispute resolution is best suited to you and your family, the benefits of mediation, the anticipated number of sessions, the likely costs of using mediation, and understanding whether you are eligible for publicly funded mediation via legal aid. To be eligible for legal aid, you will need either to be in receipt of passporting benefits such as universal credit or on low income.

Once you have attended your own MIAM, the other party is invited to attend mediation. They will attend their own MIAM. If they are also deemed suitable for mediation, then you will both proceed to joint mediation sessions. At the MIAM, the family mediator will walk you through the various types of mediation and which is best suited to you. These formats include joint mediation, shuttle mediation and child consultations.

Next, is the Agreement to Mediate. This is a document which covers how mediation works and outlines the rules of mediation, and will be provided to you in your first joint session. Both you and your former partner are required to sign this before starting the session.

The mediation process is about working with your mediator and ex-partner to reach an agreement about how you and your family will live post-separation. There is no fixed time frame for mediation and it can span over several sessions depending on

447 Grosso K (2011) *Do Couples Divorce Because of Autism?* [online]. Available at: www.psychologytoday.com/gb/blog/autism-in-real-life/201103/do-couples-divorce-because-autism (accessed February 2024).

448 Ibid.

the intensity of the conflict and the number of items to address. To benefit most from mediation, you should build an agenda of items that you would like addressed, which can be addressed in your sessions.

At the end of the family mediation process, your mediator will explain to you how you can seek legal advice regarding any proposals you have agreed to, and how they can become legally binding agreements or court orders. The fundamental core of mediation is that the mediator will never tell you what to do. Instead, they may suggest consulting with another relevant professional, or discuss what options are available to you.

If an agreement is not found, your mediator will provide you with a signed certificate that will enable you. nevertheless, to begin the court process.

Mediation is a voluntary, self-directed and court-adjacent method of dispute resolution open to all clients. You can discuss your autism with your mediator and explain any adjustments that need to be put in place for you. During the MIAM, you will be able to voice your concerns regarding the mediation process and work together with your mediator to resolve these issues. The nature of mediation is to promote constant back-and-forth communication, which generally involves plenty of questions. Mediators who understand autism will make these questions as short and specific as possible, avoiding open-ended questions that may have confusing and multiple answers. The most important aspect of the mediation process is communication – and remembering that it goes both ways.

Participants with autism – whether adults or children – may benefit from the presence of a support person in the mediation process. This is especially useful in cases involving children with autism, as a support person may help the child vocalise his or her concerns, thoughts, and emotions – particularly in cases where there are gaps in communication. While third parties are not typically invited to mediation sessions, exceptions can always be made in these circumstances. However, this individual may be present only if all involved parties consent to their attendance.

Although many parents are keen to resolve matters out of court, unfortunately this is not always possible. If court proceedings become necessary, parents – whether autistic or not –are often at an extremely low ebb. It is usual for parents to be distressed and anxious to protect their children and ensure that their best interests are met by way of a court order. It is imperative that parents involved in the family court feel heard and understood when dealing with matters regarding their children. This is especially true in matters where a parent is autistic.

Amanda Bucklow, of IPOS Mediation, has years of experience mediating disputes where a party is neurodivergent:

> 'Sometimes, the neurodivergent person has been diagnosed, sometimes they haven't, and sometimes they've been diagnosed but haven't "come out". A mediator's job isn't to "out" them or to emphasise their neurotype. It is our job to craft the mediation process so that parties, whatever their neurotype, can fully participate. For me, that starts with a pre-mediation meeting to get a better understanding of any party's style of communication. I'll listen for their speech pattern and vocabulary. I notice when

> they seem to lose concentration or become distracted, and what their stress triggers are. It's not about labelling them or judging them – it's about awareness and knowing how best to support them. I might ask: "What are your coping strategies when you're under stress?" Or I ask them to think about the physiological signals that show up when they feel under pressure, such as fidgeting or playing with their hair, so when I spot them during the mediation, I can suggest a break. I don't make assumptions about certain behaviours, because what might look like stress can be their personal approach to help improve their concentration and process information.'[449]

Bucklow says she always introduces reasonable adjustments which are appropriate to the individual's specific needs:

> 'My personal style of mediating is to keep going without taking lots of breaks, but if it means the neurodivergent party is better able to participate, I'll make sure there are a sufficient number of breaks. I may call a break if I can see one is needed, or we might have a pre-agreed signal for when the party wants one. For some people, maintaining eye contact can often be difficult. Here, instead of sitting across the table in the classic adversarial arrangement, I'll suggest parties sit alongside each other. Similarly, if I have something important to explore with the party that might generate real discomfort for them, I'll suggest going for a walk so we can talk side by side. I may also spend a little more time with the neurodivergent party than the neurotypical party in a private session.' [450]

In cases where the neurotypical party does not know that the other party is neurodivergent, Bucklow will say to them:

> 'I've been thinking about how we might manage the day and here are a couple of ideas that I think would help. What do you think? If they don't work, we can try something else. Are you OK with that?' If the neurotypical party is aware of the situation, I'll be clear about wanting to make adjustments so that the other side can fully participate in the mediation. I've never had push-back from the neurotypical party over this. They've been grateful for my guidance and seen it as a practical and helpful adjustment to the process. In fact, it's added a hugely positive dynamic because we're not stuck with: "What do we do here because I can't communicate with this person?".'[451]

Bucklow says that both neurodivergent and neurotypical people can benefit greatly from engaging in the mediation process:

> 'Neurodivergent people won't necessarily need a 'specialist' mediator – simply one who takes the time to understand the nuances, can read the signals and will suggest appropriate adjustments. Which is what any good mediator worth their salt will do. If I see that something isn't working during mediation it's my job, my responsibility, to make an adjustment so that people can refresh, reboot and re-engage. A mediator

449 Bucklow M (2022) *Mediation and Neurodiversity* [online]. IPOS Mediation. Available at: https://mediate.co.uk/blog/mediation-and-neurodiversity/ (accessed February 2024).

450 Ibid.

451 Ibid.

will always do what they can to make mediation a productive and less stressful experience. And that means making it possible for everyone to engage in the process and be able to contribute to reaching agreement.'[452]

Useful resources and guidance

- Family Law in Partnership is an award-winning team of specialist family lawyers, mediators, arbitrators and family consultants based in Covent Garden. They have wide experience of representing parents in family proceedings (divorce, separation, private children proceedings) where there is the additional issue of autism within the family (either parent or child). For more information, see www.flip.co.uk
- IPOS Mediation can be contacted at https://mediate.co.uk/contact-us
- Direct Mediation Services:
  - National Help Line: 0113 468 9593.
  - Website: www.directmediationservices.co.uk/autism-and-divorce/ (accessed February 2024).

Summary

Civil justice issues may seem less important to most of us but to an autistic individual, they can become a source of overwhelming distress. Such issues can include minor disputes with neighbours over noise, overhanging trees, or the much more upsetting divorce battles. Like civil law, the family justice system addresses disputes between private parties (family members) and seeks fair resolutions. But family law also shares characteristics with the criminal justice system, especially in cases involving domestic violence or child abuse, where the state may intervene to protect individuals and uphold societal interests. Delays in the diagnosis of autism can create problems right across the court system but are arguably most acute in family courts, which deal with pressing considerations such as the well-being of children and how divorcing couples might divide their assets. Although there has been very little research on autistic people's experiences as users of the family justice system, the nature of the condition suggests that accessing the family courts may be particularly challenging for autistic individuals. To help 'vulnerable' witnesses in criminal cases, the role of the intermediary was created by the Youth Justice and Criminal Evidence Act (1999). It has since spread to be included in family court proceedings. Any litigant who is not legally represented has the right to reasonable assistance from a layperson. This person is sometimes known as a McKenzie Friend. Autistic individuals involved in a divorce will understandably find the experience especially distressing. Obviously, it is preferable to reach an agreement out of court. To do this, mediation is essential.

452 Ibid.

Chapter 8: Other vulnerabilities in autistic adults and the law

This chapter will focus on:

- The dangers of the internet.
- Autism and drugs.
- Cuckooing.
- Disability hate crime and autism.
- Alleged links with terrorism.
- Autistic victims of the asylum battle.

The dangers of the internet

The social model of disability recognises that many people with disabilities do not consider themselves to be 'vulnerable' and may be offended by the use of that word to describe their position. In terms of the criminal justice system, the UK charity the Mental Health Foundation has issued guidelines which set out the factors to be taken into consideration when reviewing cases and prosecuting offences classified as disability hate crimes (DHC). It also addresses the approach to be taken in other cases in which disability is a factor. For the purposes of Section 66 of the Sentencing Act (2020) (which applies to all convictions on or after December 1, 2020), 'disability' means any physical or mental impairment. Section 66 is also relevant to cases where the offender has assumed a person is disabled, whether or not that assumption is correct. In some cases, disabilities can be masked or exacerbated by alcoholism and drug dependency. Some people have a combination of disabilities. Some disabilities are obvious, some are hidden. Some people may not wish to disclose the fact that they have a disability.

International law enforcement agencies have reported an apparent preponderance of autistic individuals among perpetrators of cyber-dependent crimes such as hacking or spreading malware. Nevertheless, little empirical evidence exists to support such a relationship. In 2021, Katie Maras *et al* conducted the first study empirically to explore potential relationships between cyber-dependent crime and autism, autistic-like traits, explicit social cognition and perceived interpersonal support. The researchers wrote that one possibility was that 'the anecdotal evidence of apparent autism-like behaviour in cyber-dependent criminals may actually be reflecting people with high levels of autistic-like traits who do not have a diagnosis of autism' (see Chapter 6 on the criminal justice system).[453]

453 Katie Maras et al (2021) Revisiting the relationship between cybercrime, autistic traits and autism. *Journal of Autism and Developmental Disorders* **53** (12).

More alarming, on the contrary, is the proliferation of online material which may prove dangerous for those autistic internet users who are particularly vulnerable or impressionable. In some tragic instances, people have even taken their own lives after reading material online. This led parents to campaign for an amendment to the UK's Online Safety Bill. The Online Safety Act received Royal Assent in the Houses of Parliament on October 26, 2023. The Act puts an obligation on social media companies to keep the internet safe for children and to offer adults more choice over what they see online. Ofcom (the UK's communications regulator) immediately began work on tackling illegal content and protecting children's safety.

The Online Safety Act places legal responsibility on tech companies to prevent and rapidly remove illegal content, like terrorism and revenge pornography. They also have to prevent children from seeing material that is harmful to them, such as bullying, content promoting self-harm and eating disorders, and pornography. If they fail to comply with the rules, they will face significant fines that could reach billions of pounds, and if they do not take steps required by Ofcom to protect children, their bosses could even face imprisonment.

Baroness Kidron, the online safety campaigner, has worked with the bereaved families of autistic children in calling for this crucial legal amendment. The group of families – which also includes the father of Molly Russell, who died after viewing suicide content online – had written to the UK Prime Minister, the Justice Secretary and the Secretary of State for Science and Technology, calling for the law to be changed. Baroness Kidron said there needed to be 'a proper formal route for parents and for coroners to get the kind of information we need to see'. She told the BBC that the inquest into Frankie Thomas's death had 'opened and closed' without all the information the family needed from the tech firms. 'My inbox is full of bereaved families who want access to data,' she says. 'The coroner service has not managed to get that information, families have not managed to get that information. It is inhuman, and the sort of distress that is happening all of these years later is unacceptable.' She said the amendment had support across both houses of Parliament.[454]

The letter sent to the government – and seen by the BBC – said:

> 'We have each lost a child in circumstances relating to the digital world, and we have each struggled to gain information we needed to understand more about their deaths. Sadly, each year, there are hundreds of families who find themselves in similarly distressing circumstances. The process of attempting to access data has been inhumane. In some cases, it has taken years, and we have been left in automated loops, speaking to online bots, as though we were contacting lost property.'[455]

After the passage of the Online Safety Law, the British Technology Secretary Michelle Donelan, said:

> 'The Act takes a zero-tolerance approach to protecting children by making sure the buck stops with social media platforms for content they host. It does this by making sure they: remove illegal content quickly or prevent it from appearing in the first place, including content promoting self-harm; prevent children from accessing harmful and age-inappropriate content including pornographic content, content that promotes, encourages or provides instructions for suicide, self-harm or eating disorders, content depicting or encouraging serious violence or bullying content; enforce age limits and use age-checking measures on platforms where content harmful to children is published; ensure social media platforms are more transparent about the risks and dangers posed to children on their sites, including by publishing risk assessments; provide parents and children with clear and accessible ways to report problems online when they do arise.'[456]

For his part, the Lord Chancellor and Secretary of State for Justice, Alex Chalk, said:

> 'No one should be afraid of what they or their children might see online so our reforms will make the internet a safer place for everyone. Trolls who encourage serious self-harm, cyberflash or share intimate images without consent now face the very real prospect of time behind bars, helping protect women and girls who are disproportionately impacted by these cowardly crimes.'[457]

---

454 Kuenssberg L & Andersson J (2023) *Mother of Frankie Thomas wants answers from tech firms over daughter's death* [online]. Available at: www.bbc.co.uk/news/uk-64854204 (accessed January 2024).

455 Ibid.

456 Gov.co.uk (2023) *UK children and adults to be safer online as world-leading bill becomes law* [online]. Available at: www.gov.uk/government/news/uk-children-and-adults-to-be-safer-online-as-world-leading-bill-becomes-law (accessed January 2024).

457 Ibid.

In addition to protecting children, the Act also empowers adults to have better control of what they see online. It provides three layers of protection for internet users which will:

- Ensure illegal content is removed.
- Enforce the promises that social media platforms make to users when they sign up, through terms and conditions.
- Offer users the option to filter out content, such as online abuse, that they do not want to see.

If social media platforms do not comply with these rules, Ofcom could fine them up to £18 million or 10% of their global annual revenue, whichever is larger – meaning fines handed down to the biggest platforms could reach billions of pounds.

Dame Melanie Dawes, Ofcom's Chief Executive, remarked:

> 'Ofcom is not a censor, and our new powers are not about taking content down. Our job is to tackle the root causes of harm. We will set new standards online, making sure sites and apps are safer by design. Importantly, we'll also take full account of people's rights to privacy and freedom of expression. We know a safer life online cannot be achieved overnight; but Ofcom is ready to meet the scale and urgency of the challenge.'[458]

Case study 29: Frankie Thomas

A British mother said she was left 'in the wilderness' trying to obtain information from tech companies after her autistic daughter took her own life. Judy Thomas's 15-year-old autistic daughter, Frankie, died from suicide in 2018 after viewing self-harm material online. The family repeatedly tried to obtain information from tech companies and were left 'absolutely at a loss', Thomas told the BBC's *Sunday with Laura Kuenssberg* programme in 2023.[459]

Frankie was found dead at her home in Witley in Surrey in September 2018. An inquest heard she had taken her own life after spending months viewing graphic content about suicide and self-harm on school laptops and iPads. In an emotional interview, Thomas told the BBC that the family had 'no idea why Frankie had taken her own life. We wrote online to Instagram. This went on for about a year with no answers... We wanted to speak to somebody and just say, would you help us? We were devastated ... we just wanted to know. We would have really appreciated the platforms coming to the inquest, as they were requested to.'[460]

Meta, which owns Instagram – one of the sites accessed by Frankie – apologised to her family for their experience when they first contacted them. A spokesperson for Meta said:

> 'What the Thomas family have been through is devastating and our deepest sympathies are with them and anyone affected by suicide. This is a challenging and complex issue, and we must comply with our privacy and data protection obligations. We've been in touch with the family and want to be as helpful as we can during this time.'[461]

➔

458 Ibid.

459 See www.bbc.co.uk/news/uk-64854204#: ~ :text = A%20mother%20said%20she%20was,viewing%20 self%2Dharm%20material%20online. (accessed March 2024).

460 Ibid.

461 Ibid.

The inquest into Frankie's death heard that she had gone on a platform called Wattpad, where users can write and share stories, with the last piece she read mirroring the method she used to take her own life that afternoon.

Judy and other bereaved families said they wanted an amendment to the Online Safety Bill which would allow families and coroners to enlist the support of the regulator, Ofcom, in helping them legally to obtain information from tech companies about the material their children were accessing before they died. However, the Online Safety Act, which received Royal Assent in the Houses of Parliament on October 26, 2023, did not include any such amendment.

Autism and drugs

While autistic individuals are less likely to use substances, those who do so are more likely to self-medicate for their mental health symptoms, according to new research from the University of Cambridge and published in 2021 in *The Lancet Psychiatry*.[462] There is considerable debate over substance use by autistic adolescents and adults. Some studies indicate that autistic individuals are less likely to use substances, whereas others suggest that autistic individuals are at greater risk of substance misuse or abuse. The team at the Autism Research Centre in Cambridge used a 'mixed methods' design to consider both the frequency of substance use among autistic individuals, as well as their self-reported experiences of substance use. Overall, 1,183 autistic and 1,203 non-autistic adolescents and adults (aged 16-90 years) provided information about the frequency of their substance use via an anonymous, online survey; of this group, 919 individuals also gave more in-depth responses about their experiences of substance use. Autistic adults were less likely than non-autistic peers to use substances. Only 16% of autistic adults, compared to 22% of non-autistic adults, reported drinking on three or more days per week on average. Similarly, only 4% of autistic adults reported binge drinking compared to 8% of non-autistic adults.[463]

There were also some sex differences in patterns of substance use: autistic males were less likely than non-autistic males to report ever having smoked or used drugs. In contrast, the team did not find differences in the patterns of frequency of smoking or drug use between autistic and non-autistic females. However, despite lower rates of substance use overall, the qualitative findings of the study provide a much less hopeful picture: autistic adults were nearly nine times more likely than non-autistic peers to report using recreational drugs (such as marihuana, cocaine and amphetamines) to manage unwanted symptoms, including autism-related symptoms. Drugs were used to reduce sensory overload, help with mental focus, and provide routine, among other reasons.[464]

Several autistic participants also indirectly referenced using substances to mask their autism. Past research has shown that this behavioural management (also known as 'camouflaging' or 'compensating') has been linked to emotional exhaustion, worse mental

462 Weir E *et al* (2021) Understanding the substance use of autistic adolescents and adults: a mixed-methods approach, *Lancet Psychiatry* **8** (8) 673–685.

463 Ibid.

464 Ibid.

health, and even increased risk of suicide among autistic adults. Autistic adolescents and adults were also over three times more likely than others to report using substances to manage mental health symptoms, including anxiety, depression and suicidal thoughts. Several participants specifically noted that they used drugs for self-medication. However, this self-medication was not always viewed as negative by participants, and several noted that using recreational drugs allowed them to reduce the doses of prescribed medications for mental health conditions, which was for some a welcome relief from the significant side effects of their prescribed medications. Another area of concern was the strong association between vulnerability and substance use among autistic teenagers and adults. Previous work from the Cambridge team suggests that autistic adults may be much more likely to have adverse life experiences and be at greater risk of suicide than others.[465]

The findings of the new study indicate that autistic individuals are over four times more likely to report vulnerability associated with substance use compared to their non-autistic peers, including dependence/addiction, using drugs to deal with past trauma, and substance use associated with suicide. In addition, the study identified two new areas of vulnerability not previously reported: being forced, tricked, or accidentally taking drugs; and childhood use of substances (at the age of 12 years or younger). [466]

Elizabeth Weir, a PhD student at the Autism Research Centre in Cambridge and the lead researcher of the study, said:

> 'Whether or not the substances currently classed as "recreational" could be used medically remains an open question. It is evident that the current systems of health and social care support are not meeting the needs of many autistic teenagers and adults. No one should feel that they need to self-medicate for these issues without guidance from a healthcare professional. Identifying new forms of effective support is urgent considering the complex associations between substance use, mental health, and behaviour management – particularly as camouflaging and compensating behaviours are associated with suicide risk among autistic individuals.' [467]

Dr Carrie Allison, Director of Research Strategy at the Autism Research Centre and a member of the research team, observed:

> 'While some of our results suggest lower likelihood of substance use overall, physicians should not assume that their autistic patients aren't using drugs. Drug use can be harmful, so healthcare providers should aim to establish trusting relationships with autistic and non-autistic patients alike to foster frank and honest conversations about substance use.'[468]

Professor Sir Simon Baron-Cohen, Director at the Autism Research Centre and a member of the team, explained:

465 Ibid.

466 Ibid.

467 Ibid.

468 Ibid.

> 'We continue to see new areas in which autistic adults experience vulnerability: mental health, physical health, suicide risk, lifestyle patterns, the criminal justice system, and so on. Substance use is now another area that we need to consider when developing new forms of support for autistic individuals. It is essential that we ensure that autistic people have equal access to high-quality social and healthcare that can appropriately support their specific needs; and, unfortunately, it seems clear that our current systems are still not meeting this mark.' [469]

This Cambridge study did not differentiate between those with learning disabilities and those without. Ekaterina Harrison has affirmed that, if an autistic individual comprehends the consequences of his or her actions (in this case, using drugs), 'there need to be very strong arguments to excuse them from liability based on the disability argument'.[470] However, many of those without a learning disability are still in the dark about why they have been found guilty. Andrew Robertson (not his real name), the father of the now 40-year-old autistic man, 'Rob' (see **Case study 30** below), says that his son remains scarred by his arrests and spells behind bars and that he is displaying many of the features of post-traumatic stress disorder (PTSD): 'Lapses are all too possible. His family are left to pick up the bits, an open-ended commitment. His reputation remains radically compromised and rehab is uphill work. You could say it's up to him to climb out of the pit. It is, of course, but, with Rob's make-up, it's more like scaling Annapurna – without crampons.'[471]

Case study 30: 'Rob'

Mind-altering drugs played a part in the 2019 case of a 35-year-old autistic man, Rob (not his real name), who was convicted of harassment by a magistrates' court. According to his father, Andrew Robertson (also not his real name), his son has a faulty understanding of why he was found guilty and was punished with a community sentence: unpaid work, probation and a restraining order. Robertson said:

> 'Some will say that the mess was all about drugs, but this is nonsense. Rob was using drugs to make his existence tolerable – he was self-medicating. Expert observers of high-functioning autistic people recognise that mind-altering drugs are often part of the picture, especially when combined with mental health problems.'[472]

According to Robertson, when Rob was off drugs, he was:

> '...mildly odd, a bit paranoid and depressed, difficult to engage but harmless, in fact, generous spirited. When using, he became acutely psychotic, a different person. I've lost count of the number of times an ambulance was called because of psychotic escapades which threatened to cause him serious harm or put him at odds with the law.'[473] ➔

---

469 Ibid.

470 Ekaterina Harriso, personal communication.

471 Transform Justice (2021) *A different understanding? How the CJS discriminates against those with autism.* Available at: www.transformjustice.org.uk/news-insight/a-different-understanding-how-the-cjs-discriminates-against-those-with-autism/ (accessed January 2024).

472 See www.transformjustice.org.uk/news-insight/a-different-understanding-how-the-cjs-discriminates-against-those-with-autism/ (acceased March 2024).

473 Ibid.

During one episode, according to his father, Rob broke his restraining order by sending a one-word text message ('Hi'); during another, he was sectioned for a few days because he was found walking on a railway line. In another, he drove a car into a pond, then squatted in what he believed was an empty house. Here, he moved a bicycle from a garage to the drive as a get-away option. He planned to return it later, had no intention of stealing (owning two bikes already), and was later astonished when charged with burglary – in the eyes of the law as it stands, outhouses such as garages count as dwellings and moving an item is theft.

> 'When the police arrived, he fled through dense woods, temporarily evading police helicopters and dogs, diving into a lake and remaining submerged (it was mid-winter) as long as he could, thinking he'd be invisible to his pursuers. He was tazered, arrested, admitted to hospital and later a police cell. As usual, the local mental health team refused to get involved, because drugs were in the picture. At interview, he said he believed he had been in a video game.'[474]

As outlined in Chapter 6 (see p.179), while Rob was awaiting trial on a burglary charge his already poor relationship with his probation officer hit rock bottom. Rob failed to attend court and was therefore arrested and remanded in custody for breaching his supervision order, and because he was awaiting trial for burglary. On his first night in prison, Rob should have been placed on the vulnerable prisoners' wing. Instead, according to his father, he was put on a regular wing which he shared with a violent individual. There was a disagreement. Rob was beaten up by his cellmate, aided by others in nearby cells.[475]

His solicitor now moved his case to the crown court in the hope of a more expert approach. An 'exceptionally humane and intelligent' judge (in Robertson's words) said that this was not about criminality, but mental health problems and gave Rob a suspended sentence. Unfortunately, Rob had another episode just six weeks later, again on drugs. According to his father, Rob thought that there were people in his house intent on killing him. Police and ambulance were called and, as usual, he was not admitted to a mental health unit but returned to prison. The arrest was forceful and painful, his father said. Rob's reaction was to lash out with an 'air bite' (he literally bit the air). For this, he was charged with assault – a breach of his suspended sentence.[476]

Cuckooing

Cuckooing is a practice whereby people take over a person's home and use the property to facilitate exploitation. It takes its name from cuckoos, who take over the nests of other birds. Autistic people are particularly vulnerable to this practice. According to Yo Dunn, autistic individuals can be 'book-smart' but not street-smart:

> 'Many of them can learn through studying but they will let a stranger into the house. Even highly educated, apparently very capable people with no support needs who are autistic are also very naïve and easy to exploit. It can be because we can't process fast enough, or we are not good at detecting the possibility that somebody may not actually be telling us the truth.'[477]

---

474 Ibid.

475 Ibid.

476 Ibid.

477 Yo Dunn, personal communication, January 5, 2023.

There are various types of cuckooing:

- Using the property to grow, deal, store or take drugs.
- Using the property for sex work.
- Using the property to store weapons.
- Taking over the property as a place for them to live.
- Taking over the property in order to abuse the tenant financially.

The most common form of cuckooing is where drug dealers or gang members take over a person's home and use it to store or distribute drugs. They may begin by befriending the adult at risk. They will then offer the adult something of interest to them. This could be a relationship, friendship, drugs and/or alcohol, money or clothing. In exchange, they may ask to 'borrow' a room to store something or meet other 'friends' at the property. In some cases, the gang may make it clear that this is for criminal purposes, for example, drug supply, or they may use an excuse as to why they want to use the property. Gradually, the 'benefits' will reduce and may eventually come to an end, and more and more people will come and go from the address. The gang members/drug dealers may threaten the adult at risk verbally or physically if they try to put a stop to their criminal activity. They will also discourage family, friends and support workers from visiting the vulnerable adult's address.[478]

In 2023, a prominent Labour MP, Jess Phillips, and the former Conservative Party leader, Sir Iain Duncan Smith, led calls for cuckooing to be criminalised as part of an overhaul of the 2015 Modern Slavery Act. Duncan Smith, the MP for Chingford and Woodford Green, said:

> 'It cannot be right that the invasion of someone's home by gangs for criminal purposes is out of the reach of the Modern Slavery Act. This isn't a drug crime or a property crime, it is a crime that devastates vulnerable people in the very place that should be their sanctuary.'[479]

The proposal to make cuckooing a crime is part of calls to update the law on modern slavery. The Centre for Social Justice (CSJ) think-tank said nearly four times as many modern slavery victims were formally identified and referred for support in 2021 compared with the year the laws were introduced. One rescued victim of cuckooing told the CSJ:

> 'It was the bereavement of my mum; I was taken advantage of. They was [sic] feeding me free drugs. 'Cos I was so wasted on what they were giving me I didn't even see the change until it was too late when people started moving in and then when the prostitution started.'

Another survivor said:

> 'It's scary, your house is taken over, you don't know who's knocking on your door. People coming to your door every two minutes looking for them. They're

478 See https://thebasementproject.org.uk/articles/what-you-need-to-know-about-cuckooing/ (accessed March 2024).

479 See *The Observer*, February 26, 2023. www.theguardian.com/uk-news/2023/feb/26/jess-phillips-and-iain-duncan-smith-lead-calls-to-criminalise-cuckooing (accessed January 2024).

> threatening people in your home, threatening me in my home. It totally takes over your life.'[480]

The Crown Prosecution Service says cuckooing can be out of reach of the Modern Slavery Act if the victim has done nothing apart from acquiesce to drugs being supplied from their home. But if they are forced into labour, threatened or attacked, charges could be brought under existing laws.

The UK government announced in May 2022 that it planned a new modern slavery Bill to 'strengthen the protection and support for victims of human trafficking and modern slavery and increase the accountability of companies and other organisations to drive out modern slavery from their supply chains'. However, it did not specifically mention addressing cuckooing.

A Home Office spokesperson said: 'Cuckooing is wholly unacceptable and the government is determined to tackle it and those who perpetrate this abuse. There are a range of tools that can be applied to disrupt this behaviour which can result in criminal sanctions if breached.' It said police had closed down more than 2,900 lines, made more than 8,000 arrests, and engaged more than 9,500 people through safeguarding interventions.[481]

Case study 31: Curt Hennells

Curt Hennells, a 40-year-old autistic man, was spared jail in 2020 because he had been forced into selling drugs by others who had taken over his flat, a court heard. Hennells was caught red-handed dealing in MDMA and cannabis but was a victim of 'cuckooing', a judge was told.[482]

Neighbours in Stonehouse, near Plymouth, in south-west England, called the police after smelling the plants being grown, Plymouth Crown Court heard. Judge James Townsend said that dealing in Class A drugs such as MDMA could have brought Hennells a sentence of up to four-and-a-half years in prison – minus discounts for his guilty plea and good character.

The judge added, however:

> 'I am taking an exceptional course. I am satisfied that you have been the victim of pressure put on you by other people. It was pressure to which you succumbed. You should not have done, but without that pressure you would not be in this situation. I have read a lot about you and you have difficulties, and difficulties which you are trying to tackle. This is your last chance.'[483]

Hennells pleaded guilty to possession of a Class A drug and possession of a Class B drug with intent to supply on April 22, 2018. Herc Ashworth, for the Crown Prosecution Service, said that police had found plants growing around the house with the aid of specialist lights. The barrister added that Hennells' mobile phone showed he had been dealing in both drugs.

The court heard that the total value of the cannabis was £2,550 and the street worth of the MDMA was £60.

---

480 Ibid.

481 Ibid.

482 See www.plymouthherald.co.uk/news/plymouth-news/vulnerable-plymouth-dealer-cuckooed-people-4258135 (accessed January 2024).

483 Ibid.

Useful resources and further guidance

Guidance for Working with Adults at Risk of Exploitation: Cuckooing, by Leicestershire Safeguarding Adults Board, 2020, is available at: www.llradultsafeguarding.co.uk/guidance-for-working-with-adults-at-risk-of-exploitation-cuckooing/ (accessed January 2024).

Disability hate crime and autism

The Equality Act (2010) generally defines a disabled person as someone who has a physical or mental impairment which has a substantial and long-term adverse effect on his or her ability to carry out normal day-to-day activities. People with learning disabilities are 'invisible' in UK government hate crime statistics, even though there is widespread evidence of people being targeted in hate crime attacks, according to a report published in 2018. The report entitled *A Life Without Fear?* argued that learning disability hate crime needed to be prioritised by the government and better monitoring was required to develop more effective ways of addressing the issue.[484]

Disability hate crimes and non-crime incidents are acts which target a victim because of the offender's hostility to a disabled person or disabled people in general. So any incident or crime which is perceived by the victim to be a disability hate crime will be recorded as such. If the offender is to have a sentence enhanced by the court, then prosecutors must provide evidence to prove that hostility, but such proof is not required for recording purposes. Hate crimes can be committed against a person or property.[485]

Hate crimes targeted at people with learning disabilities included fraud, violence and taking over people's property for the purposes of criminal activity such as drug dealing or prostitution – a practice known as cuckooing (*see previous section*).

There are approximately 1.4 million people in the UK identified as having a learning disability, and a recent national survey found that almost three in four autistic people and/or people with learning disabilities had experienced hate crime. The effects of these crimes on the mental health of these victims can be very serious. An additional study showed that one in four of those targeted because of their learning disabilities were more likely to report feeling suicidal as a result of their victimisation.[486]

In response to this issue, the Foundation for People with Learning Disabilities recently established the National Forum for Learning Disabilities and Autism Hate Crime. The objectives of this group are to keep a watchful brief in addressing the under-reporting of learning disability hate crimes, reduce the barriers for victims, ensure reasonable adjustments are available, support the work of the #I'm with Sam Campaign, and ensure that victims with a learning disability and autism are leaders in this campaign.

---

484 See www.mentalhealth.org.uk/about-us/news/new-report-shows-people-learning-disabilities-are-high-risk-targeting-hate-crime-yet-remain (accessed March 2024).

485 See www.cps.gov.uk/legal-guidance/disability-hate-crime-and-other-crimes-against-disabled-people-prosecution-guidance (accessed March 2024).

486 See www.mentalhealth.org.uk/about-us/news/new-report-shows-people-learning-disabilities-are-high-risk-targeting-hate-crime-yet-remain (accessed March 2024).

Learning disability hate crime is any criminal offence that is perceived – by the victim or any other person – to be motivated by hostility or prejudice based on a person's learning disability or perceived learning disability. It can take many forms, including verbal abuse, physical abuse, threatening behaviour, bullying/teasing, online/phone abuse, damage to property/theft and can even lead to death.

There is no offence of stirring up hatred based on disability, which contrasts with the position in relation to offences of stirring up hatred on grounds of race, religion and sexual orientation.

The Director's Guidance on Charging requires offences that are classified as hate crimes under CPS policies to be referred to a prosecutor for early consultation and a charging decision, whether admitted by the suspect or not. (The CPS prosecutes criminal cases in England and Wales.) There is no aggravated offence of disability hate crime, but Section 66 of the Sentencing Act (2020) imposes a duty upon courts when considering the seriousness of an offence, to treat as an aggravating factor that either:

- At the time of committing the offence, or immediately before or after doing so, the offender demonstrated towards the victim of the offence hostility based on a disability (or presumed disability) of the victim; or
- The offence was motivated (wholly or partly) by hostility towards persons who have a disability or a particular disability.[487]

Case study 32: Verbal abuse in North Shields

Paul Lyness, 41, was convicted of threatening his autistic neighbour and verbally abusing her with a string of disgusting slurs. The 31-year-old autistic woman, who has not been named, had lived with her partner at the flat they shared in North Shields for two years before Lyness moved in next door. In 2019, South Tyneside Magistrates' Court heard how he proceeded to play loud music and host parties with friends into the early hours of the morning. His behaviour left his autistic neighbour extremely distressed, as her disability left her sensitive to loud noises and disruption to her normal routine.[488]

She submitted a complaint to her local council and the court was told how this had led to friction between her and Lyness. Tensions eventually boiled over on the evening of April 19, 2018, when Lyness began throwing objects around his own back yard while screaming obscenities at her at the top of his voice. The autistic woman began to video his behaviour, at which point he said: 'I'm going to rip your throat out'. She fled inside and called the police to report the incident. Officers later arrested Lyness on suspicion of a public order offence.[489]

The court was told how the offence was then investigated as a hate crime due to the references to the victim's autism. On January 16, 2019, Lyness admitted the public order offence in court and was given a 13-week prison sentence, suspended for 12 months. He was also ordered to pay compensation of £100, a £115 victim surcharge and £300 in costs. ➔

487 See www.cps.gov.uk/legal-guidance/disability-hate-crime-and-other-crimes-against-disabled-people-prosecution-guidance (accessed January 2024).

488 See www.chroniclelive.co.uk/news/north-east-news/cruel-north-shields-thug-threatened-15746415 (accessed January 2024)

489 Ibid.

Following the case, his autistic victim thanked officers at Northumbria Police: 'I hadn't been diagnosed with autism for that long before this happened and I was going through a really difficult time. On that particular night, he had been making a lot of noise in the garden and I was already feeling worried about it. When he saw me recording what he was doing, he got even more angry and that's when he threatened to rip my throat out. It was then that I knew I had to get the police involved, but even that worried me as I didn't know whether it would just make things worse. The officers who came out were really comforting and made me feel safe again, after months of feeling like I was treading on eggshells. They treated me with respect, reassured me that it wasn't my fault and I'm glad that this man has been dealt with in court for how he treated me. If anyone else is in my shoes and doesn't think the police will believe them, then I want you to know that the best thing to do is to report it.'[490]

Useful resources and further guidance

- You can report a hate crime in a number of different ways, either directly to the police, by calling the 101 number, or through a third-party reporting centre.
- The police and their partners at the charity Dimensions have produced a guide for people who support disabled victims. The guide offers information to help keep people safe including how to spot signs of abuse and how to support the victim to get the service to which they are entitled in order to prevent future abuse. You can download the guide here: www.report-it.org.uk/files/disability_hate_crime_guide_for_carers_and_supporters_september_2020.pdf (accessed January 2024).

Alleged links with terrorism

A 'staggeringly high' number of autistic people – including children – are being 'drawn into' terrorism, according to Jonathan Hall QC, the Independent Reviewer of Terrorism Legislation. His comments came after police revealed that more than one in ten terror suspects arrested in the UK was now a child, and that most were linked to Right-wing extremism.

Hall said that autism was a 'relevant factor' for people being drawn into terrorist violence, alongside other cognitive difficulties and a person's family background. He told an event hosted by the think-tank, Bright Blue, in 2021: 'My understanding is that the incidence of autism in Prevent referrals is also staggeringly high. It is as if a social problem has been unearthed and fallen into the lap of counter-terrorism professionals.'[491] (Prevent is the UK government's counter-extremism programme.)

Hall questioned whether criminal prosecution was the right outcome in all cases, such as those over the possession of 'material likely to be useful to a terrorist'. He asked: 'Is the use of strong powers to detect and investigate suspected terrorism in children justified? I believe it is, because of the potential risk to the general public, but is the criminal justice outcome the right one in all cases?'

490 Ibid.

491 See www.theguardian.com/uk-news/2021/jul/07/staggeringly-high-number-of-people-with-autism-on-uk-prevent-scheme#: ~ :text = Hall % 20will % 20say % 20 % E2 % 80 % 9Cautism % 20plus,or % 20some % 20other % 20cognitive % 20 difficulty % E2 % 80 % 9D. (acced March 2924).

He added that possessing terrorist material: 'does not necessarily mean you are going to do something with it. What about autistic people who simply develop what is called a "special interest" in this sort of material? Police and prosecutors fret about whether there is an alternative to arrest and prosecution.'[492]

Hall's most recent report on the operation of terror laws in the UK said that evidence suggested autism was 'over-represented in lone-actor terrorist samples, compared to the general population... Unpalatable though it may be, a large number of lone-actor plots are believed by counter-terror police, rightly or wrongly, to involve individuals on the autistic spectrum.'[493]

In his 2021 speech, Hall drew attention to several autistic teenagers who had been convicted of plotting terror attacks in recent cases, including the Isis supporter Lloyd Gunton (see **Case study 34** on p.224), and the neo-Nazi Jack Reed. Reed, one of the UK's youngest terror plotters, was jailed for six years and eight months in 2020, aged just 17, for preparing neo-Nazi acts of terrorism. Reed had detailed plans to firebomb synagogues and other buildings in the Durham area as part of what he believed was an upcoming 'race war'. He was given a new prison sentence at the end of 2020 for child sex offences. His lawyers had applied for a ban on identifying him a day before his birthday on Christmas Eve, 2020, when the automatic anonymity afforded to child offenders was due to expire. The Recorder of Manchester, Judge Nicholas Dean QC, granted an extension to the restrictions but threw the application out following a challenge by the Press Association agency.[494]

Sentencing Reed for terror offences, the previous Recorder of Manchester, Judge David Stockdale QC, found the teenager's subsequently diagnosed autism had played some part in his offending. He described the teenager as 'highly intelligent, widely read, quick-thinking and articulate' but told him that it was 'a matter of infinite regret that you pursued at such a young age a twisted and – many would say – a sick ideological path.'[495]

The role of autism in terror offending was considered by the Court of Appeal in January 2021, when another neo-Nazi, Paul Dunleavy, then 17, appealed his conviction. He was jailed for five-and-a-half years for preparing acts of terrorism by researching how to convert a blank-firing gun into a live weapon and providing 'advice and encouragement' to others online.

The Court of Appeal heard evidence that, 'many autistic people have intense and highly focused interests', such as Dunleavy's obsession with guns, but judges ruled that autism did not 'make it reasonable for him to possess [terrorist] information for a particular purpose, when it would not be reasonable for anyone else to do so.'[496]

Lawyers defending autistic people accused of terror offences frequently argue that associated traits and characteristics played an instrumental part in their actions.

---

492 Ibid.

493 See www.independent.co.uk/news/uk/home-news/autism-terrorism-children-cases-radicalisation-b1879719.html (accessed March 2024).

494 Ibid.

495 Ibid.

496 Ibid.

In November 2020, a barrister representing another teenage neo-Nazi propagandist, Harry Vaughan, said his autism and a 'deficiency in emotional intelligence' made him susceptible to influence from online groups.

All these cases have primarily involved online radicalisation, either where the defendants have 'self-initiated' or have come into contact with other extremists through social media, gaming and chat forums.

The national coordinator for the Prevent programme, Chief Superintendent Nik Adams, had previously told *The Independent* that autistic people were 'more vulnerable to ... obsession, fascination, fixation'. He warned that online terrorist propaganda 'plays entirely into that, because what it seeks to do is mobilise people very quickly to do something really terrible'. He added that the number of people being referred to Prevent with mixed or unclear ideological beliefs was also rising and included those with 'complex needs', including autism and mental illness.[497]

Clare Hughes, criminal justice manager at the National Autistic Society, said many autistic people and families were concerned that high-profile cases could:

> '...warp public understanding... The vast majority of the 700,000 autistic people in the UK are law-abiding – sometimes particularly so, because of a propensity to know and stick to the rules. If autistic people do come into contact with the criminal justice system, it's absolutely essential that professionals working in the system really understand autism and that specialist support is available for autistic children and adults when it's needed. At the same time, the right early support must be available to stop people getting into dangerous situations, including mental health support to help autistic people to navigate what can feel like a chaotic and overwhelming world.'[498]

Back in 2017, Britain's National Counter-Terrorism Security Office (NaCTSO) ran a counter-terrorism campaign for the travel industry. It included a video, entitled 'How To Identify and Respond to Suspicious Behaviour'. For David ('Panda') Mery, an autistic man who was wrongfully arrested in 2005 (see **Case study 33** on p.223), this campaign was highly problematic, since, he says:

> '...we autistics tend to have our idiosyncratic behaviours everywhere we go, and increased stress in a public space is likely to exaggerate our atypical behaviours... This counter-terrorism campaign is likely to exacerbate some of the very behaviours NaCTSO deems suspicious.'[499]

Mery pointed out that a leaflet accompanying the campaign listed examples of 'suspicious behaviour', which also tended to be common autistic behaviours:

- Loitering in restricted or public areas.
- Paying significant interest to entrances, exits, CCTV or security staff, taking photos.

497 Ibid.

498 Ibid.

499 Mery P (2017) Counter terrorism campaign, a risk for autistics [online]. Available at: www.autangel.org.uk/counter-terrorism-campaign-a-risk-for-autistics/ (accessed January 2024).

- Concealing face/identity.
- Asking unusual or security-related questions.
- Avoiding security staff.
- Activity inconsistent with the nature of the building or area.

As Mery noted: 'I have done all of them. I am autistic, not a terrorist.'[500] He quoted one police officer as suggesting that autistic members of the public should carry an autism card that can be verified by police. 'Anyone being stopped due to their autistic traits could produce their card and (in theory) be on their way quickly, once their details have been confirmed', the officer said. To this, Mery responded:

> 'How autistics are being treated should not rely on the presence of such a card. The card has a role in helping communications by indicating some common or specific issues and possibly indicating ... someone to contact in an emergency. It is especially useful for non-verbal neurodivergents and those who become non-verbal in stressful situations, such as an arrest.... The main issue with such a system is about who has the power over our autistic identities. Currently, the medical profession acts as a gatekeeper of the diagnosis. This is based on the medical model and is far from ideal. Services should be available on the basis of needs, not medical diagnosis, and one's identity should not require an external gatekeeper, We should move towards the social and neurodiversity models, not towards an even more authoritarian model.' [501]

Mery added that the problem was exacerbated by:

> '...the ease with which some police forces may arrest people, compared to their reluctance to apologise and offer compensation for erroneous and unlawful arrests. For instance, after my unlawful arrest, it took me more than four years for the Metropolitan Police Service to admit the arrest was unlawful and apologise (and 12 years later, their legal department still retains some files about that arrest). The traumatising impact of ending in police custody for autistics, and other neurodivergent individuals, potentially targeted for their atypical behaviours by this counter-terrorism campaign, can be serious if it ends up causing more wrongful arrests, while not making us safer from terrorism.' [502]

In 2021, Dr Rachel Moseley, a principal academic in psychology at Bournemouth University, spoke at a panel debate as part of the UK government's Open Innovation (OI) Team, which liaises with academics and experts to generate ideas for policy and provide policy analysis. 'The participants were keen to get to the bottom of what they perceived to be a link between autism and radicalisation – their idea being that people with autism are more likely to become involved in terrorist activities. However, there is no credible evidence to suggest that autistic people are more likely than non-autistic people to hold sympathetic views on violent protest or terrorism. There is even some evidence that terror

---

500 Ibid.

501 Ibid.

502 Ibid.

networks are more reluctant to recruit people with any kind of mental health problem or neurodivergence, perhaps due to social stigma:

> 'So, my first job on the panel was to speak up and set the record straight. While there is no evidence to suggest that autistic people are more likely to be radicalised, there is evidence to suggest that they are disproportionately likely to be referred, inappropriately and unfairly, to prevention programmes. This is likely because those around them lack a nuanced understanding of autism, so that certain behaviours and interests can be easily misconstrued. Furthermore, while the evidence base for a link between autism and terrorism is exceedingly weak, numerous studies have shown us that autism stigma puts autistic people at risk of mental ill-health and suicidality. I wanted the OI Team to be aware of this, so their work would be better informed. Knowing the harm caused by such misperceptions and the stigma they generate, I also felt it was especially important to steer the discussion in the right direction.'[503]

Case study 33: Panda Mery

On July 28, 2005, David ('Panda') Mery, a British technology journalist, was arrested at Southwark Underground Station while heading to meet his wife after work. In his own words:[504]

> 'I was carrying a backpack. While waiting for the Tube, I looked at people coming on the platform, I played with my mobile phone, I took a piece of paper from inside my jacket. The police found my behaviour suspicious and instigated a security alert. They surrounded me. They asked me to take off my backpack. They handcuffed me in the back. They closed and cordoned off the Tube station. They stopped and searched me under Section 44 of the Terrorism Act 2000. They emptied my pockets. They loosened my belt. Explosive officers checked my backpack, gave the all-clear and joked about my laptop. The handcuffs were taken off (for a few minutes) and some of the stuff I was carrying in my pockets was given back to me.
>
> This should have been the end of the matter. Instead, an officer informed Mery that he was under arrest on suspicion of causing a Public Nuisance. 'They then took me to Walworth police station. They processed me. They took photographs, DNA samples, fingerprints and palm prints. They searched our flat. They interviewed me. Nine hours later, I was granted bail. One month later, when I surrendered to custody, they said they had decided to take no further action. It takes a further month and half to get my possessions back. Three months after the arrest, the Police National Computer was still listing me as under arrest... Despite all the available evidence (bar CCTV footage in the station, which the police never seized), investigators from the Met's Directorate of Professional Standards failed to find that my arrest was unlawful. [They said that there were] "reasonable grounds to suspect an offence had been committed by Mr Mery and, as such, the arrest was both lawful and justified." ... The Independent Police Complaint Commission was of no help as "[i]t is not within the remit of the IPCC to direct the Metropolitan Police Service to issue a formal and public apology for their action".' ➔

503 See: www.bournemouth.ac.uk/about/regional-engagement/public-affairs-policy-impact/setting-record-straight-around-autism-radicalisation (accessed March 2024),

504 (see: https://gizmonaut.net/blog/uk/2009/09/mps_apologises.html) Reproduced with the kind permission of Panda Mery.

It was not until 2009 that Chief Superintendent Wayne Chance, Metropolitan Police Service Borough Commander for Southwark, apologised to Mery and his wife.

Mery wrote:

> 'Being aware of the long-term impact of their actions will encourage police officers to realise that arresting innocents is not the only option available to them. Letting innocents go free and safe must be possible and has to be the preferred option. I hope that lessons will be learned and that in future, when mistakes are made, they will be acknowledged immediately. My DNA samples were destroyed and my DNA profile, fingerprints, palm prints and PNC record deleted two years ago. The litigation files maintained by the Directorate of Legal Services and the investigation files compiled by the Directorate of Professional Standards will be retained for a further six years, after which there should be no trace at the Metropolitan Police Service about this innocent.'

Since this experience, Mery has become an active campaigner on a number of human and civil rights issues.

Case study 34: Lloyd Gunton

Lloyd Gunton, a 17-year-old autistic boy who was 'hours away from committing an act of atrocity' in Cardiff, was detained indefinitely in 2018 and told he had to serve at least 11 years. Gunton was arrested after researching the security arrangements of a Justin Bieber concert, Birmingham Crown Court heard. The jury was told he had plotted to commit mass murder in an Islamic State-inspired vehicle attack.[505]

Gunton, from near Llantrisant, in South Wales, was arrested after he uploaded social media content to the photo-sharing social media site Instagram, in late-June 2017, which promoted jihad and supported al-Qaeda. Police found the password for the account was 'truck attack'. One post read: 'May Allah bring terrorism to Cardiff on 30th June'. He had researched how to carry out a vehicle ramming attack and how to stab and kill and had also looked into the security arrangements of the Justin Bieber concert in Cardiff's Principality Stadium.[506]

Gunton's defence counsel, Delroy Henry, likened the teenager's interest in Isis to rubberneckers on a motorway. 'He was drawn into it, curiosity getting the better of him,' Henry said. However, the judge, Mark Wall QC, told Gunton: 'The police found a rucksack in your room which contained a knife, a hammer and what has been referred to as a suicide note or a martyrdom letter. In the martyrdom letter, you referred to yourself as a 'soldier of Isis'. The letter was written in such terms that it was obviously to be found and read after you had carried out a terrorist attack.'[507]

Gunton was found guilty of one charge of engaging in the preparation of a terrorist act, two charges of encouraging terrorism, and a further two charges of possessing terrorist information.

➔

505 See www.theguardian.com/uk-news/2018/mar/02/teenager-lloyd-gunton-jailed-cardiff-pop-concert-terrorist-attack-plot (accessed March 2024).

506 Ibid.

507 Ibid.

The judge told him:

> 'At the time of your arrest, you were within hours of committing an act of atrocity on the streets of Cardiff. It is not possible to estimate how many people would have been murdered or seriously injured by your actions as the attack was foiled before you could undertake it. I am sure that you planned not just the killing of one person but rather mass murder.'[508]

Gunton showed no obvious emotion in the dock as he was told that his autism, young age and previous good character had saved him from an even longer minimum term. The judge informed him that the 'usual range' of minimum sentences for someone convicted of similar offences was 21 to 30 years. The judge said of Gunton's autism:

> 'This condition made you something of a loner and someone more easily impressed by the things you read on the internet. Yours is not a condition from which you will recover. It is important that, having been tempted to commit a serious offence such as this, you are under some form of supervision for the rest of your life.'

Autistic victims of the asylum battle

The concept of political asylum as a basic right was first expressed in Article 14(1) of the 1948 Universal Declaration of Human Rights, prompted by the experience of those fleeing Nazi persecution in the run-up to and during the Second World War. The 1951 Convention Relating to the Status of Refugees (the Refugee Convention) broadened the criteria under which states would grant asylum to include not just those fearing persecution on traditional political grounds but also those with a 'well-founded fear of being persecuted for reasons of race, religion, nationality, membership of a particular social group' (see Article 1A(2) as amended by the 1967 Protocol). In particular, the Refugee Convention granted a broad range of specific entitlements to those recognised as falling within its criteria.[509]

Although the international legal framework for the protection of refugees was established in the immediate aftermath of the Second World War, asylum did not become a significant issue in most Western countries until after the end of the Cold War when the number of asylum seekers rose significantly. Attention has been focused on the gap between the rights of foreign nationals under UK law vis-à-vis the rights of UK citizens. Although the Refugee Convention grants a broad range of rights for those recognised by the state as refugees under the Convention, it is largely silent on the position of those applying for refugee status, that is, asylum seekers. (The Refugee Convention does provide some limited protection, including Article 31, which prohibits states from imposing penalties on refugees who entered the country illegally.) In the absence of such protection, the provisions of the European Convention on Human Rights (ECHR), by way of the Human Rights Act (1998), have been used to safeguard the rights of asylum seekers.

---

508 Ibid.

509 For further details on the history of asylum legislation, see https://justice.org.uk/asylum-human-rights/

There have been a number of cases affecting the fate of autistic children in the UK, with very varying outcomes. In some cases, the best interests of the autistic child are respected and he or she is permitted to remain in the UK. In others, the best interests of the child 'lose out' to the interests of national security or well-being (see two contrasting examples below).

An example of a positive outcome was that of a Brazilian mother who had arrived in the UK in 2002 as a student. She had been given leave to remain in that capacity until January 2004 and then overstayed. Her son was born in Britain in 2011 and was subsequently diagnosed as autistic. His mother contended that it was in his best interests to remain in the UK. She applied for permission to stay on human rights grounds but was refused in 2017. Her appeal against this decision was dismissed by first-tier Tribunal Judge Wyman in 2018. However, permission to appeal again was granted by Judge of the First-tier Tribunal Birrell on the basis that it was arguable that the first-tier judge had erred in law in failing to identify the best interests of the child and failing to factor these into the proportionality assessment under Article 8 of the European Convention on Human Rights.[510]

It was accepted by both parties that the appeal would be determined by application of Section 117B(6) of the Nationality, Immigration and Asylum Act (2002), in light of the second appellant (the autistic child), now having been in the UK for over seven years. The child's exceptional circumstances were highlighted: namely, that he was doing very well at his English school with special support, that any change would be distressing for him and that he had friends in the UK. His mother did a great deal of voluntary work at her son's school, where she helped parents who did not speak English and those who had autistic children who were going through the process of getting a diagnosis and obtaining support. She also helped at a children's centre running a support network for parents of disabled children. The child's father, a British Muslim, had refused to have anything to do with his son.

Since his diagnosis of autism in November 2014, the boy had received assistance from educational psychologists, occupational therapists and speech and language therapists and had a place in a specialist autism unit in a state primary school in south London. The Court of Appeal heard that he found all change very challenging and resorted to hitting himself or his mother or others or closing down and not speaking if even minor things did not follow his predictable routine, such as his not being able to have his 'normal' seat on the bus or his regular teacher not being present at school. The boy could not speak Portuguese because his mother had spoken English with him since his birth.

With the help of all of the professional support, the boy had made considerable progress: he was now toilet trained, he could clean his teeth, was learning social rules and, thanks to working with an occupational therapist, was doing exercises and using a sensory room to help him when stressed. His mother believed that it would not be in her son's best interests for him to have to go and live in Brazil. She said she was unaware of any appropriate educational provision or services for autistic people there and she did not think he would cope with the change. Indeed, she believed he would be bullied. Her

510 See https://tribunalsdecisions.service.gov.uk/utiac/hu-15387-2018-ors (accessed March 2024).

legal advocate argued that the boy's best interests were overwhelmingly to remain in the UK and that this must be a primary consideration in the proportionality assessment. In Brazil, the boy would not only be in a completely new and different place, as he had never been to Brazil or met or had contact with any of his mother's family there, but he would not be able to understand anyone, as he did not speak Portuguese and had shown he was resistant to learning this language. Furthermore, the support he was now receiving in the UK had been tailored to fit his needs. To return the child to Brazil would lead to an impairment in his development and would thus be contrary to his best interests, the advocate argued.

The appeals court judge finally ruled in 2018 that the best interests were clearly that the boy should remain in the UK:

> 'I find that the first appellant is integrated into UK society, and is contributing to the community through volunteer work to the Early Years Centre and ... the Primary School and to the community at St Luke's Church; and that she speaks fluent English which is to be seen as a neutral matter. On the other side, in considering whether it is reasonable to expect the second appellant to leave, is firstly the fact that the first appellant has overstayed her leave to remain in the UK, although there is nothing further in terms of deception, use of false identities or criminality. Secondly, it is the case that, at the current time, the appellants are not financially independent as the first appellant does not have work permission, and thus they are a financial burden on the taxpayer. When the negative matters are balanced against the best interests of the second appellant, however, I conclude that it is not reasonable or proportionate to require the second appellant to leave the UK, and that the appeal should therefore be allowed under Article 8 of the ECHR.' [511]

In stark contrast, in another case, an autistic boy, referred to as L., was ordered to return to Nigeria even though it was suggested there was strong evidence that he would be subjected to considerable stigma there, or might be even accused of witchcraft. The boy's Nigerian mother had arrived in the UK in 2009 with leave as a dependent of her husband, who was a student in the UK and who himself had leave to remain in the UK until 2010. Subsequently, the mother's leave was extended in line with that of her husband until 2013. However, on March 8, 2013, the UK Secretary of State refused the mother's claim for asylum and four days later ordered her to return to Nigeria.[512]

The judge accepted that L. was autistic, that he was currently attending a mainstream school but that, if he remained in the UK, he would attend a school for children with special educational needs in the autumn:

> 'L. currently shows little communicative intent. His ability to communicate is at a pre-verbal level, with a reliance on the use of vocalisation, simple physical gestures and adult interpretation of his needs. L. is reported to respond well to music and songs and will attempt to join in. He presents as having a limited understanding of spoken language... L. is totally dependent on adult assistance, as he is not able

511 Ibid.

512 See https://tribunalsdecisions.service.gov.uk/utiac/aa-03101-2013 (accessed March 2024).

> to help with dressing or undressing and is not yet toilet trained... L. requires daily teaching and consistent use of an augmentative approach to communication (e.g. Picture Exchange Communication System – PECS) across different settings (school and home)... L. needs continued access to a range of specialists (e.g. speech and language therapy/Autism Support) in order to carry out ongoing assessments of his needs and provide advice and support in addressing those needs...'

Advocates for L's family contended:

> 'L. will certainly benefit from being nurtured within a stable home and school environment. Therefore, moving L. and his family to Nigeria is likely to significantly impede his development, as it is unlikely that L. will receive the support and understanding that he undoubtedly needs... Children with autism do a great deal better with appropriate early intervention in respect of promoting communication, behaviour and social interaction. These interventions are not available in Nigeria; in fact, I think it is doubtful that the condition of autism is generally recognised in that society, certainly outside of a few medical psychiatric communities. Therefore, repatriation will definitely have a detrimental impact on the severity of his autism in later childhood and adulthood. The fact that Nigerian children with disabilities such as autism are particularly at risk of being accused of witchcraft is well-established and the wide-ranging stigma and denial of their fundamental human rights that they may suffer due to such beliefs has been documented in numerous reports and papers.'

Summing up, however, the judge declared:

> 'I accept that there is a risk that he may face some level of discrimination in Nigeria because of his autism but he will do so in the context of his caring immediate and wider family. The evidence also shows that there are organisations dedicated to raising awareness of autism and to promote the interests of individuals with autism and their families, for example the Nigerian Autistic Society. I do not accept that there is any real risk, given that he will not be abandoned by his family, of him being accused of being a witch...
>
> 'I must strike a balance between the rights and interests of L and his parents and the public interest. The effect of L's autism on both him and his family is evident from the evidence of his parents and those involved with his care, and it is accepted that it is in his best interests to remain in the UK. I fully take that into account. Nevertheless, having regard to all the evidence and matters I have set out above, I am satisfied that L's best interests are outweighed by the weighty public interest of the economic well-being of the UK, as set out in Article 8.2 of the Convention.'[513]

513 Ibid.

Summary

The social model of disability recognises that many people with disabilities do not consider themselves to be 'vulnerable' and may be offended by the use of that word to describe their position. Nevertheless, there has undoubtedly been a proliferation of online material which may prove dangerous for those autistic internet users who are particularly vulnerable or impressionable – occasionally with tragic consequences. While autistic individuals are less likely to use substances, those who do so are more likely to self-medicate for their mental health symptoms. In some cases, this has resulted in distressing encounters with the criminal justice system. Autistic people are particularly vulnerable to the practice of cuckooing, whereby people take over a person's home and use the property to facilitate exploitation. More needs to be done to condemn and prevent this abuse. A recent national UK survey found that almost three in four autistic people and/or people with learning disabilities had experienced hate crime. Learning disability hate crime is any criminal offence that is perceived – by the victim or any other person – to be motivated by hostility or prejudice based on a person's learning disability or perceived learning disability. It can take many forms, including verbal abuse, physical abuse, threatening behaviour, bullying/teasing, online/phone abuse and damage to property/theft. Despite a number of high-profile cases, there is no credible evidence to suggest that autistic people are more likely than non-autistic people to hold sympathetic views on terrorism. In fact, evidence suggests that autism is 'over-represented in lone-actor terrorist samples, compared to the general population.' The vast majority of autistic individuals are law-abiding – sometimes particularly so, because of a propensity to know and stick to the rules. There have been a number of asylum cases affecting the fate of autistic children in the UK, with very varying outcomes. In some cases, the best interests of the autistic child are respected and he or she is permitted to remain in the UK. In others, the best interests of the child 'lose out' to the interests of national security or well-being.

Chapter 9: Mis-medication, malpractice, quack 'cures' and the MMR controversy

This chapter will focus on:

- Medical or clinical negligence and the law.
- The MMR story.
- Regulation of untested treatments.

Medical or clinical negligence and the law

In November 2022, it was announced that mandatory training was to be launched for health and care staff in England to support autistic people and/or people with a learning disability, following the four-year campaign of a grieving mother. Paula McGowan's 18-year-old son, Oliver, who was autistic and had a learning disability, died after doctors gave him anti-psychotic medication, despite his family's warnings that it was unsuitable (see **Case study 35** on p.232). McGowan expressed relief that her years of campaigning had resulted in change and said she took comfort knowing that others would have a better chance of receiving the correct care: 'There is more work to be done, but the journey has now started, and I truly believe we are on the right trajectory to achieve better health and care outcomes for neurodivergent people'.[514]

McGowan said:

> 'When Oliver died, it was obvious that health and care staff had little understanding of his neurodivergent needs. They did not understand the importance of making reasonable adjustments for him; they did not see him as a person first. People who have a learning disability die up to 26 years younger than the general population because of their healthcare needs not being met. This is unacceptable, not only for patients and their families but also for the health and care staff who have not been provided the appropriate training.'[515]

514 Morris S (2022) *Health staff in England to be trained on learning disability and autism* [online]. Available at: www.theguardian.com/society/2022/nov/01/health-staff-in-england-to-be-trained-on-learning-disability-and-autism (accessed January 2024).

515 Ibid.

Case study 35: Oliver McGowan

Thomas Oliver McGowan was only 18 years old when he died in 2016. Known as Oliver to his family and friends, the young autistic man from Bristol was taken to Southmead Hospital in the city after he suffered simple partial seizures on October 22, 2016. Complications in his care at the hospital meant Oliver never left and his condition deteriorated. His life-support machine was switched off on November 7 that year and Oliver died on November 11.[516]

An inquest in 2018 called witnesses to take the stand, and included family and medical staff involved in Oliver's care. It looked at what happened to Oliver when he was taken to the hospital by ambulance and his treatment in the intensive care unit (ICU). Among the key points to be explored at the inquest was why Oliver was given anti-psychotic medication – Olanzapine – despite protests from his parents and himself. There were also questions about restraint and about any alternative methods to manage Oliver's behaviour.

Oliver's family said he had always been a fighter. When doctors told his parents as a baby he would not survive, he proved them wrong. When he suffered two episodes of meningitis at just three weeks old, he battled through. And even though he was left with cerebral palsy, epilepsy and autism, he did not let his disabilities hold him back. He went to Culverhill School in Yate, where he was hugely popular with his peers, and he was a talented sportsman.

At the inquest, Oliver's father, Thomas McGowan, said that doctors' 'arrogance' had led to his son's death. Oliver was 'very scared and agitated' when he arrived at the hospital because the police officers, security guards, nurses and doctors had all asked him questions at the same time. He had to be restrained by police. Doctors and family raised concerns about the treatment. The court also heard about Oliver's and his parents' protests against anti-psychotic medication. But unknown to his parents, this medication had already been prescribed to Oliver. The parents discovered this only after speaking to a nurse.

Dr Nigel Langford, a consultant in clinical pharmacology, told the court it was 'possible' that Oliver would still be alive if Olanzapine had not been prescribed. Dr Russell Delaney, a pathologist, said that Olanzapine had caused neuroleptic malignant syndrome (NMS), which was a 'significant contributory factor' in Oliver's death. His temperature had spiked and his brain swelled until it was coming out of the base of his skull. There was no chance of a 'meaningful recovery,' doctors said.

In his conclusion, assistant coroner Dr Peter Harrowing said doctors had done the right thing in prescribing the medication which eventually led to Oliver's death. After the inquest, Oliver's family said they felt the coroner had been 'ferociously protective' of the doctors and that they were 'extremely disappointed' with his conclusion. They added that they wished the doctors could learn from their mistakes, but they had been 'arrogant and dismissive' of Oliver's needs.[517]

Ekaterina Harrison notes that a crucial point in Oliver's tragic case seems to be that his family was advocating for a non-medication approach. The suggestion is that, if proper reasonable adjustments had been implemented, there would have been no need to administer Olanzapine.[518]

516 See www.bristolpost.co.uk/news/bristol-news/full-story-day-oliver-mcgowan-1474471 (accessed March 2024).

517 Ibid.

518 Ekaterina Harrison, personal communication, December 12, 2023.

Between 30,000-50,000 people, many in residential care, are prescribed long-term anti-psychotics or anti-depressants (or both) despite often not being diagnosed with any specific mental illness.

Reasonable adjustments

It is instructive to see the term 'reasonable adjustments' used in a medical context here, rather than in an employment context (see Chapter 4). The McGowan family claims that the doctors were both negligent and failed to provide reasonable adjustments. The NHS is legally obliged to make it as easy for disabled people to use the health services as it is for people who are not disabled. As in the world of employment, this is known as introducing reasonable adjustments.

Reasonable adjustments include having:

- A carer stay in hospital overnight with you.
- Information in Easy Read or plain English.
- Time to meet your learning disability nurse before you go into hospital.

If you are being referred to hospital by your doctor (GP), you can ask them to check whether the hospital has a learning disability nurse. This is a specialist nurse who supports you if you have a learning disability while you are in hospital. Their job is to ensure that you receive good care. You might be able to choose a different hospital, if the one you are going to does not have a learning disability nurse. It is important that the nurse meets you and your carer as soon as possible after you arrive at the hospital, or before you go into the hospital, to allow the nurse to find out as much as possible about you and understand the help you may need while in the hospital.

Hospital passports are documents containing information about you and your health needs. They also carry other useful information, such as your interests, likes, dislikes, how you communicate and any reasonable adjustments that you might need. This Patient Passport may include details on how a patient communicates. Does he or she have complex communication needs? If so, how does the health professional know whether the patient is in pain? Before admission to a ward from A&E, for example, the patient and carer should be asked what support they might need in the hospital, such as a cubicle, due to behaviour problems or a corner bed within a bay, etc. Will the carer have support while caring in a hospital setting – that is, is someone such as a friend or staff member known to the patient available to allow the carer to have a break?

While you are in hospital, the doctors will ask you whether you give your consent to receiving treatments, including operations. If you are over 16 years old, you can usually give consent yourself. If you are under 16, or over 16 but not able to do this, your parent or carer can do this for you. The doctor must explain what is involved in the treatment, why you need it, how it will help and if there might be any risks involved. The doctor should explain everything in a way you find easy to understand, and you can ask as many questions as you like. You can also ask a carer or friend to help you.[519]

If you are not able to agree to a treatment yourself, you can ask someone else to make decisions for you. This is called having a lack of capacity to make decisions. Some people will have someone called a deputy. Other people will have someone who has a Lasting Power of Attorney. If someone is a deputy or has a Lasting Power of Attorney, they can make important decisions for you if you are not able to do so. A deputy is given this role by the Court of Protection. A deputy can be a family member, friend, carer or member of staff. A deputy can make decisions on health and welfare, as well as making decisions about money (see Chapter 3 on mental capacity). They can make decisions only when the court tells them they can. Someone who has a Lasting Power of Attorney is someone who knows the person well. They will be able to make decisions for a person whenever they are needed. They do not need the court to tell them when they can do so. If you have a Lasting Power of Attorney, you need to be able to agree to this. This means that, if you cannot agree to having a Lasting Power of Attorney, you might have to get a deputy instead. If you have a Lasting Power of Attorney, you do not usually need a deputy as well.

No one is permitted to give consent for an adult if that individual has capacity to make his or her own choices. But doctors may sometimes treat an adult without consent if the individual does not have capacity and the treatment is necessary and in the person's best interests.[520]

Oliver McGowan mandatory training on learning disability and autism

The new training programme has been named the 'Oliver McGowan mandatory training on learning disability and autism' in memory of the teenager. Section 181 of the Health and Care Act (2022) introduces a mandate into the Health and Social Care Act (2008) and

519 NHS (2022) *Support if you are going into hospital* [online] Available at: www.nhs.uk/conditions/learning-disabilities/going-into-hospital/ (accessed January 2024).

520 Ibid.

Regulation 18 of the Health and Social Care Act (2008) (Regulated Activities) Regulations 2014 that, effective from July 1, 2022, service providers registered with the Care Quality Commission (CQC) must ensure their staff undergo training on learning disability and autism relevant to their respective roles. This obligation extends to all registered providers involved in health and adult social care across England. A two-year trial took place involving more than 8,000 health and care staff. Believed to be the only training of its kind in the world, it was developed from the beginning with expertise from people with a learning disability and autistic individuals, as well as their families and carers. The Oliver McGowan mandatory training is divided into two tiers. Tier 1 is for staff who need a general awareness of the support autistic people or people with a learning disability may need, while Tier 2 is for people who may need to provide care and support.

Both tiers will complete a 90-minute e-learning package. It includes learning from autistic people and people with a learning disability, their carers, family members and subject matter experts. It also features Oliver's story. Those completing Tier 1 will then be required to take part in a 60-minute online interactive session, while those finishing Tier 2 will attend a one-day, face-to-face training session co-delivered by trainers who have a lived experience with learning disability and autism. The consultation period was in progress until September 19, 2023, and welcomed responses from all interested individuals and groups. The government concluded the consultation in late 2023 and the feedback is currently undergoing analysis.

The Oliver McGowan training has generally been welcomed by both the autistic community and healthcare professionals in the hope that it will lead to the introduction of reasonable adjustments in medical settings, where necessary, and prevent the repetition of a number of profoundly disturbing cases of medical malpractice involving autistic patients.

Nevertheless, Luke Clements, professor of law at the University of Leeds, for one, is sceptical about the efficacy of the new training:

> 'I'm not sure it's a magic bullet. There is a huge need for awareness-raising, but a lot of these things are embedded in the culture of organisations. Mandatory training is useful, but we are coming across a lot of disability teams who say "I've done autism training!" – but it's actually just three hours one afternoon – and they consider themselves experts on autism. Whereas we all know that every autistic person is different. So it's not a good situation, because of the pressure they are working under. They simply do not have time to deal with people who are not neurotypical. I do think the change of culture will happen, but social care is on its knees, so it will take a while. Much more money is needed, but there also needs to be managerial change. In my book, Clustered Injustice and the Level Green, I talk about top-down managerialism, where social workers have to fill out forms and have no discretion.'[521]

521 Luke Clements, personal communication, February 20, 2023.

The idea behind Clements' thinking is that 'the toxic experiences of many parents of disabled children result from a systems failure: from a target-driven neoliberal nightmare of a system, dominated by command-and-control managerialism and chronic underfunding.'[522]

According to Belinda Schwehr, a lawyer and a leading authority on England's Care Act (2014), the Oliver McGowan training does not apply to the statutory sector doing all the assessments:

> 'I think it applies to registered providers of care only. It is staggering that no one has mentioned this. Unless there is a crossover between the definition of competence in the Care Act and having the Oliver McGowan training under your belt, I do not think it applies to public sector social workers. I believe it applies to the people from whom they Commission services but not to those responsible for the constituent elements of a competent Care Act assessment.'[523]

Yo Dunn agrees:

> 'Most of the Oliver McGowan training is completely geared to health and is irrelevant to what social care professionals need to know. Most of it amounts to tick-boxing information, not practical information. What they really need to know about is things like processing time, the need to write stuff down and draw diagrams.' [524]

Dunn is implying that the training is too theoretical. Her final comment hints at the importance of knowing how to create the correct environment, which relates to the concept of reasonable adjustments mentioned above.

Dr Michael Fitzpatrick concurs with these reservations about mandatory autism training as a box-ticking exercise:

> 'I think an emphasis on the need for higher levels of better-paid and generally better-trained staff (in social care, as well as the health service) is the way forward. I think STOMP – and the British Institute of Learning Disability emphasis on skilled behavioural support – deserve a higher profile.'[525]

The STOMP campaign

The STOMP campaign, aimed at 'Stopping Over-Medication of People with a learning disability or autism or both,' was established in 2016, following the revelation that some 30,000 to 50,000 people, many in residential care, were being prescribed long-term anti-psychotics or antidepressants, or both, although they had often not been diagnosed with any specific mental illness. Following the disruption caused by the COVID-19 pandemic, STOMP was relaunched in 2022 by NHS England, with the support of the Challenging

---

522 Clements L (2021) *Disabled children and their families – a damning ITV Wales news story* [online]. Available at: www.lukeclements.co.uk/disabled-children-and-their-families-a-damning-itv-wales-news-story/ (accessed January 2024).

523 Belinda Schwehr, personal communication, November 21, 2023.

524 Yo Dunn, personal communication, January 5, 2023.

525 Dr Michael Fitzpatrick, personal communication, November 24, 2023.

Behaviour Foundation and a coalition of professional and voluntary organisations. A parallel campaign focuses on children, with the goal of 'Supporting Treatment and Appropriate Medication in Paediatrics' (STAMP).

As Dr Fitzpatrick has written:

> 'Though there is little evidence of the efficacy of these medications among either adults or children with learning disabilities, there is considerable evidence of their potential adverse effects, which include weight gain, diabetes and heart disease. It is clear that these drugs have come to be widely used to contain "challenging behaviour", effectively as a "chemical constraint" or "liquid cosh".' [526]

At the focus group in late 2022 to promote the relaunch of STOMP and STAMP, leading clinicians noted that there had been little progress over the past seven years in achieving the campaigns' targets. A slight decrease in prescriptions for anti-psychotics was accompanied by a greater increase in those for antidepressants. For one psychiatrist, Dr Roger Banks, national clinical director of the project, it must be 'everybody's business' in this field to promote good prescribing as well as seeking 'non-drug' approaches to challenging behaviour. He urged clinicians to make sure that they were using 'the right medication, at the right time, for the right reason, and for as short a time as possible'. [527]

Dr Fitzpatrick added:

> 'Contributions from parents and carers for people with autism and learning disabilities revealed some familiar obstacles to withdrawing or reducing medication. A number of parents reported that when they sought help and support in relation to problems of challenging behaviour at home, they were often subjected to intrusive assessments, and presumed to be guilty of neglect or abuse.' [528]

According to Dr Fitzpatrick, parents whose adult children had been admitted to residential facilities found that when their behaviour deteriorated

> '...they were prescribed medication without appropriate assessment or consultation. Access to alternatives to medication – notably "positive behaviour support" programmes – remains uneven, and staff in many residential facilities are badly paid, poorly trained and overstretched. Though there are some examples of successful medication withdrawal through local teamwork, the wider success of STOMP depends on tackling these underlying problems.'[529]

The STOMP campaign is working closely with the British Institute of Learning Disability to promote the 'positive behaviour support' model as an alternative to medication.

---

526 Fitzpatrick M (2022) *Over-medication is not the solution* [online]. Available at: www.telegraph.co.uk/health-fitness/body/over-medication-not-solution/ (accessed January 2024).

527 Ibid.

528 Ibid.

529 Ibid.

Clinical negligence

A number of families have won legal cases against hospitals after their child suffered brain damage at birth and went on to develop autism. One seven-year-old boy was born by caesarean section at University College Hospital, London, in June 2012. At birth, he had encephalopathy, hypoglycaemia, sepsis, seizures and pulmonary hypertension caused by a delay in delivery. He was labelled 'naughty' for most of his life and was excluded from school on a daily basis. His family suffered five years of misdiagnosis following his birth. Medical evidence revealed that the child's volatile behaviour was due to a birth injury. The instructed medical expert, a paediatric neuropsychiatrist, provided a diagnosis of autism and concluded that the boy would not have had this condition but for the brain injury. The High Court approved a settlement of £30 million to fund his ongoing problems. University College London Hospital NHS Trust Foundation apologised over the birth injury and said they hope the money will help provide for his future.

A spokesman for University College London Hospital NHS Foundation Trust stated that 'Experts found it difficult to assess the cause of injury and establish whether there was a genetic reason for some, or all, of the neurodevelopmental problems'. However, the claimant's expert, a paediatric neuropsychiatrist, was able to demonstrate that the brain injury had caused him to have autism and a severe form of ADHD.[530]

Of course, the notion of autism being attributed to brain injury is potentially controversial, as it could reinforce the model of 'impairment'. In 2007, I conducted an extraordinary interview with two of the true pioneers in the neurology of autism, Dr Margaret Bauman and Dr Thomas Kemper, in Boston, Massachusetts. When I asked them whether autism could be described as 'brain damage', they were unable to agree – even though they had been working together for a quarter of a century – and they broke off our interview for a few moments to debate the issue with one another.[531]

With a clinical negligence claim, there is a time limit to bring the claim. This is three years from the date of the negligent act or the date of knowledge of the negligent act. For minors, this time limit starts running from the date of their 18th birthday. As noted in Chapter 3 on health and welfare deputies, the exception to this rule is claimants who lack litigation capacity. For these individuals, there is no time limit.

The majority of clinical negligence claims via many solicitors are funded by way of a 'Conditional Fee Agreement', also known as a 'no win no fee agreement'. This means that the client is not required to pay fees if his or her case is unsuccessful. In successful cases, the opponent will pay compensation and cover some of the legal costs.

---

530 Ibid.

531 See Adam Feinstein: *A History of Autism – Conversations with the Pioneers*. Chichester: Wiley-Blackwell, 2010, p. 293.

Case study 36: Connor Sparrowhawk

Connor Sparrowhawk, an autistic, epileptic teenager affectionately nicknamed 'Laughing Boy', drowned in a bath at an NHS care unit in Oxford on July 4, 2013. Four years later, a medical tribunal found that a senior psychiatrist had failed to carry out any risk assessments on Connor before he had a seizure and died at the age of just 18.

Dr Valerie Murphy was the lead clinician responsible for treating Connor. The psychiatrist admitted 28 failings but a Medical Practitioners Tribunal Service (MPTS) found a further nine failings and 18 not proved. In its finding of fact, the 2017 tribunal said Murphy had appeared 'evasive' and 'defensive' when giving evidence, but that she now 'accepted more responsibility for your actions' than she did at the time of Connor's death or in subsequent inquiries.

Connor, who also had learning difficulties, was admitted to Slade House, a residential care unit run in Oxford by Southern Health NHS Foundation Trust, on March 19, 2013. Connor's death there led to the discovery that Southern Health had failed properly to investigate the deaths of more than 1,000 patients with learning disabilities or mental health problems over four years. The Trust accepted responsibility for Connor's death and faced prosecution by the Health and Safety Executive. [532]

In its finding of facts, the MPTS declared: 'The tribunal determined that, as a consultant psychiatrist at Slade House, you [Valerie Murphy] had a duty to conduct and record risk assessments and that they were ultimately your responsibility'. The tribunal found that Murphy had failed to carry out any risk assessments in relation to Connor, an allegation the psychiatrist had denied. It said there was 'no documentary evidence' she had carried out a risk assessment or delegated it to her juniors. There was also no mention in medical notes of a risk assessment having taken place, the tribunal found.[533]

Among the other allegations found proven by the tribunal were failing to explain the risks and side effects of taking the drug, risperidone, which can lower the threshold for experiencing an epileptic seizure, and psychotropic medication more generally. Murphy was also found not to have made an assessment of Connor's mental state when she first became responsible for his care, although she did on subsequent occasions. She has accepted she did not consider the implications of allowing him to use a bath alone, although he was checked on by staff every 15 minutes.[534]

Murphy faced a sanction, although she relinquished her licence to practise in the UK in 2014, before moving to Cork, in Ireland.

Giving evidence to the tribunal in August 2017, Murphy was questioned about two occasions when Connor was believed to have had unwitnessed epileptic seizures at Slade House. On the first occasion, on May 20, 2015, Connor bit his tongue and was later assessed as being lethargic, two possible indicators of a seizure. Murphy told the tribunal that another nurse had witnessed Connor bite his tongue and believed that it had been in anger.[535]

The tribunal heard that Connor's mother, Dr Sara Ryan, had visited her son later that day and immediately raised concerns with nurses that he had experienced an epileptic seizure. She was subsequently reassured by email that epilepsy tests would be undertaken and a monitor ➔

532 See www.theguardian.com/society/2017/aug/21/connor-sparrowhawk-risk-assessments-death-tribunal-finds (accessed March 2024).

533 Ibid.

534 Ibid.

535 Ibid.

would be placed in his bedroom overnight to spot any further signs of seizures. However, the tribunal heard that, by the time he died nearly two months later, those tests had not been undertaken.

In the other incident, on June 15, 2013, Connor was found with a bloody nose after taking a bath. When questioned by a nurse, Connor said he had been punched in the face. In medical notes read to the tribunal, a nurse said she thought it 'unlikely' that Connor had been struck in the face while alone in the bath. Asked whether the incident should have raised alarm bells, Murphy said: 'It should have. I didn't pick up on it. I can't explain why I didn't. It should've been an alarm, but it wasn't.'

On the day Connor died, a nurse said he had popped his head around the bathroom door to check on Connor about ten minutes after the bath had been run. The two did not speak but the teenager seemed fine, he said. About 20 minutes later, a fellow staff member told the nurse that Connor was submerged and his face blue. He was pronounced dead in hospital.[536]

An inquest jury in 2015 found that a number of serious failings by Southern Health had contributed to the death of the teenager. Connor's stepfather, Richard Huggins, told the 2015 inquest that he had found the hospital unit 'bleak' and staff had made them feel they were an 'inconvenience'. But he added: 'At no point did we think our son would die in a National Health Service specialist unit.'[537]

Case study 37: Alfie Anthony Nicholls

Alfie Anthony Nicholls, a seven-year-old, non-verbal autistic boy, died during the Covid pandemic after doctors failed to spot that he was severely malnourished, an inquest at South Manchester Coroner's Court in Stockport heard in January 2024. Alfie suffered a cardiac arrest and died on December 17, 2021, after collapsing at home. He had been battling an undiagnosed eating disorder. The inquest heard that he had significant sensory difficulties, which manifested themselves in his severely restrictive diet. However, problems with his diet were not picked up by medical professionals, who had failed to spot that he was severely malnourished and told his mother, Lucy Morrison, that it was 'part of his autism'. It was not until after his death that Alfie was diagnosed with avoidant/restrictive food intake disorder (ARFID), which is not uncommon in autistic children, but was not detected by medics.

The inquest heard that before starting school, Alfie was under the care of an early years team and there was a 'good understanding' of what he was eating, with efforts made to ensure his diet was as nutritional as possible. However, this all changed when he started at school in September 2019. The inquest heard that during the school day, Alfie was consuming just 'a few biscuits and a little bit of water'. During his time at school, Alfie was never seen by the school nurse and there was no attempt to understand what or how much he was consuming, the court heard.[538]

In June 2021, Alfie was referred to the speech and language team which ran food clinics, after concerns were raised by the school, but the referral focused solely on his hydration levels. The children's services, meanwhile, offered support with Alfie's sleeping and respite, but not his eating. Due to the Covid-19 pandemic, Alfie was not weighed in a paediatric setting throughout 2020 and 2021. He was finally weighed by a professional at Stepping Hill Hospital ➔

536 Ibid.

537 See www.theguardian.com/society/2015/oct/16/neglect-teenager-connor-sparrowhawk-death-nhs-unit-inquest (accessed March 2024)/

538 See www.dailymail.co.uk/news/article-12959437/Heartbroken-mother-tells-beautiful-happy-autistic-son-seven-died-cardiac-arrest-eating-disorder-left-surviving-just-biscuits.html (accessed March 2024).

during an appointment on November 2021 and then again in December by a paediatrician. Within that period of just over two months, he had lost 2.4kg - 10% of his body weight. No plan was drawn up on how Alfie was going to regain the weight he had lost. His mother remained 'extremely concerned' and felt she had not been heard, the inquest was told.[539]

Three days after the December appointment, Alfie collapsed at home. Despite efforts by paramedics to resuscitate him, he died later at Stepping Hill Hospital. Because of Alfie's sudden and unexpected death, a post-mortem examination was carried out. The pathologist, Dr Gemma Petts, found that three of Alfie's ribs had been fractured during CPR. Dr Petts sent a section of Alfie's ribs to be examined by David Manghamon, a professor of Musculoskeletal Pathology, who found evidence of 'atrophy' (wasting away) of bone marrow, most commonly caused by anorexia or a nutrient deficiency condition. Professor Mangham told the inquest that, apart from finding 'chronic malnutrition' in the bone marrow, he also found that Alfie's bone had thinned, which he said was consistent with a 'chronic malnutrition state'. Dr Petts gave an initial conclusion of 'sudden death in a child with features of malnutrition on a background of developmental delay and an autistic spectrum disorder', based on the balance of probabilities and the information she had received. She added that she believed malnutrition had caused Alfie's heart not to function properly, leading to a sudden cardiac arrest, and that the deficit in micronutrients was a significant factor in his cause of death.[540]

Giving evidence during the inquest, consultant paediatrician Dr Elizabeth Newby, who saw Alfie several days before his death, said she and no other health professionals realised Alfie was suffering from malnutrition when he was alive and that there was no detailed dietary record of what he was eating in the last two years of his life. She added that, although the management of anorexia had come on 'leaps and bounds' in recent years, but the same was not the case for ARFID up until 2022.[541]

The Senior Coroner, Alison Mutch, said it was her job to determine from the evidence how malnutrition could contribute to a child's death in 'modern Britain'. She described Alfie as 'much loved' by not only his family but all those in his care and said that the 'force of his personality shone through'. She added: 'Alfie was not an autistic child, he was a child with autism and it's important to remember that, because he was first and foremost a child. A child who died unexpectedly in December 2021.' She said that looking at the evidence, it was clear that by November 2021 the agencies responsible for Alfie's care did not have an understanding of how much he was eating and there was a 'lack of communication and professional curiosity' about the nutritional value of his diet. Mutch recorded a narrative conclusion that Alfie had 'died suddenly where his death was contributed to by malnutrition, which was caused by a severely restricted diet and where the level of malnutrition and consequential risk it posed was not recognised by professionals until after his death.'[542]

Following the inquest, a coroner criticised doctors for failing to detect Alfie's malnutrition until after his death and Stepping Hill Hospital bosses have since apologised to Alfie's family for the 'missed opportunities' to help him.

Alfie's mother had taken him to hospital and to his GP on a number of occasions in the weeks leading up to his death, knowing something was wrong. She said she had 'spent years going crazy', and she is now calling for more awareness of ARFID and how to manage the condition, in order to ensure children get the nutrients they need.

539 Ibid.

540 Ibid.

541 Ibid.

542 Ibid.

Useful resources and further guidance

STOMP was launched in 2016 by NHS England, the Royal College of Nursing, the Royal College of Psychiatrists, the Royal College of GPs, the Royal Pharmaceutical Society and the British Psychological Society. These organisations pledged to work together to stop the over-medication of people with a learning disability, autism or both. Since then, the number of official STOMP partners has grown to include: the Voluntary Organizations Disability Group (VODG), the British Association of Social Workers, the Royal College of Speech and Language Therapists, the Learning Disability Professional Senate (NHS England, Care Quality Commission, clinical commissioning groups, Challenging Behaviour Foundation, Department of Health and Health Education England), the British Association of Music Therapy, the Royal College of Occupational Therapists, the British Dietetics Association, the British Association of Art Therapy, the British Association of Dance Therapy, the British Association of Drama Therapy, the British Association of Art Therapy and VoiceAbility. You can find more about their campaign here: www.england.nhs.uk/publication/stomp-stopping-the-over-medication-of-people-with-a-learning-disability-autism-or-both/ (accessed January 2024).

The MMR story

The totally debunked notion that autism may be the result of vaccine injury or some other environmental causative factor had a major impact on the world of autism as a result of the campaign against the MMR (measles, mumps, rubella) vaccine from the late 1990s onwards. Although the claims associated with the gastroenterology researcher Andrew Wakefield were scientifically discredited (and Wakefield himself was struck off the medical register in the UK), they led to several thousand families in the UK and the USA pursuing litigation which ultimately proved futile. The MMR campaign has left a lasting legacy, as cases continue to appear in the courts arising from parental disputes over administering the MMR vaccine. One case, in which parents sought to sue solicitors over delays in taking action against the vaccine manufacturers, dragged on for a decade. In the words of Dr Michael Fitzpatrick, whose 2004 book *MMR and Autism: What parents need to know*, is an authoritative account of the controversy from the perspective of a GP who is also a parent: '...the Wakefield campaign caused enormous distress to parents of children with autism and, as a result of declining uptake of the MMR vaccine over a decade, contributed to a number of outbreaks of measles as well as many cases of mumps'.[543]

In 1998, Andrew Wakefield and 12 of his colleagues published a case series in the journal *The Lancet*, which suggested that the measles, mumps and rubella (MMR) vaccine may predispose children to behavioural regression and pervasive developmental disorder.[544] Despite the small sample size (n = 12), the uncontrolled design, and the speculative nature of the conclusions, the paper received wide publicity, and MMR vaccination rates began to drop because parents were concerned about the risk of autism after vaccination. Almost immediately afterwards, epidemiological studies were conducted and published, refuting the posited link between MMR vaccination and

543 Dr Michael Fitzpatrick, personal communication, November 24, 2023.

544 Wakefield AJ *et al* (1998) Ileal-lymphoid-nodular hyperplasia, non-specific colitis, and pervasive developmental disorder in children. *The Lancet* **351** 637–41.

autism. The logic that the MMR vaccine may trigger autism was also questioned because a temporal link between the two is almost predestined: both events, by design (MMR vaccine) or definition (autism), occur in early childhood.

The next episode in the saga was a short retraction in 2004 of the interpretation of the original data by ten of the 12 co-authors of *The Lancet* paper. According to the retraction, 'no causal link was established between MMR vaccine and autism as the data were insufficient'.[545] This was accompanied by an admission by *The Lancet* that Wakefield et al had failed to disclose financial interests (for example, Wakefield had been funded by lawyers who had been engaged by parents in lawsuits against vaccine-producing companies). However, *The Lancet* exonerated Wakefield and his colleagues from charges of ethical violations and scientific misconduct.[546]

The Lancet completely retracted the Wakefield *et al* paper in February 2010, admitting that several elements in the paper were incorrect, contrary to the findings of the earlier investigation. Wakefield *et al* were held guilty of ethical violations (they had conducted invasive investigations on the children without obtaining the necessary ethical clearances) and scientific misrepresentation (they reported that their sampling was consecutive when, in fact, it was selective). This retraction was published as a small, anonymous paragraph in the journal, on behalf of the editors.[547]

The final episode was the revelation that Wakefield *et al* were guilty of deliberate fraud (they had picked and chosen data that suited their case and they falsified facts).[548] The *British Medical Journal* also published a series of articles on the exposure (by the journalist Brian Deer) of the fraud, which appears to have taken place for financial gain.[549]

On the basis of the original 1998 article in *The Lancet*, parents across the world refused to vaccinate their children out of fear of the risk of autism, thereby exposing their children to the risks of measles and the well-documented complications related to it. Measles outbreaks in the UK in 2008 and 2009 as well as pockets of measles in the USA and Canada were attributed to the non-vaccination of children. It should also be noted that another consequence of the Wakefield article was to set up an image of autism as being more dangerous, deadlier and bleaker than measles, whereas children began to die of measles after parents delayed vaccinating their children or withdrew from the vaccination process altogether.

A requirement to produce evidence of immunisation at school entry, as in the US, was suggested in the National Immunisation Study in 1989, a year after the introduction of the MMR vaccine, but this requirement was not instigated in the UK. The continuing decline in the uptake of MMR – and increasing concerns over the outbreaks of measles

545 Murch SH *et al* (2004) Retraction of an interpretation. *The Lancet* 363:750.

546 Horton R (2004) A statement by the editors of *The Lancet*. The Lancet. 363:820–1

547 Eggertson L (2010) Lancet retracts 12-year-old article linking autism to MMR vaccines. *CMAJ* **182** E199–200.

548 Godlee F (2011) The fraud behind the MMR scare. *BMJ* **342** d22.

549 Deer B (2010) Wakefield's 'autistic enterocolitis' under the microscope. *BMJ*, **340**:c1127; Deer B. (2011): How the case against the MMR vaccine was fixed. *BMJ* **342** c5347; Deer B (2011) Secrets of the MMR scare. How the vaccine crisis was meant to make money. *BMJ* **342** c5258;. Deer B (2011) Secrets of the MMR scare. *The Lancet's* two days to bury bad news. *BMJ* **342** c7001.

– revived discussion of various methods of making immunisation compulsory. At the annual conference of the British Medical Association in 2002, for instance, a resolution proposing compulsory vaccination was discussed – and rejected.[550]

The MMR controversy brought back the culture of guilt and blame instigated by Leo Kanner, who in a notorious interview with the American magazine *Time* in 1960 declared that autistic children were 'the offspring of highly organised, professional parents' who 'just happened to defrost enough to produce a child'. Although Kanner recanted nine years later, announcing that he 'absolved' parents, the so-called 'refrigerator mother' theory raged on, expounded most notably by Bruno Bettelheim.[551]

As Dr Fitzpatrick has noted, parents' testimonies of their conviction that MMR had rendered their children autistic had great emotional force:

> '...especially when reinforced on television with selections from family videos showing the regression of thriving infants into disturbed autistic behaviour. The appearance in the media of these parents posed a difficult problem for doctors, scientists or politicians charged with upholding official immunisation policy: however persuasive their rational arguments in favour of MMR, they were no match for the images of anguished parents and their damaged children.'[552]

In 1994, the former Legal Aid Board agreed to fund a number of claims for compensation for injury allegedly caused by MMR. The Legal Services Commission (LSC) brought this legal campaign to an end in September 2003, calling a halt to the MMR case before it went to court because it finally realised it had negligible chances of success. After taking expert advice, the LSC acknowledged that, given the failure of research to establish a link between MMR and autism, the litigation was 'very likely to fail'. In its statement on the decision to withdraw legal aid, the LSC indicated that the MMR case had been the first in which such funding had been used to finance scientific research. The Commission declared that it had concluded that, 'in retrospect, it was not effective or appropriate for the LSC to fund research', emphasising that 'the courts are not the place to prove new medical truths'. According to Dr Fitzpatrick, 'the enormous waste of public funds on the abortive MMR litigation was largely the result of the provision of legal aid for "research" conducted under a team of scientifically incompetent solicitors'.[553]

In 2016, the actor Robert de Niro, who has an autistic son, announced that he was cancelling the planned screening of *Vaxxed: From Cover-Up to Catastrophe* at his Tribeca Film Festival in New York. This controversial documentary set out to prove Andrew Wakefield's theory, in part by claiming it had new evidence that the US Centers for Disease Control and Prevention (CDC) had suppressed an important study about the now-discredited link between the MMR vaccine and autism. *Vaxxed's* inclusion in the festival's proposed line-up prompted a wave of criticism from doctors, researchers and

550 Fitzpatrick M (2004) *MMR and Autism: What parents need to know*. London: Routledge, 2004, p. 32.

551 For an in-depth analysis of the history of the parent-blaming movement, see Adam Feinstein's *A History Of Autism: Conversations with the pioneers*. Chichester: Wiley-Blackwell, 2010.

552 Fitzpatrick, op. cit., page 33.

553 Ibid. p113.

activists against the science behind the film. De Niro had initially chosen to defend his decision to programme the documentary, since the issue was 'very personal to me and my family' as the father of an autistic child. After coming under severe criticism, the actor issued a second statement announcing the film would be removed altogether. 'We do not believe it contributes to, or furthers, the discussion I had hoped for', he said.[554]

The legacy of parental disputes over vaccination continued during the Covid pandemic beginning in 2020, with the rise of similar attacks on the Covid jab and rampant conspiracy theories, promoted by Andrew Wakefield, who is now living in voluntary exile in Texas. Cases of litigation against lawyers were, in the words of Michael Fitzpatrick, the 'last bitter gasp. There was a litany of recrimination and failure, encouraged by bad science, dubious expert witnesses and credulous journalists.'[555]

In 2013, Philippa Dolan, a family law partner at the West Country and London firm Ashfords acted in the High Court for a mother whose two daughters, aged 15 and 11, did not want to have the MMR vaccination. The mother and father of the girls, now divorced, decided not to vaccinate them because of the supposed link between MMR, and autism and bowel disease. That link, as we have seen, has since been discredited and, following recent measles outbreaks, the father changed his mind in the interests of the girls' health. He wrote to the mother, but she remained adamant that the girls should not be vaccinated. The father responded by taking the mother to court.

Mrs Justice Theis ruled that vaccination was in the best interests of the children. Commenting on this case in the *Law Society Gazette*, Jonathan Rayner wrote:

> 'It took less than four months from the first application to trial, which anyone familiar with the family courts will know is very fast. The case may have been fast-tracked because of the public policy implications of MMR safety. The girls had taken an interest in MMR and were assured that they would be listened to.'[556]

Case study 38: Coote vs Ullstein

A professional negligence claim against a litigation firm was thrown out by the High Court in April 2022 after it was concluded that the evidence relied upon would never have stood up to scrutiny, according to the *Law Society Gazette*. The claimant in Coote v Ullstein brought proceedings against Augustus Ullstein QC and a London firm, Hodge Jones and Allen, after missing the chance to bring a potential claim relating to the MMR vaccine against the drug manufacturer, SmithKline Beecham (SKB).[557]

➔

554 Smith NM & Child B (2016) *Makers of controversial anti-vaccination film fire back after Robert De Niro Tribeca snub* [online]. Available at: www.theguardian.com/film/2016/mar/30/vaxxed-robert-de-niro-tribeca-film-festival (accessed January 2024).

555 Dr Michael Fitzpatrick, personal communication, November 24, 2023.

556 www.lawgazette.co.uk/lawyer-in-the-news/court-rules-that-girls-must-have-mmr-jab/5038284.article (accessed March 2024).

557 See www.lawgazette.co.uk/news/negligence-claim-thrown-out-as-court-rejects-mmr-evidence/5112261.article (accessed March 2024).

Sitting in Leeds, Judge Gosnell approved applications for summary judgement from both defendants, effectively preventing the claim from proceeding any further. The judge emphasised that this was not a 'trial within a trial' but said the quality of the evidence Coote would have relied on was not enough to give her any prospect of success – especially compared with the conflicting evidence SKB would have put before a court.[558]

Judge Gosnell said: 'On an objective assessment of the expert evidence, the claimant had no real prospect of success against SKB ... she therefore has no real prospects of success in this litigation, because the loss of a chance on my assessment is less than 10% by some distance'[559].

The court heard that proceedings had been issued in 2021 against Ullstein and HJA in relation to allegations of harm suffered by Rachael Coote, who received the MMR vaccine at the age of 18 months in 1989. She was diagnosed with epilepsy and developmental regression the following year. The Coote claim was part of group action seeking to make claims against the manufacturers of the vaccine in the late 1990s. Most claimants were dealt a fatal blow when research linking the MMR with autism was discredited, but the Coote claim survived and eventually had legal aid re-instated. It was finally discontinued in 2008 over an issue with limitation, and Coote subsequently claimed for damages against her lawyers to compensate for the value of claim she would have pursued against SKB if properly advised.

The claimant in this case relied on the expert medical evidence of Dr Marcel Kinsbourne, who claimed that the MMR vaccine was a biologically plausible cause of seizures. Lawyers for the claimant urged the court not to engage in a 'mini-trial' and suggested further supporting evidence might emerge later.

Judge Gosnell declared that some analysis of the parties' respective evidence was required, adding that the Kinsbourne findings ignored various other papers and research related to MMR. The judge said the chances of a court in 2009 accepting the Kinsbourne evidence were 'nil or virtually nil' and the doctor had 'made a number of conclusions which are logically unsupportable', cherry-picking data which suited his opinion while discarding conflicting evidence. Judge Gosnell added that, on the basis of the evidence, the Legal Services Commission would have withdrawn legal aid funding and the claimant would have been compelled to discontinue the claim.[560]

Useful resources and further guidance here

- Michael Fitzpatrick: *MMR and autism: What Parents Need to Know*. Routledge, 2004.

Regulation of untested treatments

Another area of recurring controversy arises from periodic claims of dramatic therapeutic benefits for autistic children for interventions which lack good scientific evidence of efficacy or safety. In another of his books, *Defeating Autism: A damaging delusion* (2009), Dr Michael Fitzpatrick detailed and discredited a wide range of alternative treatments, including exclusion diets, medicinal supplements, so-called detoxification regimes, immune system treatments and diverse medications. Treatments with so-called

558 Ibid.
559 Ibid.
560 Ibid.

MMS and stem cell therapies have attracted widespread publicity – and proposals for improved regulations from the authoritative Westminster Commission on Autism in 2018 (see below).

In the UK, the Medicines and Healthcare Products Regulatory Agency (MHRA) is responsible for the quality, efficacy and safety of medicines. The Food Standards Agency is responsible for food safety. This includes any product for human consumption to be taken orally which is not a 'medicine'. The Advertising Standards Authority seeks to ensure that advertisements are responsible and trustworthy. Trading Standards teams protect consumers from scams, counterfeit products or unfair practices. The National Institute for Health and Care Excellence produces evidence-based guidance and advice for health, public health and social care practitioners. The Care Quality Commission is the independent regulator of health and social care in England.

Some autistic campaigners and others in the UK are calling for new legislation, similar to the Cancer Act (1939), to make it illegal to offer to treat, prescribe or promote anything as an intervention (social or biological) for autism unless you are a certified professional. Currently, it is far too difficult to determine which agency is responsible for the regulation of the manufacture, promotion, distribution, sale and use of harmful physical, medicinal, psychological or social interventions for autism. It is extremely hard to establish the remit of each agency. The Westminster Commission for Autism has recommended that the government should urgently convene all agencies with regulatory responsibility in order to conduct a thorough investigation.[561]

MHRA jurisdiction covers only products which are deemed to be medicines. In order to be a medicine, a product must seek to treat disease and have a physiological action which is consistent with a medicine. The Westminster Commission on Autism conducted an extremely valuable inquiry into the regulation of untested treatments, therapies and products, before offering guidance and advice on choosing interventions.[562] The Commission noted that the name 'Food Standards' was unhelpful since the Food Standards Agency's remit was much broader than what is conventionally considered to be 'food'. This is confusing for individuals seeking advice or to report dangerous products. In the view of the Commission, expanding the remit of the MHRA from regulating medicines to all health products would be enormously beneficial.

The Advertising Standards Authority can require evidence, including clinical trials, from those making claims that an intervention can help an autistic person. If the proponents of a particular method cannot provide the requisite evidence, they can be asked to remove the claims. They would still be permitted to sell the product. However, they would not be allowed to claim that the product could do something for which they do not have the associated evidence.

561 Westminster Commission on Autism (2018) *A spectrum of harmful interventions for autism* [online]. Available at: https://westminsterautismcommission.files.wordpress.com/2018/03/a-spectrum-of-harmful-interventions-web-version.pdf (accessed January 2024).

562 Ibid.

The Westminster Commission on Autism was made aware of interventions being sold which do not claim to be a treatment for autism, but associated claims are made in books, social media posts and in face-to-face consultations, all of which are beyond the remit of the Advertising Standards Authority. The interventions offered to treat or 'cure' autism include social, psychological, medicinal, chemical, dietary and behavioural. Drugs administered include 'atypical anti-psychotics' – so-called because they were developed as alternatives to the major tranquillisers, such as chlorpromazine or haloperidol, long-used in the treatment of schizophrenia. Yet they have come to be widely used in people with learning disabilities to contain 'challenging behaviour', effectively as a 'chemical restraint'. [563]

Tragically, one biomedical method, known as chelation (involving the removal of heavy metals from the body), proved fatal in the case of a five-year-old autistic boy, Abubakar Tariq Nadama, who went into cardiac arrest and died in August 2005. The boy's parents had moved from England to the Pittsburgh area to seek treatment for his autism. They filed a wrongful death suit against Dr Roy E. Kerry and the doctor was charged with involuntary manslaughter in 2007. Chelation is approved by the US Food and Drug Administration for treating acute heavy metal poisoning, but not for treating autism. Some people who believe autism is caused by a mercury-containing preservative once used in vaccines continue to maintain, without scientific evidence, that chelation may also help autistic children.

The UK's National Institute for Health and Care Excellence (NICE) has ruled out the use of chelation, as well as several other biomedical interventions, for the management of the core characteristics of autism. These interventions include: exclusive or restrictive diets, including gluten-free, casein-free or ketogenic diets, hormone therapies or testosterone regulation, hyperbaric oxygen, vitamins, minerals and dietary supplements, drugs which are usually given for problems with memory and thinking, anti-convulsants, antidepressants or anti-psychotics (unless other conditions are present, for example epilepsy and depression) and secretin.[564]

NICE has no legal power to enforce a ban on any of the interventions. Some of them may be used by autistic people to manage co-existing conditions. However, the NICE guidelines for children are clear that secretin, hyperbaric oxygen and chelation should never be used in any context.[565]

The Westminster Commission on Autism's inquiry surveyed more than 500 people from the UK autism community. It was found that autistic people had been offered treatments such as crystal therapy, ear candles, vitamins, spiritual intervention, aromatherapy, chelation, juice plus diet, hyperbaric oxygen therapy, exorcism, stem cell transplants, exposure therapy (including slapping), rerum, acupuncture, DAN (Defeat Autism Now) therapy, MMS (bleach), turpentine and many more. None of these interventions has been subjected to scientific testing. Some are dangerous and their use could result in serious

563 Ibid.

564 NICE (2013) CG170: *Autism spectrum disorder in under 19s: support and management* [online]. Available at: www.nice.org.uk/guidance/cg170/chapter/recommendations (accessed January 2024).

565 Ibid.

harm. Yet there is no single legal mechanism, at present, to report any form of intervention that is suspected of causing harm or being unethical. Establishing such a mechanism must be prioritised.[566]

Case study 39: Miracle Mineral Solution (MMS)

In 2015, the BBC exposed a self-styled 'reverend' who claimed that autism could be 'purged' by swallowing bleach.[567] Leon Edwards sold sodium chlorite and hydrochloric acid to a reporter posing as the relation of an autistic child. Combined, the chemicals form bleach, which Edwards called Miracle Mineral Solution (MMS). Experts said it was untrue any such mixture could cure autism and warned its use could lead to serious harm or death. Edwards was linked to the Genesis II Church, an American organisation which described itself as a 'non-religious church of health and healing'. The BBC researcher met Edwards at King's Cross Station in London for a paid-for demonstration as to how the bleach should be mixed and imbibed. He claimed that '170 children have had their diagnosis removed of autism in four years'. In 2013, a jury in the US state of Washington convicted a Genesis II member, Louis Daniel Smith, for selling MMS as a 'miracle cure'. He faced a maximum of 34 years in prison.

Carol Povey, of the UK's National Autistic Society, said:

> 'No evidence of any kind exists to support the preposterous claims made for MMS as an intervention for autism. It is shocking that dubious companies continue to promote potentially very harmful products like these. Autism is a complex neurological condition, without a cure.'[568]

Dr Sarah Jarvis, a GP, said ingesting bleach could cause scarring to the oesophagus, damage to the stomach and even death. She explained: 'A very small amount of concentrated bleach has the possibility of doing great harm. This is particularly true of a child's gut lining, which is thinner than an adult's.'[569]

Professor Richard Goldberg, an expert in pharmaceutical law at Durham Law School, warned that selling sodium chlorite for consumption breached the Food Supplements England Regulations. 'This is a potential criminal offence,' he said. 'The Food Standards Agency has to inform the relevant local authority and the authority has to take action.' Fiona O'Leary, a mother of two autistic children and a leading campaigner against MMS, warned:

> 'This has been offered as a cure for autism in 60 countries. What worries me is people normalising this treatment – it does not even warrant the word "treatment". Autism is not a "disease" that you can "cure" with bleach. We need legislation so that people offering it are always prosecuted, but we don't see the authorities addressing this issue. The suffering children are going through is shocking – it's child abuse.'[570]

Over the past few years, many parents of autistic children have been turning to social media to exchange information on stem cell clinics, which have proliferated in the US and abroad over the past few years. These online forums play down the fact that only a

566 Westminster Commission on Autism (2018) *A spectrum of harmful interventions for autism* [online]. Available at: https://westminsterautismcommission.files.wordpress.com/2018/03/a-spectrum-of-harmful-interventions-web-version.pdf (accessed January 2024).

567 See www.bbc.co.uk/news/uk-england-london-33079776 (accessed March 2024).

568 Ibid.

569 Ibid.

570 Ibid.

small fraction of stem cell treatments – specifically, those for generating blood cells – have been proven safe or effective. And experts are warning that some of these 'therapies' can cause significant harm. A widely criticised 2019 paper describing a study that used stem cells to treat autistic children was retracted in 2021 after the authors failed to disclose that participants had paid thousands of dollars to take part.

Stem cells can become many types of cells in the body, from muscle to brain, and can repair damaged tissue. But they are approved only for treating some blood conditions, for skin grafts and the repair of damaged corneas. There is growing evidence that stem cells may help other conditions, including multiple sclerosis – but only after full clinical trials can these procedures be declared safe, effective and better than existing treatments. Until then, they are experimental.

The legal situation in the UK is as follows: if someone's own cells are removed and re-injected into their body without being substantially changed, the process falls outside usual European Union legal regulation. In any case, the UK is no longer a member of the EU. However, the Department of Health said the Medicines and Healthcare Products Regulatory Agency would take tough action against any clinic not following strict safety rules.

Nevertheless, according to a BBC investigation in 2020, some private UK clinics were charging patients thousands of pounds for unproven and unregulated treatments using the 'healing powers' of stem cells. Autism Regenerative Centre (ARC) in London was offering stem cell treatments for autism for children over the age of two. According to its website, bone marrow cells were taken from the child under general anaesthetic and re-injected into a vein or their spinal canal. Up to three treatments, each costing £9,500, could be prescribed. An ARC manager told a UK mother that the procedure might be carried out at a hospital near London's prestigious Harley Street. [571]

Professor Declan Murphy, a leading figure in autism research at King's College London, told the BBC he was horrified that such treatment was being offered because there was 'no evidence it was reliable or safe'.[572]

Several clinicians and researchers told BBC Radio 4's 'Stem Cell Hard Sell' programme in 2020 that the treatments could not be justified by the quality of evidence[573]. Stem cell therapies continued to be promoted at conferences organised by Treating Autism in 2022/2023. Dr Michael Fitzpatrick noted that Treating Autism's organisers were formerly very active campaigners on behalf of Andrew Wakefield, adding: 'Britain's General Medical Council could take a more active role in policing medically qualified purveyors of dubious interventions, although there are signs that they are keeping a closer eye on this'. [574]

571 Curwen L (2020) *The risks behind the hype of stem-cell treatments* [online]. Available at: www.bbc.co.uk/news/health-51006333 (accessed January 2024).

572 Ibid.

573 Ibid.

574 Dr Michael Fitzpatrick, personal communication, November 24, 2023.

- The Westminster Commission on Autism's report on the regulation of medical treatments for autism can be read here: https://westminsterautismcommission.files.wordpress.com/2018/03/a-spectrum-of-harmful-interventions-web-version.pdf (accessed January 2024).

Summary

The Oliver McGowan mandatory training has been launched for health and care staff in England to support autistic people and/or people with a learning disability. The McGowan family claim that the doctors were both negligent and failed to provide reasonable adjustments in the tragic death in hospital of their autistic son, Oliver. The new training has generally been welcomed by both the autistic community and healthcare professionals (with some reservations) in the hope that it will lead to the introduction of reasonable adjustments in medical settings, where necessary, and prevent the repetition of a number of profoundly disturbing cases of medical malpractice involving autistic patients. Although the suggestions of a link between the MMR vaccine and autism have been totally discredited, the legacy of parental disputes over vaccination continued during the Covid pandemic beginning in 2020, with the rise of similar attacks on the Covid jab and rampant conspiracy theories. Meanwhile, in the face of the promotion of various scientifically unproven 'treatments' for autism – some of them extremely dangerous – autistic campaigners and others in the UK are calling for new legislation, similar to the Cancer Act (1939), to make it illegal to offer to treat, prescribe or promote anything as an intervention (social or biological) for autism unless you are a certified professional.

Chapter 10: The rights of older autistic people

This chapter will focus on:

- The benefits maze.
- Older autistic people and the criminal justice system.
- Ageing and ethics.

The rights of older autistic people

Little is known or has been written about autism in older people. Most research on autism has focused on children and young people, but the majority of autistic individuals are adults and there is increasing awareness of the needs of adults and the lack of research on ageing in these individuals. On estimates of at least a one per cent prevalence for autism[575] the number of autistic adults aged over 65 will be 155,000 by 2035 in the UK alone. A 2016 study[576] found that, within the autistic sample, older age was associated with higher ratings of autism traits and superior cognitive performance. One interpretation, the researchers commented, was that 'general cognitive ability and the development of coping strategies across the lifespan did not necessarily reduce autistic traits but might mitigate their effects.' As the authors of the 2016 study note, the increase in both the number of older adults and older autistic adults 'represents a significant change in the population, and will require hitherto un-provided services... It is therefore important to understand the trajectory of well-being, cognitive and social abilities' in autism and the needs of autistic individuals as they age.[577]

575 In fact, according to the latest figures from the US-based Centers for Disease Control and Prevention (CDC), released in 2024, the prevalence of autism in *children* could be as high as 1 in 36, See https://publications.aap.org/aapnews/news/23904/CDC-Autism-rate-rises-to-1-in-36-children?autologincheck=redirected In the CDC's first-ever estimate of prevalence in *adults* in 2017, it put US adult prevalence at approximately 2.21%. See www.cdc.gov/ncbddd/autism/features/adults-living-with-autism-spectrum-disorder.html

576 Francesca Happé *et al* (2016) Demographic and cognitive profile of individuals seeking a diagnosis of Autism Spectrum Disorder in adulthood. *Journal of Autism and Developmental Disorders* **46** (11) 3469.

577 Ibid.

Research on risk of mortality

In 2015, a Swedish study found that people with autism were more than twice as likely as their peers in the general population to die prematurely.[578] Previous studies had hinted at premature death among people with autism, but most of them explored mortality risk in small populations and focused on specific causes of death, such as accidental injury or epilepsy. The 2015 study, from the Karolinska Institutet in Stockholm, relied on data from more than 27,000 people with autism and 2.7 million controls from the Swedish population. The researchers found that autism increased mortality risk regardless of the underlying cause of death. The study's large sample size allowed the researchers to explore diverse causes of death. The most common cause of death among people with severe autism was epilepsy, which affects roughly eight per cent of autistic people. In contrast, the most likely cause of death among people with 'mild' autism was circulatory disease. Suicide was the only cause of death that is more common among individuals with 'mild' autism than those with severe autism. The risk of suicide in individuals with less severe forms of autism is about ten times higher than in the general population. Autistic women were more likely than autistic men to commit suicide. A new study published in November 2023 and led by researchers at University College London confirmed that autistic people experienced a reduced life expectancy. However, the number of years of life lost may not be as high as previously claimed.[579] The UCL team used anonymised data from GP practices throughout the UK to study people who had received an autism diagnosis between 1989 and 2019. They studied 17,130 people diagnosed as autistic without a learning disability and 6,450 participants diagnosed as autistic with a learning disability. They then compared these groups with people of the same age and sex, who had not been diagnosed as autistic. The researchers found

578 Tatja Hirvikoski *et al* (2016) Premature mortality in autism spectrum disorder. *Br J Psychiatry* **208** (3) 232–8.

579 See www.ucl.ac.uk/news/2023/jun/number-autistic-people-england-may-be-twice-high-previously-thought (accessed March 2024).

that autistic men without a learning disability had an average estimated life expectancy of 74.6 years, and autistic women without a learning disability, around 76.8 years. Meanwhile, the estimated life expectancy for people diagnosed with autism and learning disability was around 71.7 years for men and 69.6 years for women. These figures compare to the usual life expectancy of around 80 years for men and around 83 years for women living in the UK.

Nevertheless, the lead investigator of the study, Professor Josh Stott, of UCL, said:

> 'Autism itself does not, to our knowledge, directly reduce life expectancy, but we know that autistic people experience health inequalities, meaning that they often don't get the support and help that they need when they need it... We know that when they have the right support, many autistic people live long, healthy and happy lives.' [580]

The study's joint-lead author, Dr Elizabeth O'Nions (UCL), said:

> 'Autistic people are rightly and increasingly pushing for recognition that autism reflects natural and expected variation in how brains function, and that society must make space for all. This means that services must be inclusive and accommodating of those who have particular support needs by adapting how they operate. We believe that the findings of this study reflect inequalities that disproportionately affect autistic people.'

Professor Stott said:

> 'Very few autistic adults have been diagnosed, meaning that this study focuses on only a fraction of the total autistic population. Those who are diagnosed may be those with greater support needs and more co-occurring health conditions than autistic people on average. We think this is particularly the case for women diagnosed with autism and learning disability – the larger reduction in life expectancy may reflect a disproportionate under-diagnosis of autism and/or learning disability in women. It's likely that not all autistic people experience a reduced life expectancy – indeed, some autistic people may be better at sticking to healthy routines than average, potentially increasing their life expectancy.'

Dr Judith Brown, Head of Evidence and Research at the National Autistic Society, said:

> 'These findings demonstrate that autistic people continue to face unacceptable inequalities through a lack of understanding, barriers to vital services and inadequate care, which lead to poorer mental and physical health outcomes. Without investment, improved understanding, inclusion and the correct level of support and care, autistic people will continue to see reduced life expectancy, with the most at-risk group in this study being autistic women with learning disabilities. This research should be a wake-up call for government, the NHS, healthcare professionals and society as a whole that we must tackle the health inequality autistic people face.'

580 Ekaterina Harrison commented that 'This observation is intriguing; it appears that the environment plays a more significant role in life expectancy than autism itself.' Personal communication, January 10, 2024.

In October 2009, the Autism Act (in England) was passed, which put an expectation on local authorities to recognise the needs of autistic adults. This landmark legislation resulted in *Fulfilling and Rewarding Lives: The strategy for adults with autism in England*.[581] This strategy described a vision where all autistic adults are able to live fulfilling and rewarding lives within a society that accepts and understands them. In July 2021, the UK government released a national strategy, *The National Strategy for Autistic Children, Young People, and Adults: 2021 to 2026*. [582]

Issues affecting older autistic people

The vision exists, and so do the legal provisions. But what can we do in practice to ensure that autistic people have the same opportunities as other citizens to live healthy, fulfilled lives as they age? Recognising the needs of autistic adults is now an expectation enshrined in law, but little attention has been paid to the issues affecting older people with the condition. The findings of one survey point to a population who are struggling to have their needs recognised and met. A significantly higher percentage of 40- to 64-year-olds had not received an assessment (a statutory assessment of their needs under the Community Care Act (1990)) compared with 18–29-year olds, and the survey showed that a considerable number of adults with autism aged 40 and over remained reliant on family for their support. Very few autistic individuals in any age group received most of their support from friends, and the evidence points to people with autism becoming more and more isolated as they grow older.[583]

As parents age, they may no longer be able to support their autistic children, but there is evidence that they are not supported by professionals or friends either. This puts a great responsibility on other family members.

Despite the studies cited above, we still know relatively little about outcomes for autistic adults, especially the older age group, or whether there are changes in autism symptoms and behaviours related to the ageing process. Digby Tantam's studies from the 1980s and 1990s revealed a desperate picture of social isolation, high unemployment and mental ill health among the more able population. This view was confirmed by recent work by Stuart-Hamilton and colleagues comparing autistic adults over the age of 40 with those of the general population, which also points to significant levels of unemployment, anxiety and depression in older autistic adults.[584] Just as autistic children become autistic adults, so autistic adults grow older. As with our response to the transition from childhood to adulthood, we need to deal with the new transition from adulthood into older age. According to the British charity Autistica, research into autistic adults amounts to just 60p per person per year. The charity's chief executive, James Cusack, who is autistic himself, says: 'We don't even have a

581 For more, see: www.gov.uk/government/news/fulfilling-and-rewarding-lives-the-strategy-for-adults-with-autism-in-england (accessed February 2024).

582 See www.gov.uk/government/publications/national-strategy-for-autistic-children-young-people-and-adults-2021-to-2026

583 Crane L *et al* (2018) Autism Diagnosis in the United Kingdom: Perspectives of Autistic Adults, Parents and Professionals. *J Autism Dev Disord* **48** (11) 3761–3772.

584 Howlin P (2021) Adults with autism: Changes in understanding since DSM-111. *J Autism Dev Disord* **51** (12). Available at: www.ncbi.nlm.nih.gov/pmc/articles/PMC8531125/ (accessed February 2024).

basic understanding of how to support adults with autism as they age.'[585] Focus on childhood research means that many older adults with autism today may not have been diagnosed and risk having autistic symptoms mistaken for mental illness or dementia. And concurrent with a lack of research and knowledge is a lack of understanding and training in adult health and social care. 'This matters, as the isolation that many autistic people experience due to social and communication difficulties is likely to worsen with age. When you have very limited support networks, you may become increasingly reliant on social care.'[586]

Many care staff who work with autistic individuals are accustomed to managing younger groups and therefore may have had little experience in being with older autistic people. Without good training, they may struggle to understand the issues they face. We also need better mechanisms for the diagnosis and treatment of comorbid conditions. Dementia rates are increasing, and dementia in the learning-disabled population is much higher than in the general population, even excluding Down's syndrome. Nevertheless, changes in behaviour are not necessarily related to dementia. There could be many alternative explanations.

Local authorities are frequently unaware of the number or circumstances of older autistic adults, especially the more able who are not receiving funded services. Their social isolation may be compounded by the sudden loss of carers, retirement or loss of employment and related network of support. When dealing with autism, the boundaries of responsibility for health and social care are blurred, particularly for the more able group. Will their changing needs be recognised and responded to appropriately? Will the new UK central government strategy really help, especially if local discretion is at the heart of entitlement?

Cathie Long, a social worker, was diagnosed with autism at the age of 56. She says the diagnosis has been life-changing:

> 'I wish I had it younger. It's given me a lot of understanding of who I am, how I relate to other people, why I find some things difficult that other people might not find so difficult. For a long time in my life, I was thinking: "Right, one day I'll wake up and it'll all fall into place and I'll have everything sussed." I think the diagnosis has actually enabled me to suss things out and understand why I felt different. I don't put myself under such great pressure any more to please all the people all the time – I think that was something I was doing a lot. I realised that if I don't pace myself, I'm going to get to a place where I'm completely overwhelmed and I can't function. I shut down for a few days. It's that sort of thing. I'm having to really think about what I need to do for me rather than trying to meet everybody else's needs and ignore my own. That's a really big change.'[587]

585 Bawden T (2023) *More than 9 in 10 autistic people over 50 don't have a diagnosis, study finds* [online]. Available at: https://inews.co.uk/news/health/autistic-people-over-diagnosis-study-2427578 (accessed January 2024).

586 Ibid.

587 Ibid.

Long says it required a great deal of effort to obtain the diagnosis: 'I don't know if I would have ever got it through the NHS – I did have to go privately, but I'm glad I did. Even with private, there are really long waiting lists, so I had to wait months to just have the assessment.'[588]

She says she enjoyed:

> '...becoming part of a community of like-minded people, connecting with other neurodivergent people. And something I think that is really interesting is that some of my really long-standing friends, who I've connected with all my adult life have, one by one, come out as autistic, or have ADHD, or both. And I think it just shows how we subconsciously attract people with the same difference.'[589]

Cos Michael was diagnosed with autism at the age of 50. She spent several years at Britain's National Autistic Society, leading their Autism and Ageing projects and winning the Autism Professionals Award for Outstanding Adult Services in 2014, and has specific knowledge of issues around autism and growing older. She explained:

> 'The problem is that older autistic people are routinely and consistently excluded from every policy document relating to autism. These same keywords are absent from the Autism Act and Strategy documents. They are also omitted in the output of every policy document I have looked at, that might drive actions to support older autistic people. I have campaigned on this matter, ever since I left the NAS in 2014. I have spoken at APPGA meetings, at many conferences and to the campaign department at the NAS, but nobody has been interested... So nobody could say that they are unaware of the existence of over one-third of the autistic population – those aged over 40. As autistic people, we are an excluded population in English law.' [590]

Another neglected area is that of the carers for elderly autistic people. Michael Baron, the father of an adult son with autism (and one of the founders of Britain's National Autistic Society), has experienced the difficulties of becoming an elderly carer. He is now 95 years old. When Baron's wife became ill and died in 2012, he became the remaining carer for their middle-aged autistic son, Timothy. The process of his wife's rapid decline into dementia and a number of other age-related conditions had led Michael to believe that, in finding solutions for autistic adults and their ageing parents:

> '...the incidence of dementia in the older population should not be neglected, since it affects about 20% of people who are over 80 years of age. This risk is underplayed. When a carer quickly develops dementia, they are not only unable to provide consistent care for a person with autism, but they may also be unable to seek other care solutions. If they are a sole carer, this could have dramatic consequences for the person with autism.'[591]

---

588 Ibid.

589 Ibid.

590 Cos Michael, personal communication, December 11, 2023.

591 Autism Europe. *Towards a Better Quality of Life: The rights of aging people with autism* [online]. Available at: www.autismeurope.org/wp-content/uploads/2017/08/ageing-report-en-sml.pdf (accessed March 2024).

Ekaterina Harrison goes even further. She believes the risk of dementia in older autistic individuals 'does not even appear to be acknowledged, let alone downplayed.'[592]

Many older autistic people find it very difficult to cope with loneliness, changes or the struggle to form friendships. Indeed, a 2023 Kingston University study found that several people with learning disabilities and autism in the Netherlands chose to die legally through euthanasia and assisted suicide due to these feelings of helplessness.[593] Commenting on the findings, the study's lead author, Professor Irene Tuffrey-Wijne, said that, alongside the need for a wider debate on the ethics of dealing with requests from vulnerable groups, the research also highlighted the importance of investing in highly individualised support services around the world, Tuffrey-Wijne has made it her life's mission to campaign on behalf of people with learning disabilities and autism when it comes to end-of-life care and bereavement. She observed:

> 'What these individuals needed was a society where they felt they belonged, with people around them who not just accept and accommodate, but welcome their unique ways of being. There is no doubt some people feel helpless, suffer deeply and profoundly and the support needed is complex but hopefully there can be a culture shift and a big investment in services that are significantly under-resourced.'[594]

Receiving a diagnosis later in life

Diagnosing older people with autism is important so that they can benefit, as others do, from the greater understanding and access to services that a diagnosis can bring. People face some key transitions as they age, such as retirement and bereavements, and it is important they receive appropriate support. A significant transition faced by many people with autism as they get older comes when their parent-carers are no longer able to support them at home. Many autistic people continue to live at home with carers well into adulthood, and parent-carers are therefore likely to be nearing and entering old age while still providing care to people with often very high needs.

Given the historical context of autism and the progress made in the development of diagnostic techniques, it is probable that there will be many adults receiving a diagnosis after the age of 50, and it is crucial that health care professionals, social workers and clinicians spot signs of the condition in older adults.

Recent research suggests that receiving a diagnosis should be followed up with professional help to enable the individual to manage the change to his or her life and identity. While past research has also focused on poor aftercare, one particular study

592 Ekaterina Harrison, personal communication, January 10, 2024.

593 Irene Tuffrey-Wijne et al (2023) Euthanasia and physician-assisted suicide in people with intellectual disabilities. *BJPsych Open* **23** 9 (3):e87.

594 Kingston University. *Factors associated with learning disabilities and autism led to requests for euthanasia and assisted suicide in the Netherlands, Kingston University study finds* [online]. Available at: www.kingston.ac.uk/news/article/2843/05-jul-2023-factors-associated-with-learning-disabilities-and-autism-led-to-requests-for-euthanasia-and-assisted-suicide/ (accessed February 2024).

also highlighted the need for special consideration in the workplace.[595] Advocacy work, backed by the Equality Act (2010), can support this process by helping the newly diagnosed individual to reshape their work environment to best suit their needs. Clinicians and health workers need to be more aware of the possible signs of undiagnosed autism, to avoid misdiagnosing depression, anxiety or other mental health conditions. A thorough study of the client's early childhood and their current relations (family, work colleagues) can help.

More work also needs to be done to support older adults after they receive a diagnosis. They and their families need to be supported through this transitional phase, and emphasis needs to be placed on future potential and possibilities.

The potential for sudden breakdowns in caring arrangements is high, and too many autistic people may find themselves hurriedly placed in settings that may be expensive, distant, inappropriate, or all three. Other people may be left living at home without adequate support. This is a key cause for stress and concern for parents and carers as they approach older age. It is important, therefore, that careful planning, involving the autistic individual and their family, takes place well in advance of a change to the family situation. This will help to address the concerns of both the autistic person and his or her carers. Emergency plans, detailing what support will be put in place for someone if their care arrangements break down, can alleviate anxiety, and lessen the likelihood of an emergency residential placement.[596]

Entering the healthcare system at the point of severe health decline can result in expensive nursing home placements or hospitalisations. People may also be less likely to ask for adaptations to their property, or for home help. The Care Act (2014) includes a duty to provide independent advocacy services for those who find navigating the care system difficult and have no support networks to assist them. Older autistic people may find this helps them to access services.[597]

As one woman with Asperger's syndrome, Susan Dunne, declared:

> 'I hope by the time I need age-related support that health and social care professionals will appreciate the importance of consistency and routine in managing anxiety in autism. I'd like it if they understood why loud noises, unexpected touch and doors left open can be anathema. I'd prefer it if I'm not assumed to have mental health issues or the onset of dementia because my brain processes information differently. Given the present lack of research, knowledge and training in ageing and autism, I'm not optimistic that any of this will have happened by then.' [598]

595 Davies J, Romualdez AM, Malyan D, Heasman B, Livesey A, Walker A, Pellicano E and Remington A (2024): Autistic Adults' Priorities for Future Autism Employment Research: Perspectives from the United Kingdom, *Autism Adulthood*. March; 6(1): 72–85. Published online 2024 Feb 28. doi: 10.1089/aut.2022.0087 Available at www.ncbi.nlm.nih.gov/pmc/articles/PMC10902279/ (accessed March 2024).

596 SCIE (2017) *Growing older with autism* [online]. Available at: www.scie.org.uk/autism/adults/transition/older (accessed JMarch 2024).

597 Ibid.

598 Dunne S (2015) 'I'm scared to be an older person with autism'. The Guardian, November 11.

How ageing affects autistic and neurodiverse people

Even after the passage of the Autism Act (2009), the UK lacks a coordinated strategy for providing health and social care for older autistic adults. Steven Kapp, a researcher at the University of Portsmouth, put it this way: 'We knew it was wrong for people with disabilities to be institutionalised on a massive scale, but we seem to look the other way when they're older.'[599]

When dealing with autism, the boundaries of responsibility for health and social care are blurred, particularly for the more able group. Will their changing needs be recognised and responded to appropriately? An ongoing UK government review into the present system of funding for social care reflects the growing concern over the anticipated numbers of the elderly in need and the inability or unwillingness of the state to meet this need.

Research by Professor Rebecca Charlton (whose work at Goldsmiths, University of London, examines how ageing affects autistic and other neurodiverse people in terms of health, cognition and well-being) has shown that age and severity of autism are linked, and that 'as age increased, so did the severity of autism symptoms in social situations, communication and flexible thinking (such as coping with change or generating new ideas or solutions).' She also found that autistic older people were more likely than younger people to extract rules from situations or to prefer structure.[600]

It has been pointed out that the Covid pandemic exacerbated what for many older autistic individuals was already a hard and dislocated existence:

> 'It has led to very real challenges for those organisations and charities which support people, and it has limited the appropriate access to clinical and medical interventions. It has prevented or halted some positive developments which were focused on training frontline health and care staff to get better at recognising and responding to late-age autism... People with autism may develop robust coping mechanisms from which we can learn but equally transitions of age may result in sharp deterioration and decline.'[601]

For autistic people, the ageing process may be challenging as their health and social care needs change with age, as the authors of a 2023 study observed: 'These changes are likely to intersect with autism-related support needs such as anxiety and difficulties with change and uncertainty, difficulties with executive function, autobiographical memory and the ability to think about the future.' According to the researchers, autistic individuals reported a lack of understanding and knowledge among professionals relating to how best to work with them as they aged. 'Autistic people reported a sense of fatigue that they have to continually train others in how to work with them. Older autistic people are not receiving the support they require to thrive. It is important that professionals are adequately trained to both work with autistic people and in working with age-related changes.'[602]

599 See www.spectrumnews.org/features/deep-dive/growing-old-with-autism/ (accessed March 2024).

600 See https://scottishcare.org/citizens-of-another-world-autism-and-older-age/ (accessed March 2024).

601 Ibid.

602 See: Mary Elizabeth Stewart *et al.* (2023). Older Autistic Adults, Ageing, and Social Care. Paper presented at INSAR 2023 Annual Meeting, Stockholm, Sweden.

Social prescribing (SP) is the referral of patients to non-clinical services for practical, physical or psychosocial support. Recent guidelines from NHS England mean that SP will become commonplace for people with complex healthcare needs. Since autistic adults make up over one per cent of the population and commonly have co-existing physical and mental health conditions, they are likely to be referred to SP services. This can include helping to organise everyday activities, support to access services, craft and art hobbies, physical activities or support for mental health problems. Recently, NHS England has made social prescribing a priority and funding will provide a staff member to support social prescribing in every GP surgery.

As Ekaterina Harrison points out, some argue that social prescribing may contribute to the medicalisation of social issues by viewing them through a healthcare lens: 'Critics suggest that social and economic problems require broader societal solutions beyond healthcare interventions.'[603]

As the authors of a 2023 open letter on SP, led by Professor Rebecca Charlton,[604] point out, the factors that influence engagement are not clear and are likely to reflect both differences in service characteristics (what is available), provisions for access (physical location, accessibility, direct and indirect costs), as well as differences in client characteristics, interests, and needs.

> 'For example, is a client with intellectual impairment living in supported accommodation as likely to be referred to a SP service as someone living independently without intellectual impairments? Even if both individuals were referred to SP, barriers to access are likely to be different. For an individual in supported living, a barrier may be the availability of a carer to accompany the individual to an appointment, but for the carer to make and at prompt to attend the appointment may be supportive. Different barriers and supports may exist for someone living independently. Many of these issues are similar for autistic people and a general population sample.'[605]

The 2021 open letter goes on to note that successful SP services:

> '...are likely to be those which enable autistic people to feel empowered, communicate their needs, and establish and maintain social relationships at their level of preference. SP services that take account of individual strengths and difficulties are more likely to effectively support autistic people across the lifespan and, therefore, deliver more long-term benefit... Autistic adults are most likely to be referred to existing services that support a wide range of people (e.g. a general walking group) or target people with a specific need (e.g. singing for older adults), rather than autism-specific services. However, services unfamiliar with autistic people may need to make adjustments in order to succeed.'[606]

603 Ekaterina Harrison, personal communication, January 10, 2024.

604 Charlton RA *et al* (2021) Social prescribing for autistic people: A framework for service provision [version 2; peer review: 2 approved]. *AMRC* Open Res **2** 19

605 Ibid.

606 Ibid.

The crisis in funding for social care in the UK naturally represents severe problems for older autistic people, as well. Indeed, as Carol Povey, Richard Mills and colleagues asked in a 2011 paper:

> '...could this be a double whammy for people with autism? Already socially isolated and disadvantaged by their condition and responses to it, will they face additional problems from a system more attuned to the needs of the majority? What of those already settled in residential services? Will their entitlement to funding be lost? Could they be forced to move on from familiar surroundings and people as a consequence of arbitrary budgeting on the part of a local authority? Who will defend or fight for them when their parents are no longer around? The issues related to autism and ageing are a growing challenge for society. We need to develop ways for people to continue to enjoy fulfilled and productive lives as they grow older. By its very nature, autism provides strong predisposition to a host of social and medical problems (eg, fragile X) and these may be exacerbated with age. We need to ensure that as far as possible, we intervene in a timely fashion to prevent this predisposition becoming a reality. Just as children with autism become adults with autism, adults with autism grow older. As with our response to the transition from childhood to adulthood, we need to deal with the new transition from adulthood into older age. The question from parents, "What happens after I'm gone?", is as relevant today as ever.'[607]

The United Nations Convention on the Rights of Persons with Disabilities and older autistic individuals

Under the United Nations Convention on the Rights of Persons with Disabilities (UNCRPD), an international human rights instrument intended to protect the rights and dignity of people with disabilities, autistic individuals, their families or representatives, and relevant organisations must gain a strong understanding of their rights and governments must fulfil their obligation. The UN Convention, which the UK ratified in 2009, can potentially influence British court decisions. Parties to the Convention are required to promote, protect, and ensure the full enjoyment of human rights by people with disabilities on an equal basis with others.[608]

Nevertheless, as Ekaterina Harrison has observed, the UNCRPD 'does not establish direct obligations within UK domestic law, nor does it create independent rights for individuals. Instead, it may be used as an interpretive aid in the construction and understanding of UK law.'[609] Many signatories to the Convention have not taken into account the intersection of age and disability. Older people with disabilities have suffered a double disadvantage, as seen in their relatively low priority in health and social care policies and provision.

---

607 Povey C, Mills R, Gomez de la Cuesta GG (2011) Autism and ageing: issues for the future. *Clinical Practice* **41**: 230–232.

608 Equality and Human Rights Commission (2010) *The United Nations Convention on the Rights of People with Disabilities Equality and Human Rights Commission Guidance What does it mean for you?* [online]. Available at: www.equalityhumanrights.com/sites/default/files/uncrpdguide_0.pdf (accessed January 2024).

609 Ekaterina Harrison, personal communication, January 10, 2024.

Article 19 of the UNCRPD guarantees the right to an independent life and self-determination. Autistic people requiring a high level of support have the right to make decisions for their future, and to ask for the provisions of the UN Convention to be respected.

Article 25 of the Convention guarantees the right to maintain or improve the quality of health. Autistic individuals should be provided with the necessary means to ensure:

- Health problems related to ageing are prevented, notably through regular check-ups and screenings.
- Accurate diagnosis and accurate information on their specific health condition/s.
- Problems related to their specific health conditions (for example osteoarthritis) are prevented.
- Treatment of individual health conditions.[610]

Articles 9 and 26 of the UNCRPD protect the right to maintain and improve communication and social interaction. Older autistic individuals should be provided with access to adapted/alternative means of communication and visual information. Where possible, inter-generational dialogue involving older autistic people should be fostered by:

- Participating in cultural events and other leisure or sports activities with younger people in the broader community.
- Supporting contact between schools, youth organisations and structures for older autistic individuals.[611]

Article 26 of the UN Convention guarantees the right to appropriate intervention. Multi-disciplinary assessment and co-ordination of interventions should be provided for autistic people throughout their lifespan, including during old age, while taking into account the functional abilities of the older person and the interests and wishes of the older person and his/her family.[612]

Individualised support plans for autistic people should be designed and put into practice with the principal objectives of improving and maintaining skills for autonomy in the home or residence, and improving and maintaining social skills in community activities.[613]

The same Article of the UNCRPD (Article 26) protects the right of access to services which provide a good quality of life. Older autistic people should be fully and directly involved throughout the process of designing, implementing and evaluating services that aim to meet their needs. Families, care providers and friends should also be involved in these processes since appropriate services should be the result of a dialogue between relevant stakeholders. A diversity of accredited services must also be available. Autistic service users and their families/representatives must have permanent contact and dialogue with the staff, the opportunity to express their needs, priorities, hopes and desires, and to

610 Equality and Human Rights Commission (2010) *The United Nations Convention on the Rights of People with Disabilities Equality and Human Rights Commission Guidance What does it mean for you?* [online]. Available at: www.equalityhumanrights.com/sites/default/files/uncrpdguide_0.pdf (accessed January 2024).

611 Ibid.

612 Ibid.

613 Ibid.

participate fully in the development, monitoring and review of individual support plans. In order to achieve these goals, services should provide specific, qualified interventions consequent to contemporary knowledge in the field of autism. Services should also have a stable and reliable structure that adopts quality standards related to the quality of life of the users and is based on a set of rules defining responsibilities, day-to-day routines and procedures. These measures will enable family and staff members to identify the individual needs of autistic people and will also provide a way of reducing the risk of isolation and exclusion.[614]

Article 24 of the Convention guarantees the right to education and life-long learning. With this in mind, relevant services must offer a learning environment and education facilities adapted to older autistic people: 'Life-long education is necessary to compensate for the great difficulties that people with autism have in extracting meaning from simple experiences (something most other people are capable of without specific educational support) and to attain the highest possible degree of self-sufficiency.'[615]

Article 30 of the UN Convention protects the right to leisure. Older autistic people also have the right to take part in leisure activities and enjoy cultural life. They should be provided with adequate support, according to their individual needs, in order to benefit from culture, entertainment, recreation and sport.

The right to housing facilities is enshrined in Articles 19 and 23 of the UNCRPD. Autistic people must be supported to remain in their own homes as long as they can, like other ageing people, or live in places where they were accustomed to spending time before retiring from 'active life'. Preparation for the changes in living arrangements must be carefully planned. New environments must be adapted to the specific needs of each person with autism. For those living at home, specific support (medical or technical aids, housekeeping, adaptation to the environment, etc) must be provided, and support for ageing family members who care for older autistic individuals must also be offered. For those living in supported housing facilities, autistic people must be supported to live in the home to which they are accustomed, with no age limit. If this is not possible, they should be placed in a nearby residence to restrict the changes to their daily life. In addition, complementary medical and health support (nurses, other support staff, hospital care, technical aids, accessibility, etc) must be provided at the requisite level of intensity.[616]

Article 28 of the UN Convention also guarantees the right to realistic and adequate financial support (see the following section on the 'benefits maze').

The benefits maze

The financial situation of disabled people in relation to pensions can vary and depends on various factors, such as the nature and severity of the disability, an individual's employment history and social support systems. In some cases, disabled individuals

614 Ibid.

615 Ibid.

616 Ibid.

may face challenges in building a robust pension due to barriers in the workforce, such as discrimination or limited access to suitable employment opportunities. Disabilities might have an impact on a person's ability to work, affecting his or her earnings and, subsequently, that individual's pension contributions. In addition, some disabled individuals may incur extra costs related to their disability, diverting resources that could otherwise contribute to pension savings. However, it is important to note that disability does not automatically lead to pension poverty, and government assistance, workplace accommodations, and supportive social policies can play crucial roles in mitigating financial challenges for disabled individuals. The level of pension security for disabled people can vary based on the effectiveness of these support systems.[617]

The face-to-face assessments in the personal independence payment (PIP) process can prove as nightmarish as a job interview or a police interview for many autistic individuals. They, their family members and advocates claim that the emphasis on such assessments is leading to them losing this benefit or receiving downgraded awards (see **Case study 40** on p.269). Undergoing an assessment may provoke extreme anxiety. If the assessment takes place at a busy centre, there may be no quiet rooms available, and the sensory overload may prove overwhelming. This is exacerbated by a general lack of awareness about autism among the assessors, which can lead to the bizarre situation of a health visitor, nurse or paramedic acting as an assessor, contradicting the view of a senior consultant.[618]

Non-autistic people find the pensions maze difficult enough to negotiate. Imagine how daunting it can seem for some older autistic individuals! This section provides some extremely useful advice from specialists on how to ensure your pension rights are fully respected.

Benefit entitlement changes in the UK when you reach each of two important ages: state pension age and pension credit qualifying age. From these ages, you can move from working-age benefits to benefits for older people. Women born before April 6, 1950, reach state pension age on their 60th birthday. Men born before December 6, 1953, reach state pension age on their 65th birthday. Anyone born after these dates will have a higher state pension age. Under current UK legislation, the state pension age for everyone reached 66 in October 2020. It will be 67 by 2028 and 68 by 2046.[619]

The Pensions Act (2014) allows for the state pension age to be increased at a faster rate in the future, and will be reviewed every five years. It will then be set according to a range of factors, including average life expectancy. It is intended that, on average, you should spend no more than one-third of your adult life in retirement. This means that, if life expectancy rises as predicted, the state pension age may rise to age 68 by the middle of the 2030s, age 69 by the late 2040s and age 70 by the 2060s. You can check your state pension age online.[620]

617 Ekaterina Harrison, personal communication – my thanks to her for making these important points.

618 See https://morningstaronline.co.uk/article/people-autism-spectrum-conditions-are-unfairly-treated-pip-claims ((accessed March 2024).

619 See www.autism.org.uk/advice-and-guidance/topics/benefits-and-money/benefits/benefits-you-can-get/benefits-for-older-people (accessed March 2024).

620 See www.gov.uk/government/publications/state-pension-age-review-2023-government-report/state-pension-age-review-2023#:~:text=The%20Pensions%20Act%202014%20brought,whether%20this%20pathway%20is%20appropriate. (accessed March 2024).

The State Retirement Pension (SRP) has existed since the early 20th century and is linked to the amount of national insurance contributions paid over a working lifetime, or national insurance credits received by being in receipt of certain benefits, such as Jobseekers' Allowance or Employment and Support Allowance. Since 2010, 30 years of contributions or credits are required to give a full category A pension. It is also possible for widowed people to receive a pension based on their late spouse's contribution record (category B pension). The Pension Service should write to you if you are approaching pension age and invite you to apply. If you have not heard three months before you will reach pension age, you can apply by calling 0800 731 7898 and making a claim over the phone or asking for a paper claim form to be sent to you online at www.gov.uk/claim-state-pension-online.

Attendance Allowance (AA), Disability Living Allowance (DLA) and Personal Independence Payment (PIP) are benefits paid to people who have a disability. You can be entitled to only one of these three benefits at a time. Which of them you are entitled to depends on your age and the time you first claim. DLA and PIP are for people who first claimed a disability benefit when they were aged under 65. DLA is being abolished and gradually replaced by PIP. Adults (aged over 16) can no longer make a new claim for DLA. If you get DLA and were born on or before April 8, 1948, you can carry on receiving DLA for as long as you meet the criteria. If you get DLA and were born after April 8, 1948, your DLA will stop and you will be invited to claim PIP at some point. AA, DLA and PIP are non-means-tested and non-contributory benefits for people with long-term illnesses or disabilities resulting in significant care needs. This means that they are not affected by savings, earnings or other benefits and do not depend on having paid national insurance contributions to receive them. They can be paid in conjunction with all other benefits without negatively affecting the level those benefits are paid at and can lead to an increase in these benefits as well.[621]

Pension Credit (PC) is payable to people who have reached the qualifying age and who have an income below the weekly minimum level the government expects someone to live on. It can act as a 'top-up' on an SRP, or provide complete provision to people who do not qualify for an SRP. Pension Credit can be paid to single people or to couples. Following a change to the rules in May 2019, both members of a couple now need to be over the state pension age to claim. You will need to claim universal credit if one of you is under state pension age.

Pension Credit is means-tested, which means that income such as earnings and some benefits will affect the amount paid, as will savings. Pension Credit can be claimed by calling 0800 99 1234.

A new Flat Rate (or single tier) state pension was introduced for anyone reaching state pension age after April 5, 2016. It replaces other pension elements (such as the second state pension and savings pension credit) and is set at a rate above the basic level of means-tested support (that is, guarantee pension credit level for a single person). This requires 35 years of national insurance contributions or credits to receive the full amount; a minimum of ten years' contributions or credits to qualify for a smaller pro rata amount provides transitional payments for those who would have received a higher SRP under the previous system.

621 See www.autism.org.uk/advice-and-guidance/topics/benefits-and-money/benefits/benefits-you-can-get/benefits-for-older-people (accessed March 2024).

New research by the Pensions Policy Institute (PPI) revealed in 2022 that people with disabilities face huge barriers to pensions saving, resulting in a private pension pot just 36% of the UK average. The research found that people with a disability who were approaching retirement age (age 60-64) had £47,980 average pension wealth compared to the average UK pot size of £130,928, a difference of almost £83,000.[622]

Disabled people are more than twice as likely to be unemployed as non-disabled people and even those who can work are often limited by the amount and type of work they can do. They may find themselves trapped in low-paying or part-time jobs. The high prevalence of part-time work means that many are excluded from automatic enrolment. As pointed out by NOW: Pensions, a UK pension provider for almost two million people, an employee is enrolled in a workplace pension scheme 'only once he or she earns over £10,000 a year in a single job. Even those earning more than the £10,000 threshold in a job and enrolled still miss out on potentially significant contributions from each of their employments due to the Lower Earnings Limit. The lower limit is set at £6,396, meaning that only earnings over that amount are pensionable. Instead of saving 8% into a pension, those earning £10,000 are only contributing 3.6% of that total figure, meaning they are missing out on crucial employer contributions.'[623]

Joanne Segars, Chair of Trustees at NOW: Pensions, declared:

> 'People with disabilities are one of the under-pensioned groups that we have been campaigning on behalf of for some time. We believe it is imperative that we continue to raise awareness of the discrimination that many people go through which has a huge impact on the ability of people to save for their later life. We want to make pension saving fairer for everybody in the UK and our policy proposal to remove the £10,000 earnings threshold would help get a further 500,000 disabled people saving for their retirement.'[624]

Laurie Edmans co-chair of GAIN – Group for Autism, Insurance, Investment and Neurodiversity – said: 'GAIN is campaigning for a radical improvement in the employment prospects of neurodiverse people, many of whom – like people with non-visible disabilities – face very similar employment challenges to those with physical disabilities.'[625]

---

622 Now: Pensions (2022) People with disabilities have a pension wealth just 36% of the average UK pension [online]. Available at: www.nowpensions.com/press/people-with-disabilities-have-a-pension-wealth-just-36-of-the-average-uk-pension/ (accessed January 2024).

623 Ibid.

624 Ibid.

625 Ibid.

Case study 40: Arabella Tresilian

Arabella Tresilian, 47, a disabled mother from Bath who was left with no income for three years after her PIP claim was rejected because she 'didn't seem autistic enough', has described her disability benefit assessment as 'inhumane and traumatising'.[626] Tresilian was forced to stop working due to several conditions – including autism, post-traumatic stress disorder, anxiety, depression and chronic fatigue – which make her prone to burnout.

In 2016, she applied for support from both universal credit and PIP. This was the beginning of a three-year battle to secure the payment. The amount was eventually awarded through a tribunal. 'It was the most inhumane system I had come across at a time when I desperately needed compassion, care, understanding and the financial support that I was entitled to,' she told the I newspaper.

> 'I was greeted by a woman who took me into the waiting room pre-assessment, who then revealed herself to be my assessor. As an autistic person, I desperately need clarity, and it really unnerved me. I felt like I had to defend myself right from the beginning of the assessment. I was being asked these complex, difficult and personal questions, and my verbal tics began. It felt like she caught the wind under her sails and was interrogating me. I had tears down my cheeks.'[627]

The assessor tried to cancel the assessment mid-way through because of Tresilian's increasing distress:

> 'I felt like my financial security was in this woman's hands and she was going to rewind this process and start again. I urged her to not make me come again. Later on, when we started, her supervisor rang. The assessor said she was so worried about me, she thought she'd have to call an ambulance. I was right there and could hear the entire conversation.'[628]

Although she presented with symptoms of the complex illnesses and issues she faced, she received a letter declining her assessment for PIP and declaring she was 'completely fine and fit for work'. The following year, she reapplied for PIP, but was turned down again:

> 'They said because I didn't need prompting during the assessment and that I had adequate eye contact, I didn't need it. It was their way of saying: "Well if you can do those things, you can't be very autistic." I was assessed by a physiotherapist, and I wondered how much she knew about autism.'[629]

In the run-up to the tribunal, Tresilian was in debt and unable to work or pay her rent or for food. 'As a mother, that is a really scary place to be,' she said. 'My 16-year-old daughter became a young carer and worked a part-time job to make ends meet.'

Tresilian has since returned to work but said she had been traumatised by the experience of applying for disability support:

> 'It took me a long time to clear my debts and recover from the emotional and physical toll of it. I don't know how we can say a system is working if we ask our most vulnerable people to present themselves at court to defend their need for money.' [630] ➔

626 See https://inews.co.uk/news/health/pip-assessment-lived-without-income-three-years-not-autistic-enough-1344728 (accessed March 2024).

627 Ibid.

628 Ibid.

629 Ibid.

630 Ibid.

The latest government figures show that at least two-thirds of disability benefit assessment decisions are overturned at tribunal. According to the disability charity, Scope, this is the equivalent of one every minute of the working day.

James Taylor, executive director of the charity, observed:

> 'These wrong decisions throw a person's life into turmoil. Having to fight for financial support puts a huge toll on disabled people's mental and physical health and can plunge families into poverty. We've heard from huge numbers of disabled people who felt their assessors did not understand their condition or how it affects their life. An assessor with appropriate knowledge will be able to understand the true impact of someone's condition and how it might fluctuate, as well as giving disabled people confidence they will get a fair assessment and the right decision first time round.'[631]

A Department for Work and Pensions (DWP) spokesperson said:

> 'We are very sorry for the distress caused to Ms Tresilian. Since we handled this case, we have changed our approach to decision-making for PIP to help ensure we make the right decision as early as possible... We urge anyone who believes they may be eligible for extra support to speak to their work coach.' [632]

Older autistic people and the criminal justice system

As we saw in Chapter 6, autistic people are frequently being failed by the criminal justice system. No specific research has investigated the plight facing older and elderly autistic individuals who first come into contact with the CJS. However, between 2007 and 2010, Cos Michael managed a project called Learning Matters, for the Prisoners' Education Trust. The project aimed to raise awareness of the need for distance learning within prisons. Between those years, Michael visited many prisons and spoke to many prisoners:

> 'I was made aware of the difficulties of ageing in prisons, particularly the older and more basic environments. Apart from the environmental and sensory issues that affect all neurodivergent people, older people face additional, punitive challenges. Most older prisons have no lifts, and the stairs can be steep. I never saw a lift in newer prisons either, but I assume there may be some. The hard mattresses in cells can be punishing on older, arthritic bones. When my work took me into prisons, I was unaware of any level of occupational therapy for prisoners with physical or post-operative needs. These conditions apply to all older people in prisons, but as is well known, healthcare is extremely basic: even if clinicians and psychologists have some level of autism knowledge, I can practically guarantee that this will not have covered ageing, as it is extremely rare to include ageing in any autism training.' [633]

631 Ibid.

632 Ibid.

633 Cos Michael, personal communication, December 11, 2023.

As Michael points out, prison will be additionally punishing for older autistic people:

> 'Lack of adjustments for the noise, smells, overcrowding and other environmental hardships is likely to exacerbate mental health problems for autistic elders. And of course, if an older autistic person repeatedly has meltdowns, they are far more likely to be diagnosed with dementia, by psychologists who do not understand autism in older people, rather than be treated with the humanity and dignity that we all deserve.'[634]

The new National Autism Training Programme (NATP) does include ageing training, to which Cos Michael has contributed, but this needs to be rolled out into Prison Service training:

> 'If nobody is looking, then nobody is finding evidence relating to older autistic people in the CJS. And if nobody is finding evidence, then nobody is being commissioned to take any action relating to them. Therefore, there are no services or adjustments in the legal system that specifically support older autistic people. To the best of my knowledge, there are no policies in place to change this. In summary, as far as I am aware, older autistic people are being abandoned by policy and so are abandoned in CJS processes at all stages.'[635]

Ageing and ethics

The granting of euthanasia and assisted suicide (EAS) to autistic people with learning disabilities in the Netherlands raises an 'ethical dilemma' about society's duty of care to vulnerable people, according to a 2023 report led by Professor Irene Tuffrey-Wijne, professor of intellectual disability and palliative care at Kingston University in the UK. The report expressed concerns that 'disablism' was a potential factor at play in cases involving autistic people and/or people with learning disabilities.[636]

Professor Tuffrey-Wijne's new report, which she authored alongside Leopold Curfs, Sheila Hollins and Ilora Finlay, looked at 39 cases of EAS involving autistic people and/or people with intellectual disabilities between 2012 and 2021. For an assisted dying application to be granted in the Netherlands, six criteria must be met, including that the patient must be deemed by multiple medical professionals to be subject to 'unbearable suffering without prospect of improvement'. The researchers found that, in around two-thirds of the 39 cases analysed, the characteristics of autism or intellectual disabilities were the 'sole or major' cause of suffering, which were found to be severe enough to approve assisted dying. In eight of the 39 cases, this unbearable suffering was related only to the learning disability or autism. In these, the suffering related to issues such as feeling unable to cope with the world due to overstimulation, or being unable to make friendships or connections with people.[637]

---

634 Ibid.

635 Ibid.

636 Irene Tuffrey-Wijne *et al* (2023) Euthanasia and physician-assisted suicide in people with intellectual disabilities. *BJPsych Open* 23 **9** (3):e87.

637 Church E (2023) *'Ethical' debate needed on assisted suicide for people with learning disabilities* [online]. Available at: www.nursingtimes.net/news/research-and-innovation/ethical-debate-needed-on-assisted-suicide-for-people-with-learning-disabilities-11-07-2023/ (accessed January 2024).

In a third of the cases, doctors said the fact that a patient's learning disabilities or autism was untreatable was a 'key consideration' in whether assisted dying should be granted. One excerpt from an EAS case report read: 'According to [the physician], the huge burden of suffering had to be seen in the context of the patient's limited resilience and coping, which was a result of his limited intelligence and near-absence of the ability to reflect'. Professor Tuffrey-Wijne said: 'These cases raise ethical dilemmas that society must face in defining the extent of its duty of care to its citizens, particularly those with disabilities.'[638]

Her report was published shortly after Professor Tuffrey-Wijne gave evidence at an inquiry into whether assisted dying should be legalised in the UK. She told the inquiry, led by the UK Health and Social Care Select Committee, that she was 'not reassured by the safeguards in place in countries where it is already legal, such as in Holland.

The report's authors said unconscious bias and health inequality experienced by autistic people with learning disabilities had played 'a not insignificant part' in people applying for assisted dying in the cases examined. They wrote:

> 'Disablism – society's unconscious bias against physically or intellectually disabled people, often subliminally expressed – can constitute a coercive pressure on someone with a disability. Furthermore, people with disabilities experience stark inequities in health and social care provision, severe enough to put some patient groups at real risk and to lead to premature and avoidable deaths. These inequities, including societal failures to accept and provide adequate support for disabled people to manage their lives, appear to have played a not insignificant part in the EAS requests of people with intellectual disabilities and/or ASD in our study.'[639]

The report went on to refer to how, within Dutch law, suffering must have a medical basis and that this 'raises real questions' about using symptoms of a learning disability or autism as considerations for assisted dying. It added:

> 'The implicit message communicated to patients in granting EAS requests on the basis of intellectual disability or ASD-related suffering is that such conditions are indeed hopeless. This is of concern, as is the risk that the option of EAS hampers investment in appropriate treatments and societal changes.'[640]

The report concluded with a call for more debate around whether further safeguards for vulnerable patients seeking assisted dying should be introduced in countries where it is legal. It also said that 'further investigation' was needed into how doctors assess the criteria of 'hopelessness'.[641]

Professor Tuffrey-Wijne added that the report also highlighted a need for more investment in 'individualised' support services for people in these vulnerable groups. She said:

---

638 Ibid.

639 Ibid.

640 Ibid.

641 Ibid.

> 'What these individuals needed was a society where they felt they belonged, with people around them who not just accept and accommodate, but welcome their unique ways of being.
>
> 'There is no doubt some people feel helpless, suffer deeply and profoundly and the support needed is complex but hopefully there can be a culture shift and a big investment in services that are significantly under-resourced.'[642]

In the UK, the Health and Social Care Select Committee continues its inquiry into whether assisted dying could be legalised here. More than 250 pieces of written evidence have been submitted to the inquiry, which has been heard from UK lawmakers, academics specialising in palliative and end-of-life care, experts from countries where it is currently legal, and the Swiss 'right to die' organisations, Dignitas and Exit.

Ekaterina Harrison has correctly pointed out that a key consideration relating to the issue of assisted suicide for autistic individuals is the differentiation between autistic individuals with and without learning disabilities, because the approach to concerns about comprehension and decision-making capacity may vary:

> 'Can autistic individuals understand the implications of assisted suicide, especially those with learning disabilities? Safeguards are needed to prevent coercion and external influences, focusing on preserving individuals' independence. Concerns arise if assisted suicide is seen as an option due to a lack of access to good end-of-life care.'

Harrison adds that there may be broader societal implications 'including potential changes in how we view disability, independence and the value of life.'[643]

Summary

Recognising the needs of autistic adults is now an expectation enshrined in law, but little attention has been paid to the issues affecting older people with the condition. The findings of one survey point to a population who are struggling to have their needs recognised and met. A significantly higher percentage of 40- to 64-year-olds had not received an assessment, compared with 18–29-year olds, and the survey showed that a considerable number of adults with autism aged 40 and over remained reliant on family for their support. It is crucial that health care professionals, social workers and clinicians spot signs of autism in older adults. Moreover, if an older autistic individual repeatedly has meltdowns, he or she is far more likely to be diagnosed with dementia, by psychologists who do not understand autism in older people. Recent research suggests that receiving a diagnosis should be followed up with professional help to enable the individual to manage the change to his or life and identity. People face some key transitions as they age, such as retirement and bereavements, and it is important they receive appropriate support. They also need to be escorted through the benefits maze. Very little research exists on older and elderly autistic individuals caught up in

642 Ibid.

643 Ekaterina Harrison in communication with the author, January 10, 2024.

the criminal justice system. Apart from the environmental and sensory issues which affect all neurodivergent people in prison, older people face specific challenges such as the absence of lifts and the steepness of the stairs. Finally, a 2023 report on the granting of euthanasia and assisted suicide (EAS) to autistic people with learning disabilities in the Netherlands raised an 'ethical dilemma' about society's duty of care to vulnerable individuals in the UK and elsewhere.

Chapter 11: Broader legislation

This chapter will focus on:

- Autism and the UNCRPD (2008)
- Autism and the Human Rights Act (1998)
- Autism and the European Convention on Human Rights (1950)
- European Parliament Resolution harmonisng the rights of autistic persons (2023)

Autism and the UNCRPD (2007)

The UK is a signatory to a number of international human rights treaties which are legally binding in international law. They include the United Nations Convention on the Rights of Persons with Disabilities (UNCRPD). Article 19 of this Convention provides for the right of disabled people to live independently in their communities. The CRPD is sometimes described as a 'new paradigm' of disability rights, which moves away from paternalistic welfare approaches and emphasises respecting 'individual autonomy including the freedom to make one's own choices' and non-discrimination.[644]

Article 12 of the CRPD stipulates the 'right to equal recognition before the law'. It has four core elements:

- Disabled people are recognised as persons in law.
- Ensuring that disabled people are not discriminated against in exercising their legal rights to make decisions.
- Ensuring that disabled people have access to the support they need in order to make legal decisions for themselves.
- Ensuring that people's rights, will and preferences are respected.[645]

The Mental Capacity Act (2005) (MCA) was drafted before the CRPD was adopted by the United Nations, and in some respects it sits in tension with the empowering approach of Article 12 of the CRPD. Advocates' are obliged to work within the MCA framework under UK domestic law. Both the MCA and the Care Act (2014) contain important tools that can be used by advocates to promote the empowering ethos of the CRPD.

Article 12 of the CRPD is closely linked to Article 19 – the right to independent living. Disabled people around the world have campaigned for independent living for decades, and for the first time in the CRPD this was enshrined in international human rights law.

The CRPD is based on the social model of disability. This means that disability is regarded as the outcome of an interaction between physical, mental, intellectual or

644 Department of Health et al (undated) *Providing Independent Advocacy under the Care Act* [online]. Available at: www.local.gov.uk/sites/default/files/documents/self-study-pack-669.pdf (accessed January 2024).

645 Ibid.

sensory 'impairments' and various barriers which hinder people's full and equal participation in society. The social model of disability emphasises the importance of addressing environmental and social barriers, such as accessibility measures, and tackling discriminatory attitudes, rather than treating disability as solely an individual or medical phenomenon. In the context of decision-making, the social model of disability means focusing on what changes can be made to people's environments, and what supports they need, to help them make decisions – rather than focusing on individual deficits in decision-making skills. It also means addressing discriminatory attitudes which hold disabled people to higher standards of decision-making than others, or are treated as unable to make decisions because they may communicate or make decisions in unusual ways.[646]

How far are autistic people specifically protected under the CRPD? The UN Committee on the Rights of Persons with Disabilities (the 'CRPD Committee'), has itself expressed concern about the adverse treatment of autistic youths in the context of equal access to (and participation in) education. In 13 country reports, the Committee said it was concerned about the disparate treatment of autistic people over a range of CRPD rights, including the lack of access to early-intervention services for autistic children and the lack of services for families with disabled members (particularly autistic individuals).[647]

Autism and the Human Rights Act (1998)

The Human Rights Act (1998) (HRA) was enacted in the UK on October 2, 2000. It incorporates the Articles and Protocols of the European Convention on Human Rights (1950) that are considered applicable in the UK (Schedule 1, HRA). While not all provisions of the Convention are explicitly included in the HRA, it mandates that all UK courts interpret legislation in a manner that aligns, to the extent possible, with the principles of the Convention.

The Convention recognises two types of rights: absolute rights and qualified rights. Absolute rights, such as the right to life, cannot be infringed by a member state under any circumstances. In contrast, qualified rights, such as the right to respect for private and family life, may be subject to regulation by a member state through legislation. However, such regulation must have a specific legitimate purpose and be deemed necessary in a democratic society.

The Human Rights Act requires all public authorities (such as government departments, councils, hospitals, the police and those acting on behalf of public authorities) to act in a way which respects and protects an individual's human rights. A human right is an entitlement which belongs to every person, regardless of whether he or she has a learning disability or not. The Human Rights Act applies to every person resident in the UK. The Act places a duty on public authorities to ensure that all actions and decisions that they make take these rights into account. If a public authority does not, it may be in breach of an individual's human rights and they could be taken to court.

646 Ibid.

647 See https://cerebra.org.uk/wp-content/uploads/2020/08/2020-07-Final-Report-Autism-Plus.pdf

UK courts are obligated, to the greatest extent possible, to interpret all legislation in a manner consistent with the Convention (Section 3, HRA). Public authorities are prohibited from acting in a way that contradicts the Convention (Section 6, HRA). Government ministers are required to provide a statement on the compatibility of proposed legislation with the Convention during its introduction. Nevertheless, any legislation deemed incompatible by UK courts remains effective until Parliament decides otherwise.

- **Article 3 of the HRA:**

Freedom from torture and inhuman or degrading treatment – is crucial for autistic people with or without learning disabilities. People with learning disabilities have the right to receive care and support that is dignified and respectful. A public authority must intervene if a person deliberately inflicts mental or physical harm on a person with a learning disability, which includes physical and/or psychological abuse in a health or care setting. The state has a duty to protect people from such treatment and investigate allegations.

- **Article 8:**

A right to respect for private and family life – is also a very important right. Autistic people and/or people with learning disabilities have a right to live their lives privately, to enjoy family relationships (including the right to live with their own family), and to enjoy their homes peacefully without interference from public authorities.

As Ekaterina Harrison has noted, courts have generally adopted a broad interpretation of the term 'private and family life', encompassing respect for various aspects of an individual's identity, including name, sexual orientation, and personal relationships. For example, in the case of *ST (A Minor) and another v L Primary School [2020] EWHC 1046 (QB)*, the High Court determined that a school, by sending a letter to parents addressing the disruptive behavioural issues of a disabled pupil to reassure them about the staff's ability to manage the situation appropriately, was found liable for misusing private information and violating the Data Protection Act (1988) and the Human Rights Act (1998).[648]

- **Article 12:**

The right to marry – means that people with learning disabilities have the right to marry and to start a family, just like everybody else. This Article specifically addresses the union of 'men and women' and does not establish a right for same-sex couples to marry. The UK government introduced the legislation introducing same-sex marriage in England and Wales as an equality measure.

- **Article 14:**

Protection from discrimination – requires all rights and freedoms set out in the Human Rights Act to be applied without discrimination (direct or indirect). In other words, people with learning disabilities should not be prevented from enjoying any of the other rights in the Act because of their disability. As Ekaterina Harrison has correctly observed, there will often be an interaction in the UK between the Equality Act (2010) and the anti-discrimination provisions of the HRA, such as Article 14. In the European Convention on Human Rights, there is no universal prohibition on all forms of

648 Personal ccommunication, November 30, 2023 – my thanks to Ekaterina Harrison for pointing this out.

discrimination. Instead, it prohibits the state from discriminating in the way individuals can enjoy the rights outlined in other Articles of the Convention. For instance, Article 14 is violated if one ethnic group has more freedom of expression than another or if one gender receives more respect for their private lives. Therefore, individuals cannot rely solely on Article 14 in an action against a member state. They must invoke it in conjunction with another Article. Article 14 also outlines specific characteristics on which the state cannot discriminate concerning the enjoyment of Convention rights, including sex, race, colour, language, religion, political or other opinion, national or social origin, association with a national minority, property, birth, or other status. This list is not exhaustive.[649]

Useful resources and further guidance

If you think that a public authority has interfered with an individual's human rights or has failed to act to ensure that their rights have been protected, you can try to resolve it informally at first. If this does not work, you can make a formal complaint to the public authority or take legal action. See the Citizens' Advice Bureau website for more information.

For more information, see:

- www.equalityhumanrights.com/en/human-rights/human-rights-act (accessed January 2024).
- www.equalityhumanrights.com/sites/default/files/human-rights-act-learning-disabilities.pdf (accessed January 2024).

Autism and the European Convention on Human Rights (1950)

Elements within the UK's current Conservative government – notably those who supported Brexit – are also campaigning for the country to leave the European Convention on Human Rights. This would represent a further blow to the rights of the UK's autistic individuals.

On February 12, 2020, the Equality and Human Rights Commission (EHRC) launched a legal challenge accusing the UK's Department of Health and Social Care of 'repeated failure to move people with learning disabilities and autism into appropriate accommodation'. By doing so, the EHRC maintains, the department is violating the European Convention on Human Rights. 'This suggests a systemic failure to protect the right to a private and family life and the right to live free from inhuman or degrading treatment or punishment', said a spokesperson for the EHRC.[650]

The previous year, a September 2019 report revealed a dire lack of support for autistic people in the UK: 58% needed counselling, for example, but only 21% received it.[651] Tim Nicholls, head of influencing and research at the National Autistic Society, said: 'There is

649 Ekaterina Harrison, personal communication, November 30, 2023.

650 See www.bmj.com/content/368/bmj.m578 (accessed January 2024).

651 NHS Digital (2021) *Learning Disability Services Monthly Statistics (AT: November 2019, MHSDS: September 2019 Final)* [online]. Available at: https://digital.nhs.uk/data-and-information/publications/statistical/learning-disability-services-statistics/provisional-statistics-at-november-2019-mhsds-september-2019-final (accessed January 2024).

a crisis in social care funding, both for adults and for children. Mental health services are stretched beyond capacity at the moment.'[652]

As stated in previous chapters of this book, many autistic individuals in the UK continue to end up in hospitals, and some are detained there for many years. One reason this occurs, according to critics, is that social care workers transfer them there to deflect the costs of their care. Once an autistic person has been institutionalised, he or she can be released only when social care is in place, which is often unaffordable.

As we have seen, another problem is that the UK's Mental Health Act continues to define autism as a 'mental disorder' along with conditions such as schizophrenia, which means that people can be hospitalised purely because they have autism. By contrast, people with neurological conditions such as stroke or epilepsy cannot be hospitalised against their will.

Many advocacy groups, including the National Autistic Society, maintain that autism should also be classified as a neurological condition. However, as discussed in previous chapters, that move could have an unwelcome consequence: autistic people who exhibit 'challenging' behaviour might instead find themselves in the criminal justice system and end up in prison instead.

The following rights enshrined in the European Convention on Human Rights are particularly relevant to the detention of young autistic people and/or people with learning disabilities in mental health hospitals:

- **Article 2:**

This article places an obligation on public authorities to protect the right to life, a prohibition on the taking of life and a procedural obligation to investigate deaths. Where deaths occur in detention, or there is an imminent risk of death, Article 2 is engaged.

In the case of *R (Maguire) v HM Senior Coroner for Blackpool and Fylde [2019] EWHC 1232 (Admin)*, the court examined whether the coroner had erred in determining that Article 2 (right to life) was not applicable to the circumstances of the death of J.J. who had Down's syndrome and moderate learning difficulties, and who died in a hospital at the age of 52 after more than 20 years in a care home. The coroner concluded that allegations of individual negligence, raised during the inquest, did not fall within the state's obligations under Article 2. The court clarified that Article 2 might be engaged in cases where the state assumed responsibility for an individual's welfare or safety, particularly when there was a high degree of control, such as in detention situations. The established positive duty also extended to situations where the state exercised legal or practical control, but without systemic dysfunction or a specific assumption of responsibility, the state would not be held accountable under Article 2.

Mental incapacity justifying deprivation of liberty under the Mental Capacity Act (2005) alone was insufficient to trigger Article 2, and the coroner's role was to delineate the line

652 Marshall M (2020) *UK government faces lawsuit over mistreatment of autistic people* [online]. Available at: www.spectrumnews.org/news/u-k-government-faces-lawsuit-over-mistreatment-of-autistic-people/ (accessed January 2024).

between state responsibility and individual actions. In this case, the court found that the coroner's approach did not reveal any error.[653]

- **Article 3:**

Article 3 prohibits torture, inhuman or degrading treatment. Where conditions in detention reach a certain level of gravity, Article 3 may be engaged. The family court case of *A & S (Children) v Lancashire County Council [2012] EWHC 1689 (Fam)* is an illustration. The High Court declared Lancashire County Council (LCC) in violation of the HRA for numerous breaches in its duties towards two children, A and S, who were in its care after being freed for adoption. A and S, initially placed in foster care due to neglect and domestic violence, were eventually freed for adoption under the Adoption Act (1976). LCC abandoned the search for adoptive families but failed to revoke freeing orders, leaving A and S as 'statutory orphans' for 11 years. Placed with multiple foster families, some abusive, they suffered severe emotional and behavioural difficulties. The High Court found LCC's actions incompatible with Articles 3, 6, and 8 of the HRA as follows: LCC's failure to revoke the freeing orders deprived A and S of any contact with their mother or birth family, protection under the Children Act (1989) and access to the court and the protection offered by a guardian (Articles 6 and 8); LCC's failure to provide A and S with an opportunity to secure a permanent adoptive placement and a settled and secure home life (Article 8); LCC's permitting A and S to be subjected to degrading treatment and physical assault by foster carers and failing to adequately protect them (Articles 3 and 8); LCC's failure to provide accurate information concerning A and S's legal status to the IRO and ensuring procedures for Looked After Child Reviews' recommendations (Article 8); LCC's failure to promote the rights of A and S to independent legal advice (Article 6).[654]

- **Article 5:**

Article 5 prohibits arbitrary deprivation of liberty. A person of 'unsound mind' may be lawfully deprived of their liberty if it is necessary and proportionate. Where a person is detained on the grounds of mental ill-health or mental incapacity, Article 5 is engaged. Article 5 primarily pertains to criminal proceedings but could also be invoked in mental health and deprivation of liberty cases. For instance, in *R (H) v Mental Health Review Tribunal, North & East London Region and another [2001] EWCA Civ 415*, the Court of Appeal found that requiring a patient to prove they should no longer be detained under the Mental Health Act (1983) was incompatible with Article 5. The mental health tribunal must order the discharge of a patient if the criteria justifying the detention no longer exist.

- **Article 8:**

Article 8 provides the right to respect for a private and family life. This requires public authorities to protect the right to personal autonomy, physical and psychological integrity, and the maintenance of relationships with others. Where an individual's autonomy or integrity is interfered with, or where individuals are removed from their families, Article 8 is engaged.

653 My thanks, again, to Ekaterina Harrison for citing this important case.

654 See www.casemine.com/judgement/uk/5a8ff76260d03e7f57eabf8b (accessed March 2024).

- **Article 14:**

Article 14 provides for the right not to be discriminated against in relation to the other Convention rights. Where young autistic people and/or people with learning disabilities are discriminated against in relation to the enjoyment of their Convention rights, Article 14 is also engaged.

European Parliament Resolution harmonising the rights of autistic persons (2023)

On October 4, European Union lawmakers endorsed a non-binding Resolution to harmonise the rights of autistic people in Europe, recommending mutual recognition of diagnoses, better access to employment and the prohibition of forced sterilisation.[655] However, it remains unclear whether this Resolution affects the UK in any way, after its decision to leave the EU in 2016.

The Resolution, adopted by Members of the European Parliament (MEPs) during the plenary session, aims to better consider autistic people's needs in a move towards a more inclusive society. While it does not carry the force of law, this 'soft law' reflects the majority view of Parliament about the need for a common autism status recognised by all member states. In the EU, 100 million people are disabled, and five million of them (more than 1%) are autistic, according to European Parliament figures.

A French MEP, Anne-Sophie Pelletier, called the Resolution 'a strong message sent by the European Parliament for full recognition of autistic people in our society. It's time now for diagnoses to be recognised in all member states.'

The Resolution argues that the lack of common recognition between countries 'greatly complicates their movements from one EU member state to another' – preventing them from 'seeking the support they need'. As such, MEPs called for the first time for 'the adoption of a European legal status for people with disabilities, enabling mutual recognition and accreditation in all member states'.[656]

The text also aims to make access to employment more inclusive for autistic individuals and, as required by the Employment Equality Directive, to 'ensure that recruitment and positive action programmes, as well as quotas, lead to tangible employment opportunities'.

Of those Europeans who are autistic, 40% do not have an intellectual disability. This can create barriers to gaining a certificate of disability recognition, according to European Parliament data. It could also prevent them from accessing a European Disability Card, an initiative proposed by the European Commission on September 6, 2023. The European Commission proposed the European Disability Card as an EU-wide cross-border proof of disability. While welcomed, the proposal was also criticised as

655 For more information, see: www.europarl.europa.eu/doceo/document/TA-9-2023-0343_EN.html (accessed January 2024).

656 Bauer-Babef (2023) *EU Parliament calls for harmonisation of rights of autistic people in Europe* [online]. Available at: www.euractiv.com/section/health-consumers/news/eu-parliament-calls-for-harmonisation-of-rights-of-autistic-people-in-europe/ (accessed January 2024).

insufficient by disability organisations, which now urge co-legislators to take action, particularly on work and study matters.

The Resolution adopted by the plenary session on October 4, 2023, covers many other areas affecting the daily lives of autistic people in Europe: diagnosis, work, education, healthcare, accessible transport and combatting violence. Regarding violence, the Resolution notes that there are 'clearly illegal procedures involving serious physical abuse of children, including bleach enemas, which are still widespread and insufficiently regulated in most member states'. Bleach enemas, in the context of autism, refer to a dangerous and scientifically unsupported method to 'treat' autism which involves introducing chlorine dioxide, a powerful bleach, into the body. It can cause serious health risks, including chemical burns, dehydration, electrolyte imbalances, organ damage and psychological harm (see Chapter 9).

The director of Autism Europe, Aurélie Baranger, declared: 'This Resolution is non-binding, but it's a strong call for action both at the European level and at the national level, for policymakers to take further action to address the discrimination and adapt for autistic people.'[657]

Summary

The UK is a signatory to a number of international human rights treaties which are legally binding in international law. The United Nations Convention on the Rights of Persons with Disabilities (UNCRPD) is based on the social model of disability, which emphasises the importance of addressing environmental and social barriers, such as accessibility measures, and tackling discriminatory attitudes, rather than treating disability as solely an individual or medical phenomenon. In the context of decision-making, this means focusing on what changes can be made to people's environments, and what supports they need, to help them make decisions – rather than focusing on individual deficits in decision-making skills. The Human Rights Act requires all public authorities (such as government departments, councils, hospitals, the police and those acting on behalf of public authorities) to act in a way which respects and protects an individual's human rights. Elements within the UK's current Conservative government – notably those who supported Brexit – are also campaigning for the country to leave the European Convention on Human Rights. This would represent a further blow to the rights of the UK's autistic individuals, since the ECHR contains a number of important Articles which are of considerable relevance to Britain's autistic community. It remains unclear, likewise, whether the Resolution to harmonise the rights of autistic people with autism in Europe affects the UK in any way, after its decision to leave the EU in 2016. The Resolution, which in any case is non-binding, recommends mutual recognition of diagnoses, better access to employment and the prohibition of forced sterilisation.

657 Ibid.

Select Bibliography

Attwood, Tony; Hénault, Isabelle and Dubin, Nick: *The Autism Spectrum, Sexuality and the Law – What Every Parent and Professional Needs to Know*. London: Jessica Kingsley, 2014

Atwood, Will: *Asperger's Syndrome and Jail – A Survival Guide*. London: Jessica Kingsley, 2018

Booth, Janine: *Autism Equality in the Workplace – Removing Barriers and Challenging Discrimination*. London: Jessica Kingsley, 2016

Brewer, Neil and Young, Robyn L: *Crime and Autism Spectrum Disorder – Myths and Mechanisms*. London: Jessica Kingsley, 2015

Broach, Steve and Clements, Luke: *Disabled Children – A Legal Handbook*. London: Legal Action Group, 2020

Buchan, Andy: *Autism and the Police – Practical Advice for Officers and Other First Responders*. London: Jessica Kingsley, 2020

Clements, Luke: *Community Care and the Law*. London: Legal Action Group, 2019

Clements, Luke: *Clustered Injustice and the Level Green*. London: Legal Action Group, 2020

Debbaudt, Dennis: *Autism, Advocates and Law Enforcement Professionals*. London: Jessica Kingsley, 2002

Dubin, Nick: *Autism Spectrum Disorder, Developmental Disabilities and the Criminal Justice System – Breaking the Cycle*. London: Jessica Kingsley, 2021

Dunn, Yo: *Social Work with Autistic People – Essential Knowledge, Skills and the Law for Working with Children and Adults*. London: Jessica Kingsley, 2020

Graham, James: *Autism, Discrimination and the Law – A Quick Guide for Parents, Educators and Employers*. London: Jessica Kingsley, 2008

Feinstein, Adam: *A History of Autism – Conversations with the Pioneers*. Chichester: Wiley-Blackwell, 2010

Feinstein, Adam: *Autism Works – A Guide to Successful Employment Across the Entire Spectrum*. London: Routledge, 2019

Fitzpatrick, Michael: *The Tyranny of Health – Doctors and the Regulation of Lifestyle*. London: Routledge, 2000

Fitzpatrick, Michael: *The MMR and Autism – What Parents Need to Know*. London: Routledge, 2004

Flynn, Eilionóir; Arstein-Kerslake, Anna; de Bhailís, Clíona and Serra, María Laura (eds.): *Global Perspectives on Legal Capacity Reform – Our Voices, Our Stories*. London: Routledge, 2020

Gainsborough, Judith (ed.): *Educational Psychology Perspectives on Supporting Young Autistic People – Insights from Experience, Practice and Research.* London: Jessica Kingsley, 2022

Jarrett, Simon: *Those They Called Idiots: The Idea of the Disabled Mind from 1700 to the Present Day.* London: Reaktion Books, 2020

Nussbaum, Martha: *Hiding from Humanity – Disgust, Shame and the Law.* Princeton: Princeton University Press, 2004

Quarmby, Katharine: *Scapegoat – Why We are Failing Disabled People.* London: Portobello Books, 2011

Quinn, Alexis: *UNbroken - Learning to Live Beyond Diagnosis.* New York: Balance, 2022

Volkmar, Fred; Loftin, Rachel; Westphalia, Alexander and Woodbury-Smith, Marc (eds.): *Handbook of Autism Spectrum Disorder and the Law.* Cham: Springer, 2021

Index